Brokering Culture in Britain's Empire and the Historical Novel

Brokering Culture in Britain's Empire and the Historical Novel

Matthew Carey Salyer

LEXINGTON BOOKS
Lanham • Boulder • New York • London

Published by Lexington Books
An imprint of The Rowman & Littlefield Publishing Group, Inc.
4501 Forbes Boulevard, Suite 200, Lanham, Maryland 20706
www.rowman.com

6 Tinworth Street, London SE11 5AL, United Kingdom

Copyright © 2020 by The Rowman & Littlefield Publishing Group, Inc.

All rights reserved. No part of this book may be reproduced in any form or by any electronic or mechanical means, including information storage and retrieval systems, without written permission from the publisher, except by a reviewer who may quote passages in a review.

British Library Cataloguing in Publication Information Available

Library of Congress Cataloging-in-Publication Data

Names: Salyer, Matthew C., author.
Title: Brokering culture in Britain's Empire and the historical novel / Matthew C. Salyer.
Description: Lanham : Lexington Books, 2020. | Includes bibliographical references and index. | Summary: "Brokering Culture in Britain's Empire and the Historical Novel radically recontextualizes conventional views of the relationship between the British Empire and the emergence of the nineteenth-century historical novel. The author focuses on how literary translations of eighteenth-century experiences of empire established the genre as a site of critique for nationalism and historical progress"-- Provided by publisher.
Identifiers: LCCN 2020005976 (print) | LCCN 2020005977 (ebook) | ISBN 9781498562904 (cloth) | ISBN 9781498562911 (epub) | ISBN 9781498562928 (pbk)
Subjects: LCSH: English fiction--19th century--History and criticism. | American fiction--19th century--History and criticism. | Historical fiction, English--History and criticism. | Literature and history--Great Britain--History--19th century | Literature and history--United States--History--19th century | National characteristics, British, in literature. | National characteristics, American, in literature. | Romanticism--Great Britain. | Romanticism--United States.
Classification: LCC PR878.R7 S25 2020 (print) | LCC PR878.R7 (ebook) | DDC 823/.809--dc23
LC record available at https://lccn.loc.gov/2020005976
LC ebook record available at https://lccn.loc.gov/2020005977

For James Purcell, an eighteenth-century butcher at Ormond Quay.

Contents

Acknowledgments ix

Introduction: When We "Empired in the Empire"; or, The Problem of Narrating Imperial Time and Place in an Imperial Time and Place 1

1 "A little false geography": Edmund Burke as Edward Waverley 19

2 "The empire of the father continues even after his death": *Edgar Huntly*, James Annesley, and the Eighteenth-Century Orphan Redemptioner Narrative 43

3 Still "Under Sir William": *Locum Tenens*, Cooper's Leatherstocking, and the Tragic View of the American Revolution 75

4 "Revolution is a work of blood": Nationalism, Horror, and Mercantile Empire in Frederick Marryat's *The Phantom Ship* 97

5 "Buried in their strange decay": Lost Letters, Lost Races, and Imperial (Mis)translations 117

6 "Just as Government's a mere matter of form": *Blackwood's Edinburgh Magazine*, Imperial Romanticism, and the Art of "Personation" 149

7 Coda: "And to show us your books": Kipling's Peachey Taliaferro Carnehan as "Romance-Monger" and Reader 175

Works Cited 201

Index 223

About the Author 227

Acknowledgments

Foremost, I would like to thank my mother for reasons that are too numerous and diverse to adequately disclose in this short space. Given the themes and situation of this book, however, I want to sketch in brief some reasons that seem particularly germane to matters at hand. Growing up with my mother and grandmother, I saw the passing of a certain way of life in factory cities of the American Northeast, and I felt the resonant echoes of collective memory in what Sir Walter Scott called "'Tis Sixty Years Since." I will always be able to picture my mother as she was in her own girlhood: a precocious convent-school girl named Diana Carey—"Diana" because it struck my grandmother as a more American-sounding name than my grandfather's first choice, "Brigid." At Notre Dame Academy, though, the nuns called her "Beautiful Dreamer" and told her that Virgin Mary would cry if she whistled in the halls. She once put this claim to the test in front of the statue of Our Lady, just to see what would happen, and Our Lady did not cry. I have, however, seen my mother almost come lovingly to tears on several occasions as she described her time at Notre Dame, recalling the nuns who gave her what would now be considered a "classical" education. Indirectly, then, I would also like to thank the long-dead Sisters of the Congrégation de Notre Dame in their *Madeline* habits who tricked my mother—and indirectly myself—into growing up with the habit of thinking that literature, history, and culture belong to everyone, not just to a professional academic elite or particular social class. Like all good-hearted tricksters, they told the truth. I continue to be inspired by my mother's voracious reading, her dogged pursuit of sources and references, and her deep sympathy for those whose lives she reads about. At seventy-two, she braved the seven-hundred-foot climb to the top of Skellig Michael, as her father before her had done in his seventies. I walked behind her, listening to her describe the lives of its fifth-century monks in minute detail, and scolding her as she bent down to pick sea-spurrey and reach her hand into the puffin holes—just to see. Perhaps like all people, her curiosity is sparked most by those whom my uncle Raymond would call "our own ones," but as an inner-city day-care teacher, her gentle, intelligent, curious, and mischievous inner life is a gift and support to children who often have too few of their "own ones." In a different life, she would have been a natural Sister Brigid. In this one, she is the mother who taught me how to read and teaches me how to whistle.

I am grateful to Wayne Franklin for advising and mentoring me during graduate school. His input on earlier versions of material in this book, often in the form of one or two decisive comments, has been invaluable. Most of all, though, he modeled the kind of intellectual openness, care for textual details, and regard for the human dimension of the past that I continue to aspire to in my own scholarship and teaching. Richard D. Brown's graduate course in history taught me something of the discipline of his discipline, to which I am perhaps more temperamentally suited than my own, as well as the stylistic and narrative possibilities of microhistory. I also want to thank Charles Mahoney for his creative, expansive reframing of the Romantic canon, without which I would have overlooked several writers for whom I have grown to have deep affinities. I would be remiss if I did not also thank Dwight Codr, whose time at UCONN never intersected with mine as much as I would have liked, but whose work makes a powerful case for eighteenth-century studies as an exciting and relevant field. I am thankful, as well, to the peer readers and editors at *Nineteenth-Century Studies*, *Gothic Studies*, *Victorian Periodicals Review*, *Four Score of American Literature*, and *Studies in Burke and His Time*, where previous versions of material in some of this book's chapters have appeared. Special thanks in this regard is due Ian Crowe for his editorial willingness to entertain an unconventional critical focus on the "poetic" Burke.

I have been fortunate at West Point to share intellectual camaraderie, long-standing friendship, and a proper drink now and then with the talented Victorianist and poet, Justin Sider. Patrick Query, Gerard MacGowan, Seth Herbst, and Lieutenant Colonel Jeff Gibbons have been wonderful course directors, administrators, scholars, professional advocates, and stewards of the humanities. Colonels David Barnes and Anthony Zupancic have always extended considerable trust in my ability to "get results" and I am thankful for their support and confidence. For three years, I had the great pleasure of working for and with Colonel John Nelson and Lieutenant Colonel Sean Cleveland, both now retired. I am consistently impressed with the intellectual seriousness, excitement, and compassionate earnestness of rotating military instructors at West Point. Justin Cunningham, Elizabeth Lazzari, Nathan Pfaff, Adam Karr, Marissa Dey, Joe Mazzocchi, and Hannah Williams come to mind among numerous others. I am particularly grateful to Colonel Dave

Harper, the head of West Point's English Department, for being a strong advocate of scholarship and the humanities at West Point, as well as a serious Miltonist and scholar of book history. While I am quite sure that John Milton would have wanted to see me hanged, Dave Harper has been remarkably generous in his support of my unconventional career progression and employment at West Point. I am grateful for the continued intellectual inspiration I receive from students. Several of the ideas in this book were inspired by classroom discussions in my upper-level American Literature course. Outside the classroom, I would like to single out Reed Johnson, Hunter Daniels, Kiana Stewart, and Josh Smoak as people who make academic life worth the effort.

Finally, I think that all honest scholars in the humanities will admit that their critical interests are driven by their own personal anxieties, desires, and personalities. If the subtext of this book often concerns the lives of small, furtive men scrambling to advance their families, then it is because I am not interested in anything in this life nearly as much as watching my hard-minded wife, Meghan Maguire Dahn; my beautiful, wild daughters, Rory and Vivian; my fine, strong son, Éamon; and whatever children or grandchildren may have joined them by the time you read this.

Introduction

When We "Empired in the Empire"; or, The Problem of Narrating Imperial Time and Place in an Imperial Time and Place

"his yong sone, when he Empired in the Empire"—*Disciplina Clericalis* c. 1500

On July 22, 1761, the world warred again while Horace Walpole, the Eton-educated fourth Earl of Orford and youngest son of the Prime Minister, Sir Robert Walpole, lived in a pretty "little play-thing house" by the river. Horace had built his "toy house" some ten miles from Whitehall at Twickenham, a quiet, gentrifying suburb noted for Alexander Pope's gardens, where the heathland was mostly gravel save two patches of brick-earth and a strip of alluvium that ran with the Thames. There had already been a house on the site since 1698, a plain affair built by a retired coachman for the Earl of Bedford. It abutted an otherwise unremarkable plot of land called Strawberry Hill Shot that someone had long since nicknamed "Chopped Straw Hill." The name stuck, being a good coachman's joke about cheating earls, hints of reselling the straw meant for the earls' horses, getting one over on life.[1] By the 1730s, the borough boasted more respectable villas like Orleans House and Marble Hill, built for more respectable owners like George III's mistress, Henrietta Howard. In 1822, the novelist Laetitia Matilda Hawkins would remark that such places "contributed to give Twickenham its epithet *classic*," but in 1761, "classic" Twickenham ran in parallel circuits with a coachman's world, one built for less fortunate sons and driven by the twin engines of domestic industrialization and overseas empire. In 1736, for example, the famous quack, Joshua Ward, began manufacturing sulphuric acid at Great Vitriol works. Think what stink. Then you had Hounslow Mills, a great network of factories on the banks of the Crane used for the industrial production of gunpowder.[2] No doubt this contributed to the existence of "The Folly," a kind of fixed hostel-barge "wherein divers loose and disorderly persons [were] frequently entertained who have behaved in a very indecent Manner and [did] frequently affront divers persons of Fashion and Distinction who often in an Evening Walk[ed] near that place."[3] But there was none of that bustle at the rechristened "Strawberry Hill." The Earl of Orford found it distasteful, as he did most things. He preferred his design for a "gingerbread castle," his "paper house," to be clever, antiquarian, and a bit campy.[4] The grounds were pinaster, almond trees, Spanish broom, carefully unkempt and scattered with *objets d'art*. There was a quaint Gothic chapel, a model cottage, and a garden seat fashioned into a seashell. Walpole preferred things to "hang somewhat poetical like that" while the barges and mudlarks and merchantmen and frigates slunk to the Port of London, burdened, bloodied, from faraway. In 1772, five of the Hounslow mills exploded, killing three laborers and shattering "parts or all of eight of [Strawberry Hill's] painted windows."[5] It was, Walpole remarked, a "cruel misfortune" for his poor windows.[6]

In a manner of speaking, Reader, this book is about His Lordship's broken windows. In 1761, when the shift-work boys in the mill were still running around on both legs, each pane was still painted, planned, and intact. It was Walpole's view of the world beyond them—the ideological corollaries to Strawberry Hill's guiding architecture of curation, of control—that was broken. His Lordship acknowledged as much in his diaries, which were also fine examples of brilliant but inward-looking intellectual architecture. For that matter, so was the metropolitan "Britishness" he exemplified. Walpole's eighteenth century was an "intensely creative period in terms of patriotic initiatives and discussion of national identities,"[7] but the creative patriotism of British public discourse most often occurred within narrow assumptions about political life and the nation's historical dialectic. Whig political-historical mythmaking, for example, was largely at odds with the longer arc of political instability and civil war that framed everyday life for diverse Britons well into the eighteenth century—the Bishop's Wars (1639–1640), the Scottish Civil War (1644–1645), the Irish Confederate Wars (1641–1653), the First, Second, and Third English Civil Wars (1642–1651), the Williamite War (1689–1692), the Invasion of 1708, the Jacobite Risings of 1715, 1719, and 1745. Even as late as 1759, the "Young Pretender," Charles Stuart, contemplated returning to Britain a second time, capitalizing on discontent among the Tories.[8] As Jeremy Black remarks, these patterns of conflict should be "properly to the fore in any political account, for they serve to underline the uncertainty of developments" in eighteenth-century Britain.[9]

More to the point, they underscore the conceptual disconnect between Whig presentism and the lived historical experience of many Britons. As Jonathan I. Israel remarks, what "in the end mattered most in the Whig view . . . was the contention that [the Glorious Revolution of 1688] . . . was the crucial turning-point in England's constitutional development."[10] Perhaps in consequence, the cacophonous, sudden growth of the British Empire "simply did not loom that large at all in the minds of most men and women back in Europe," and "often went strangely unacknowledged—even by those who benefitted from it most."[11]

Of course, this was not the case for a range of civil servants, adventurers, soldiers, merchants, colonial agents, spies, merchant seamen, convicts, and a host of other emigrants whose livelihoods, families, social statuses, and opportunities for advancement outside of metropolitan England depended on the Empire. Quite often, these were men and women—to include a notable number of High Tories, Catholics, ("crypto-") Jacobites, and other malcontents, men and women displaced, whether directly or indirectly, by Britain's eighteenth-century nation-building—whose peripheral status in the dominant national narrative meant that the terms of their "Britishness" were more fraught at "home" and more easily renegotiated abroad. In consequence, they tended to share with Edmund Burke and Adam Smith a historicizing, imaginative self-understanding that "rested upon the ancient perception of an extended *civitas*—a single polity that embraced both the mother country and its colonies, however remote."[12] The case I would like to sketch in this book is twofold and focuses on the recursive brokering of value—and therefore on the position of the value-broker—implied in this "Burkean" mode of imagining and experiencing empire. First, I would like to argue for the significance of the popular literary "romance" as a context used by eighteenth-century imperial Britons for translating between the contradictions of national and imperial Britishness, as well as for developing a sense of the intercultural broker's speaking position and significance in reframing the definitional problem—and possibilities—of Britishness beyond the Whig "Glorious Revolution" narrative. Second, insofar as the nineteenth-century *Waverley*-style historical romance took special interest in accounts of eighteenth-century imperial lives, finding "romantic" genre-based value in the historical dislocations of, for example, *Waverley*'s Jacobites or Leatherstocking's Tories, I would suggest that the eighteenth-century problem of brokering the political-literary meaning of imperial Britishness gained a double valence through its translation for nineteenth-century audiences as a paradigm for understanding historical change. Indeed, the encoded cognitive dissonances of the meanings brokered between England's "Whig-historical" nationalism and the ambiguities of Britishness abroad came to serve, in the nineteenth century romance, as a counterfactual space for critiquing narratives about historical justice, progress, and the national identities in both Britain and America.

The recent turn to what has been called "New Imperial History," emphasizing the circulation of power through global networks rather than "nation-centered historical models,"[13] foregrounds this. As Linda Colley remarks, British imperium "always involved dependence on non-whites and non-Christians, and not merely the experience of ruling them."[14] Moreover, it depended on the constant circulation of information, currencies, goods, and persons between different "nodes" in the Empire's global networks. As Edmund Burke observed in 1763, the "extent of the commercial empire of Great Britain is such, and it engages her in such a vast variety of difficult connections, that it is impossible for any considerable length of time to pass over, without producing an abundance of events," special and temporal alternations between "peace [that] seem[s] so well settled," and locations where "the theater of hostility . . . [is] infinitely enlarged."[15] To a great extent, the New Imperial History offers a historiographical recursion to Burke's descriptive, journalistic understanding of Britain's empire during the Seven Years' War. In so doing, it highlights principles of political, economic, and social circulation that presupposed, at least to eighteenth-century empire-builders, the ability to translate not just information but *value* between different locations and strata of empire-production. In 1755, for example, Lord Halifax predicted that "an alliance with any one of the wild nations of North America, would be of more service to us, than an alliance with the powerful empire of Russia."[16] Not surprisingly, the "imperial interlocutor" in Colonial encounters was often assumed to possess "the power to speak for [multiple parties] rather than be spoken to," and this "power to speak supervenes all comment on alienation and indeed reinforces the ownership established" through writing.[17] The most obvious example of this kind of mediation was the commercial "factor," or "agent of a merchant abroad," who often held "a general commission to act for the best . . . [and] do for him as he sees fit." In 1797, Thomas Edlyne Tomlins observed that the factor was "accountable for all lawful goods which shall come into his hands," empowered "in express words," but otherwise indemnified against losses incurred on the principal's account.[18] The most famous use of an agent's work as a literary occasion for describing Colonial manners is certainly Ebenezer Cooke's multivalent 1708 satire, *The Sot-Weed Factor: Or, a Voyage to Maryland*,[19] but the copious "how-to" literature on factoring grew concurrently with the importance of the agent's positional speaking authority on public matters, as in the case of 1758's *Sentiments of a Corn-Factor*,[20] as well as through the inevitable metaphorical extension of "factoring" to countless noneconomic situations, strikingly exemplified by 1704's *The Town Spy, or, the Devil's Factors Discover'd*.[21]

Likewise, the factor's position, itself, prismed along with both the metaphorical extensions of his work and the growing complexities of British rule. As early as 1705, Willem Bosman described the Guinea administration in terms of "Under-Factors" and "Sub-factors" who were "accountable to the Factor, or chief Factor."[22] Similarly, numerous legal cases of the period illustrate both the factor's power to determining his relationship with numerous principals and the general tendency to replicate, defer, and extend an agent's influence through proxies. Thomas Godfrey's suit against Thomas Saunders, for example, during Easter Term of 1770, parsed complex litigation involving "the said T.G. and sundry other persons as factor, as well as solely as jointly with other factors" at Fort Saint George.[23] Such copious professional and legal literature concerning the practice (and malpractice) of factoring offers a window into the sort of apparatuses that imperial interlocutors used to negotiate, translate, and "smooth out" the British Empire's "vast variety of difficult connections." Moreover, it identifies imperial interlocution as a speaking position that was relatively distinct from both metropolitan and peripheral outlooks, and one that was so often subject to replication, deferral, and subdivision because it was, at least in practice, communal. Even if we are more conservative than the author of *Devil's Factors Discover'd*, limiting the factoring's metaphorical net past commercially focused administrative or colonial activities to include those whose livelihoods, more broadly, depended on significant forms of intercultural brokerage, the range of Britons within that net seem to constitute a distinct British Imperial class, at least in E. P. Thompson's sense of the word: "men as they live[d] in their own [collective] history" and who often tended to see themselves as such.[24]

Of course, Imperial Britons largely aspired to Britishness, not "Imperialness" or the factor's paradoxically fixed intermediacy. Sir William Johnson, for example, went to great lengths to "legitimize" his colonial position, employing his brother, Warren, in Dublin to have a proper "Coat of Arms Cut in a very neat manner" (stolen, though it was, from the O'Neills of Tyrone) in 1749/50, 1763, and 1774.[25] Before he slit his own throat with a penknife in 1774, Robert Clive had retired to a fine house at Claremont, retaining the popular landscape architect, Lancelot "Capability" Brown, whose sentiments, Walpole decided, "rose much above his birth." But Johnson, Clive, and others like them were perhaps most British abroad because they were consummate traffickers in—and "factors" of—various forms of cultural capital. As Eric Hinderaker remarks, it is helpful, at least in this regard, to think of empires as "processes rather than structures, and more as creations of people immediately engaged in colonization than of policy directives."[26] For many Britons, Britishness was as transactional as empire-building, a "symbol and commodity that was constantly threatened, as well as redefined, by the predatory wars of the period."[27] Certainly from a Marxian outlook, it is ideologically incoherent to lump Robert Clive together with, say, Irish indentured servants, common soldiers, or transported convicts. But that is largely the point. The British Empire, itself, particularly after the Seven Years' War, was ideologically incoherent, a characteristic noted by most of its astute participants and observers. What remained constant were its administrative processes of substitutional authority and brokerage. In addition, these processes of being "written under" another's authority, of "sav[ing] writing," of "impos[ing] a heavy task of writing,"[28] and so forth, with their high emphasis on facts, details, and errors, tied the practice of representation-as-empowerment to confessional and pseudo-autobiographical writing from the "middle-ground" positions of British Imperial networks. In the case of Edward Kimber, whose *Life and Adventures of Joe Thompson* recounted his own experiences as an East India company agent, his coequal emphasis on his role as reader elides his professional "Charge of [the] Books" with his gifted "choice Collection of Books," just as his "Narrative Founded on Fact" elides his particular life experiences with a more universalized set of pseudo-romantic "adventures" framed by an epigraph from Pope that seeks to "wake the Soul, by tender Strokes of Art."[29] Most significantly, these processes of reading, writing, imperial brokerage, and imaginative, quasi-fictionalized self-representation did not occur at the behest of London; they emerged apart from dominant centers of culture and mediated the metropole's understanding through the framework of "adventure."

This book seeks to trace the development of a "factored" speaking position in the British First Empire, and thus I am interested in eighteenth-century writing "agents" in both senses of the word. The word, "factor," of course, is a hair apart from "factum," meaning "a man's own act and deed . . . any thing stated and made certain,"[30] and both words derive from the Latin term for creating, "making" in the sense of the Credo's "*factorum caeli et terrae*." In the light of this double valence, I am interested in the aesthetic of "factum"—the twinned imaginative fictions of imperial deeds and certainties—that reproduced eighteenth-century forms of cultural brokerage for nineteenth-century readers through the *Waverley*-style historical romance. Hannah Arendt remarks that the "nineteenth century offered us the curious spectacle of an almost simultaneous birth of the most varying and contradictory ideologies" about the modern nation state and its counterpoint in the "imperialist legend."[31] For Georg Lukács, the publication of Walter Scott's *Waverley* in 1819 ushered in a vogue for novels that depicted mass historical experience in terms of national identities, offering "concrete possibilities for men to comprehend their own existence as something historically conditioned, for them to see in history something which deeply affects their lives and immediately concerns them."[32] Of course, this is hard to square with the profound political-historical consciousness that the Seven Years' War inspired in Burke or, more broadly, the degree to which any number of "imperial" Britons understood, experienced, and wrote about their lives in terms of historical contingencies. Nineteenth-century historical romancers, in turn, both in England and America, had relatively little interest in depicting Napoleonic Europe or, for that matter, equivalent "mass historical" revolutions in

America. But irrespective of their own political beliefs, British and American romancers tended to set their novels in the eighteenth-century British Empire with striking regularity. Scott, for example, did not need Napoleon to understand that "our children [in the nineteenth-century present] are as naturally exported to India as our black cattle were sent to England."[33] However, his sense of the historically systematic depended on an imaginative response to patterns of "Burkean" empire. Indeed, in this, the link between nineteenth-century fictions and their eighteenth-century source contexts—which organizes the chapters of this book—is more than an archival observation, for it presents Britain's "vast variety of difficult connections" abroad as the historical constant between eighteenth-century lives and their nineteenth-century readers. In a sense, the constant recursion of imperial networks made antiquarian narratives about representative past "lives and adventures" abroad feel potentially more vital, more of the "present," than Whig narratives about the constitutional history of England.

I argue that the synergistic historical and experiential frame of eighteenth-century empire, far more than what Lukács had in mind when he wrote of a mass historical consciousness after Napoleon, gave rise to the Romantic historiography of writers who followed in Scott's wake. The literary culture of *Waverley*-style fictions converted the eighteenth-century imperial problem of brokering cultural space into allusive historiographies that characterized what *Blackwood's* called "romance-mongering." The progress of this book, which begins with the representative negotiations between nineteenth-century romancers (Scott, Cooper, Marryat) and their eighteenth-century imperial contexts, thus moves to a consideration of how the circulation of imperial-historical romance helped redefine the Romantic speaking position of the "factor," as well as reading audiences in the Victorian "imperial commons" through circuits that paralleled the eighteenth-century cultural mediations that romancers mined for their source material.[34] Indeed, as Richard Maxwell observes, the promiscuous borrowing of plots and tropes between romancers "shaped the literary habits of the British Empire" in concert with practical limits on commerce and transit, giving rise to different relationships between space and time for imperial and metropolitan audiences.[35] In India, for example, the Waverley Novels arrived "in tandem with Eugene Sue's *Mysteries of Paris*, which draws substantially from *Notre-Dame*, itself a creative variation of *Ivanhoe*."[36] Whereas English audiences read works in chronological production sequence, the sort of mass-market readers that Kipling alluded to in his depictions of Daniel Dravot and Peachey Carnehan were less "up do date" than their domestic peers, but had more latitude in terms of how they engaged with texts and constructed alternative structures of meaning between them. In effect, a genre delimited by an allusive background of imperial cultural brokerage asked its imperial readers to replicate the "factoring" processes represented in the lives and adventures depicted. In

1893, for example, Rudyard Kipling defended the present-day realism of his classic tale, "The Man Who Would Be King," with the precedent that "men even lower than Peachey Carnehan made themselves kings (and kept their kingdoms too) in India not 150 years ago."[37]

Finally and foremost, this book seeks to outline, at the intersection of imperial readerships and imperial sources, authorial practices that nineteenth-century British and American romancers used to translate the tenuous, real-world speaking position of eighteenth-century interlocutors into the formulaic problem of the Scott-Cooper plot, wherein the hero is "caught between two opposing [historical or cultural] forces . . . but [in which] the relationship of the hero to those forces [often] varies considerably."[38] This is, of course, intrinsically bound to the genre's paradoxical relationship to what Paul Ricoeur calls the "fundamental bifurcation between fictional and historical narrative," which William Godwin, among other Romantic practitioners, tried to delineate in terms of the fictive "study of individual men from the past" and the proper historical approach to "terms of abstraction . . . [of] which the nation is composed."[39] Yet as Colley remarks, the first-hand accounts that eighteenth-century (and nineteenth-century) Britons gave of their own imperial lives were often "at once startlingly atypical and remarkably revealing, strange and representative" at the same time.[40] The employment of such "startlingly typical" incidents as *Waverley*-style fiction's most "representative" general descriptions of the past tended, in turn, to encode the often-ambivalent, sometimes-antagonistic, and always-ambiguous stance of eighteenth-century imperial brokering "classes" toward the dominant metropolitan culture. For the Victorian historian, John Seeley, the Whig(gish) tradition, which tended to "emphasize certain principles of progress in the past," missed the "true point of view in describing the eighteenth century," namely the production of empire in a "fit" of national "absent-mindedness."[41] Its growth, he argued, was "not only greater but far more conspicuous [than 'Constitutional England'] though it has been less discussed, partly because it proceeded more gradually, partly because it excited less opposition."[42] But to the extent that the eighteenth-century "factoring" heroes of Anglophone romances underwent their adventurous peripli through global empire, the genre's aesthetic of historical verisimilitude tended to reflect cultural dynamics in Walpole's Britain that catalyzed their life-and-adventures plots with experiences of social exclusion, disenfranchisement, and displacement. In turn, the genre, itself, emerged as a key site for reviving and brokering long-standing critiques of the liberal nation state, dialectical progress, and the limits of historical justice, so much so that the genre's fundamental mode might well be thought of as *The Counter-Constitutional History of England* or *The Unconstitutional History of the British Empire* in which the particularized, ironized, feckless-seeming, and ideologically ambivalent imperial interlocutor displaces the abstract, univocal national citizen as political subject.

As J. C. D. Clark remarks, "history labours under a major handicap in societies suffused with a sense of their own righteousness and inevitability."[43] This is not because "all we can say for sure [about the historical process] is that it is condemned to increasing disorder by entropy,"[44] but because, as Ricoeur notes, "humanized" narrative "attains its full meaning when it becomes a condition of temporal existence."[45] Great "turning points" such as the Glorious Revolution seem to presuppose what Frank Kermode calls "the sense of an ending," projecting "the clock's tick-tock" as the "model of what we call a plot, an organization that humanizes time by giving it a form,"[46] but as Alasdair MacIntyre remarks, "narrative form is neither disguise nor decoration," for we can only begin to pose questions about choices in the present once we have tried to "answer the prior question, 'Of what story or stories do I find myself a part?'"[47] Since the Glorious Revolution, ultra-Tories and others had portrayed modern Britain as "the product of serial illegitimacies" culminating with the "usurpation of the Stuarts by the House of Hanover, the last battle of which had only recently been fought (1746)."[48] Great Whigs, in turn, made a "fetish of the Gothic constitution [the Magna Carta] that glossed these multiple usurpations as evolutionary progress."[49] On Walpole's part, for example, this led to unshakable convictions about being on the "right side" of history, and that "history"—his story—would triumph against even the "greatest monsters exhibited" by global affairs.[50] In 1795, for example, he penned a letter to the moralistic novelist, Hannah More, suggesting a tale about the French Revolution "to show, that though we must not assume the pretension to judging of divine judgments, yet may we believe that the economy of Providence has so disposed causes and consequences, that such villains as Danton, Robespierre, &c. &c. &c. do but dig pits for themselves."[51] As in a Gothic novel, "Providence" resolved all.

The conceptual threat to this outlook is a temporal, the idea that mass historical experience is "not governed by Reason, the class struggle or any other deterministic law,"[52] but in both the historical Long Eighteenth Century and its afterlife as historical-romance tableau, this threat manifested as conceptualized imperial space. At the Seven Years' War's height, for example, in 1758, the Duke of Newcastle, Thomas Pelham-Holles, confessed that "Ministers in this country, where every part of the World affects us, in some way or another, should consider the whole Globe" in policy-making.[53] This could not help but decenter the "fetish of the Gothic constitution," in no small part because it revealed the "serial illegitimacies" that constituted the empire's day-to-day brokered production of power. In 1772, for example, Robert Clive bluntly told the House of Commons that his "line ha[d] been military and political," a kind of speculative adventurism.[54] "I owe all I have in the world," he continued, "to having been the head of an army,—and as for cotton,—I know no more about it than the Pope of Rome!"[55] Clive fully understood that cotton mattered to Britain. Whig Britain, on the other hand, did not quite fathom how optional or negotiable its historical archnarrative had become to men like Clive. Indeed, the "forces that created a hollow British empire" during the Seven Years' War frustrated "metropolitan attempts to infuse meaning and efficacy into the imperial connection" from the outset.[56] For imperial brokers of all strata, there *was* relative parity between "wild nations of North America" and the "powerful empire of Russia."[57] Walpole, for his part, might dismiss William Johnson, the Indian Agent who ruled most northern New York like a private fiefdom, as a mere "Colonel . . . of Irish extraction, settled in the West Indies, and totally a stranger to European discipline,"[58] but in North America, that mattered less than "one word" from Molly Brant, Johnson's Mohawk consort, whose assent went "further with [the Iroquois] than a thousand words from any white man without exception."[59] Similarly, in 1760, Edmund Burke's *Annual Register* estimated Clive's wealth at "£1,200,000 in cash, bills, and jewels . . . so that he may with propriety be said to be the richest subject in the three kingdoms."[60] What did it matter that Walpole, whom the Tory pamphleteers of the time slandered as a "hermaphrodite horse just brought to town,"[61] thought Clive equally absurd with his "scimitar, dagger, and other matters covered in brilliants?"[62] What was striking about Clive, as a characteristically imperial life, was his ability to self-deal from a brokered position of cultural equivalence, a fact borne out by the remarkable similarities between English concerns about "nabobs" who returned to "marry into your families" and "enter into your senate,"[63] and the resentment of Indian elites who trafficked with "a handful of traders who have not yet learned to wash their bottoms."[64] Newcastle's country, "where every part of the world affects us," seemed increasingly outside the rational dispositions of Providence. "Thunder go the Tower guns," wrote Walpole, "and . . . Lord Granby is become a nabob."[65]

On July 22, 1761, Horace Walpole found this all distasteful, as he did most things. He walked through the "little play-thing house" to his desk as he always did, his "knees bent and feet on tip toe as if afraid on a wet floor."[66] Perhaps he appeared as he does in the portrait by Sir Joshua Reynolds—that is, as a man "not merely tall, but slender to excess" under the black-velvet weight of the loose, oil-painted coat, the gradient ambers of candlelight that haloed his cold, noncommittal wit.[67] The pallid, oblong face drew taut across the cheeks from thin, indolent lips as if by hooks; beneath them, the delicate jawline propped on a hand. As in the Reynolds portrait, perhaps each finger extended, bent like the architecture of a bird's wing-bones. An icon of thoughtfulness, boredom, privilege. Then, perhaps, the avian hands uncurled to clutch the scrolled papers and the potted quill beside his elbow. Reached again, wrote:

> For my part, I believe Mademoiselle Scuderi drew up the plan of this year. It is all royal marriages, coronations, and victories: they come tumbling so over one another from different parts of the globe, that it looks just like the handywork of a lady romance writer, whom it costs nothing but a little false geography to make the Great Mogul in love with a Princess of Mecklenburg, and defeat two marshals of France as he rides post on an elephant to his nuptials. I don't know where I am. I had scarcely found Mecklenburg Strelitz with a magnifying-glass when I am whisked to Pondicherry—well, I take it and raze it . . . how the deuce in two days can one digest all this? Why is not Pondicherry in Westphalia? I don't know how the Romans did, but I cannot support two victories a week.[68]

Of course, the 4th Earl of Orford understood empires perfectly well. His privilege depended on one. He liked to collect the antiquarian artifacts brought home by overseas networks of power and exchange: Aztec sacrificial objects, the "magic mirror" of Dr. John Dee, a finely-decorated lance from Moghul India, things like that.[69] But had the Seven Years' War actually been more like *Artamenes, or the Grand Cyrus* and *Almahide, or the Slave Queen*, two meandering Scudéry novels, it would have seemed like a more reasonable representation of empire to Walpole, the Gothic novelist. Indeed, just as Scudéry's overwrought romances were vehicles for celebrating "the vitality of [those] years during which the making of history was approached as a literary enterprise" in the French Enlightenment,[70] Walpole's *Castle of Otranto* attempted to "transfer [Whig] Saxonist myth from the realms of politics and architecture to that of literature."[71] Conversely, the "false geography" of Britain's imperial "romance" suggested that the genre's descriptive modes posed an implicit political threat, disclosing underlying Whig anxieties about the certitudes of national-historical consciousness as a legitimate "mass" experience. In 1750, for example, Thomas Nugent reminded Britons that "it is natural for a republic to have only a small territory, otherwise it cannot subsist for long,"[72] and Britain's global reach conspired with its own colonial past to offer no exception. Among numerous other works, Gibbon's *Decline and Fall* templated imperial, not national, order as one "firmly established by the coalition of its members," through which "subject nations, resigning hope, and even the wish of independence, embraced the character of Roman citizens."[73] Similarly, William Camden's *Britannia* portrayed Imperial Rome as "that common Mother [who] challenges all such for her citizens, *Quos domuit, nexuque pio longinqua revinxit*. Whom conquer'd she in sacred blood hath tied. And 'tis easy to believe that the Britains and Romans, by a mutual engrafting for so many years together, have grown up into one Nation . . . [that] was called *Romania*, and the *Roman Island*."[74] For Gibbon, the central characteristic of imperial power was a principle of complete diffusion; for Camden, empires both preceded and produced nations through "engrafting."

Both men, however, assumed the fundamental bifurcation between empire and nation as principle of political commonwealth. Neither historian entertained what Henry St. John, Lord Bolingbroke, called "the greatest absurdity imaginable," the principle of "Imperium et Imperio," or "state-within-a-state."[75] But as Dermot Ryan notes, the growing recognition, at least in some quarters during the eighteenth century, of "a new imperial formation: an imperial network integrated through exchange with no permanent sovereign center," effectively "provincialized England" in the minds of its advocates.[76] To a notable extent, this laid conceptual "groundwork for relating romantic theories of the imagination to the processes of empire-building," suggesting that the "sympathetic imagination allows us to occupy not only the place of another, but also other places."[77] In the case of the *Waverley*-style historical romance, this inheritance was not simply a series of modalities for imagining empire-building and nation-building. Primarily, it sought to emphasize the historical architects of Bolingbroke's "Imperium et Imperio," the eighteenth-century "factoring" classes that recursively articulated Britishness as a "recent, fragile and contested ideology of power," mediating between a "still friable sense of British identity and British statehood."[78] To the extent that nineteenth-century romancers, whether British or American, bound the sympathetic imagination to genre norms concerning eighteenth-century imperial settings, life-and-adventures reportage, and social-historical verisimilitude, the valorized (self-)translation of the figure of the British Imperial "factor" from peripheral, mediatorial speaker to heroic actor evoked Walpole's "little false geography" as the substitutional landscape for nineteenth-century readers to explore both radical individuation and radical critiques of the justice and inevitableness of their own national-historical milieu.

At Hounslow, though, "whose heath sublime terror fills, [and] with her gibbets lend[s] her powder mills," consider how the world ran on July 22, 1761.[79] His Lordship had no use for brokering empire. By the year's end, he would grow bored with the "opportunity of conquering all the world, by being at war with all the world."[80] As Walpole remarked to his longtime friend, George Montagu, "'tis a busy world, and well adapted to those who love to bustle in it;" it was a world in which one must "love or hate," and he had the "satisfaction of doing neither."[81] All throughout nearby Hounslow-heath, that "fresh robbery of villages, hamlets and farms and labourers' buildings and abodes," the bodies of criminals, madmen, and traitors hung from gibbets, their bodies rotting in suspension over "all that [was] bad in soil and villainous in look."[82] For imperial-minded Britons, Walpole's neighborhood was nothing if not an analogous landscape for the problem of understanding what it meant to broker global power. During the Hastings Impeachment, for example, Edmund Burke argued against the exercise of "arbitrary power" in India by comparing its justifications to "robberies on

Hounslow Heath," about which "a man [might] as well say, I have robbed upon Hounslow Heath, but hundreds have robbed there before me."[83] For Burke, this metaphor helped him imagine the imperial "voice" as an engine set against national elites, common law for "the security of the people of England . . . the security of the people of India . . . [and] the security of every person that is governed, and every person that governs."[84] This was one possibility. In 1857, an editorial in *The Quarterly Review* defended the Chinese practice of suspending decapitated heads in bamboo cages at Chantoung, where "several of them were coming to pieces, and the heads were hanging to the bars by the beard or had fallen to the ground."[85] It was worth recalling, the *Review* explained, that such spectacles had been routine on Hounslow-heath, and "barbarous as this reads, it need not astonish educated Englishman" who know the "days of Burke and Fox and Pitt."[86]

But in those days, what made His Lordship, the 4th Earl of Orford, think that he was on history's side? Providence? "All the freebooters," he remarked of Hounslow Heath," that are not in India, are taken to the highway."[87] Indeed, it was true. Villains like Captain Macheath, the antihero of John Gay's *Beggar's Opera* (1728) and its colonially based sequel, *Polly* (1777), had a habit of reappearing, remade, as it were, in far-flung "false geographies" of Britain's empire through their own brokered, self-brokering "handywork."[88] Indeed, it was metropolitan Whigs like Horace Walpole whose global outlook reflected Erich Auerbach's sense of causal relations in naïve romances where the "geographical relation [or societies] to the known world, their sociological and economic foundations, remain unexplained."[89] On January 6, 1772, for some reason, "nine thousand powder-mills broke loose . . . [at] Hounslow-heath; a whole squadron of them came hither" to Walpole's fine "toy house" and broke eight painted-glass windows.[90] Providence saw fit to preserve "those in the cabinet, and Holbein-room, and galley, and blue-room, and green-closet, &c."[91] The following day, Horace Walpole, the Eton-educated 4th Earl of Orford and youngest son of the Prime Minister, Sir Robert Walpole, wrote an elegant letter to the Hon. H. S. Conway, Lieutenant of Ordinance, who was responsible for overseeing Hounslow Mills, informing him that "the two [stained-glass] saints in the hall have suffered martyrdom! They have had their bodies cut off, and nothing remains but their heads."[92] How provincial His Lordship would have seemed to Macheath. How unfit for a beggar's opera like empire.

NOTES

1. Horace Walpole, letter to Horace Mann, 7 June 1748, in *The Yale Edition of the Correspondence of Horace Walpole*, vol. 19 (New Haven: Yale University Press, 1937–1983), 486.
2. Laetitia Matilda Hawkins, Anecdotes, *Biographical Sketches and Memoirs; Collected by Laetitia Matilda Hawkins*, vol. 1 (London: F. C. and J. Rivington, 1822), 89.

3. Complaint to the Court of Alderman, 28 May 1745; see D. H. Simpson and E. A. Morris, *Twickenham Ferries in Story and Song*, Borough of Twickenham Local Historical Society Paper No. 43, 1980.

4. For Walpole's residence at Twickenham, see Michael Snodin and Cynthia E. Roman, *Horace Walpole's Strawberry Hill* (New Haven: Yale University Press, 2009).

5. Walpole, letter to Lady Ossory, January 1772, in *Correspondence*, 1:75.

6. Walpole, letter to Lady Ossory, January 1772.

7. D. Baugh, *The Global Seven Years' War, 1754–1763* (New York: Routledge, 2014), 1.

8. Doron Zimmerman, *The Jacobite Movement in Scotland and in Exile* (London: Palgrave Macmillan, 2003), 159.

9. Jeremy Black, *A Short History of Britain* (London: Bloomsbury Academic, 2015), 49.

10. Jonathan I. Israel, *The Anglo-Dutch Moment: Essays on the Glorious Revolution and Its World Impact* (Cambridge: Cambridge University Press, 2003), 10.

11. Linda Colley, "The Imperial Embrace," *The Yale Review* 81, no. 4 (1993), 92.

12. Anthony Pagden, "Afterward: From Empire to Federation," in Balachandra Rajan and Elizabeth Sauer, *Imperialisms: Historical and Literary Investigations, 1500–1900* (New York: Palgrave MacMillan, 2004), 263.

13. For context, see Kathleen Wilson, ed., *A New Imperial History: Culture, Identity and Modernity in Britain and the Empire, 1660-1840* (Cambridge: Cambridge University Press, 2004).

14. Linda Colley, *Captives: Britain, Empire, and the World, 1600–1850* (New York: Anchor, 2004), 71.

15. Edmund Burke, "History of Europe," *The Annual Register, for the Year 1763* (London: J. Dodsley, 1763), 1.

16. 10 December 1755. R. C. Simmons and P. D. G. Thomas, eds. *Proceedings and Debates of the British Parliaments Regarding North America, 1754–1783*, 6 vols (Milkwood, 1982–1986), I.115.

17. Bill Ashcroft, "Travel and Power," in Julia Kuehn, ed., *Travel Writing, Form, and Empire: The Poetics and Politics of Mobility* (New York: Routledge, 2009), 232.

18. Thomas Edlyne Tomlins, *The Law-Dictionary: Explaining the Rise, Progress, and Present State, of English Law, in Theory and Practice, Defining and Interpreting the Terms or Words of Art; and Comprising Copious Information, Historical, Political, and Commercial, on the Subject of Our Law, Trade, and Government* (London: Andrew Strahan, 1797), n.p.

19. Ebenezer Cook[e], *The Sot-Weed Factor; or, A Voyage to Maryland. A Satyr. In which is describ'd The Laws, Government, Courts and Constitutions of the Country, and also the Buildings, Feats, Frolicks, Entertainments and Drunken Humours of the Inhabitants of that Part of America* (London: D. Bragg, 1708).

20. Anonymous, *Sentiments of a Corn-Factor on the Present Situation of the Corn Trade* (London: J. Richardson, 1758).

21. Anonymous, *The Town Spy, or, the Devil's Factor's Discover'd. In Several Witty and Ingenious Dialogues . . . The Whole Laying Open, Their Cunning Intrigues, and Subtile and Wicked Designs* (London: Robert Gifford).

22. William Bosman, *A New and Accurate Description of the Coast of Guinea, Divided into the Gold, the Slave, and the Ivory Coasts* (London: J. Knapton, 1705), 94.

23. Godfrey vs. Saunders, Easter Term 10 Geo. 1770, in George Wilson, *Reports of Cases Argued and Adjudged in the King's Courts at Westminster* (London: H. Baldwin and Son, 1799), 82.

24. E. P. Thompson, *The Making of the English Working Class* (New York: Vintage, 1966), 11.

25. Henry St. John Bolingbroke, "Concerning Authority in Matters of Religion," *in The Philosophical Works of the Late Right Honorable Henry St. John, Viscount Lord Bolingbroke*, vol. 3 (London, 1754), 49.

26. Eric Hinderaker, *Elusive Empires: Constructing Colonialism in the Ohio Valley, 1673–1800* (Cambridge: Cambridge University Press, 1997), xi.

27. Kathleen Wilson, *A New Imperial History*, 12.

28. John Mair, *Book-Keeping Modernized: Or, Merchant-Accounts by Double Entry, according to the Italian Form . . . To Which is Added, A Large Appendix.* (Edinburgh: John Bell, and William Creech, 1786), 515.

29. Edward Kimber, *The Life and Adventures of Joe Thompson. A Narrative Founded on Fact* (London: John Hinton, 1775), 92, 124.

30. Tomlins, *Law-Dictionary*, n.p.

31. Hannah Arendt, *The Origins of Totalitarianism* (New York: Harcourt, 1976), 208.

32. Georg Lukacs, *The Historical Novel* (Lincoln: University of Nebraska Press, 1962), 24.

33. Walter Scott, "Letter to Lord Montagu, June 1822," qtd. in Douglas M. Peers, "Conquest Narratives: Romanticism, Orientalism and Intertextuality in the Indian Writings of Sir Walter Scott and Robert Orme," *Romantic Representations of British India*, ed. Michael J. Franklin (New York: Routledge, 2005), 244.

34. Horace Walpole, Letter to George Montagu, 22 July 1761.

35. Richard Maxwell, *The Historical Novel in Europe, 1650–1950* (Cambridge: Cambridge University Press, 2009), 10.

36. Maxwell, *The Historical Novel*, 110.

37. Seeley, *Expansion*, 10.

38. George Dekker, *James Fenimore Cooper: The American Scott* (New York: Barnes and Noble, 1967), 59.

39. William Godwin, "Of History and Romance," *Enquirer* [1797] http://www.english.upenn.edu/~mgamer/Etexts/godwin.history.html. 17 August 2014.

40. Linda Colley, *The Ordeal of Elizabeth Marsh: A Woman in World History* (New York: Anchor, 2007), xx.

41. Colley, *The Ordeal of Elizabeth Marsh*, xx.

42. Colley, *The Ordeal of Elizabeth Marsh*, xx.

43. J. C. W. Clark, "British America: What If There Had Been No American Revolution?" in Niall Ferguson, ed., *Virtual History: Alternatives and Counterfactuals* (New York: Basic Books, 1999), 125.

44. Clark, "British America," 89.

45. Paul Ricoeur, *Time and Narrative*, vol. 1, tran. David Pellauer (Chicago: Chicago University Press, 1984), 52.

46. Frank Kermode, *The Sense of an Ending: Studies in the Theory of Fiction with a New Epilogue* (Oxford: Oxford University Press, 2000), 45.

47. Alasdair MacIntyre, *After Virtue* (London: Gerald Duckworth & Co., 1981), 215.

48. Marie Mulvey-Roberts, *Dangerous Bodies: Historicizing the Gothic Corporeal* (Oxford: Oxford University Press, 2016), 19.

49. Robert Miles, qtd. in Mulvey-Roberts, *Dangerous Bodies*, 19.

50. Walpole, *Correspondence* 31:397.

51. Walpole, *Correspondence* 31:397

52. Niall Ferguson, ed., *Virtual History: Alternatives and Counterfactuals* (New York: Basic Books, 1999), 89.

53. Qtd. in John Brewer, *The Sinews of Power: War, Money and the English State, 1688–1783* (London: Unwin Hyman, 1989), 175.

54. Robert Clive, Speech to the House of Commons, 30 March 1772, qtd. in Philip Henry Stanhope, *The Rise of Our Indian Empire. By Lord Mahon. Being the History of British India from Its Origin till the Peace of 1783. Extracted from Lord Mahon's History of England* (London: John Murray, 1858), 27.

55. Clive, qtd. in Stanhope, *Rise of Our Indian Empire*, 27.

56. Fred Anderson, *Crucible of War: The Seven Years War and the Fate of Empire in British North America, 1754–1766* (New York: Vintage, 2000), xxi–xxii.

57. Q. Horatius Barbatus, "Journal of the Proceedings and Debates in the Political Club," *The Gentleman's and London Magazine: and Monthly Chronologer* 26 (Dublin: John Exshaw, 1757), 393.

58. Horace Walpole, *Memoires of the Last Ten Years of the Reign of George the Second*, vol.1 (London: John Murray, 1822), 404.

59. William Claus, letter to Frederick Halimand, 1779, National Archives of Canada, MG24, Series B, BI 14:63, D.

60. *The Annual Register, Or a View of the History, Politics, and Literature, for the Year 1760* (London: J. Dodsley, 1760), 120.

61. William Guthrie, *An Address to the Public, On the Dismission of a General Officer* (London: W. Nicoll, 1764), 7.

62. Horace Walpole, Letter to Horace Mann, 20 July 1767, in *Correspondence* 22:540.

63. Edmund Burke, "Speech on Fox's East India Bill," in David Bromwich, ed., *On Empire, Liberty, and Reform* (New Haven: Yale University Press, 2000), 311.

64. Narayan Singh, qtd. in William Dalrymple, "The East India Company: The Original Corporate Raiders," *The Guardian*, 4 March 2015.

65. Walpole, *Correspondence* 9:378.

66. Eliza Cheadle, *Manners of Modern Society* (London: Cassell Petter & Galpin, 1875), 44.

67. Sir Joshua Reynolds, *Horace Walpole*, oil on canvas, c. 1756–1757, 50 1/8 in. x 40 1/8 in., National Portrait Gallery, UK.

68. Walpole, *Correspondence* 9:378.

69. See H. Tait, "The Devil's Looking Glass," in Warren Hunting Smith, ed., *Horace Walpole, Writer, Politician, and Connoisseur* (New Haven: Yale University Press, 1967), 195–212.

70. Joan de Jean, *Tender Geographies: Women and the Origins of the Novel in France* (New York: Columbia University Press, 1991), 46.

71. Laura Doyle, *Freedom's Empire: Race and the Rise of the Novel in Atlantic Modernity, 1640–1940* (Durham: Duke University Press, 2008), 217.

72. Charles-Luis de Secondat, Baron de Montesquieu, *The Spirit of Laws: A Compendium of the First English Edition*, ed. David Wallace Carrithers (Berkeley: University of California Press, 1977), 176.

73. Edward Gibbon, *The History of the Decline and Fall of the Roman Empire*, vol. 2 (New York: Harper and Brothers, 1845), 444.

74. William Camden, *Camden's Brittania Abridg'd . . . with above Sixty Maps Exactly Engraven* (London: Joseph Wild, 1701), 35.

75. Bolingbroke, Henry St. John., "Concerning Authority in Matters of Religion," *The Philosophical Works of the Late Right Honorable Henry St-John, Lord Viscount Bolingbroke* (London, 1754), 49.

76. Dermot Ryan, *Technologies of Empire: Writing, Imagination, and the Making of Imperial Networks, 1750–1820* (Newark: University of Delaware Press, 2013), 34.

77. Ryan, *Technologies of Empire*, 34.

78. C. A. Bayly, "The British and Indigenous Peoples, 1760–1860: Power, Perception, and Identity," in Martin Daunton and Rick Halpern, eds., *Empire and Others: British Encounters with Indigenous Peoples, 1600–1850* (Philadelphia: University of Pennsylvania Press, 1999), 19.

79. William Mason, "An Heroic Epistle to Sir William Chambers, Knight," in Thomas Campbell, *Specimens of the British Poets; With Biographical and Critical Notices, and an Essay of English Poetry*, vol. 7 (London: John Murray, 1819), 314.

80. Horace Walpole, letter to George Montagu, 30 December 1761, in *Correspondence* 9:416.

81. Walpole, letter to Montagu, 30 December 1761.

82. William Cobbett, *Rural Rides . . . with Economical and Political Observations Relative to Matters Applicable to, and Illustrated by, the State of Those Counties Respectively* (London: William Cobbett, 1830), 61.

83. Edmund Burke, "Impeachment of Warren Hastings," in *The Writings and Speeches of Edmund Burke* (New York: Cosimo, 2008), 11:224.

84. Burke, "Impeachment," 225.

85. Robert Fortune, "Travels in China," *The Quarterly Review* 102.203 (London: John Murray, 1857), 161.

86. Fortune, "Travels in China," 161.

87. Horace Walpole, qtd. in James Thorne, *Handbook to the Environs of London, Alphabetically Arranged, Containing an Account of Every Town and Village, and of All Places of Interest, within a Circle of Twenty Miles Round London* (London: John Murray, 1876), 370.
88. John Gay, The Beggar's Opera *and* Polly (Oxford: Oxford University Press, 2013).
89. Erich Auerbach, *Mimesis: The Representation of Reality in Western Literature*, tr. William Trask (Princeton: Princeton University, 2013), 130.
90. Auerbach, *Mimesis*, 130.
91. Auerbach, *Mimesis*, 130.
92. Auerbach, *Mimesis*, 130.

Chapter One

"A little false geography"

Edmund Burke as Edward Waverley

As George Dekker remarks, *Waverley*'s "contest between the principles of reaction and progress assumes the shape of an imperialistic conflict between Gaelic-speaking Roman-Catholic feudalists . . . and an English-speaking Anglo-Saxon Protestant army, professionally trained and equipped to defend an advanced agrarian and mercantilist state."[1] But when Edward Waverley finally meets Bonnie Prince Charlie, the real "state of the Chevalier's Court," which contains, like "an acorn of the future oak, as many seeds of *tracasserie* and intrigue, as might have done honour to the Court of a large empire," shocks the naïve hero.[2] One of Walter Scott's subtler historical insights in *Waverley* is this recognition that Jacobite political cultures often produced a jarring telescopic effect between small-scale feudal interests and large-scale cosmopolitan networks with imperialistic ambitions. The tendency of Scott's critics to emphasize an element of Romantic nationalism in *Waverley*[3] obscures the novel's tendency to argue that "'progressive' history is not the story of humanity, but the story humanity tells itself in order to conceal the deeper reality which is the business of the world, as a counterhistory to tell."[4] In fact, none of Scott's Jacobites—Edward Waverley included—really care one way or the other about British national-historical ideologies. Instead, "every person of consequence" surrounding Charles Stuart pursues "some separate object . . . with a fury" in a counterfactual miniature of unrealized empire. The scene leaves Waverley with the impression that personal or familial interests are "altogether disproportioned to [their] importance" at the Chevalier's Court,[5] but by the end of the novel, even Edward follows suit. He worries about the "Prosperity of the united Houses of Waverley-Honour and Bradwardine," and ensures that his father-in-law's manor, Tully-Veolan, has "been disposed as much as possible according to the old arrangement; and [that] the new moveables . . . [have] been selected in the same character with the old furniture."[6] The decorators hang a "large and spirited painting, representing Fergus Mac-Ivor and Waverley in their Highland dress," on the wall, alongside "the arms which Waverley had borne in the unfortunate civil war."[7] The final disposition of Tully-Veolan, which ought to embody Scott's nineteenth-century observations about the "total eradication of the Jacobite party," the "gradual influx of wealth, and extension of commerce" after 1745,[8] is thus what secures the Jacobite ethos as an evolving, historically responsive understanding of familial identity for the Waverley-Bradwardine family.

In practical terms, Edward's conflation of literary romance with real life—the basic catalyst for *Waverley*'s plot—pays dividends for him. It is true that at the end of the novel he must compromise the nostalgic Jacobitism of the MacIvor clan to accommodate post-1745 political realities, but he does so as the new patriarch of the Waverley-Bradwardines. The fact that Edward gains a paterfamilias worth *making* compromises for suggests that he was essentially correct in deciding to stake his fortunes on an unreasonable conflation of chivalric romance and the real world of politics, executions, rebellions, and land titles; in effect, Waverley-Honor's dusty library prepared its latch-key ward, Edward, quite well for success. But the practical triumph of romance in *Waverley* is not Edward's acquisition of Tully-Veolan, per se. While this resolves the novel's heroic register into the domestic, a characteristic maneuver of Walter Scott's plots, it also gives Edward and the Bradwardines an increased scope of moral action. In becoming heir to the Bradwardines, title-holder to their estates, and interlocutor between the treasonable paterfamilias and Britain, Edward is able to save his new wife, father-in-law, and dependent tenants from humiliation and dispossession.

I would like to assume some of Edward Waverley's risk by suggesting that the *interpreted* life of Scott's fictional romance-hero lets us infer a useful biographical context for drawing the cultural paradoxes of Edmund Burke and others like him into clearer focus. Scott's interest in Burke extended beyond their mutual affinities for the traditional. Scott corresponded with Burke acquaintances such as Mary Leadbeater; he drew on anecdotal accounts of Burke's involvement with Dr. Johnson's circle; he was certainly versed in the details of Burke's upbringing and private life from his readings of James Prior's popular *Life of Burke*.[9] Reconsidering Burke through the lens of "kinship" to Edward weaves the various strands of Burke's legacy—the "American" Burke, the "Indian" Burke, the "Irish" Burke, the "French" Burke—back to a single source paradox. Burke's was the first real public life of the British Empire, and with the publication of *Thoughts on the Causes of the Present Discontents* in 1770,[10] he seems to have sprung from the floor of Parliament with what William Hazlitt called his "profound and restless imagination" violent and fully formed.[11] Because of his instinct for "knit[ting] . . . two ideas together . . . so that no man can put them asunder,"[12] his were the also first mature treatments of the British Empire as such in eighteenth-century politics. He was also the first eighteenth-century Briton of standing to articulate political issues from a British Imperial *stance*. But what a curious thing: it was not the fortunate sons of the Great Whig Families who were best prepared to take the long view of Britain's global role during and after the Seven Years' War; it was the Irish Edmund Burke, who had spent much of his youth in the Blackwater region of Ireland's West, surrounded by Jacobite relations, valorized political criminals, and a literate folk culture of politicized romance. The great historical intuition of Scott's characterization of Edward Waverley foregrounds Burke's Blackwater youth as a kind of "garden" that bore fruit—the "acorn of the future oak" of Burke's mature thought on the British Empire's structure, meaning, and potential. The romanticized "state of the Chevalier's Court" in Burke's youth echoed in his adult conception of "the Court of a large empire," due in part to the same habit of "knit[ting] . . . two ideas together" that established Edward Waverley in the practical affairs of the world.

To eighteenth-century metropolitans who *were* invested in the success of Whig ideologies, the sense of political disproportion that Scott would later portray as Edward's psycho-historical drama made both the Jacobite specters of British history and the unfolding history of the British Empire seem like jarring fictions brought to life. In 1755, for example, Horace Walpole asked Richard Bentley to imagine a "great sea-victory, or defeat; or that the French are landed in Ireland, and have taken and fortified Cork; that they have been joined by all the wild Irish, who have proclaimed the Pretender."[13] It was as likely, Walpole explained, as "thirteen gold-fish, caparisoned in coats of mail, as rich as if Madame Scuderi had invented them," embarking "on a secret expedition."[14] It was the same Scuderi whom, Walpole would refer to six years later as the author of empire's "false geography," and the fantastical romance "handywork" of the news of the world. Of course, Walpole had never been particularly concerned that the "Pretender's boy" could give the "comfortable [Walpole] apartments in the Exchequer and Custom-house to some forlorn Irish peer, who [would choose] to remove his pride and poverty to some large unfurnished gallery."[15] But what would the disproportions of the Seven Years' War have looked like to someone who *had* been "charmed by the prospect of being governed by a true descendent of the Mac-na-O's?"[16] After his adventures at the Chevalier's Court, how would Edward Waverley, happily retired to Tully-Veolan, have understood the subsequent growth of Britain's imperium?

Given Edward Waverley's bookish inclinations, he probably would have reencountered the Court's dissonance a decade later through Edmund Burke's 1757 treatise, *A Philosophical Enquiry into the Origin of Our Ideas of the Sublime and Beautiful*, where proportion—acorn and oak and all—appeared as a matter of teleology and natural law. "To judge of proportion," Burke writes, "we must know the end for which any work is designed. According to the end the proportion varies."[17] In 1758, Edward Waverley would just as likely have read about the byzantine policy entanglements of the Seven Years' War—the cognitive disproportions of Walpole's romance-written British Empire—in Burke's essay, "History of the Present War," published serially in *The Annual Register* until 1763. In the *Register*, Waverley would have encountered news of familiar characters from the Chevalier's Court such as Thomas Arthur Dillon, Count Lally Tollendal, who ended his long military career withstanding a British siege at Pondicherry, the last French stronghold in India, on "but a half pound of rice a day . . . without any wet provisions."[18] Waverley probably would have found an echo of his own experience in the *Register*'s editorial voice, as well. After meeting Edmund Burke in 1761, Horace Walpole described the future politician, who had recently written "a book in the style of [the Jacobite exile] Lord Bolingbroke,"[19] as a "sensible man, but [one who had] not worn off his authorism yet, and thinks there is nothing so charming as writers, and to be one."[20] Like Edward Waverley, whose historical agency was the product of reading "an exhaustless collection of memoirs, scarcely more faithful than romances, and of romances so well written as hardly to be distinguished from memoirs,"[21] Burke romanced politics. And as recent critical attention to the "Irish" or "postcolonial" element of Burke's thought suggests, his emergence on the public stage of the 1750s was marked by negotiations of a distinct Jacobite cultural inheritance.[22] For Burke, the act of writing performed the personal and historical transformations of *Waverley*'s Court; it reframed his youthful flirtations with Jacobite disreputability as a historiographical approach to central definitional questions about the meaning of the British Empire. And if Burke's historical consciousness during the 1750s is any measure, Edward Waverley's immersion in a treasonous Jacobite counterculture of the 1740s would have left the retired rebel better prepared to understand the "future oak" of British imperium than the Great Whigs who retained their apartments at the Exchequer.

"POLITICAL AND RELIGIOUS BALLADS OF THE VILEST DOGGEREL": EDMUND BURKE AT WAVERLEY HALL

Scott's portrait of Richard Waverley, Edward's pragmatic father, is a particularly insightful characterization of eighteenth-century men like Richard Burke, Edmund's ambitious father, who had little interest in the more "controverted parts of religion; [and] therefore brought up his sons in the profession of what he thought the most public road to preferment—the religion of the country, established by law."²³ While Richard Waverley's older brother, Sir Everard, inherits "from his sires the whole train of Tory or High-Church predilections and prejudices which had distinguished the house of Waverley since the Great Civil War," Richard sees "no practical road to independence save that of relying on his own exertions," and thus adopts "a political creed more consonant to both reason and his own interest" than his family's Jacobitism.²⁴ Scott's narrator in *Waverley*—and it is always a tricky matter to identify Scott with his speakers—reserves judgment on this Hanoverian conformer, noting that the "mixed motives which unite to form the motives of our actions" are often as difficult to unravel as artists' depictions of "compound passions in the same features at the same moment."²⁵ Edmund Burke, on the other hand, tended to define personal identities almost exclusively in terms of inherited traditions and thus came to view recantation, at least by 1795, as a primal violation of the individual. "Let three millions of people," he reflected, "but abandon all that they and their ancestors have been taught to believe sacred, and to forswear it publicly in terms the most degrading, scurrilous, and indecent . . . and to abuse the whole of their former lives, and to slander the education they have received,—and nothing more is required of them."²⁶ The ailing, intellectually violent Burke of the 1790s, who imagined the peeled skin of his corpse "made into a drum, to animate Europe to eternal battle" in *Letter to a Noble Lord*,²⁷ is thus a striking counterpoint to the central historiographical fiction in *Waverley*, the idea that a generational remove from the site of trauma ameliorates its effects. At the approximate remove of Waverley's "sixty years since," the inverse seems to have been true for Burke, who wrote that he could "hardly overrate the malignity of the principles of Protestant ascendancy . . . or of Indianism . . . or of Jacobitism . . . this last is the greatest evil. But it readily combines with the others, and flows from them."²⁸ Had he lived a little longer, a post-Terror, post-Napoleonic Edmund Burke would likely have been a particularly unsympathetic reader of Richard Waverley's life—and probably Richard Burke's.

Edmund Burke was fully aware of the extent to which he and his brothers had benefited from their father's decision to conform to the Established Church, and it was unquestionably advantageous, once Edmund became a public figure, to bury the Irish or Catholic "layer" of his psyche in the oblivion that scions of the Great Whig Families imagined was Irish history.²⁹ As it was, caricaturists such as James Gilray portrayed Burke accepting rosaries and whips from a black Satan, "Old-Orthodox,"³⁰ and writers like John Courtnay pointed out the Irish orator's "panegyric on the service of High Mass [in the *Reflections*], where the State is offered up as a propitiatory oblation to the Church."³¹ But while fear of political implications partly accounts for the fact that an "elemental part of [Burke's] psychological makeup was the need for personal privacy," his passionate figuration of the conformer—the prodigal heir reduced to the "most degrading, scurrilous, and indecent" public performances—hints at a deeper and more proto-Romantic psychological element. Burke's "abuse[rs of] the whole of their former lives" were figures drawn from a standard trope in Jacobite folk cultures, particularly in the immediate aftermath of failed rebellions and public political trials. As negative tropes, Jacobite portrayals of men who abandoned their natural allegiances to kith, kin, and king simply inverted the community values embodied by heroic figures. Whereas Burke's conformer commits a kind of social suicide by betraying his inheritance, Jacobite lyricists of Burke's youth celebrated doomed Stuart loyalists as martyrs, Catholic figurations of the "Great Good Man, whom Fortune does Displace," or the "Sacred Person" who, "Prostrate, Seems as Great, as when he Stood."[32] Suggestions that Richard's conversion inscribed a guilty debt on his son's psyche tend to miss this point: Jacobitism was not an ideology; it was a range of communal, feudal identities expressed through political hero-worship with mythic undertones.[33] Burke could not have responded to the paternal weight of conformism with such a tone of tragic nostalgia unless he intimately understood what it meant to admire men who refused compromise with the Whig Ascendancy. And by 1795, Burke's long engagement with British affairs in Ireland, India, and America—reflected through the violent theater of French politics during the 1790s—illustrated the persistence of a tonally Irish iteration of Jacobite hero-worship, one in which history was not imagined as the repetitious story of good men ruined, but as the grinding, unfolding process of their murder.

Although unrepentant English Jacobites of the Sir Everard Waverley type faced recriminations that typically included the forfeiture of titles and estates, the execution of James Cotter of Anngrove in 1720 suggested to members of Ireland's Catholic gentry that Jacobite Gaels were liable to become the objects of judicial murder as well.[34] In Jacobite circles, the Cotter trial was probably "the most important political event in Ireland during the first half of the eighteenth century, for it reduced the supporters of the Stuarts to subservient meekness."[35] Cotter, a notorious rake and Tory sympathizer, had assumed mastership of one of the few remaining Catholic estates in Ireland after the death of his father, Sir James Fitz Edmund Cotter, a prominent cavalier who commanded James II's Irish armies after the Battle of the Boyne.[36] Beginning in 1711, the validity of Cotter's extensive lease was repeatedly challenged in court,[37] and when the former Lord Chancellor of Ireland, Alan Brodrick, accused Cotter of raping a young Quaker woman, Elizabeth Squibb, many Catholics were of the opinion that the charge against Cotter had been fabricated by his numerous enemies among the Protestant Ascendancy.[38] Despite the fact that a number of prominent Whigs involved in the proceedings pressed for clemency, it seemed to observers that the actual merits of the case had been subsumed by 1720 into a pure political drama performed by the Lord Justice, William Conolly, and others "to win favour in court circles in London where there were private grudges against the Cotter family."[39] Conversely, any "nuances [in the case or its handling] were lost in the [Jacobite] literary rhetoric of lament."[40]

Richard Burke seems to have acted as Cotter's attorney for at least some portion of the famous trial and likely continued to assist Cotter's executor and brother-in-law, Garrett Nagle, long after the case ended.[41] In fact, the outcry about Cotter's execution, which resulted in widespread rioting and sporadic attacks on Quakers, may have influenced Richard's decision to recant Catholicism and conform to the Established Church in 1722, shortly before his marriage to Mary Nagle. As Breandán Ó Buachalla observes, the Nagle circle of influence in the Blackwater Valley was "an island of Catholic hegemony in a sea of Protestant ascendancy,"[42] and the Cotter trial, if nothing else, illustrated what a dangerous liability a famous Catholic name could be in Ireland. For the better part of a century, the Nagle family figured prominently in British fears about Irish insurrection. In the 1690s, Sir Richard Nagle served as James II's Secretary of State at the Court of Saint-Germain;[43] in the 1720s, Joseph Nagle, the attorney "most disliked by the Protestants of any Catholic in the kingdom,"[44] was accused of recruiting Irish soldiers for the King of Spain; in the 1730s, Joseph Nagle and Garrett Nagle were investigated on suspicion of being Jacobite agents; in the 1760s, Garrett Nagle was arrested during the Whiteboy riots, along with Edmund Burke's cousin, Father Nicholas Sheehy, who was executed in 1766.[45] While "conformity for the sake of securing family lands was a way of life in eighteenth-century Ireland,"[46] Richard Burke's conversion allowed him to establish himself professionally and socially apart from the Nagle world.[47] It also secured prospects for his three sons—Garret, Edmund, and Richard—in spite of the tainted family politics of the Cotter era.

However, poetic recollections of Cotter and other celebrated Jacobites, whose exploits inspired a voluminous oral and written literature, may have had a very different effect on Edmund, who spent much of his childhood in the care of Patrick Nagle and other maternal relatives around Castletown-Roche.[48] As Breandán Ó Bauchalla remarks, "Irish political poetry for most of the eighteenth century is essentially Jacobite . . . its underlying values, its rhetoric, its ideology can be readily classified" as such.[49] A number of Jacobite poets found their muse in Cotter of Anngrove, including Domhnall Ó Colmáin, whose radical tract, *Párliament na mBan*, was dedicated to the Tory heir,[50] but for the Blackwater gentry, Jacobite folk literature tended to have a distinct personal or genealogical element. The numerous lyrics composed by Edward Nagle, for example, on the popular subject of Cotter's "Unfortunate tho' much Lamented Death," are not reducible to a series of ideological tropes; they bemoan the real loss of kith and kin.[51] While it is impossible to know exactly what books, tales, anecdotes, and poems circulated in the Nagle household, the connection between literary production, Jacobitism, and family identity in Burke's childhood landscape is undeniable, as is the influence of that landscape on Burke's intellectual development. His abiding love of Edmund Spenser's "extremely fine and poetical" language, for example, was sparked playing in the ruins of Kilcolman Castle, where "that excellent writer" had composed parts of *The Faerie Queen*.[52] Like James Cotter, Edmund Spenser was related to the Nagle family through marriage; like Edward Nagle's elegies for Cotter, Burke's 1747 nostalgic pastoral poem, "The Blackwater," framed personal longing in terms of the public inheritance of his famous relation, populating childhood haunts with Spenser's river nymphs from Book VII of *The Faerie Queen*.[53] As James Prior remarks, the "partiality which [Burke] always entertained for the spot, in addition to his long residence in it, and familiarity with the neighboring objects, gave rise to the belief of his having been born there."[54] Burke very well may have wished that this had been the case. As his friend, William Dennis, remarked in 1747, Edmund led "a very unhappy life from his Father's temper," and often formed "desperate resolutions" because of it.[55] Conversely, Burke remembered his uncle, Patrick Nagle, as a beneficent surrogate father. "For all the men I have seen in any situation," Burke reflected, "I really think he is the person I should wish myself, or anyone I dearly loved, to most resemble."[56]

Richard Burke lost or discarded his son's final draft of "The Blackwater," but surviving fragments suggest an important aspect of Edmund's psyche.[57] It was the imaginative work of writing that afforded him the opportunity to cast a private counterhistory against the scripted respectability that Richard imposed on him; it was through the assumption of lyrical and rhetorical identities that Edmund was able "to most resemble" an idolized Patrick Nagle and his Catholic, Jacobite family. In *Waverley*, this is also the crux of Edward's transformation from sentimental reader to political adventurer. Like Richard Burke, who sent Edmund to the Blackwater after extended health complications in 1735, Richard Waverley sends his ill son to recover at Waverley Hall while he pursues his own "official duties . . . [and] the prosecution of . . . his plans of interest or ambition" elsewhere.[58] Thus, despite Richard's fear of maintaining an "intimate commerce with a man of Sir Everard's habits and opinions," Edward grows up with "the same intimate relation to both families."[59] But "the library at Waverley-Honour, a large Gothic room, with double arches and a gallery, contained such a miscellaneous collection of volumes as had been assembled, during the course of two hundred hears, by [the] family," and it is "throughout this ample realm [that] Edward was permitted to roam at large . . . through a sea of books, like a vessel without a rudder."[60] Waverley-Honour's library does, in fact, provide one important parameter for the intellectual formation of its heir: it projects Sir Everard's historical paterfamilias onto the imagined literary domain of Shakespeare, Milton, Spenser, Drayton, Classical writers, Continental chivalric tales, "picturesque and interesting passages from our old historical chronicles . . . and poets who have exercised themselves on romantic fiction."[61] While this ruins Richard Waverley's plan for his son by rendering him "intellectually undisciplined as well as something of a social misfit," Edward's "enthusiasm for romance," fostered at Waverley-Honour, is ultimately what "exposes Waverley personally to the Cause his family reveres."[62]

Curiously, Edward Waverley's undirected and "somewhat desultory" meanderings in Sir Everard's family library probably resemble aspects of the formal education that Burke would have received during the Blackwater years. As the ward of Catholic gentry, Edmund attended illegal "hedge schools" until his father sent him to Abraham Shackleton's Quaker school at Ballitore in 1741.[63] Hedge-school curriculum varied with the schoolmaster, but most ensured that students received at least a basic education in literature, mathematics, bookkeeping, and catechism. Wealthier students who showed promise, such as Edmund's cousin, Honora Nagle, were often sent abroad to further their Catholic education on the Continent, and it is certainly possible that Patrick Nagle entertained such plans for his bookish nephew at some point.[64] Echoes of the Vulgate, the Ordo Missae, and Thomas Aquinas's *Summa Theologica* in Burke's mature writing lend credence to claims that a Blackwater schoolmaster "first put a Latin grammar into the hands of Edmund Burke."[65] They also resonate with modes of catechetical instruction described by Nano Nagle, who was likely educated at the same hedge school as her cousin.[66] But even at its most cosmopolitan, the hedge-school system was primarily oriented toward the continuation of local communities and their traditions. Indeed, its prevalence in nonconforming areas illustrates a broader shift in Jacobite political cultures away from the unviable royalism of seventeenth-century partisans and toward the paternalistic populism of eighteenth-century movements such as Lord Bolingbroke's Country Party.[67] While most pupils came from relatively modest backgrounds, their instruction often included promiscuous samplings of Latin, Greek, Irish, and English texts, and it was not uncommon to find "a classic work of history or literature . . . in a laborer's shelf in the townland cabins" alongside "cheap reprints from the publishers of 'sixpenny books' in Dublin, Cork, and Limerick."[68] Like the "bold and decisive activity" of Fergus Mac-Ivor's political intellect in *Waverley*, the social imaginations of hedge-school pupils were thus "sharpened by the habit of acting on a preconceived and regular system, as well as by extensive knowledge of the world."[69]

Perhaps the most surprising aspect of the hedge-school curriculum is the extent to which pupils "exercised themselves on romantic fiction" as part of a markedly Jacobite social pedagogy. Quite understandably, children who were expected to "hear Mass every day, say their morning and night prayers, [and] say the Catechism . . . by question and answer" also read popular hagiographical romances such as "the Lives of the Saints, of St. Patrick, of

St. Columbkill, of St. Teresa, St. Francis Xavier, [and] the Holy Scapular."[70] Partly as a result, educational reformers regularly complained that "disloyal principles were insinuated into [pupils'] minds by [hedge-school] teachers, every one of whom was a leader of some illegal association."[71] At least in some instances, this was certainly true. A popular Castletownroche schoolmaster named Liam Inglis, for example, who appears to have worked for some time as Edmund's tutor, was also a Jacobite poet of some note who eventually became an Augustinian priest in 1749.[72] Ironically, Protestants also criticized what they imagined was the "total [moral] neglect of the Roman Catholic clergy" when it came to the type of secular literature used in hedge schools. As Antonia McManus observes, the "diversity of the reading material read . . . [spanned] the pious polemical romance fiction of Penelope Aubin, namely *The Noble Slaves* (1722) and *Adventures of Lady Lucy* (1726) to the novels, *Clarissa* (1747–1748) by Richardson," Defoe's *Moll Flanders*, and popular retellings of *The Story of Guy, Earl of Warwick*.[73] William Carleton lists "the history of Reynard the Fox, the Chevalier Faublax . . . the Battle of Aughrim, Seige of Londonderry, History of the Young Ascanius, a name by which the Pretender was designated and a Renowned History of the Seige of Troy; the Forty Thieves, [and] Robin Hood's Garland."[74] P. J. Dowling finds evidence of *Don Quixote*.[75] In 1808, Hely Dutton compiled a list of long-standing "cottage classics" that included tales about "Montelion, Knight of the Oracle, Parismus and Parismenes, Irish Rogues and Rapparees, Freney, a notorious robber . . . the celebrated pirates, Jack the Bachelor, a noted smuggler, History of Rosamund and Jane Shore, two prostitutes, Dona Rosina, a Spanish Courtezan, Ovid's Art of Love, History of Witches and Apparitions, [and] The Devil and Dr. Faustus."[76]

Critics of the educational system that formed Burke in the Blackwater had deep reservations about a system oriented toward the kind of Jacobite bildungsroman that Scott would later enact as *Waverley*. They viewed the romance of treason as an effect of reading countercultural stories that regularly celebrated saints and martyrs alongside the "lives of pirates, dexterous thieves, witches, smugglers, and illustrious prostitutes"—altogether a mix of "political and religious ballads of the vilest doggerel, miraculous legends of holy friars persecuted by Protestants, and of signal vengeance inflicted by the divine power on those who persecuted them."[77] There is no record of what romances Burke's teachers may have used during his Blackwater years, or if they used them at all. However, it would have been unusual for Edmund's education to have excluded Jacobite folk stories and poetic romances, particularly given Nagle connections to rebel literary circles. Jacobite popular culture of the eighteenth century, much of it oral, was marked by a deeply-ingrained secretiveness; it left deliberately few records for outsiders to examine—and prosecute.[78] Finding a record is thus often a question of finding echoes in a communal vernacular of memory, gesture, and personal association.

In 1792, Edmund acknowledged as much to his son, Richard Jr., then on business in Ireland for the Catholic Committee.[79] "When you go to the Blackwater," Edmund advised Richard, "if we have got any friends alive, and not quite ruined there, hinder them from shewing you honours in the way which in old times was not unusual with them, but which since are passed away, for in the present age and reign of newspapers they would be very mischievous."[80] Circumspect as he was, Burke nurtured a remarkable private knowledge of the "old times." He asked Richard Jr. to track the provenance of a collection of "many curious letters, manuscripts of all sorts, and printed books" that he remembered encountering in 1764; he maintained a polemical interest in obtaining "a volume of journals of the confederate Catholics in Kilkenny" and "a short printed manifesto of [Jacobite folk hero] Phelim O'Neil, on his taking arms in 1641."[81] Burke had a special interest in refuting Protestant histories of Ireland, particularly with respect to O'Neill and "the pretended massacre[s of English settlers] of 1641."[82] In the early 1760s, he planned his own historical work on the subject, but never completed this project, probably because his nostalgic, partisan interpretation of Ireland's past threatened the careful personal reserve that secured his political future.[83] Moreover, Burke did not have recourse to the genre distinctions that allowed historical romancers of the early nineteenth century to portray Jacobites, High Tories, and other political undesirables as sympathetic historical actors with human motivations for mainstream British audiences. While the prose accounts that comprised Burke's "manuscripts of all kinds" had distinct polemical and literary elements, they also tended to claim a high degree of historic verisimilitude. Had he lived at a later date, though, it is not hard to imagine Burke as a historical novelist, rendering the story of James O'Neill through an Irish *Waverley* or James Cotter's trial in a Blackwater version of *The Heart of Mid-Lothian*.

"I AM A RUNAWAY SON FROM A FATHER, AS YOU ARE": BURKE AND THE REACTIONARY ADVENTURE OF EMPIRE

Before 1757, the literary possibilities of Jacobite personae offered Burke a means of negotiating his public-private matrices of communal sympathy, personal frustration, and filial guilt. A letter written shortly after Culloden describes his "general compassion" toward the Chevalier's followers, his wish that the whole affair might be "terminated without bloodshed," and his "melancholy" reflections on "the state of those unhappy gentlemen who engaged in this affair, (as for the rest they lose but their lives,) who have thrown away their lives and fortunes, and destroyed their families forever, in what . . . they thought was a just cause."[84] The letter is cryptically and deliberately misdated as "April 26, for fear I should forget 1745."[85] Clearly, though, Burke did not forget the public drama of *Waverley*'s Court. In fact, the celebrated public trials of the Chevalier's "unhappy gentlemen" likely inspired the *Enquiry*'s key description of "a State criminal of high rank . . . on the point of being executed in the adjoining square."[86] Although Burke distrusted the way "lurid displays of violence facilitated a kind of aesthetic detachment,"[87] his "literal-minded theory of tragedy," which effaced "the distinction between tragic events in real life and dramatic tragedy as an imitation of reality,"[88] celebrated the power of tragic catharsis to expose the "weakness of the imitative arts, and proclaim the triumph of real sympathy."[89] In the *Enquiry*, representations of the tragic sublime thus attain their full meaning through the audience's recognition of the limit of aesthetic experience and the autodestruction of fictive distance between real and unreal, viewer and victim. As a theory of the tragic process, Burke's description of the State criminal celebrates the promiscuous reading program of Edward Waverley, the blurring of romance and literality; it posits that mimesis is less a copy than a skin which must be lived through and shed through experience. In the case of *Waverley*, the real failures of the Chevalier's Court allow Edward Waverley to judge the limits of Sir Everard's political romance, but the adventure stories of Waverley-Honour also allow Edward to rehearse the proper sympathetic response to the actual tragedy of Fergus Mac-Ivor's execution at the novel's end.

Although the *Enquiry* was not published until 1757, Burke composed much of its basic argument in the late 1740s while still a student at Trinity College.[90] And just as the *Enquiry*'s "aesthetic categories [outline] a unifying element of [his mature] social and political outlook,"[91] the *Enquiry*, itself, emerges from a context of Burke's early literary experiments which, like Waverley's romances, rehearse the potential application of Jacobite personae to Hanoverian politics. At Trinity, for example, Burke actively participated in debates about the fate of Simon Fraser, a controversial Highland chieftain whose scandalous life, widely-reported treason trial, and dramatic beheading provided British audiences with a spectacle akin to the one described in the *Enquiry*.[92] He also followed the political trials of Jacobite lords such as George Mackenzie, William Boyd, and Arthur Elphinstone, all of whom were executed with bloody fanfare in 1746.[93] In later years, the tragic Jacobite celebrities of the 1740s provided Burke with analogues for emergent political crises in the British Empire: Fraser's trial gave precedent to the impeachment charges brought against Warren Hastings in the 1780s,[94] and recollections of "that great, but unhappy man," Elphinstone, spoke to the honor of treasonous American sailors in the 1770s.[95] To the extent that Burke's political writing inherited the *Enquiry*'s rhetoric of mimetic tragedy, it resonated with Jacobite mythmaking about the Forty-Five and the suffering bodies of actual State criminals. But the political lives of such "unhappy gentlemen" also presented the young Burke with an expressive personal vernacular, a lyrical counterpoint to Richard Burke's conformism and stifling ambitions. One of Burke's early literary sketches, for example, describes a model Irishman in hell as a "fellow that made his way to this world through the Gallows, and lived by his gallantrys in the other," where "the women . . . were so solicitous to save him that their husbands resolved to hang him."[96] If there is a ghost in the piece, it is that of James Cotter, who lends Burke his volatile, cavalier, and self-consciously Irish sexual persona. Similarly, Burke may have borrowed Nagle airs on a 1752 trip through Monmouth with William Burke, during which many "of the lower sort apprehended . . . that we were spies, from Spain" or France, plying "their trade."[97] Burke did nothing to dissuade them. Instead, he reveled in the "very mysterious" figure that he cast in the mercantile town and relished the company of Monmouth's "hearty Jacobites, that is, a sort of people, whose politics consist in wishing that right may take place; and their religion, in heartily hating Presbyterians."[98]

Burke's "adventures at Monmouth" produced—at least in their hero's mind—a *Waverley*-style bildungsroman in germinal form; as Burke later told Shackleton, they "would almost compose a novel, and that of a more curious and entertaining kind, than some of those we are entertained with from the press."[99] To the extent that they do, they touch on the crux of Burke's first published work, *A Vindication of Natural Society*, in which he chose to frame his unrelenting assault on "the evils of the existing political institutions," presented "with incomparable force of reasoning and lustre of eloquence,"[100] as an epistolary fiction, "not so much because he wish[ed] to conceal his thought, or merely to ridicule that of another, but because he [found] fiction to be the best form by which to convey his ideas about politics."[101] The *Vindication* is less about political ideologies—whether presented seriously or satirically—than about the relationship among three figures: a disillusioned Noble who, near death, surveys the failures of political history and doubts "whether or not the Creator did ever really intend Man for a State of Happiness;"[102] a young Lord at the beginning of his political career who is the recipient of the Noble's "general melancholy" about the state of "political Societies, their Origin, their Constitution, and their Effects;"[103] and an Editor who has managed to acquire and publish their private correspondence, but who will not reveal "by what Means it came into [his] Hands."[104] Burke's choice of a date—the "following Letter," the Editor notes, "appears to have been written about the Year 1748"[105]—establishes these relationships in terms of a historical proto-novel, an "Under-plot," which aligns the *Vindication*'s attack on political society with Culloden, the trials of the Chevalier's "unhappy gentlemen," Burke's own youthful flirtation with the romance of playing the Jacobite "spy," and the *Enquiry*'s initial development. This specific historical setting also accounts for the tenor of despair and secrecy that runs throughout the Noble's last testament and the fictional circumstances of its publication. Admittedly, no single character in the *Vindication* neatly corresponds to Burke's political thought, but the imagined community of the whole text serves as an image of his mind in the 1750s: nostalgic, secretive, inquisitive, both drawn to and repelled by blood, rebellious and deferential, religious at turns, despairing at others, distrustful of respectability. Burke, in effect, transitions from Blackwater romance to Whig opposition politics through a pitch-perfect impersonation of the most politically successful ex-Jacobite and populist Tory, Bolingbroke.

Because the *Vindication* was, in many ways, a later project than the *Enquiry*, Burke's choice of persona and the political cynicism in the work are hard to parse from the historiographical approach that he assumed quickly thereafter in "The History of the Present [Seven Years'] War," published serially, as indicated earlier, as part of the *Annual Register* starting in 1758.[106] Like *Waverley*, the *Vindication*, with its parting nod to Jacobite disappointment, contained an "acorn" of the British Imperial landscape that confounded the Great Whig, Walpole, but provided Burke with the recurrent theme of his political career. As the *Vindication*'s Noble remarks, "history is dark and uncertain" apart from the knowledge that "there were Conquerors, and Conquests . . . and consequently, all that Devastation, by which they are formed, and all that Oppression by which they are maintained."[107] In the *Register*, Burke frames his evolving, annual, narrative history of the War this way from the outset. "It would be difficult," he remarks, "to perfectly understand the operations of the several powers at war, during the last year [1757], without . . . examining the causes which more nearly or remotely operated to produce those troubles that have involved so many parts of the world in one common distraction."[108] But in the *Register*, the meaning of that "common distraction" remains lost in the *Vindication*'s obscure past, and the "war in which all parties and interests seem now to be so perfectly blended, arose from causes which originally had not the least connection."[109] Notably, Burke's "History" does not "pretend to decide concerning the right of either nation in [the] contest," finding it "evident enough that right had much less influence on both parties than the consideration of conveniency," and probable enough that "the ruling men [who] influence all public interests and concerns as much as the public interests themselves . . . [had] other causes to hasten this breach."[110] If there is a genuine thesis in the midst of the *Vindication*'s general despair, it is simply that "all Empires have been cemented in Blood."[111] Throughout his evolving narrative of the Seven Years' War, Burke treats British foreign affairs as the evidence.

Burke's "History of the Present War" is not ultimately about the progress of a war. Like the *Vindication*, it is about the imperial landscape as a political mimesis for the multivalent possibilities of natural law and the human condition. Thus, while the Treaty of Paris wrote a national-historical conclusion to the *Register*'s printed Imperial history, Burke effaced it immediately by continuing his project of writing present-history as a new, episodic "History of Europe." Hardly European, Burke's focus in the work lay elsewhere: Manila, Madras, Malacca, and all manner of places where "the theater of hostility was infinitely enlarged," despite the false "peace [that] seemed so well settled."[112] The "extent of the commercial empire of Great Britain is such, and it engages her in such a vast variety of difficult connections," he explained in 1763, "that it is impossible for any considerable length of time to pass over, without producing an abundance of events."[113] The alienation of Bolingbroke and other Jacobite figures from the center of British political history seems to have informed Burke's curious perspective on Britain's role in world affairs, as well as the insight that the meaningful historical processes, events, and actors tended to operate far from the metropolitan center. As John C. Weston, Jr. remarks, Burke believed that he could "see, through a survey of societies of the present world, every 'state of gradation of barbarism' and every 'mode of refinement' which man has experienced, but he never expressed a view of any sort of progress in universal history."[114] To the contrary, he believed that "we know that *we* have made no discoveries, and we think that no discoveries are to be made, in morality,—nor many in the great principles of government, nor in the ideas of liberty, which were understood long before we were born altogether as they will be after the grave has heaped its mould on our presumption."[115] His *Register* histories were thus a circumvention of what he perceived as the hollowness of national-historical narrative on a grand imaginative scale. But by the commencement of his active political career in 1763, Burke had effectively exchanged margin for margin in the *Register*, translating the Blackwater's nostalgic draw into the unfolding futurity of the British Empire.

As Geoffrey Plank observes, the "Jacobite rising influenced the administration of the empire," both through the "military confrontation itself, which affected all of Britain's domains ... [and the military establishment's subsequent] prominence in the governance of the Highlands and in the empire as a whole."[116] For Burke, however, the imperial shift meant a return to the domain of individualistic romance rather than bureaucratic progress, adventure-plot rather than dialectics, and an "abundance of [discreet] events" that confronted a range of imperial heroes, just as they had for the pirates, highwaymen, State criminals, and cavaliers of the "cottage classics." In fact, the "doggerel" romances of Burke's youth, reflecting the diasporic realities of life on the British cultural margins, often had an imperial outer limit. Even the pro-Hanover romance, *Vertue Rewarded; or The Irish Princess*, counterpointed Ireland's Williamite War of the 1690s with Spanish Colonial adventures in Peru.[117] Not surprisingly, Burke culled a series of "extraordinary adventures" from the British Empire for his first issue of the *Register*, reflecting that "the human mind can have no entertainment at once more congenial and useful to it, than . . . [stories] of extraordinary distresses, and wonderful deliverances,"[118] such as those of John Zephaniah Holwell, a prisoner in the Black Hole of Calcutta, and Robert Eastburn, a Pennsylvania blacksmith captured by an Iroquis raiding party in 1756.[119] But the representative adventurers that Burke chooses are hardly uncommon men. Robert Eastburn, for example, marches "behind an Indian, who had a large bundle of scalps hanging at his back, which was increased as often as some straggling wretch was overtaken."[120] The cardinal virtue of Eastburn, who must keep "this object perpetually before his eyes" and can do nothing about his own misfortune, is essentially that of Edward Waverley—he is drawn into historical violence and manages to simply survive.

Ian Duncan suggests that, "like the treatises of Burke . . . Scott's first novel represents rebellion, for all the variety of motive for those involved, as a reactionary adventure, so making it more difficult to imagine in any other terms."[121] Although the form of the novel tends to repress the possibility of a "sole verbal and semantic center of the ideological world," the reactionary adventure-plot ensures that *Waverley*'s poetic strain, through which Edward negotiates the dialogic aspects of the shifting historical landscape as "pure and direct expression[s] of his own intention," triumphs in the end.[122] This is a key distinction between the revolutionary outlook, which anticipates radical shifts in culture, and that of rebellion, which presupposes that cultures writ large can retain their coherence as private states of mind. In a sense, this psychological lyricism is what gives the *Vindication*'s Noble, who has "played long enough [on the world's stage] to be tired of the Drama," the last word in the tragic "ancient Theatre" of history's "immense and rapid Conquests" and "usual Carnage."[123] But for Burke, the social psychology that constituted the foundational aspiration of commonwealths was the idea that a "stable family, the acquisition of property, and freedom go together."[124] While the Noble's anarchism makes him an apostate in civil society, *Vindication*'s imperial setting also draws his familial impulse into high relief. "Happy, my Lord," he concludes, "if instructed by my Experience, and even by my Errors, you come to make such an Estimate of things, as may give Freedom and Ease to your Life. I am happy that it promises me some Comfort at my Death."[125]

As in the case of the Noble's last testament, the great reversal in *Waverley* is not the failure of Jacobite aspirations, but the Waverley-Bradwardines' poetic translation of historical principles into the domestic psychology of a stable paterfamilias. Similarly, the progress of Burke's imagination from Blackwater romance through the Noble's death in the *Vindication*, and, finally, to the "extraordinary adventures" of the midcentury British Empire, involved both an expansion of the idea of the political family to global scale of Empire as well as a reformulation of Jacobite cultural identity as a language of kinship. Scott's final resolution of Edward Waverley's adventure is thus an astute historiographical intuition, although not because—as is often claimed—it illustrates how the Jacobites were subsumed into the dialectical "inevitabilities" of life in modern Britain. Instead, it illustrates the reduction of the values and aspirations of "the Chevalier's Court" to the small scale of the domestic paterfamilias; but given the extent of the diaspora of former Jacobite families and their associates throughout the British Empire, the "Court," in this sense, took seed everywhere that the House of Hanover ruled. Often, it also made cosmopolitan encounters with Imperial subjects abroad empathetic or potentially empathetic—like to like, kin to kin—even when it served little utilitarian logic to do so.

When Burke actually established his own family in the 1750s, it echoed his Blackwater upbringing rather than his father's ambitions. Despite the fact that Richard spared no expense to maintain Edmund at Middle Temple, Edmund ruined his prospects for the law by marrying a sixteen-year-old Catholic, Jane Nugent, whose family had Nagle connections; he mortified Richard by flirting with conversion to "the Romish faith" in 1750; he attempted to immigrate to the Middle Colonies, a common option for Jacobites with poor prospects at home.[126] Edmund guiltily reassured his father that he dreaded "anything that look[ed] ill-judged in [his] conduct,"[127] but his "frustration, his questioning, and his deep, fundamental unhappiness . . . went far beyond the common anxiety about a suitable profession."[128] By the 1770s, this logic of the Jacobite paterfamilias seems to have influenced the continuing role that Burke played in the Nagle family: he was Garret's leaseholder under the Penal Laws; he helped to raise his nephew, Edmund, after the death of Edmund, Sr. in 1763.[129] And despite Richard's example, Edmund's sense of the Irish past remained the most inflexible, the most colored in terms of a romancer's heroes and villains, on the question of conformers who adopted an "unaccountable Anglicism, whiggism, and Protestantism, which in those days stood with many, particularly with all the rising men, in the place of honour, conscience, and public spirit."[130] In a sense, he was far more the adopted son of the *Vindication*'s Noble and the kinsman to an ever-increasing number of reactionary adventurers—some from history, some from romance, and some from far abroad. Kinship tied his innermost yearnings for home to Blackwater romances; the politics of empire provided a telescopic lens for seeking those continuities abroad. He often made little distinction. As he explained to his friend, the Armenian rebel, Joseph Emin, in 1756, "I am a runaway son from a father, as you are."[131]

NOTES

1. George Dekker, *The American Historical Romance* (Cambridge: Cambridge University Press, 1987), 39.

2. Walter Scott, *Waverley; or, 'Tis Sixty Years Since*, ed. Claire Lamont (Oxford: Oxford University Press, 1986), 250.

3. See, among others, Georg Lukács, *The Historical Novel*, trans. Hannah Mitchell and Stanley Mitchell (Lincoln: University of Nebraska Press, 1983); Stuart Ferguson, "At the Grave of the Gentile Constitution: Walter Scott, Georg Lukács and Romanticism," *Studies in Romanticism* 44, no. 3 (2005): 423–437; Katie Trumpener, "National Character, Nationalist Plot, National Tale and Historical Novel in the Age of *Waverley*, 1806–1830," *ELH* 60, no. 3 (1993): 685–731.

4. Cairns Craig, *Out of History: Narrative Paradigms in Scottish and English Culture* (Edinburgh: Polyglon, 1996), 72.

5. Scott, *Waverley*, 250.

6. Scott, *Waverley*, 336–337.

7. Scott, *Waverley*, 336–338.

8. Scott, *Waverley*, 338.

9. James Prior, *Memoir of the Life and Character of the Rt. Hon. Edmund Burke; with Specimens of His Poetry and Letters, and an Estimate of His Genius and Talents, Compared with Those of His Contemporaries* (London: Baldwin, Cradock, and Joy, 1826); for Scott's knowledge of Burke, see, for example, vol. 1 of *Biographical Memoirs of Eminent Novelists, and Other Distinguished Persons* (Edinburgh: Robert Cadell, 1834), 243–244.

10. Edmund Burke, *Thoughts on the Causes of the Present Discontents* (London: J. Dodsley, 1770).

11. William Hazlitt, "Character of Mr. Burke," in Daniel E. Ritchie, ed., *Edmund Burke: Appraisals and Applications* (New Brunswick: Transaction, 1990), 15.

12. Hazlitt, "Character of Mr. Burke," 15.

13. Horace Walpole, letter to Richard Bentley, April 24, 1755, in W. S. Lewis, ed., *The Yale Editions of Horace Walpole's Correspondence* (New Haven: Yale, 1937–1983), 35:221.

14. Walpole, letter to Richard Bentley, *Correspondence*, 35:221.

15. Walpole, *Correspondence* 1:380.

16. Walpole, *Correspondence* 35:221.

17. Edmund Burke, *A Philosophical Enquiry into the Origin of Our Ideas of the Sublime and Beautiful*, in T. O. McLoughlin and James T. Boulton, eds., *The Writings and Speeches of Edmund Burke*, vol. 1 (Oxford: Oxford University Press, 1997), 1757.

18. Thomas Arthur Dillon, Count Lally Tollendal, *Memoirs of Count Lally, from His Embarking for the East Indies, as Commander in Chief of the French Forces in That Country . . . to Illustrate His Civil and Military Character* (London: Charles Kiernan, 1766), 93–94.

19. Walpole refers to Burke's *A Vindication of Natural Society: or, A View of the Miseries and Evils Arising to Mankind from Every Species of Artificial Society* (London: M. Cooper, 1756).

20. Walpole, *Correspondence* 9:378.

21. Scott, *Waverley*, 14.

22. See, for example, the recent work of Katherine O'Donnell, including "The Image of a Relationship in Blood: *Párliament na mBan* and Burke's Jacobite Politics," *Eighteenth-Century Ireland* 1, no. 1 (2000): 98–119, and "Burke and the *Aisling*: 'Homage of a Nation," *Journal for Eighteenth-Century Studies* 30, no. 3 (2007): 405–422; see, also, Sean Patrick Donlan, ed., *Edmund Burke's Irish Identities* (Dublin: Irish Academic Press, 2007); Luke Gibbons, *Edmund Burke and Ireland: Aesthetics, Politics and the Colonial Sublime* (Cambridge: Cambridge University Press, 2003).

23. Richard Shackleton, qtd. in *The Leadbeater Papers; A Selection from the Mss. and Correspondence of Mary Leadbeater. Vol. 2. Unpublished Letters of Edmund Burke: And the Correspondence of Mrs. Richard Trench and Rev. George Crabbe* (London: Bell and Daldy, 1862), 113.

24. Scott, *Waverley*, 4.

25. Scott, *Waverley*, 4.

26. Edmund Burke, "A Letter to William Smith," in Peter Stanlis, ed., *Edmund Burke: Selected Writings and Speeches* (Chicago: Regnery Gateway, 1963), 323.

27. Edmund Burke, *A Letter from the Right Honourable Edmund Burke to a Noble Lord, on the Attacks Made upon Him and His Pension, in the House of Lords, by the Duke of Bedford and the Earl of Lauderdale, Early in the Present Sessions of Parliament* (London: J. Owen, 1796), 3.

28. Edmund Burke, *The Correspondence of Edmund Burke*, ed. Thomas W. Copeland, et al. (Cambridge: Cambridge University Press, 1958–1978), 8:254.

29. As George Montagu remarked to Horace Walpole in 1761, "Mr. Bourke that you saw at Mr. Hamilton's at Hampton Court is going to write an history of Ireland, and then you will know what little there is to be known of this kingdom," in Walpole, *Correspondence* 9:405.

30. James Gilray, *Crumbs of Comfort* (1782). BM 6027; British Museum, London.

31. John Courtnay, *A Poetical and Philosophical Essay on the French Revolution. In a Letter Addressed to the Right Hon. Edmund Burke* (London: J. Ridgway, 1793), 31.

32. Alexander Balloch Grosart, ed., "On the Departure of King James yc 2d 1688," *English Jacobite Ballads, Songs & Satires, etc. From the MSS. At Towneley Hall, Lancashire* (Manchester: Charles E. Simms, 1877), 86.

33. Convert's guilt is a foundational part of Connor Cruise O'Brien's psychological interpretation of the Burkes in *The Great Melody: A Thematic Biography and Commented Anthology of Edmund Burke* (Chicago: Chicago University Press, 1992); for the culture(s) of eighteenth-century Jacobitism, see James J. Sack, *From Jacobite to Conservative: Reaction and Orthodoxy in Britain, c. 1760–1832* (Cambridge: Cambridge University Press, 1993); Peter Kleber Monod, *Jacobitism and the English People, 1688–1788* (Cambridge: Cambridge University Press, 1993).

34. For the effects of the Williamite Confiscation and the land settlement of the early eighteenth century, see, especially J. G. Simms, *The Williamite Confiscation in Ireland, 1690–1703* (London: Greenwood Press, 1956); David Hayton and Gerard O'Brien, eds., *War and Politics in Ireland, 1649–1730* (London: Hambledon Press, 1986); D. W. Hayton, *Ruling Ireland, 1685–1742: Politics, Politicians and Parties* (Suffolk: Boydell Press, 2004); for contemporary attitudes toward the Cotter estates during the Confiscation, see Anonymous, *Proposals for Raising a Million of Money out of the Forfeited Estates of Ireland: Together, with the Answer of the Irish to the Same, and a Reply Thereto* (London: T. Goodwin, 1694).

35. Basil O'Connell, "Richard Burke and James Cotter, Jr.," *The Burke Newsletter* 6, no. 1 (1964), 361.

36. For James Cotter of Anngrove, see William Logan and Liam O'Buachalla, eds., "The Letters and Papers of James Cotter Junior, 1689–1720," *Journal of the Cork Historical and Archaeological Society* 68 (1963): 66–95; see, also, "A Collection of Transcripts of Deeds, Letters and Other Documents (Some in Irish) Relating to Members of the Cotter Family, from the 17th to 19th Century, Compiled by the Rev. George E. Cotter, c. 1878," MS 711, National Library of Ireland, Dublin. His father, Sir James, was widely hated in Whig circles for carrying out the assassination of John Lisle, Charles I's regicide, in 1664; for the plot to assassinate Lisle, see Alan Marshall, *Intelligence and Espionage in the Reign of Charles II, 1660–1685* (Cambridge: Cambridge University Press, 2002), 291–300; for Sir James Fitz Edmund Cotter, see B. Ó Cuív, "James Cotter, a Seventeenth-Century Agent of the Crown," *Journal of the Royal Society of Antiquaries of Ireland* 89, no. 2 (1959): 135–159.

37. Josiah Brown, *Reports of Cases, upon and Writs of Error, in the High Court of Parliament from the Year 1701, to the Year 1779. With Tables, Notes and References* (London: P. Uriel, 1779), 4:81.

38. For the Cotter trial, see Neal Garnham, "The Trials of James Cotter and Henry, Baron Barry of Santry: Two Case Studies in the Administration of Criminal Justice in Early Eighteenth-Century Ireland," *Irish Historical Studies* 31, no. 123 (1999): 328–342; James Kelly, "'A Most Inhuman and Barbarous Piece of Villainy': An Exploration of the Crime of Rape in Eighteenth-Century Ireland," *Eighteenth-Century Ireland* 10 (1995): 78–107.

39. David Dickson, *Old World Colony: Cork and South Munster, 1630–1830* (Cork: Cork University Press, 2005), 270.

40. Dickson, *Old World Colony*, 270.

41. Logan, "Letters and Papers," 135.

42. Breandán Ó Buachalla, "The Making of a Cork Jacobite," in P. O'Flannagan and C. G. Buttimer, *Cork: History and Society: Interdisciplinary Studies on the History of an Irish County* (Dublin: Geography Publications, 1993), 472.

43. Edward T. Corp, *A Court in Exile: The Stuarts in France, 1689–1718* (Cambridge: Cambridge University Press, 2004), 116–120; see, also, T. C. Barnard, "Lawyers and the Law in Later Seventeenth-Century Ireland," *Eighteenth-Century Ireland* 24 (2009): 11–35.

44. "The Life of Miss Nano Nagle: Foundress of the Presentation Order," *The Bengal Catholic Herald* 7 (1844), 97.

45. Gibbons, *Colonial Sublime*, 21–24.

46. Elizabeth Lambert, *Edmund Burke of Beaconsfield* (Cranbury: Associated University Presses, 2003), 23.

47. O'Brien, *Melody*, 3–11; see, also, Luis Cullen, "Catholics under the Penal Laws," *Eighteenth-Century Ireland* 1 (1986): 22–36; S. J. Connolly, *Religion, Law and Power: The Making of Protestant Ireland, 1660–1760* (Oxford: Oxford University Press, 2002).

48. Arthur P. J. Samuels, ed., *The Early Life Correspondence and Writings of Rt. Hon. Edmund Burke: With a Transcript of the Minute Book of the Debating "Club" Founded by Him in Trinity College Dublin* (Dublin: University Press, 1923), 8.

49. Breandán Ó Bauchalla, "Irish Jacobite Poetry," *The Irish Review* 12 (1992), 40.

50. Domnhall Ó Colmáin, *Párliament na mBan*, ed. Brian Ó Cuiv (Dublin: Dublin Institute for Advanced Studies, 1952). Ó Colmáin, a Munster priest, addressed this discourse on the importance of women's education to his student, Cotter, and used the names of prominent Munster families for his characters. Some sense of the importance and popularity of the text can be gleaned from the fact that, although unpublished, over forty manuscript copies exist.

51. Unsigned, *Elegy on the Unfortunate tho' Much Lamented Death of James Cotter, Esq., Who Was Executed at Cork on the 7th May, 1720, for Ravishing Elizabeth Squibb, a Quaker. A Broadside* (n.p, 1720).

52. Burke, *Philosophical Enquiry*, 316; for Burke's habit of quoting Spenser, see *Enquiry*, 251, and *The Reformer*, in *Writings and Speeches*, 91.

53. Edmund Burke, "The Blackwater," in Samuels, *Early Life*, 9.

54. Prior, *Memoir*, 10.

55. William Dennis, qtd. in Samuels, *Early Life*, 96.

56. Burke, *Correspondence*, 1:346.

57. Samuels, *Early Life*, 10.

58. Scott, *Waverley*, 11.

59. Scott, *Waverley*, 11.

60. Scott, *Waverley*, 11–13.

61. Scott, *Waverley*, 14.

62. Marjorie Garson, *Moral Taste: Aesthetics, Subjectivity, and Social Power in the Nineteenth-Century Novel* (Toronto: University of Toronto Press, 2007), 41.

63. Mary Leadbeater's comment that Edmund already possessed an "uncommon genius" when he enrolled at Ballitore, with a mind "strongly bent to literary acquirements" and "classical taste," suggests much about the quality of Edmund's intellectual formation in the Blackwater; see Mary Leadbeater, ed., *Memoirs and Letters of Richard and Elizabeth Shackleton . . . Including a Concise Biographical Sketch, and Some Letters, of her Grandfather, Abraham Shackleton* (London: Harvey and Darton, 1822), 4.

64. For Honora Nagle, founder of the Presentation Sisters, see Mary Pekham Magray, *The Transforming Power of Nuns: Women, Power, and Cultural Change, 1750–1900* (Oxford: Oxford University Press, 1998), 14–32; Elizabeth Lambert, "The Law, the Nun, and Edmund Burke," in Ian Crowe, ed., *An Imaginative Whig: Reassessing the Life and Thought of Edmund Burke* (Columbia: University of Missouri Press, 2002), 158–174.

65. See, for example, *Hansard* 21:720; Burke, *Writings and Speeches*, 3:166.

66. Lambert, "The Law, the Nun," 160.

67. See J. A. W. Gunn, *Beyond Liberty and Property: The Process of Self-Recognition in Eighteenth-Century Political Thought* (Montreal: McGill-Queen's University Press, 1983), 120–194.

68. Robert James Scally, *The End of Hidden Ireland: Rebellion, Famine, & Emigration* (Oxford: Oxford University Press, 1995), 142.
69. Scott, *Waverley*, 124.
70. William Carleton, "The Hedge School," in vol. 2 of *Traits and Stories of the Irish Peasantry* (Dublin: William Curry, Jun. and Company, 1830), 187.
71. Carleton, "The Hedge School," 186.
72. O'Brien, *Melody*, 22. For Inglis [English], see Éamonn Ó Ciardha, "A Voice from the Jacobite Underground: Liam Inglis (1709–78," in Gerard Moran ed., *Radical Irish Priests, 1690–1970* [Dublin: Four Courts Press, 1998]): 16–38, and *Ireland and the Jacobite Cause: A Fatal Attachment* (Dublin: Four Courts Press, 2004), 285–286, 338–345. Inglis was one of a number of political priest-poets connected to the literary/familial circles of James Cotter and the Nagles; see, for example, poetic dialogues between Edmund Nagle and Inglis in "Collection of Historical and Other Poems, in Irish," Additional MSS. 33,567, f.49, 51, 53, 55, Department of Manuscripts, British Museum, London.
73. Antonia McManus, *The Irish Hedge School and Its Books, 1695–1831* (Portland: International Specialized Book Service, 2004), 182.
74. Carleton, *Peasantry*, 188.
75. P. J. Dowling, *The Hedge Schools of Ireland* (Cork: Mercier, 1968), 33.
76. Hely Dutton, *Statistical Survey of the County of Clare, with Observations on the Means of Improvement; Drawn up for Consideration, and by Direction of the Dublin Society* (Dublin: Graisberry and Campbell, 1808), 236–237.
77. Carleton, *Peasantry*, 187.
78. For context, see, for example, Murray G. H. Pittock, *Material Culture and Sedition, 1688–1760: Treacherous Objects, Secret Places* (New York: Palgrave Macmillan, 2013), and *Poetry and Politics in Eighteenth-Century Britain and Ireland* (Cambridge: Cambridge University Press, 1994).
79. See Burke, *Correspondence* 7; Eamon O'Flaherty, "The Catholic Convention and Anglo-Irish Politics, 1791–3," *Archivum Hibernicum* 40 (1985): 14–34.
80. Burke, *Correspondence*, 7:105.
81. Burke, *Correspondence*, 7:105.
82. Burke, *Correspondence*, 7:105.
83. See John C. Weston, Jr., "Edmund Burke's Irish History: A Hypothesis," *PMLA* 77, no. 4 (1962): 397–403; see, also, Richard Bourke, "Party, Parliament, and Conquest in Newly Ascribed Burke Manuscripts," *The Historical Review* 55, no. 3 (2012): 619–652; T. O. McLoughlin, "Edmund Burke's 'Abridgement of English History,'" *Eighteenth-Century Ireland* 5 (1990): 49–59.
84. Burke, *Correspondence*, 1:63.
85. Burke, *Correspondence*, 1:63.
86. Burke, *Enquiry*, 223.
87. Gibbons, *Colonial Sublime*, 25.
88. Frans De Bruyn, *The Literary Genres of Edmund Burke: The Political Uses of Literary Form* (Oxford: Clarendon, 1996), 201. Gibbons makes use of De Bruyn's observation in *Colonial Sublime*, 25, but De Bruyn is quick to point out that "for Burke, 'Art is man's nature,' precisely because human nature requires the external monitory check of society" (201).
89. Burke, *Enquiry*, 223.
90. Ian Crowe, *Patriotism and Public Spirit: Edmund Burke and the Role of the Critic in Mid-Eighteenth-Century Britain* (Stanford: Stanford University Press, 2012), 149.
91. Neal Wood, "The Aesthetic Dimension of Burke's Political Thought," *Journal of British Studies* 4 (1964): 42.
92. Gibbons, *Colonial Sublime*, 25.
93. See "The Whole Proceedings in the House of Peers, upon the Indictments against William Earl of Kilmarnock, George Earl of Cromertie, and Arthur Lord Balmerino, for High Treason, in Levying War against His Majesty, A.D. 1746," in vol. 18 of T. B. Howell, ed., *A Complete Collection of State Trials and Proceedings for High Treason and Other High Crimes and Misdemeanors from the Earliest Period to the Present Time* (London: Longman, Hurst, Rees, Orme, and Brown, 1813), 442–530.

94. Burke, *Writings and Speeches* 12:200; see, also, F. P. Lock, *Edmund Burke: Volume II: 1784–1797* (Oxford: Oxford University Press, 2006), 70–71; for Lord Lovat, see Duncan Forbes, *Memoirs of the Life of Lord Lovat* (London: Mr. Cooper, 1746); Simon Fraser, *A Candid and Impartial Account of the Behavior of Simon Lord Lovat . . . By a Gentleman who attended his Lordship in his last Moments* (London: J. Newbery, 1747).

95. Britanicus, *Seasonable Reflections, on the Dying-Words, and Deportment, Of that Great, but Unhappy Man, Arthur, late Lord Balmerino, Who was Beheaded . . . Published by the Authority of the Sheriffs* (London: John Noon, 1746), t.p; Edmund Burke, *A Letter from Edmund Burke, Esq; One of the Representatives in Parliament for the City of Bristol, to John Farr and John Harris, Esqrs. Sheriffs of that City, On the Affairs of America* (London: J. Dodsley, 1777), 6.

96. Edmund Burke, "A Dialogue," in H. V. F. Somerset, ed., *A Note-Book of Edmund Burke* (Cambridge: Cambridge University Press, 1957), 76.

97. Edmund Burke, Letter to Richard Shackleton, 28 September 1752, in vol. 1 of *The Works and Correspondence of the Right Honourable Edmund Burke* (London: Francis and John Rivington, 1852), 15.

98. Burke, Letter to Shackleton, *Correspondence*, 16.

99. Burke, Letter to Shackleton, *Correspondence*, 16.

100. William Godwin, *An Enquiry Concerning Political Justice and Its Influence on General Virtue and Happiness* (London: G. G. J. and J. Robinson, 1793), 10.

101. Frank N. Pagano, "Burke's Views of the Evils of Political Theory; Or, *A Vindication of Natural Society*," *Polity* 17, no. 3 (1985): 447.

102. Burke, *A Vindication of Natural Society*, i.

103. Burke, *Vindication*, 13.

104. Burke, *Vindication*, i.

105. Burke, *Vindication*, i.

106. See Thomas W. Copeland, "Burke and Dodsley's *Annual Register*," *PMLA* 54, no. 1 (1939): 223–245.

107. Copeland, "Burke and Dodsley's," 14.

108. Edmund Burke, "The History of the Present War," *The Annual Register, for the Year 1758* 1 (London: J. Dodsley, 1758), 1–2.

109. Burke, "The History of the Present War," 2.

110. Burke, "The History of the Present War," 2–3.

111. Burke, *Vindication*, 13.

112. Edmund Burke, "History of Europe," *The Annual Register, for the Year 1763* 6 (London: J. Dodsley, 1763), 1.

113. Burke, "History of Europe," i.

114. John C. Weston, Jr., "Edmund Burke's View of History," *The Review of Politics* 23, no. 2 (1961), 204.

115. Edmund Burke, *Hansard* III:345, qtd. in Weston, "View of History," 207.

116. Geoffrey Plank, *Rebellion and Savagery: The Jacobite Rising of 1745 and the British Empire* (Philadelphia: University of Pennsylvania Press, 2005), 6.

117. Ian Campbell Ross and Ann Markey, eds., *Vertue Rewarded; or, The Irish Princess* [1693] (Dublin: Four Courts Press, 2010).

118. Burke, *Annual Register* (1758), 278.

119. See John Zephaniah Holwell, *A Genuine Narrative of the Deplorable Deaths of the English Gentlemen, and Others, Who Were Suffocated in the Black-Hole . . . in a Letter to a Friend* (London: A. Millar, 1758); Robert Eastburn, *A Faithful Narrative, of the Many Dangers and Sufferings, as Well as Wonderful Deliverances of Robert Eastburn . . . With a Recommendatory Preface, by the Rev. Gilbert Tennent* (London: William Dunlap, 1758).

120. Burke, *Annual Register* (1758), 303.

121. Ian Duncan, *Modern Romance and Transformations of the Novel: The Gothic, Scott, Dickens* (Cambridge: Cambridge University Press, 1992), 53.

122. Mikhail Bakhtin, "Discourse in the Novel," in *The Dialogic Imagination: Four Essays*, ed. Michael Holquist, trans. Caryl Emerson and Michael Holquist (Austin: Texas University Press, 1981), 366, 285.

123. Burke, *Vindication*, 105, 17.
124. Francis Canavan, *The Political Economy of Edmund Burke: The Role of Property in His Thought* (New York: Fordham University Press, 1995), 32.
125. Burke, *Vindication*, 106.
126. Richard Musgrave, *Memoirs of the Different Rebellions in Ireland, from the Arrival of the English . . . With the History of the Conspiracy Which Preceded it* (Dublin: Robert Marchbank, 1802), 41.
127. Samuels, *Early Life*, 97.
128. Lambert, *Burke*, 34.
129. Burke, *Correspondence* 3:411–416.
130. Burke, *Correspondence* 7:102.
131. Joseph Emin, *The Life and Adventures of Joseph Émïn, an Armenian. Written in English by Himself* (London: N.p., 1792), 90.

Chapter Two

"The empire of the father continues even after his death"

Edgar Huntly, *James Annesley, and the Eighteenth-Century Orphan Redemptioner Narrative*

Dublin was a dirty old town in 1789, with "mass-houses, churches, mixt together," and the "masters of their servants afraid," and the servants mixing on Fishamble Street to the Four Courts with "lawyers, revenue-officers, priests, physicians; beggars of all ranks, age, and conditions."[1] In this "Dublin, if ye knew it," one Irish satirist concluded, one could see "villainy both with applause and profit crowned" where "worth scarce shows its face on the ground."[2] Here, in the fictional 1789 of Charles Brockden Brown's bizarre romance, *Edgar Huntly; or, Memoirs of a Sleep-Walker*, Clithero Edny, the poor-born servant of a prominent Anglo-Irish family, the Lorimers, has been stalking Arthur Wiatte, the estranged brother of his employer and surrogate mother, Euphemia. Wiatte is also the father of Clithero's fiancée, Clarice, and although Clithero has not met Arthur Wiatte, he knows him by reputation as someone who "exceeded in depravity the arch-foe of mankind" and "rejoiced in proportion to the depth of that distress of which he was the author."[3] Though the scion of a fine family in the Protestant Ascendancy, Arthur Wiatte is a squanderer, gambler, seducer, highwayman, and a convict who has just returned to Dublin from seven years transportation. He had left his illegitimate daughter, Clarice, whose mother "died shortly after her birth," consigned "to the care of a hireling" until Arthur's sister took her in.[4] It was not an unfamiliar situation in eighteenth-century Dublin. In the real world, for example, there would still have been "beggars of all ranks" in 1789 who would have recalled stories of a strange little child named "Jemmy" wandering "about the Streets in [a] wretched Condition" in 1729 with "Boys [who] called him always *My Lord*."[5] Of all people, His Lordship, Richard, Earl Anglesea, had taken a keen interest in finding the lad, though he called him a little "Son of a Whore."[6] Jemmy, for his part, called His Lordship "Uncle Dick," and there had been rumors that Richard's brother, Arthur Annesley, had contrived to house Jemmy at the home of Dominick Farrell, a tradesman to whom he owed unpaid debts in the sum of £6. There was talk, moreover, that when Farrell approached Altham concerning the "poor Condition" he found Jemmy in, Arthur "said I will pay you, not only for [keeping Jemmy], but what I owe you."[7] Farrell's wife would not stand for keeping the bastard of gentleman who owed her husband money, but through Dominick, Jemmy came under the care of a butcher, John Purcell, whose wife "washed the Boy, gave him Cloaths, and put a Shirt of Purcell's son on him."[8] That might have been that, but as with *Edgar Huntly*'s Wiatte, there had always "seemed something unnatural in [Richard's] Temper, of which his Brother was then the Object, and afterwards his Son."[9]

As Terry Eagleton remarks, the Protestant Ascendency "had a culture of its own," based on subjugation, differentiation, but it "was not, on the whole, a field within which the cultures of the governors and the governed could negotiate, interact, [or] inflect themselves in each other's terms."[10] In both *Edgar Huntly*'s fictional Dublin and its historical analogue, though, this was not the case when matters of inheritance or status within the Ascendancy were concerned. Earl Anglesea, for example, made several trips to Purcell's neighborhood, Ormond Quay, to kidnap Jemmy after his brother's death in 1727, visits which were remarkable for their reversals of power. Ormond Quay, where Jemmy "belonged," belonged to the Ormond Boys, Catholic "fellows of the lowest description," largely of rural origins, who had found work as "assistants and carriers from slaughter-houses, joined by cattle-drivers from Smithfield, stable-boys, helpers, and idle drunken vagabonds."[11] In eighteenth-century Dublin's shifting urban landscape, they formed a "body of fighting men, armed with falchions, as they called them,—oak staves of casks hardened by smoking in chimneys, sharpened on one side, and a hole cut in one end to admit a hand."[12] In one of His Lordships visits, Purcell, the Catholic butcher, took offense that Richard, the Protestant master, "did not think it proper to return" his salute; cudgel in hand, he threatened to "knock out the Brains of any one that should touch" Jemmy—Richard, "the Constable," "his Assistants," "some odd-looking Fellows" near the door—and give them what was known in the parlance of the time as an "Ormonde fracture."[13] At length, he "brought the Child home [again] in Defiance of them all."[14] As Purcell described it two decades later, he "went off with the Child in his Hand, and brought him Home safe to his Mammy"[15]—*Jemmy*'s adopted home, meaning Purcell's home; *Jemmy*'s surrogate "Mammy," meaning Purcell's wife.

The moment when an inconsequential butcher "took the Child (who was trembling with Fear) and put him close between his Legs," threatening to beat the world to death should it touch his "son," is supraideological, suprahistorical. Its existential greatness is perhaps tied to its futility, for Purcell could undo the central historical patterning of the world he shared with lords, constables, and orphans, one characterized by contingency, commodification, transportation, the circuits of empire. In this, the butcher's boy shared a kind of symbolic kinship with Charles Brockden Brown's fictional Clithero, who finds himself, in *Edgar Huntly*, turning down "dark, crooked, and narrow lane[s]" after collecting the "amount of a debt which had lately been recovered" on his mistress's behalf.[16] "Passing the occasional "night-officer, distinguished by his usual ensigns," he finds himself "supposing particular emergencies, and delineating the conduct that was proper to be observed on each" when Arthur Wiatte attacks him, ostensibly over the sum of the debt, shouting "this shall do your business" as he fires a pistol. In the ensuing struggle, Clithero kills him. Because Clithero is known to the attending "surgeon, the landlord, and some of the witnesses," the "case needed no explanation" the next morning.[17] But the privileges of status and belonging, as Jemmy knew, are situational. Within six months of Wiatte's death, the poor-born rich woman's servant, Clithero, would follow the reportedly rich-born butcher's boy, Jemmy, into exile and servitude on the North American frontier.

If empires have an "Under-plot," Edmund Burke recognized that it was not the obvious progress of "all that Devastation, by which they are formed, and all that Oppression by which they are maintained," but rather, as in the real case of Jemmy and the fictional case of Clithero, a more complex mediation of life between conflicting diasporic and familial pulls. Early American writers, however, almost exclusively emphasized "all that Oppression" as a trope for explaining what Crèvecoeur called the "surprising metamorphosis" of immigrants in the "great American asylum, [where] the poor of Europe" met, commingled, and thrived "by the power of transplantation."[18] In 1784, for example, Benjamin Franklin contrasted America's "general happy Mediocrity that prevails" with miseries of the "old longsettled Countries of Europe."[19] Similarly, Royall Tyler's 1787 comedy, *The Contrast*, reminded "patriot hearts" to spurn "the fashions and follies" of the Old World for "homespun habits."[20] Tyler's admonishment of "modern youths," whose "imitative sense" gravitated toward Old World models,[21] would surely have extended to Charles Brockden Brown. *Edgar Huntly*, for example, staged "incidents of Indian hostility" and "perils of the western wilderness" as homespun substitutes for Ann Radcliffe's "castles and chimeras,"[22] using imported "gothic language to challenge . . . the foundation of reason and citizenship" in the Early Republic."[23] This causes his narrator in *Memoirs of a Sleep-Walker*, a young Pennsylvania Quaker named Edgar, to "question the coherence of the external world and, more pointedly, the coherence of the perceiving self."²⁴ Although Brown's protagonist, for example, insists that he "never looked upon or called up the image of a savage without shuddering," he proves himself to be a bloodthirsty "master of the Tom hawk" and fantasizes about the "bloody retribution" he can inflict on the "prostrate bodies" of Lenni Lenape warriors.²⁵ In another scene, he fetishizes "rending some living animal to pieces, and drinking its blood and grinding its quivering fibres between [his] teeth."²⁶ As Sydney J. Krause remarks, the "conventional view on this point would be that Brown was commenting on the Age of Reason's reverence for order, sobriety, sanity, optimism, its faith in the knowledgeable state of man."²⁷ This is no doubt true, but both the idea of America in the Early Republic and critiques of it like Brown's were what Wayne C. Booth terms "stable ironies"—simplistic, self-exhausting, and "fixed, in the sense that once a reconstruction of meaning has been made, the reader is not then invited to undermine it with further demolitions and reconstructions."²⁸

Edgar hopes for as much. *Memoirs of a Sleep-Walker*, which traces his jarring periplus into "the primitive world and downward into his own consciousness" takes the form of a letter written to his fiancée that recounts his investigation into the murder of her brother, Waldegrave.²⁹ But while Edgar wants the act of writing to force his "narrative, incompatible with order and coherence," to be "terminated in repose," he admits that its "drama is brought to an imperfect close."³⁰ What would proper closure in *Edgar Huntly* mean, though? The first thing Edgar recounts is returning to the scene of Waldegrave's murder along the "craggy and obscure path which led to Inglesfield's house," a farm "on the verge of Norwalk."³¹ There, he encounters Clithero sleepwalking, spading the base of an elm. "His occupation," Edgar recalls, "was mysterious and obscure. Was it a grave he was digging? Was his purpose to explore or to hide?"³² When Edgar accuses Clithero of murdering Waldegrave—a reasonable suspicion given the circumstances—Clithero exonerates himself with a long account of his life in Ireland that implicates him in the attempted murder of his Anglo-Irish patroness, Euphemia, in a fit of madness, hoping to "save" her from living with news of her brother's death. The Irishman's reasoning, like his backstory, is remarkably convoluted, and for Donald Ringe, this "sharp contrast between the long retelling of Clithero's past and the exciting adventures of Indian fighting seriously mars the unity of the tale."³³ But "marring" Edgar's narrational lens of rationality is largely Brown's point. Edgar admits that his own "limited and uniform" worldview has left him unable to distinguish Clithero's confession from the stories of "romancers and historians," and this causes his "judgment to sink into imbecility and confusion."³⁴ Ringe's "sharp contrast" is part of the psychological aesthetic of *Edgar Huntly*'s narration—and one tied to genre—but for Edgar, psychological dissonance is the product of acknowledging that Clithero's own psychological coherence requires both New and Old World resolutions. In an aesthetic sense, romance subjects Brown's narrator to different discursive positions within *destabilizing* ironies as Edgar moves from being a "distant and second-hand spectator" of empire-driven lives depicted by "romancers" to "witnessing them" firsthand and then "partaking in their consequences."[35] In his masterful reading of *Tom Jones*, William Empson describes this as a "special kind of ambiguity," one in which "A may hold some wise balanced position between [B and C], or may contrariwise be feeling 'a plague on both your houses.'"[36] The "reason this situation can arise," Empson continues, "is that the style of Fielding is a habitual double irony."[37]

Our naïve Edgar, however, always the potential *object* of habitual double ironies, is no Henry Fielding. On the other hand, the "romancing" Clithero is a figure tied to the "special kind of ambiguity" of life within certain strata of the eighteenth-century British Empire. As Elizabeth Jane Wall Hinds remarks, Brown placed his "capitalist characters in the necessarily ascendant social position" in novels like *Edgar Huntly*, "representing in them the next generation of successful adult males, while those entrenched in the older order of insular patronage lose not only the opportunity of the new world but even the disappearing opportunity of the old."[38] Inasmuch as this helps contextualize Edgar's psychological unrest within the "social" world of the novel, it also locates the defining social relationships that make Clithero's prominent role as speaker—and happenstance "romancer"—so powerful and disorienting to Edgar. As Brown, himself, remarked in 1799, a "man is encompassed by numerous claims . . . comprised in a copious narrative."[39] In Clithero's case, central to his unfolding as habitual double-ironist is the second sense in which Brown often used the term, "claim," to mean "debt." Brown suggests that Clithero's status in America ought to be understood in terms of debt peonage, a system "more important to Pennsylvania that it was to any other colony or state [and that] continued longer in Pennsylvania than elsewhere."[40] As "redemptioner" (and romancer), Clithero is the habitual double-ironist, and he is thereby both the source and problem of closure in the novel. He figures centrally within the "disappearing opportunities" of both the New and Old Worlds and yet he remains distinct from both, a social orphan. As Cheryl L. Nixon observes, attempts to "define the form of the novel and the form of the family" paralleled each other for eighteenth-century Britons, with the orphan proving "the perfect figure to do both."[41] For Edgar, Clithero's risk as "orphan" is both class-based and genre-based: Edgar is not master of his own world and could not describe it even if he was; Clithero is the servant of two, speaking with an "accent, tremulous at first, but acquiring stability and force" the more closely tied it becomes through confessional speech to the Anglo-Irish past in Edgar's American present.[42]

"A CERTAIN TRANSACTION": INDENTURED SERVITUDE AND ROMANCE IN CHARLES BROCKDEN BROWN'S PENNSYLVANIA

Part of the "legacy [Brown] derived from his childhood as a Quaker boy growing up in Revolutionary Philadelphia" was the presence of large numbers of immigrants like the fictional Clithero for whom Crevecoeur's "power of transplantation" had meant penal "transportation" to "his Majesty's colonies and plantations in America" or debt peonage in exchange for passage.[43] In practice, the two were often spoken about interchangeably. Those who incurred debts for passage were either classified as indentured servants, who subjected themselves to "a barter transaction whereby shippers traded freight space and provisions for forward-labor contracts" that were sold on arrival "at the shipper's discretion," or redemptioners, whose method of obtaining passage was a "loan transaction secured by human-capital collateral" and who were technically free to "negotiate a labor contract to sell [themselves] for the amount they owed" upon arrival in America.[44] The spectrum of conditions under debt peonage varied, as did understandings of what indenture meant. One servant, William Moraley, who came to Philadelphia in 1729, described himself in picaresque terms as part of a "Cargo consisting chiefly of Voluntary Slaves, who are the least to be pitied."[45] For his part, Benjamin Franklin saw debt peonage as integral to the American rags-to-riches narrative, arguing that poor immigrants "begin first as Servants or Journeymen; and if they are sober, industrious & frugal, they soon become Masters . . . and become respectable Citizens."[46] But whereas Moraley's Quaker master fed him "upon Dumplings, boil'd Beef, and Udder" while his servant "became enamour'd with Mrs. Sarah, the Daughter,"[47] rewards posted for runaway indentured servants and redemptioners throughout the Mid-Atlantic described their bodies as "whipped and branded," marked with "several [scars] on [the] Arms and Body," or identifiable by "a Steel Collar round [the] neck."[48] And while redemptioners often described their bondage as a form of apprenticeship, it is in representations of suffering that the mediatorial qualities of their self-descriptions appear most pronounced. Elizabeth Sprigs, for example, who had been transported by her father, wrote him that "what we unfortunat English people suffer . . . is beyond the propibility of you in England to conceive."[49] Another servant, Baikia Harvey, "beg[ged] that none of my Relation may come to this Country . . . this is a good poor mans Country when a man once getts into a good way of living but our Country people knows nothing when they come."[50] This is the language of persons bound legally to North America and equally bound by deep familial ties to the Old World. More than that of correspondent or translator, though, it is the speaking location of the habitual double-ironist, holding "some wise balanced position between [B and C]," or else feeling, contrariwise, "a plague on both your houses."

Even if we imagine Clithero with his share of "boil'd beef and Udder" instead of the "Collar," Brown makes it clear that he is bound to Ingersold, his master. Clithero's absences from the farm are no mere gothic effect; they are noted, observed, and mediated with regard to his master. Edgar, for example, must "inquire what had become of [Ingersold's] servant"; he must "seek an interview with [Ingersold's] servant"; he must ask Ingersold's leave to "permit the absence of his servant for one day" over the course of his enquiries.[51] These are not courtesies on Edgar's part; in 1799, real-life "Clitheros" in Brown's Pennsylvania "would have [had] five days added to their service time" for "each day [they] absented [themselves] from labor" without permission.[52] And although he is one of two servants on the Ingersold farm who "occupie[s] the same apartment in the barn,"[53] Clithero is also suspect as the "only foreigner" in a neighborhood where the "scheme was, for the most part, a patriarchal one," and "each farmer [lived] surrounded by his sons and kinsmen."[54] Readers can assume that a good number of these German "kinsmen" to families like the Ingersolds, Waldegraves, and their neighbors would also have made their passage from Europe as redemptioners. As Marianne S. Wokeck remarks, British merchants in the colonial trade "found that a considerable number of Germans, successfully settled in Pennsylvania, were willing to redeem the fare costs of poor immigrants, especially when such newcomers were relatives, friends, or former neighbors."[55] Brown echoes this in his description of Waldegrave's friend, Weymouth, who embarks "in an American ship, for New York . . . destitute of all property" and relying, "for payment of the debts which [he] was obliged on contract, as well as for [his] future subsistence, on [his] remittance to Waldegrave."[56] Weymouth is no poor transplant; that he is, himself, an American entrepreneur, illustrates how ubiquitous the practice of self-commodification is in the economic world of *Edgar Huntly*. Clithero's peonage is that of a redemptioner, as well. Unlike indentured servants, whose labor was sold by the shipper, Clithero "wandered hither" to Ingersold's farm.[57]

As Matthew Pethers observes, though, Clithero is simultaneously the "apogee" of a century-old figure of the transported "felon-servant," evoking a historical specter of "alien and irrational presences" on the American landscape."[58] To the extent this is true, Clithero represents, more broadly, an older, harsher model of peonage, as well as one with distinct Irish features. His circuitous passage from Dublin through Belfast's port, where "a vessel was preparing for America," and on to Philadelphia, is an accurate reflection how most human cargo was shipped from Ireland, particularly during emigration surges in the late 1720s and 1760s–1770s.[59] It also makes him an unusual Irish redemptioner. By the 1790s, Philadelphian employers increasingly turned "from bound labor to free labor" because of a growing workforce and "because it freed them from maintaining indentured servants regardless of whether or not they could be fully employed."[60] Moreover, most Irish of the period "avoided bound labor and seem to have placed a high premium on their independence from such contracts."[61] In this regard, Clithero grows more anachronistic the closer he gets to the Early Republic. His potential signification as a kind of Irish emigrant—transport, redemptioner, indentured servant—also grows more multivalent the more grounded it is in Brown's received historical past.

The global history of British imperialism, "whether in America or in Ireland would have been a familiar one" to Brown, and several of his works reflect an "Irish subtext" that demonstrates a keen interest in the island.[62] Brown also tended to draw on what Peter Kafer describes as a Pennsylvania Quaker "underwood of tribal knowledge," one in which Irish and Scots-Irish colonial networks were often implicated.[63] Part of that lore undoubtedly touched on the strange case of James Annesley, an Anglo-Irishman who claimed to be the son of Arthur Annesley, 4th Baron Altham. The Annesley case, in turn, was also an inflection point between local colonial "tribal knowledge" in both Pennsylvania and Ireland and broader treatments of the celebrated case in Britain. In 1743, James, recently returned to Dublin after service in the West Indies aboard the *HMS Falmouth*, sued Richard Annesley, his uncle, over the loss of "extensive estates in Ireland, England, and Wales as well as four aristocratic titles, including the treasured earldom of Anglesea, one of two English peerages," and annual incomes from land of £10,000.[64] James claimed that Richard, Lord Anglesea, had conspired to have him kidnapped as a child after Lord Altham's death in order to steal his inheritance, placing the lad on a ship, aptly named the *James*, "entered outwards for . . . Philadelphia."[65] In the 1740s, James's barrister, Douglas Mackercher summed his American life up thus: little "Jemmy" was "ill-treated, kidnapp'd, transported to Philadelphia, where he was a Slave for thirteen or fourteen years, suffering unspeakable Hardships, and was come to England, to obtain his Right, Title, and Estate."[66]

As one of the longest, strangest lawsuits in eighteenth-century Britain, the Annesley case captivated a wide, diverse audience. As might be expected, that audience included "ordinary folk in Ireland, especially Catholics [who were] able to empathize with James's persecution," the sort for whom "his uncle's [potential] disgrace may have given vent to pent up animosity toward the established order."[67] Similarly, Jacobite sympathizers like the London stationer and poet, Elizabeth Boyd, whose *Altamira's Ghost* pleaded James's cause, were likely "fir'd with [such]indignant Rage" on his behalf because James's disinheritance and overseas exile mirrored their own ruin.[68] James's case had also become a *cause célèbre* for the upper class, "notwithstanding the threat that his lawsuit posed to property holders."[69] More broadly, the vilification of Arthur and Richard Annesley, both of whom had reputations for dissolute living, reflected shifting social mores in some circles. Increasingly, the Whig Britain that James returned to celebrated Defoe's middle-class idealization of the "compleat English gentleman," someone who forewent "Scotch tones & rough & roaring freedom of manners" to, as James Boswell put it, "get into a proper well-behaved plan."[70] As the case dragged on through appeals and injunctions—it remained unsettled at James's death in 1760—its public narrative evolved alongside its legal developments to include poems, pamphlets, and novels that established the "fact" of James's lordship in the space of "common knowledge" where, like James, it could assert claims and establish identities, but without resolution. Often, this involved genre-blurring. In 1745, for example, the nonfictional *Case of the Honourable James Annesley, Esq.* advertised itself as "Being a Sequel" to Elizabeth Haywood's *Memoirs of an Unfortunate Young Nobleman*, a quasi-fictional romance published two years earlier.[71] Similarly, a long, digressive tale—not unlike in structure to *Edgar Huntly*'s Clithero narrative—presented in Tobias Smollett's 1751 picaresque novel, *Peregrine Pickle*, retold James's tribulations with additional factual details conveyed to Smollett by James's barrister, Mackercher.[72] As Elizabeth Boyd remarked, the "impartial Just," from "Clans of Figure to the low Plebian, rejoice[d] the Frauds detected, and wish[ed] with [her] to see the noble Slave enjoy his lawful Right,"[73] even if only in an imagined commonwealth of readers. "Notwithstanding the verdict" in his initial suit, James never assumed his title or received so much as "one farthing from the estate for which the verdict was obtained,"[74] much of which went to fund his uncle's ongoing appeal. His "lawful right" was less firm in the law than in poems about the law's delay. Nor did his indentured servitude make him a "Slave" in the understood legal sense, noble or otherwise. However, the persona of James Annesley, a "man is encompassed by numerous claims" (in both senses), allowed him to capitalize on the multivalent ambiguities—he suffered "Transportation," he was "Indent[ured]," he was "sold as a common Slave"—in the legal description of his status.

British trial accounts tended to quickly summarize James's American servitude, his transformation from Anglo-Irish heir to American "noble Slave." Notable exceptions, such as Haywood's *Memoirs*, merged a general outline of facts—likely garnered from James, himself—with romanced elements, reflecting imperial anxieties about "the presence of savage new worlds *made by Europeans themselves*," a "zeitgeist of the disordered American frontier as viewed in Britain."[75] The reflexive alignment between Irish and Indian "savages" in Brown's fiction, most notably in *Edgar Huntly*, is here in primitive form. In *Memoirs*, for example, James's "descriptions of the landscape of the Delaware . . . mirror his own inner torments in an almost pseudo-gothic fashion" that seem to prefigure *Edgar Huntly*'s treatment of both Clithero and Edgar in the same locales.[76] But Pennsylvanian "tribal knowledge" about James's servitude tended to highlight or skew different narrative elements than British popular retellings. This is not surprising given representations of James as erstwhile frontiersman "holding a Gun and a dead Squirrel," carrying on a love affair with an Indian "slave of the Irokese nation," devising escapes through Susquehanna lands, and fighting "vengeful brothers of his Indian admirer."[77] As late as 1832, for example, summaries of Annesley's life appeared in the Philadelphia press, highlighting elements of Annesley lore—his fine singing voice, a "strong looking log cabin" near Robert Barber's "250 acres of the lower hills" where "James, afterward Lord Altham, was confined, having run away from his master."[78] American versions emphasized that James's master, like Clithero's, was an "old German" farmer living near the "forty mile-stone" on the Lancaster road.[79] They also claimed that James had a child with the Old German's daughter who died fighting Edgar's foes, the Lenni Lenapi, at some point prior to the Revolution. And whereas British versions insisted that the Quaker daughter's affections were "not reciprocated" by James, Pennsylvanian accounts reversed the Altham dispossession, claiming that James had abandoned the "plain Mennonite maid Beckie" and her son when he returned to Britain, dispossessing them of a rightful inheritance. In these versions, "Beckie" dies heartbroken and James's unnamed heir is forsaken by his Quaker grandfather, replicating his father's own orphaning.[80]

Broadly, these Pennsylvanian "tribal" versions are what Walter Scott—who used Annesley's case, himself, for the plot of *Guy Mannering*—called "traditional memorials," folk knowledge that "partake[s] in such a varied and doubtful degree" of "fiction mingled with truth" that it forms the basis for "romantic histories or historical romances, according to the proportion in which their truth is debased by fiction."[81] Of course, this is Edgar's problem with Clithero's tale; he finds himself too proximate to it to distinguish between romanced and historicized elements. In part, this is because, as Hinds observes, Edgar Huntly's central social fact is the sequential, historical movement of "successful adult males" into "ascendant social position[s]." The figure of the orphan thwarts this because it interrupts the historical succession plot, but more importantly because it uncovers the fiction of displacement-as-progress. The orphan's narrative desire—the restoration of familial dynamics in the past—is impossible and therefore its narrative end is always substitutional. Retellings of James's (North) "American" life, for example, relocate and reproduce Lord Altham's family dramas in Ireland through James's own actions as frontier protagonist, translating an Anglo-Irish aristocratic tale of disinheritance into a Pennsylvania Mennonite one. Indeed, while Cooper's Moravian-born hero, Leatherstocking, "is not lost heir to some great aristocratic family," the figuration of James Annesley's Indian-fighting orphan—whether or not he existed—shares Bumppo's position as a "virtually nameless, or name-shifting product of frontier classlessness," just as his father, in declaring himself Lord Altham's son throughout his North American frontier indenture, simultaneously reveals that, like Leatherstocking, he "really belongs to a society which he cannot feel a part of, or rather that he doesn't belong to any society at all."[82]

Leatherstocking, of course, had Cooper to advocate for the "biographical" significance of the peripheral Colonial, Bumppo, whose frequent name changes "make it impossible to *address* him and thereby pin him down geographically and socially."[83] James Annesley had "James Annesley," whose social indeterminacy, spanning the First Empire, made it possible to address him as an "Unfortunate Young Nobleman." That we have no equivalent record of James's supposed American son, whether in "romantic histories or historical romances," is partly, then, an effect of the public, discursive context for James's own self-narration in the 1740s–1750s Britain, one through which his staging as orphan "interrogate[d both] the family and narrative and, ultimately, allow[ed] family-making to be equated with fiction-making."[84] But the goal was not to reveal the family as untruth, it was to extend psychological communion between the author-orphan and the minds of constituents, speaking to the work of narrative substitution in family-making. The practical exigencies involved in seeing *Annesley vs. Anglesea* through to settlement encouraged this. *Case of the Honourable James Annesley* (1758), for example, which recapitulated the "three Trials" already in print, was published in response to the "great Pains" that Richard Annesley had taken to "eraze and extirpate the least Remembrance" of the case on the public's part through his interminable use of the appeals process.[85] James, the preface makes clear, did "not suffer alone," but was by then united in misfortune with those "ruined Friends" who had lost large sums sponsoring him during his decade-long litigation.[86] As "orphan," sustaining his surrogate family of patrons and supporters required the iterative, recursive production of his personal narrative. The inverse was equally true.

Fundamentally, then, the work of both family-making and fiction-making in James's case was interrogative. It sought to understand relationships—biological, legal, historical, and even literary—as species of truth. The author of a 1744 piece called *The Parallel: Or, A Collection of Extraordinary Cases, Related to Concealed Births, and Disputed Successions* makes this point with respect to James's claim. "We have lately seen," the author reflects, "a certain Transaction in Ireland, become the common Topic of Conversation, on account of some surprising Incidents that attended it," but the author finds it "much stranger than the Story, that in most Companies, you find People ready to determine" James's truthfulness "independent of Evidence, just as their Craft of Mind leads them."[87] Here, *The Parallel* distinguishes between two "Craft[s] of Mind," noting that "some, because the Story is strange, will needs have it true; but what is still more whimsical, is the opposite Opinion; that because it seems strange, therefore it is altogether incredible."[88] *Parallel*'s author proceeds to describe "a few examples of the same sort," including an "abundance of striking Passages" from the life of Richard III that "exercised the Pens of most of our Authors, whether Poets or Politicians."[89] What is of significance, here, is not the willing elision of fictional and political genres, but the emphasis in both instances on the idea of what *may have happened*, which of course is the defining ethos of the historical romance for writers like Charles Brockden Brown. His 1801 essay on the subject aligns the genre with "the *probable* and the certain" against official history's "tissue of untruths . . . [that] never had existence."[90] We see this echoed in Clithero's confession with its redress of Edgar whose "inferences," Clithero (and Brown) proclaim, in their "design and conduct, are a tissue of destructive errors."[91] Clithero's speaking position—both Old World foreigner and romancer—thus aligns his tale with "what *may* have happened, and what has *actually* happened."[92] Edgar, on the other hand, is "blind to the most momentous consequences of . . . [his] actions"—in Brown's understanding, a mere chronicler.[93] What *The Parallel* implies is that historicized, grounded "romancing" is not a falsification, but rather a "middle Road," a hermeneutic of reasonable doubt. In the case of James Annesley, iterative retellings of his life functioned as an interrogatory process meant to clarify, rather than obscure, causes and relationships. Significantly, *The Parallel* suggests, the "middle Road"—which, for our purposes, might be thought of as a hermeneutic of habitual double irony—is characteristic of the "common sort of People [who] are so very fond of the Marvelous, and so ready to exalt every Transaction."[94]

Similarly, Brown's authorial "Transactions" of the 1790s, which often relied on true-crime accounts and newspaper stories for their inspiration, occupied an inflection point between eighteenth-century novelists like Smollett and Fielding, who distinguished their own work apart from "monstrous Romances,"[95] and Regency-era romancers like Scott who admired eighteenth-century "traditional memorials" for their historiographical methods. Indeed, it is hard to find a clearer model of the emergent idea of a "mixed class" of literature, one that oscillated between "romantic histories, or historical romances, according to the[ir] proportion" of fact, than the decade-long production of popular "memorials" in the Annesley case. Brown, himself, was almost undoubtedly aware of James's story. His lost 1798 novel, *Sky-Walk; or, The Man Unknown to Himself*, employed numerous elements later recycled for *Edgar Huntly*, including somnambulism, an Edgar-like narrator, a frontier setting, and a secretive Irish immigrant.[96] If *Sky-Walk*, then, is something of a first draft for what eventually became *Edgar Huntly*, its Clithero figure is the suggestively named "Annesley." There are, of course, any number of possible inspirations for Brown's choice of surname. Robert Annesley, for example, was a prominent Quaker merchant on Sixth Street whose family had emigrated from County Laois shortly after the American Revolution. But in the surviving fragment of *Sky-Walk*, the Irishman's sufferings follow the orphan pattern in James's accounts; Brown's "Annesley" attempts to return to Ireland from abroad to acquire an estate, but finds himself "reduced from a state of comparative prosperity, to utter distress" through miscarriages of justice.[97] We also know from notes on the plot that Brown set much of the novel's action on the Delaware, where James lived before his "wonderful Escape from America."[98] One must assume that the narrator, ostensibly another Dubliner, replicates the disenfranchisement of "Annesley" (on whose behalf he intervenes with the law) through his own eventual "transportation" in one form or another to James's old Middle Colonies landscape.

Indeed, the travails of disenfranchised or mysterious Irishmen on the Delaware was a thematic, almost obsessive, thread in Brown's imagination. Like *Sky-Walk*'s narrator or *Edgar Huntley*'s Clithero, for example, his protagonist in the unfinished *Memoirs of Stephen Calvert* has a consciousness dominated by two poles: Dublin and the American frontier. It also set its transatlantic plot circulations in motion with an "indolent, vindictive, irascible" Anglo-Irish gentleman whose "marriage choice . . . was governed by no considerations but those of property and family," and who tore his "infant sons from the arms of their mother, and consigned [them] to the care of hirelings"—both key depictions of James's father, Lord Altham, in Mackercher's case.[99] Indeed, a basis in the Annesley case might account for Brown's claim about his own fictional account of "Annesley," Dublin, and Pennsylvania in *Sky-Walk*, namely that the novel is partway a "picture of truth," one in which "facts have supplied the foundation of the whole."[100] In a less speculative sense, what Brown's iterative "Irish" fictionalizing shares with the Annesley precedent is the production of the orphan-redemptioner's voice and cultural position through the process of open-ended revisioning of the historical and the fictional. In terms of Brown's authorial process, *Stephen Calvert* served as a kind of "intertext" to *Edgar Huntly*; Brown had "interrupted *Edgar Huntly*'s serialization to publish *Stephen Calvert*, a move made sensical as the novel begins by repeating Edny's traits and life testimony" in variation through the "Annesley" material.[101] Similarly, divergent "tribal" and "traditional memorials" of the actual James Annesley's life developed his claims for eighteenth-century audiences accustomed to "journalistic summaries and fictionalized accounts of a trial [that] freely reordered the evidence as a sequential narrative of events, usually of a biographical cast."[102]

"HE AND HIS FELLOW SERVANT": THE *PROBABLE* AND THE CERTAIN" LIVES OF JAMES ANNESLEY AND CLITHERO EDNY

A Pennsylvania redemptioner in 1800, the year after *Edgar Huntly*'s publication, was "always a person in the depths of poverty, who, for transportation to the United States, willingly became a slave."[103] It is notable, then, given James's kidnapping, to see him referred to, like Clithero, as "our redemptioner" in later American retellings. More to the point, he was, strictly speaking, an indentured servant, not a redemptioner. Richard Annesley had contracted with Thomas Henry, captain of the *James*, for his nephew's passage as "cargo," and the lad had been recorded with Dublin's town clerk as indented under "the Name of James Hennesley" in 1728.[104] "Traditional memorials," however, while often displaying a high concern for verisimilitude and factual detail, are more open-ended, geared toward providing relative contexts for the "tribe." As early as 1760, accounts circulating in America shifted elements and episodes of James's life around. His extended obituary in the *Boston News-Letter* is well worth considering in this regard:

> Mr. Annesley's birth was introduced in Ireland with almost the pomp of that of a prince, it having been accompanied with such rejoicings of every sort, as were never known in Ireland before or since, this will appear from the mouths of almost a hundred witnesses. From his birth to the age of 8 or 9 years, his dress and attendants declared him in all respects, the son of a nobleman: but soon after the scene changed; for on the death of his father he was instantaneously kid-napp'd and sold to America, where he underwent thirteen years dreadful slavery; and ever since his return from thence he has suffered the plague and torture of the law, 'till at last he has fell a victim to a broken heart. — His life, almost from his birth to his decease, and his claim, are far from being the least extraordinary in the annals of private persons of this nation; for starting from the low and ignominious state of a slave, he laid claim to a coronet and estate, and at once engrossed the attention and compassion of the three kingdoms more, I believe, than any private man ever did. — 'Tis assured that the trustees of Mr. Annesley's will attend to lose no time in prosecuting the claim in favor of the Orphan, for he has left a son.[105]

While this is not an accurate version of James Annesley's life, either according to his own account or those brought forward by others in the 1740s, its conflation of two opposed narrative arcs suggests much about the understanding of Annesley as orphan-servant, as well as the mechanics of how biographical-historical matter was "romanced." The first presents Annesley's fairy-tale fall from "pomp like that of a prince" through the American ordeal of "thirteen years dreadful slavery." This, in turn, is paralleled perfectly by an equivalent period of "plague and torture" after his return to Britain. This overarching trajectory of social descent is counterpointed by the sort of rags-to-riches tale that Franklin would admire. In this second arc, James, "starting from the low and ignominious state of a slave," rises up the social ladder to claim a "coronet and estate" as a "private person." The conclusion, such as it is, does not resolve the narrative or provide judgment on its events. Instead, it consists of reiterating the narrative process itself—"prosecuting the claim"— and locating the position of the "Orphan," who is both implied narrator and the object of narration, and at the nexus of both topsy-turvy story arcs. James Annesley's (English) son, here, is not described as an "orphan" as he is in other obituaries from 1760. He is, in effect, legitimated by the double-ironic knot tied in the position of his father.

In *Edgar Huntly*, both arcs intersect in Clithero, the literary "son" to *Stephen Calvert*'s "Orphan," "Annesley." The central thrust of his Armagh-to-Dublin bildungsroman traces his ascent through Euphemia's patronage from his parents' fields, where he would "doubtless have trodden in their footsteps," to the enjoyment of "emoluments large enough to supply [him] with every valuable instrument of improvement or pleasure" in "my lady's household-establishment."[106] However, after his attempt to kill Euphemia and subsequent ejectment from the Lorimer home, he recalls that he "threw off the garb of affluence, and assumed a beggar's attire" in Dublin before finally obtaining passage to America from Belfast.[107] Clithero's account of the intervening time is scant. "Successive incidents supplied me with a clue," he recalls, "and suggested, as they rose, the next steps to be taken."[108] While Clithero tells us at this point that his "conceptions with regard to the future were shapeless and opaque," his assessment is an equally apt description of the narrative interregnum between Dublin and his native Ulster, which is striking given his descriptive attention to detail and sequence throughout the rest of his tale. It is "accidental" that he has money on him in his beggar's clothes; in his "unabated" restlessness, he arrives at "one town" and knows "not why [he] should go farther."[109] The point of this is in part to highlight his psychological distress; on Brown's part, it is also the means of providing the quickest elision between the sort of reverse arcs that the orphan speaker holds in equilibrium. Just as "'tis assured" that Annesley's trustees will "lose no time in prosecuting the claim" in his favor, Brown loses no time in accomplishing Clithero's shift to *Edgar Huntly*'s Pennsylvania setting.

For eighteenth-century readers familiar with "Unfortunate Young Nobleman," though, Clithero's reduction to "beggar's attire" would have been a suggestive analogue to some of the most scandalous parts of the Annesley case testimonies. After his acrimonious separation from James's mother, "Moll" Sheffield, in 1716, Lord Altham had moved to Dublin with James and had taken up with a Phrapper Lane heiress of modest fortune, Sally Gregory. Altham's new mistress, who had "assumed [Moll's] Title, and was called by all her own Creatures in the family, Lady *Altham*," began "very early to shew a great Distaste to the Child, and endeavored to get him out of her Way," and finally succeeded in boarding James "at the House of Connaugh, the Dancing-Master," while encouraging Lord Altham to disclaim James's legitimacy.[110] Meanwhile, Lord Altham's "Affairs were fallen into such Confusion" during this period, "his Debts so great, and his Credit so much sunk," that he eventually conceded to suggestions that "he might raise Money upon the Anglesea Estate, to which he had a right, provided the Boy as out of the Way." He could not formalize long-term leases without his legal heir's consent, and James—"Jemmy"—was too young to grant it. One account of the Annesley affair in 1744 summed it up thusly: "[Altham's] last Humour was to make himself easy, by selling the Reversion . . . at the expense of his Family, and this led him, as he had turned his Wife out of Doors, to gratify his own Humour, to turn his Son out of Doors to satisfy his Interest."[111] When James returned to his father's house at Inchicore, he was not "so much as permitted to enter the House, but [was instead] turned out and abandoned into the wide World."[112] For the next two years, he "rambled about the Streets [of Dublin] in that wretched Condition," much to the shock of those in Altham's orbit who came across "poor Wom[e]n that sold Potatoes" and knew him well.[113] At first, his absence from Lord Altham's household caused as much trouble as his presence had, provoking a scandal with "all the Inhabitants of Dublin for witnesses."[114] It was only after Altham's death that his brother, Richard, sent his "Assistants" to hunt Jemmy outside Ormond Market at "Smithfield, College Green . . . [or] on a Sunday [at] the Long Meadows," where they finally abducted him and consigned James to the *James*.[115]

In the *News-Letter*'s 1760 obituary, this sort of material, which made up the bulk of widely publicized court testimonies, has as little purchase as the space and time between Euphemia's Dublin "household establishment" and Ingersold's farm does in Clithero's confession. This is because structurally, both orphan-servant narratives organize events around what Charles Renouvier calls the "*uchronie*, a utopia of past time" in which the author "writes history not as it was, but as it could have been."[116] In one sense, the critical value of this sort of thought experiment is counterfactual; it highlights an awareness of otherwise latent causal chains or relationships in history through a hyperfocus on key events or persons, the reconfiguration of which into speculative "what ifs?" comprises an interrogative method. This allows Clithero's confession, for example, to illuminate Brown's concerns about the Early Republic's "subjection to cruel cycles of merchant capitalism" by assuming a historical, defamiliarized version of the perspective in Annesley's *Memoirs*, where what "lurk[ed] behind the story of 'the unfortunate nobleman' was the idea that America was a kind of topsy-turvy world."[117] What makes *Edgar Huntly*'s America such a "topsy-turvy world," however, is not the manner in which it inverts the British social order. It is the novel's implication that New and Old World conflicts mirror and implicate each other, suggesting any number of unsettling possibilities, not least of which is that Edgar's America, psychologically speaking, is Clithero's Anglo-Irish counterfactual fiction.

As Richard J. Evans remarks, the "key point" in the *uchronie* is the "angle at which the imaginary trajectory departs from the real."[118] For Renouvier, this "scission point" depends on the writer's purpose in staging the *uchronie*. In the case of both orphan-servant narratives, Annesley's and Clithero's, this is complicated by their confessional mode of speech; their *uchronie* is not utopian time, but a utopian self, staged in both the past where they were whole and in the speculative future where that wholeness will be affirmed, a sort of temporal double-ironist. In consequence, what distinguishes the orphan-servant's *uchronie* from other romanced counterfactual "histories" is that it has no interest organizing sequential time from the scission point for the sake of the historical present. Instead, the "imaginary trajectory" seems to run backward from the scission point, the real or symbolic orphaning, for which New World transportation, servitude, and other attendant miseries serve as extended metaphor. In the *News-Letter*'s obituary, this manifests in the disproportionate weight given to James's pre-trans-portation life in Ireland; it is only before "soon after the scene changed" that time passes in detailed sequence—the birth "accompanied with such rejoicings," the "8 or 9 years" of childhood—and after transportation, the emphasis is on rendering Annesley's American servitude as well as his British lawsuit as a "scene." Similarly, Clithero makes it quite clear to Edgar that meaningful time, for all intents and purposes, stopped when he left Ireland and came to Ingersold's farm where he is "content to wear out [his] few remaining days."[119] Only the reconstruction of what might have been matters to Clithero in his fictional world or Annesley in his real one.

The attestation of "a hundred witnesses" in the *News-Letter*'s *uchronie*, for example, freely transposes accounts of James's widely publicized return to Ireland in 1743, during which he canvassed for plaintiff's deponents in his case against "Uncle Dick" onto his birth. While Annesley's return was, indeed, accompanied by something like "the pomp of a prince," his infancy was a different matter. Arthur Annesley had married James's mother, Mary ("Moll"), the illegitimate daughter of John Sheffield, 1st Duke of Buckingham, in 1715. Richard Annesley seems to have opposed the union, as did Altham's namesake and uncle, Arthur, 1st Earl of Anglesea. Long-standing "animosities subsisted between [Richard] and his Brother" over financial matters, and "Jemmy" Annesley's birth frustrated "Richard in his Expectations of Estate and Title," a matter he "made no Manner of Secret."[120] Anglesea, in turn, disapproved of his nephew's marriage to the daughter of his Tory political rival, Buckingham. Altham had little affection for Anglesea, to whom the birth of Altham's heir promised problems, but he needed the "Old Dog."[121] Altham depended on the diminishing returns of Anglo-Irish landlordism, a system that multiplied subleases and middlemen to prop up the opulent lifestyles of absentee masters like him. His "circumstances . . . being none of the best," though, and being of a "very roving Inclination" besides, Altham quite clearly viewed his private affairs as a form of financial speculation.[122] Although his decision to wed the "handsome" Moll Sheffield "may have been an impulsive choice," it was also an economic gamble on the Anglesea estate, as was his subsequent decision to throw her out of Dunmain House shortly after James's birth in 1716. "Lord Anglesea will not be in friendship with me," Altham reportedly claimed, "while I live with this woman . . . [and therefore] I will part with her."[123]

The Annesleys, in fact, had lived apart for a good portion of their marriage—Lord Altham in Ireland, Moll with familiar circles in England—until 1713 when Lady Altham joined her husband at Wexford. She established herself at Dunmain House, a grand, gray, granite gentleman's farmhouse that Arthur had sublet from Captain Lambert, a local Protestant squireen to whom he was, at times, indebted for loans. But unlike the charming depiction of "rejoicings of every sort" in her son's obituary, the widely publicized testimonies of Altham's servants from James's trial painted a different picture. Their recollections of Lord Altham portrayed him flinging the "China that had indecent figures on it" at his butler's head, at his wife, then demanding that Moll birth him his "Irish bull," then prompting her miscarriages whenever his darker moods struck.[124] Moll's longtime servant, Mary Heath, finally confronted Altham, remarking that "the Lady would be a fruitful Woman, [if] only for my Lord's Usage."[125] His frequent sexual infidelities were common knowledge, as well. Richard, in fact, argued at trial that James was the bastard of "Juggy" Landy, kitchen maid at Dunmain who Altham had expelled, threatening to "bring out the Hounds. and set them at the Whore."[126] Similarly, one of Altham's Dublin friends, surprised to hear about both Altham's marriage and the subsequent birth of his son, warned him that it was high time to "turn off all his whores" in the capital.[127]

To "turn off" was not the high-minded renunciation our Dublin moralist made it sound like. Samuel Johnson defined it as "to dismiss contemptuously," citing Joseph Addison's turn of "he *turn'd off* his former wife to make room for this marriage."[128] Similarly, an anonymous 1711 address to "Protestant Readers of all Circumstantial Differences" argued for "keep[ing] the Sword" against "all such who tend to debauch our lands" by reminding readers that "a Master may turn off all or any of his Servants" without cause, a context used several times throughout the Annesley depositions.[129] The phrase connoted social alienation, capricious reassignments of classes and identities, the commodification of relationships that otherwise bound through custom. In Altham's case, it also staged an "improvidence [that] masked a deeper insecurity" among the Protestant Ascendency about its own "ambivalent status within both Ireland and the empire."[130] In this regard, the power to both perpetrate and punish sexual misconduct reinscribed the Protestant establishment's power over the social economies of Irish demesnes and vice versa. During James's trial, for example, Richard's lawyers used the fact that Annesley's childhood tutor, James Dempsey, was Catholic as proof that James was a bastard, for as a Protestant, Lord Altham "must be supposed to [have] take[n] some Care that the Mind of his Child took not a wrong bias in its Infancy."[131] Similarly, James's baptismal record was discredited for listing, as godfathers, a "Person in very poor and mean Circumstances," as well a "Roman Catholick, and Papists by the Laws of this Kingdom . . . cannot become Sureties for Protestant Children."[132] In a similar vein, attorneys during the Annesley trial used this elision of sex, religion, and class to "turn off" deponents. Joan Laffin, for example, a former servant of Altham's, was discredited for having been "an obscure person in the Family," as well as "both a Whore and a Thief," and therefore someone "No-body would believe," even if "she swore all the Oaths in the Universe."[133]

By far, though, the most striking example of what it meant to "turn off" someone in James's childhood was the violent, almost farcical entrapment of Moll Sheffield and her subsequent expulsion from Dunmain House. The Sunday following his admission to "Mr. Sutton (the Surgeon), Mr. Taylor (my Lord's Receiver)," and Thomas Palliser (a young Anglo-Irishman who had "great Intimacy and Continuance in the Family)" that he intended to be rid of Moll for Anglesea's sake,[134] Lord Altham insisted that Palliser "must stay at Home, to keep [Moll] Company" during breakfast, "for that he was going to Church."[135] Although Palliser "never attempted the Virtue of Lady Altham in any Respect," Arthur "came [at length] into the Room with some Servants, and having a drawn Sword in his Hand made a Thrust" at Palliser, accusing him of having seduced Lady Altham. Dunmain's servants restrained Palliser on Altham's behalf and "cut off a Piece of his Ear."[136] They had their own reasons, it seems, for playing such an eager part in the violent charade, seeing as how the young gentleman "used to put Horse-Jallap into some of their Drink" as a joke and "tell [their] Lady Lies of them."[137] But when Altham threw his wife out of Dunmain House following the Palliser farce, few of the "sixteen or seventeen servants" in Altham's "large and disorderly household" seem to have supported his "unwillingness to part with the Child" or allow Moll to "at least give the Child a parting Kiss."[138] Despite his "strict Charge . . . to not let [their] Lady have any Access to him,"[139] Altham's servants seem to have frequently violated this rule, whether out of compassion or "for the Lucre of . . . getting a Piece of Money,"[140] and Moll's secret visits continued for some time while she lodged with Captain James Butler a few miles from Lord Altham's house. Altham, meanwhile, threatened his servants—and James—with transportation to America or being "turned out" of the house. Increasingly "Paralytick" and emotionally ravaged by her "Family and Misfortunes," Moll finally returned to England by way of Dublin in 1723, where she remained until her death in 1728.[141] By the time "her Ladyship went to London," Mary Heath recalled, "she [had] lost the Use of her Limbs and could not stand."[142] Moll's "Disorder," Heath explained, had begun in Wexford.

If it seems unnatural for Moll Sheffield to have left her son in Wexford, it is important to remember that English custody law held to the maxim that "a mother, as such, is entitled to no power, but only to reverence and respect."[143] William Blackstone elaborated on this point, arguing that "empire of the father continues even after his death; for he may by his will appoint a guardian to his children."[144] Moreover, although Arthur Annesley had contrived to establish grounds for divorce with the Palliser spectacle, he had not acted on them. In a manner of speaking, he hedged his bets with respect to the Anglesea business. Moll was therefore still bound by marital coverture laws that precluded her from signing contracts, holding properties, or filing suit.[145] Just as James, as double-ironist, would come to negotiate his own "special kind of ambiguity" between servant and lord, his mother occupied an equivalent interzone after leaving Wexford; like James, her full enfranchisement into the social position she claimed was more conceptual than factual. In a sense, her nomadic dislocations from James Butler's house in New Ross to Dublin to London foreshadow James's transportation, rendering the Anglo-Irish milieu an equivalent colonial "topsy-turvy world" to North America's and herself a "noble Slave" in the sociolegal "empire" of James's father.

Clithero's quick initial sketch of his childhood introduces familiar relationships and characterizations from the Annesley case, set against a backdrop of Irish peasant life, what Sir Charles Coote would describe as Armagh's "degrading relicks of the feudal system" a few years later in 1804.[146] The Edny family's landlord, Lorimer, is an Altham-like scoundrel, wastrel, and absentee who keeps to "the metropolis" while "stewards and retainers" upkeep his estate.[147] Like Lord Altham's pecuniary-minded marriage to Mary Sheffield, Lorimer has married the upright Euphemia Wiatte for "a great accession of [her] fortune," all the while retaining "the vices that grow out of opulence."[148] He fathers a profligate son just as inclined to "the vices inherent in wealth and rank" as himself; he causes the stoic, long-suffering Euphemia to endure, as Moll did, countless "distressing and humiliating obligations" through her connection to him; he lavishes "two-thirds of his fortune" on a mistress.[149] But *Edgar Huntly*'s signal counterpoint to the Annesley narrative is Brown's decision to quickly kill off the "Altham" father figure in a foolish duel, thereby allowing its "Moll," Euphemia, to "profit by her newly-acquired independence, [and] live conformably to her notions of right."[150] Given his allusive echoes to the Annesley saga in *Edgar Huntly*'s development, it is possible that Brown was influenced by the figure of Dorothea Annesley Du Bois, a disinherited, delegitimized daughter of James's uncle, Richard, and his first wife, Ann Simpson, who, like her cousin, unsuccessfully sued her father's estate to gain financial independence and wrote several novels, plays, and poems throughout the 1760s and 1770s that pleaded her case in fictional trappings and were sometimes confused with James's narrative.[151] Comparatively speaking, though, the structure of Clithero's narrative thus unfolds around a fascinating "what if?" from the more prominent Annesley trial. Here, what would have immediately closed the James Annesley narrative only serves to highlight Brown's overarching socioeconomic critique of the "effect of commerce on Old World expectations of inheritance based in land ownership and patronage."[152] For all her goodwill, Euphemia merely displaces Lorimer as the power-broker who has enough social capital to "turn" others "off" and "on."

Taken with Clithero's "vivacity and promptitude" during a visit to the Edny cottage, for example, she arranges to have him brought "under her own protection" (the same language he uses to describe Euphemia's adoption of Arthur's ostensible illegitimate orphan, Clarice).[153] Her design, Clithero recalls, was "that [he] should be educated with her child, and that an affection, in this way, might be excited in [him] towards [his] young master, which might render [Clithero] . . . one of his most faithful and intelligent dependents."[154] Is Clithero, then, surrogate son or servant? Whereas the social dynamics of feudal landlordism made the stakes of James's position simple—bastard or heir—Euphemia's "management of that great instrument of good and evil, money,"[155] which ostensibly repudiates Lorimer's Altham-like "prejudices of rank and luxury,"[156] allows her position as mediatrix to be both more idealistic and more volatile. Clithero, her devotee, remarks that she was "always in search of doing good, always mediating scenes of happiness, of which she was the author."[157] But he also observes that "she treated [him] in a manner in some degree adapted to the difference of rank and the inferiority of [his] station, yet wildly dissimilar from that which a different person would have adopted . . . not that of an equal and friend, but still more remote was it from that of a mistress."[158] Clithero is always revaluating his relationship to Euphemia in terms of degrees, differences, dissimilarities, remoteness. Armagh peasant that he is, Clithero is after feudal social definition. His habit of qualifying her goodwill in terms of "some" and "still more" suggests that he is psychologically a "servant" to her subjective need to compose "scenes of happiness" and that he is, by extension, subject to her "management" of its "great instrument," finance.

Clithero's confusion about his relational position is understandable. Euphemia is, after all, the aristocratic owner of the demesne where he was born. What he does not fully understand, though, is that her relationship to the source of her wealth—the land—as well as to Clithero, is capitalistic rather than feudalistic. In portraying her as someone whose personal and moral identity is linked to her ability to capitalize, leverage, and alienate traditional landholdings, Edgar Huntly places her squarely within the tradition of eighteenth-century allegories of "Lady Credit," a figure whose "delicate, indeterminate balance of "multiple subject positions" expressed new sensibilities about the link between political self-determination, moral choice, and globalizing finance.[159] For indentured servants, though, like the self-styled "Tennis-ball of Fortune," William Moraley, allegorized credit-finance had little resonance as a marker of middle-class virtue or personal freedom.[160] Indeed, Moraley could have echoed countless emigrant Britons, including the "noble Slave," Annesley, or the despondent fictional Clithero, when he reflected that a "Person like Me, Oppress'd by Dame Fortune, need not care where he goes."[161] For nearly twenty years after his freedom, moreover, James's attempts to "court" fate in the proceedings, which met with varying outcomes, quite literally hinged on his access to credit. James's friends, he reminded readers in 1758, had been "reduced, if possible, to a lower Ebb than the unfortunate Mr. Annesley himself, who ha[d] it not in his Power to afford them the least Return."[162] Brown's central insight with his own "Lady Credit," Euphemia, consisted of making her the *agent* of alienation, rather than the means for others to do so, beginning with her well-intentioned alienation of Clithero from his own natural household, his conversion, like Jemmy, from son to a "species of [psychosocial] property." It is telling in this regard that Clithero qualifies his effusive gratitude to Euphemia at almost every turn with references to his own "servitude," his "lot," the "inferiority of [his] station," and so on. By the time he makes his confession to Edgar, he has come to view even his pseudo-adoption as "an event . . . which, for a long time, [he] regarded as the most fortunate of [his] life, but which [he] now regard[s] as the scheme of some infernal agent, and as the primary source of [his] calamities."[163] What is more, this seems to go hand-in-hand with his hesitant recognition of Arthur Wiatte—the most markedly caricatured figure of the old feudal order's excesses—as human rather than devil, a person with rational interests and, like Clithero, a tale to tell upon his return from transportation abroad. He seeks him out, for example, not to threaten him or prevent his access to Euphemia, but "to get a knowledge of his situation and views"[164]—in effect, a kind of forbidden knowledge, a tale that cannot be uttered, as its potential assertions of injustice threaten the claims to moral authority that Euphemia's capricious power as "Lady Credit" is based on. "As a human being," Clithero reflects after Wiatte's death, "his depravity was never beyond the health-restoring power of repentance. His heart, so long as it beat, was accessible to remorse."[165] Notably, it is Euphemia and Sarsefield who deny this grace to Clithero when they reappear at the novel's close. While we see Euphemia's attempts to "improve" others, we never see her "restore" them. We only hear Clithero's speculations about her willingness to do so. Because he cannot imagine the sorts of radical self-creation that correspond closely to Euphemia's "enlightened" worldview (and Edgar's), he instead imagines inner life in terms of redemption, contrition—as an "orphan," his moral outlook looks for paradigms of potential *restoration*.

Although *Edgar Huntly*'s larger point seems to be that Clithero was an "Irish savage in his home country before he comes to America," his own narrative implies that the failure with Euphemia's program of social "improvement" on his behalf was not caused by her "spirit of mistaken benevolence."[166] Instead, Clithero's description of his situation in her household implicates the psychological barbarism of the commodifying impulse that characterized the social power of Anglo-Irish elites. How different, after all, is her useful "adoption" of the tenant's son from Lord Altham's calculi of social self-interest? Euphemia, it is true, suggests that Clithero has "become a member of her own family" when she grants permission for him to wed her adopted niece, Clarice. Even so, Clithero continues to understand that in conditional terms, describing his "personal ease and liberty" as being "less infringed" than that of other servants, and how his elevation allows him to manage "in some degree" the selection of other domestics in her "large and opulent . . . household establishment."[167] His enfranchisement into Euphemia's household does not exempt him from the process of commodification; it is not, for example, an upper-class parallel to Purcell's brief adoption of James Annesley. Instead, it makes him a greater stakeholder in the "free and unrestrained power of alienation" as Euphemia's rent-collector and middleman. He derives "a sort of authority," for example, from receiving and disbursing specie; Euphemia's "tenants and debtors" are "in some respects" his; they depend on the "justice and lenity" he devises "for the most part."[168] What Brown is describing, here, is a position with specific significance in Anglo-Irish landlordism. "The interference of the middleman between the landlord and occupying tenant," Sir Charles Coote opined in 1804, "is universally allowed to stand as total eclipse between agriculture and improvement," and against "useful restrictive clause[s]" that would "prohibit alienation of lands."[169] On the one hand, Clithero has in fact followed Euphemia's lead quite well in his course of "improvement," for the *nature* of his power, stripped of fine-sounding niceties, replicates hers. At the same time, what makes him an effective middleman is also at the heart of his psychic dissonance: he does not consciously accept the essential nature of Euphemia's "household establishment" and thus treats capitalistic relationships as feudal ones.

One of the most telling omissions in this regard concerns his relationship—or lack thereof—to 1780s Armagh. Brown's historical method as a novelist was more allusive than descriptive, perhaps indicative of the insider/outsider mentalities that characterize the kind of Quaker "underworld of tribal knowledge" that Kafer emphasizes. Sydney J. Krause makes this point with regard to the foreboding elm tree where Waldegrave was murdered, a reference that, while never made explicit, evoked the "meaning a strategically prominent 'Elm' would have had for eighteenth-century Pennsylvanians at all mindful of . . . the city's origins" and the pact between William Penn and the Delaware people.[170] To audiences that knew Irish affairs at all, the specific choice of Armagh as Clithero's home would not merely associate his peasant background with tensions between the Protestant Ascendancy and tenant Catholics; it would evoke a decade of well-publicized and violent sectarian disturbances that culminated in the "Armagh Outrages" of 1795–1796, which saw the forcible expulsion of several thousand peasant Catholics from Armagh and the founding of the Orange Order. Brown, like most literate Philadelphians, was certainly aware of the county's bloodshed. From 1795 to 1799, *The Philadelphia Gazette* published at least thirty-five separate stories illustrating what multiple articles referred to as "a civil war,"[171] driven in part by the Catholic peasantry's attempt to enforce traditional "legitimacy" against Euphemia's class in terms everything from "rent levels, to the collection of tithes and cess, to the occupation of land," and halt "dispossession, eviction, landgrabbing, and 'drawing straight lines.'"[172] Insofar as Clithero works as Euphemia's middleman and manager of Lorimer's Armagh estates, his utility to her becomes obvious as he provides a familiar, native-born, Catholic "face" for her financial speculations. Indeed, during the late 1780s, the period Clithero describes during his narrative, internecine fighting between the Catholic "Defenders" and Protestant "Peep 'o Day Boys" was reaching a decade-long crescendo. No wonder Euphemia's "surprise is beyond measure" when Clithero, fearing that Euphemia will deny his desire to marry her ward, declares his intention to return to Armagh and live out the rest of his days, he "hope[s], in peace."[173] The ironies of Clithero's exchange come into sharp relief in this context, reflecting not only his position as speaker, but the way in which his speaking status depends on his third position landlady's middleman situated between his antithetical identities as Euphemia's surrogate "son" and the symbolically orphaned, native-born son of her Armagh peasant tenants.

It is also worth noting in this regard that although the feudal-minded Clithero describes his attempted murder of Euphemia in scrupulous detail, he seems unable or unwilling to describe facets of her "capitalizing" social relations that threaten his vision of her as a well-meaning lady-of-the-manor. The entire subplot with her brother, Arthur, for example, is largely of her own contrivance, and each turn in its narrative progress corresponds to Euphemia's decision to "turn off" or "turn on" the fates of others through the far-reaching apparatus of Britain's commercial empire. When Arthur, for example, objects to her possible marriage with the young surgeon, Sarsefield, whose "birth was mean and [who] was without fortune," her decision to "procure," through "her interest," a "post in the service of the East India Company" is not so much a passion-driven effort to protect him from Arthur's wrath as it is a calculated attempt to "better" him, as she will eventually do with Clithero. While Sarsefield is initially reluctant because his own judgment is "obscured by passion," he eventually "grants concurrence to all her schemes."[174] Similarly, when Arthur is arrested as a highwayman, Clithero recounts that Euphemia's "intercession was solicited, when all the world knew that pardon would readily be granted to a suppliant of her rank."[175] However, although Arthur, "his kindred, his friends, and even indifferent persons" beg her intercession, she demurs.[176] Clithero reads this as a sign that "her justice was inflexible," and while that might be true, his description of the general public outcry highlights the break from traditional familial bonds and social allegiances that makes Euphemia such a volatile force, particularly in the lives of the poor, like Clithero or Sarsefield, or the destitute and ruined, like Arthur. In all three cases, the effect of her decision-making, whether to elevate or condemn, is the same. Sarsefield is captured during a war between "the Company and some native powers."[177] Arthur, "convicted and sentenced to transportation," is rumored to have been killed during a mutinous "affray" aboard the prison ship he is on.[178] Insofar as he is a variation on this theme, we meet Clithero midway through his symbolic "captivity," his cycle of transportation. For his part, Sarsefield returns to Dublin long after "he had escaped from the prisons of Hyder, [and] had wandered on foot, and under disguises" across half the globe.[179] Again, as in Clithero's case, Sarsefield has a "long and various story to tell," one that seems, at turns, as though it is about to overtake Clithero's own retelling.[180] After his similarly unexpected reappearance, Arthur attempts to gain an audience with Euphemia, ostensibly to recount his own surprising escape and survival.

Whereas Arthur is denied the space to recount, as Clithero and Sarsefield do, his own "romantic" adventures, it is Clithero, alone, who does not return to Ireland and close the structural loop in the family plot. If Euphemia's position as "Lady Fortune" allows her to serve as catalyst for Annesley-style imperial dislocations that assume the generic character of romance, and result in reappearances, self-declarations, and "magical" socioeconomic transformations, it is because the cultural values she represents generate conflict and a need for resolution in the quasifeudal world of eighteenth-century Ireland. In the rational, individualistic psychological landscape of the Early Republic, on the other hand, the overriding principle of "transplantation" as unfettered success story negates the complex mediations and backward pull of the Old World implied in the narrative contexts for "transportation." To put it bluntly, *Edgar Huntly*'s Early Republic does not acknowledge orphaning. This is perhaps the logic behind why, at the close of the novel, Euphemia's biological child with Sarsefield, "with whose future existence so many pleasures were entwined, is dead" at the same moment that her symbolic child, Clithero, is thwarted in his attempt to reconcile with her. Having gained word of Sarsefield and Euphemia's visit to America, Clithero attempted to stage a reconciliation in New York, but was thwarted in this design by Sarsefield, effectively recasting Clithero in Arthur Wiatte's position as a "madman, whose liberty is dangerous, and who requires to be fettered and imprisoned as the most atrocious criminal."[181] The novel offers very little evidence to support this claim. In fact, when Clithero is seized at Elizabethtown and "conveyed" to a "packet [ship], which immediately set sail," it is through Sarsefield's connivance with the local authorities.[182] Clithero, in turn, protests "against the injustice of his treatment" with what Sarsfield calls "perverted reason."[183] In an attempt to escape by swimming to shore, Clithero forces himself below the waves "at the moment when his flight [is] overtaken," ironically fixing him at the moment of transit that defines the orphan-servant's imperial circulation.[184]

If, as Cheryl L. Nixon argues, the "Annesley case reveals a dynamic essential to the orphan plot" insofar as it interrogates "not only the factual/fictional status of the family but also the factual/fictional status of forms used to construct the family," then Clithero's narrative extends this to a metacritique.[185] In total, his tale implies that the process of interrogating, reorganizing, and redefining familial roles and obligations, embodied for Clithero by his benefactress, Euphemia, endlessly replicates and diffuses the kinds of social, psychic, and physical violence concentrated on "the noble Slave," James Annesley, in his account of dispossession and transportation to America. The effective point of scission between the two narratives, the reversed deaths of Altham/Lorimer and Moll/Euphemia, allows the mother-figure a remarkable degree of latitude in determining what the makeup of the "household establishment" looks like. But whereas Annesley accounts like the *News-Letter* obituary resequenced events to provide a more dramatic focus on the orphan's loss of the stable, pseudofeudal paterfamilias, the purely "speculative" (in all senses) nature of Euphemia's maternal power, which allows for the free rearrangement of persons into different social/familial roles, destabilizes the familial reestablishment that is the orphan's object of desire. In the broader context of *Edgar Huntly*'s critique of the Early Republic, the simple "stable irony" is that Clithero, the "romancer" who is able to recount his own past with moral self-reflection, is labeled mad because he retains, as the psychological artifact of his desire, the familial, feudalistic Old Word mentalities that form the preconditions of both his symbolic orphaning and his coherence. Edgar, on the other hand, is a picture of sanity to the novel's other characters, most notably Sarsefield, who both recasts Clithero in the "wicked uncle" role and occupies it himself. Indeed, it is telling of Brown's craft that he makes Clithero regret the irrationally "evil" Arthur Wiatte's death, for it foreshadows his own. In *Edgar Huntly*'s America, it seems, Lady Credit makes everyone a dispossessing uncle—their own or someone else's—eventually. Happily married to Sarsefield, the social object of her own creation, she will not die impoverished and humiliated like Moll

Sheffield, though, and her infant can never be orphaned. In the Early Republic, the fertile, apotheosized, and "transplanted" landscape of her worldview, it is already born dead.

NOTES

1. Anonymous, "Description of Dublin," *The New Foundling Hospital for Wit. Being a Collection of Fugitive Pieces, in Prose and Verse, Not in Any Other Collection. With Several Pieces Never Before Published*, vol. 6 (London: J. Debrett, 1786), 167.
2. Anonymous, "Description of Dublin," 168.
3. Charles Brockden Brown, *Edgar Huntly; or, Memoirs of a Sleep-Walker, with Related Texts*, ed. Philip Barnard and Stephen Shapiro (Indianapolis: Hackett, 2006), 32.
4. Brown, *Edgar Huntly*, 35.
5. Anonymous, *A Letter to a Nobleman in the Country on the Great Affair of Mr. Annesley: Containing a Full and Distinct Account of That Extraordinary Transaction, and All Its Circumstances. Together with Some Particulars, Not Hitherto Published. By an Impartial Hand* (London: J. Roberts, 1744), 17.
6. Anonymous, *The Trial at Bar between Campbell Craig, Lessee of James Annesley, Esq; and the Right Honourable Richard Earl of Anglesea, Defendant, before the Honourable the Barons of the Exchequer, at the King's Court, Dublin, in Trinity Term, in the 16th and 17th Years of the Reign of Our Sovereign Lord George the Second, King of Great-Brotain, &c. and in the Year of Our Lord 1743* (London: R. Walker, 1744), 81.
7. Anonymous, *The Trial at Large, between James Annesley, Esq; and the Right Honourable the Earl of Anglesea, before the Barons of the Court of Exchequer in Ireland . . . the Whole Taken in Court and Revived by an Eminent Counsellor in the Cause* (Newcastle Upon Tyne: John Gooding, 1744), 23.
8. Anonymous, *The Trial . . . James Annesley*, 24.
9. Anonymous, *Letter to a Nobleman*, 15.
10. Terry Eagleton, *Heathcliff and the Great Hunger: Studies in Irish Culture* (London: Verso, 1995), 241.
11. James Dowling Herbert, *Irish Varieties from the Last Fifty Years: Written from Recollections* (London: William Joy, 1836), 83.
12. Herbert, *Irish Varieties*, 83.
13. Herbert, *Irish Varieties*, 85.
14. *Trial at Bar*, 147.
15. *Trial at Bar*, 82.
16. Brown, *Edgar Huntly*, 49.
17. Brown, *Edgar Huntly*, 51.
18. J. Hector St. John Crèvecoeur, *Letters from an American Farmer and Sketches of Eighteenth-Century Life*, ed. Albert E. Stone (New York: Penguin, 1981), 69.
19. Benjamin Franklin, "Information to Those Who Would Remove to America," *Autobiography and Other Writings*, ed. Ormond Seavey (Oxford: Oxford University Press, 1993), 319.
20. Royall Tyler, *The Contrast*, in *The Contrast: Manners Morals, and Authority in the Early American Republic*, ed. Cynthia A. Kierner (New York: New York University Press, 2007), 38.
21. Tyler, *The Contrast*, 38.
22. Brown, *Edgar Huntly*, 4.
23. Beverly R. Voloshin, "*Edgar Huntly* and the Coherence of the Self," *Early American Literature* 23, no. 3 (1988): 262.
24. Sian Silyn Roberts, *Gothic Subjects: The Transformation of Individualism in American Fiction, 1790–1861* (Philadelphia: University of Pennsylvania Press, 2014), 65.
25. Brown, *Edgar Huntly*, 111, 251.
26. Brown, *Edgar Huntly*, 110.

27. Sydney J. Krause, "Edgar Huntly and the American Nightmare," *Studies in the Novel* 13, no. 3 (1981): 298.

28. Wayne C. Booth, *The Rhetoric of Irony* (Chicago: University of Chicago Press, 1974), 6.

29. Richard Slotkin, *Regeneration through Violence: The Mythology of the American Frontier, 1600–1860* (Norman: University of Oklahoma Press, 1973), 308.

30. Brown, *Edgar Huntly*, 5.

31. Brown, *Edgar Huntly*, 8.

32. Brown, *Edgar Huntly*, 9.

33. Donald Ringe, *Charles Brockden Brown* (New York: Twayne, 1966), 6.

34. Brown, *Edgar Huntly*, 63.

35. Brown, *Edgar Huntly*, 63.

36. William Empson, "Tom Jones," *The Kenyon Review* 20, no. 2 (1958): 219.

37. Empson, "Tom Jones," 218.

38. Elizabeth Jane Wall Hinds, *Private Property: Charles Brockden Brown's Gendered Economics of Virtue* (London: Associated University Presses, 1997), 134.

39. Charles Brockden Brown, "Walstein's School of History," in *Charles Brockden Brown's Weiland, Ormond, Arthur Mervyn, and Edgar Huntly with Related Texts*, ed. Philip Barnard and Stephen Shapiro (Indianapolis: Hackett, 2009), 337.

40. Cheesman Herrick, *White Servitude in Pennsylvania: Indentured and Redemption Labor in Colony and Commonwealth* (New York: Negro University Press, 1969), 26.

41. Cheryl L. Nixon, *The Orphan in Eighteenth-Century Law and Literature: Estate, Blood, and Body* (London: Routledge, 2016), 115.

42. Brown, *Edgar Huntly*, 46.

43. Peter Kafer, "Charles Brockden Brown and Revolutionary Philadelphia: An Imagination in Context," *The Pennsylvania Magazine of History and Biography* 116, no. 4 (1992): 468; for the legal basis and norms of penal transportation, see the Transportation Act of 1717 (4 Geo. 1 c. 11).

44. Farley Grubb, *German Immigration and Servitude in America, 1702–1920* (London: Routledge, 2011), 244.

45. William Moraley, *The Infortunate: The Life and Adventures of William Moraley, an Indentured Servant*, ed. Susan E. Klepp and Billy G. Smith (University Park: Pennsylvania State University Press, 2005), 28.

46. Franklin, "Information," 324.

47. Moraley, *Infortunate*, 41.

48. Fugitive advertisements quoted in Michael V. Kennedy, "The Consequences of Cruelty: The Escalation of Servant and Slave Abuse, 1750–1780," *Essays in Economic and Business History* 22 (2012): 127.

49. Elizabeth Sprigs, "Letter to Mr. John Spriggs in White Cross Street near Cripple Gate, London, 22 September 1756," in *Colonial Captivities, Marches, and Journeys*, ed. Isabel Calder (New York: Macmillan, 1935), 151.

50. Biakia Harvey, "Letter to Thomas Biakia, Esq., 30 December 1775," William Manson Papers, Orkney Island Archives, Kirkwall, Orkney.

51. Brown, *Edgar Huntly*, 21, 24, 65.

52. John Bach McMaster, *A History of the United States, from the Revolution to the Civil War*, vol. 2 (New York: Appleton and Company, 1900), 558.

53. Brown, *Edgar Huntly*, 19.

54. Brown, *Edgar Huntly*, 12.

55. Marianne S. Wokeck, "German and Irish Immigration to Colonial Philadelphia," *Proceedings of the American Philosophical Society* 133, no. 2: Symposium on the Demographic History of the Philadelphia Region, 1600–1860 (1989): 130.

56. Brown, *Edgar Huntly*, 99.

57. Brown, *Edgar Huntly*, 62.

58. Matthew Pethers, "The Indentured Atlantic: Bound Servitude and the Literature of American Colonization [Part Three]," *U.S. Studies Online*, British Association for American Studies, http://www.baas.ac.uk/usso/the-indentured-atlantic-bound-servitude-and-the-literature-of-american-colonization-part-three/

59. Brown, *Edgar Huntly*, 62.
60. Wokeck, "German and Irish," 139.
61. Wokeck, "German and Irish," 139.
62. Mark L. Kamrath, "American Exceptionalism and Radicalism in the 'Annals of Europe and America,'" in *Revising Charles Brockden Brown: Culture, Politics, and Sexuality in the Early Republic*, ed. Phiip Barnard, Mark L. Kamrath, and Stephen Shapiro (Knoxville: University of Tennessee Press), 356.
63. Peter Kafer, *Charles Brockden Brown's Revolution and the Birth of the American Gothic* (Philadelphia: University of Pennsylvania Press, 2004), 248.
64. A. Roger Ekirch, *Birthright: The True Story That Inspired Kidnapped* (W.W. Norton & Company: New York, 2010), 14.
65. *Trial at Bar*, 148.
66. *Trial at Bar*, 346.
67. Ekirch, *Birthright*, 168.
68. Elizabeth Boyd, *Altamira's Ghost; or, Justice Triumphant. A New Ballad. Occasion'd by a Certain Nobleman's Cruel Usage of His Nephew. Done Extempore* (London: Charles Corbett, 1744), 2.
69. Ekirch, *Birthright*, 168.
70. Daniel Defoe, *The Compleat English Gentleman*, in *Selected Writings of Daniel Defoe*, James T. Bouldon, ed. (Cambridge: Cambridge University Press, 1975); James Boswell, *London Journal*, ed. Janet B. Kopito (Mineola: Dover, 2018), 203–204.
71. Anonymous, *The Case of the Honourable James Annesley, Esq; Being a Sequel to the Memoirs of an Unfortunate Young Nobleman* (London: W. Bickerton, 1745); Eliza Haywood, *Memoirs of an Unfortunate Young Nobleman, Return'd from a Thirteen Years Slavery in America Where He Had Been Sent by the Wicked Contrivances of His Cruel Uncle. A Story Founded on Truth, and Address'd Equally to the Head and Heart* (London: J. Freeman, 1743).
72. Tobias Smollett, *The Adventures of Peregrine Pickle. In Which Are Included, Memoirs of a Lady of Quality* (London: D. Wilson, 1751). For Mackercher, see Lewis M. Knapp, "Smollett and the Case of James Annesley," *Times Literary Supplement*, 28 December 1935, 199; Lewis M. Knapp and Lillian de la Torre, "Smollett, MacKercher, and the Annesley Claimant," *English Language Notes* 1 (1963): 28–33; Lillian de la Torre, "New Light on Smollett and the Annesley Case," *Review of English Studies* 22 (1971): 274–281.
73. Boyd, *Altamira's Ghost*, 2.
74. Anonymous, "A Further Account of the Contest between Lord An—sey and Mr Annesley, the Supposed Son of the Late Lord Altham," *The Gentleman's Magazine and Historical Chronicle* 26 (London: D. Henry, 1756), 428.
75. William Henry Foster, *Gender, Mastery and Slavery: From European to Atlantic World Frontiers* (New York: Palgrave, 2010), 88.
76. Catherine Armstrong, *Landscape and Identity in North America's Southern Colonies from 1600 to 1745* (New York: Routledge, 2016), 192.
77. *Trial at Bar*, 103; Haywood, *Memoirs*, excerpted in T. B Howell, ed., *A Complete Collection of State Trials and Proceedings for High Treason and Other Crimes and Misdemeanors from the Earliest Period to the Year 1783*, vol. 17 (London: Longman, Hurst, Rees, Orme, and Brown, 1816), 1450.
78. Sherman Day, *Historical Collections of the State of Pennsylvania; Containing a Copious Selection of the Most Interesting Facts, Traditions, Biographical Sketches, Anecdotes, etc. Relating to Its History and Antiquities, Both General and Local, with Topographical Descriptions of Every County an All the Larger Towns in the State* (Philadelphia: George W. Gorton, 1843), 408.
79. John Fanning Watson, *Annals of Philadelphia in the Olden Time; Being a Collection of Memoirs, Anecdotes, and Incidents of the City and Its Inhabitants, and of the Earliest Settlements of the Inland Part of Pennsylvania from the Days of the Founders* (Philadelphia: A. Hart, 1850), 268.
80. William Riddle, *Cherished Memories of Old Lancaster-Town and Shire* (Lancaster: Intelligencer Printing House, 1910), 260.

81. Walter Scott, "An Essay on Romance," in *The Miscellaneous Prose Works of Sir Walter Scott, Bart.* Vol. 6 (Boston: Wells and Lilly, 1829), 104.
82. John C. Cawelti, "Cooper and the Frontier Myth and Anti-Myth," in *James Fenimore Cooper: New Historical and Literary Contexts*, ed. W. M. Verhoeven (Amsterdam: Editions Rodopi B. V., 1993), 153.
83. Cawelti, "Cooper," 153.
84. Nixon, *Orphan*, 115.
85. Anonymous, *Case*, 5.
86. Anonymous, *Case*, 5.
87. Anonymous, *The Parallel: Or, A Collection of Extraordinary Cases, Relating to Concealed Births, and Disputed Successions* (London: J. Roberts, 1744), 2.
88. Anonymous, *The Parallel*, 2.
89. Anonymous, *The Parallel*, 2.
90. Charles Brockden Brown, "The Difference between History and Romance," in Philip Barnard and Stephen Shapiro, eds., *Charles Brockden Brown* (Indianapolis: Hackett, 2009), 341.
91. Brown, *Edgar Huntly*, 25.
92. Brown, "Difference," 341.
93. Brown, "Difference," 341.
94. Anonymous, *Parallel*, 5.
95. Henry Fielding, *The History of Tom Jones*, ed. R. P. C. Mutter (New York: Penguin, 1966), 395.
96. The only portion of Brown's novel to survive is his "Extract from 'Sky-Walk,'" published as promotional material in *The Weekly Magazine* 1, no. 8 (1798), 228–231.
97. Brown, "Extract," 229.
98. Anonymous, *Case*, 7.
99. Charles Brockden Brown, "Memoirs of Stephen Calvert," *The Monthly Magazine, and American Review* 1, no. 3 (1799), 192–193.
100. [Speratus], "Letter 1," *The Weekly Magazine* 1, no. 7 (1798): 202.
101. Stephen Shapiro, "'Man to Man I Needed Not to Dread His Encounter': Edgar Huntly's End of Erotic Pessimism," in Barnard, *Revising*, 233.
102. Alexander Walsh, *Strong Representations: Narrative and Circumstantial Evidence in England* (Baltimore: Johns Hopkins University Press, 1992), 25.
103. McMaster, *History*, 558.
104. *Trial at Bar*, 148.
105. *Boston News-Letter*, 24 April 1760.
106. Brown, *Edgar Huntly*, 26, 29.
107. Brown, *Edgar Huntly*, 62.
108. Brown, *Edgar Huntly*, 62.
109. Brown, *Edgar Huntly*, 62.
110. Anonymous, *Letter to a Nobleman*, 13.
111. Anonymous, *Letter to a Nobleman*, 15.
112. Anonymous, *Letter to a Nobleman*, 15.
113. Anonymous, *Letter to a Nobleman*, 14–16.
114. Anonymous, *Letter to a Nobleman*, 19.
115. *Trial at Bar*, 94.
116. Charles Renouvier, qtd. in Richard J. Evans, *Altered Pasts: Counterfactual in History* (Waltham: Brandeis University Press, 2013), 6.
117. Foster, *Gender, Mastery*, 88.
118. Evans, *Altered Pasts*, 6.
119. Brown, *Edgar Huntly*, 62.
120. Anonymous, *Letter to a Nobleman*, 7.
121. Arthur Annesley, qtd. in Ekirch, *Birthright*, 42.
122. Anonymous, *Letter to a Nobleman*, 12.
123. Anonymous, "Judicial Puzzles—the Annesley Case," *Blackwood's Edinburgh Magazine* 88 (1860), 568.

124. Anonymous, *Case of the Honourable*, 80.
125. *Trial at Bar*, 16.
126. Anonymous, "Cause between J. Annesley, Esq; and the E. of Anglesey," *The London Magazine, and Monthly Chronologer* 13(1744), 179.
127. Tom Barnes, qtd. in Ekirch, *Birthright*, 80.
128. Samuel Johnson, *A Dictionary of the English Language: In Which the Words Are Deduced from Their Originals, and Illustrated in Their Different Significations by Examples from the Best Writers. To Which Are Prefixed a History of the Language, and an English Grammar* (London: W. Strahan, 1773), n.p.
129. Anonymous, *An Answer to the High-Church Standers; or, A New Passive Obedience* (N.p, 1711), 14.
130. Ekirch, *Birthright*, 20.
131. *Trial at Bar*, 138.
132. *Trial at Bar*, 325.
133. *Trial at Large*, 43.
134. *Trial at Bar*, 175.
135. *Trial at Bar*, 175.
136. *Trial at Bar*, 176.
137. *Trial at Bar*, 178.
138. *Trial at Bar*, 40.
139. *Trial at Bar*, 40.
140. *Trial at Bar*, 40.
141. *Trial at Bar*, 201.
142. *Trial at Large*, 53.
143. William Blackstone, *Commentaries on the Laws of England: By the Late Sir W. Blackstone. To Which Is Added an Analysis by Baron Field, Esq.* (Philadelphia: John Grigg, 1827), 360.
144. Blackstone, *Commentaries*, 361.
145. For context, see Tim Stretton and Krista J. Keselring, *Married Women and the Law: Coverture in England and the Common Law World* (Montreal: McGill-Queen's University Press, 2013); Joanne Bailey, *Unquiet Lives: Marriage and Marriage Breakdown in England, 1660–1800* (Cambridge: Cambridge University Press, 2003).
146. Charles Coote, *Statistical Survey of the County of Armagh, with Observations on the Means of Improvement; Drawn Up in the Years 1802, and 1803, for the Consideration, and Under the Direction of the Dublin Society* (Dublin: Graisberry and Campbell, 1804), 141.
147. Brown, *Edgar Huntly*, 26.
148. Brown, *Edgar Huntly*, 26.
149. Brown, *Edgar Huntly*, 27.
150. Brown, *Edgar Huntly*, 27.
151. For the author of numerous poems, songs, plays and, most notably, the autobiographical novel, *Theodora* (1770), see, for overview, John Lempriere, *Universal Biography: Containing a Copious Account, Critical and Historical, of the Life and Character, Labors and Actions of Eminent Persons, in All Ages and Countries, Conditions and Professions. Arranged in Alphabetical Order* (New York: E. Sargeant, 1810), 442; for misattribution to James Annesley, see George Hardinge, *The Miscellaneous Works, in Prose and Verse, of George Hardinge, Esq.* (London: J. Nichols, Son, and Bentley, 1818), xl.
152. Hinds, *Private Property*, 134.
153. Brown, *Edgar Huntly*, 27, 35.
154. Brown, *Edgar Huntly*, 27.
155. Brown, *Edgar Huntly*, 29.
156. Brown, *Edgar Huntly*, 26.
157. Brown, *Edgar Huntly*, 29.
158. Brown, *Edgar Huntly*, 30.
159. Sandra Sherman, *Finance and Fictionality in the Early Eighteenth Century: Accounting for Defoe* (Cambridge: Cambridge University Press, 1996), 52; see, also, Carl Wennerlind, *Casualties of Credit: The English Financial Revolution, 1620–1720* (Cambridge: Harvard Uni-

versity Press, 2011); Marieke De Goede, "Mastering 'Lady Credit,'" *International Feminist Journal of Politics* 2, no. 1 (2000): 58–81.

160. Moraley, *The Infortunate*, 108.
161. Moraley, *The Infortunate*, 50.
162. Anonymous, *Case of the Honourable James Annesley, Esq. Humbly Offered to All Lovers of Truth and Justice* (N.p., 1758), 5.
163. Brown, *Edgar Huntly*, 26.
164. Brown, *Edgar Huntly*, 48.
165. Brown, *Edgar Huntly*, 53.
166. Christopher Stampone, "A 'Spirit of Mistaken Benevolence': Civilizing the Savage in Charles Brockden Brown's *Edgar Huntly*," *Early American Literature* 50, no. 2 (2015): 415.
167. Brown, *Edgar Huntly*, 29.
168. Brown, *Edgar Huntly*, 29.
169. Coote, *Statistical Survey*, 145.
170. Sydney J. Krause, "Penn's Elm and Edgar Huntly: Dark 'Instruction to the Heart,'" *American Literature* 66, no. 3 (1994): 463.
171. See, for example, "From One of the United Irishmen," *The Philadelphia Gazette*, 10 July 1797.
172. Kyla Madden, *Forkhill Protestants and Forkhill Catholics, 1787–1858* (Montreal: McGill-Queen's University Press, 2005), 115.
173. Brown, *Edgar Huntly*, 38.
174. Brown, *Edgar Huntly*, 42.
175. Brown, *Edgar Huntly*, 34.
176. Brown, *Edgar Huntly*, 34.
177. Brown, *Edgar Huntly*, 42.
178. Brown, *Edgar Huntly*, 34.
179. Brown, *Edgar Huntly*, 43.
180. Brown, *Edgar Huntly*, 43.
181. Brown, *Edgar Huntly*, 193.
182. Brown, *Edgar Huntly*, 193.
183. Brown, *Edgar Huntly*, 194.
184. Brown, *Edgar Huntly*, 194.
185. Nixon, *Orphan*, 125.

Chapter Three

Still "Under Sir William"

Locum Tenens, *Cooper's Leatherstocking, and the Tragic View of the American Revolution*

Like *Edgar Huntly*'s Clithero, James Fenimore Cooper's quintessential American hero, Leatherstocking, is an orphan, a frontiersman, and a "white savage." At his core, he is also—at least to the townspeople of Templeton— as much of a "degrading relic of the feudal system" as Charles Brockden Brown's half-mad Armagh lad. That we do not typically think of Leatherstocking in these terms has less to do with Cooper's characterization of Bumppo as an iconoclast than it does with the fact that Leatherstocking's "biographer" never subjected him to a *Waverley*-style narrative crisis. We never see Leatherstocking conflicted by moments when his deep personal and psychological allegiances run afoul of history's course. This is because Cooper never filled in Leatherstocking's "missing years" during the 1770s–1780s. Entangled in copyright disputes, monetary woes, and contractual issues with multiple publishers, the aging romancer found that he could only "manage a temporary enthusiasm for the old soldier and hunter and trapper" by the early 1850s.[1] However, secondhand accounts and scattered notes about the projected sixth novel remain, tantalizing readers with suggestions of a climactic scene set at Niagara Falls—Colonel Guy Johnson's Loyalist-Iroquois redoubt—as well as a hasty scenario, later adapted for *Wyandotté* (1843), that places Bumppo between two political ideologues, "listening and at a loss to decide." Wayne Franklin speculates that Cooper may have planned to grow his unwritten novel out of an "astute seed" planted in *The Prairie*, one in which Leatherstocking mentions serving under "Mad" Anthony Wayne after the events of *The Pioneers*. Wayne's "long colorful service during the Revolution," Franklin remarks, "a fair amount of it in the

Hudson Valley, would have made him an ideal commander for Natty Bumppo in that war as well." Conversely, Steven P. Hawthorn suggests that Cooper recycled much of his projected scenario because he "found himself constrained by a small but significant detail from his first Leatherstocking tale . . . wherein Natty Bumppo is revealed to be the lifelong servant (and, in old age, guardian) of Colonel Effingham, a loyalist."[2] Near the end of *The Pioneers*, Colonel Effingham's grandson, Edward Oliver Effingham, explains that Natty "was reared in the family of my grandfather; served him for many years during their campaigns at the West, where he became attached to the woods; and he was left here as a kind of locum tenens on the lands that that old Mohegan (whose life my grandfather once saved) induced the Delawares to grant him when they admitted him as an honorary member of their tribe."[3]

While this biographical sketch never explicitly states what *side*—if any—Cooper's hero took, it does identify what Leatherstocking *did* during the Revolution. He acted as an unrecognized *locum tenens* (a quasilegal term meaning *to hold the place of* or *to substitute*) at Templeton for the Loyalist Effingham family. In this sense, *The Pioneers* extends *Waverley*'s temporal horizon. While we do not see anything akin to the moment of great cultural crisis that characterizes Edward's youth in *Waverley*, Cooper presents the equally fraught drama of living with the consequences of such great historical shifts in *The Prairie*. The novel presents a backwoods epilogue to *Waverley*, one in which we see Leatherstocking assume Edward's function at the conclusion of Scott's work—to provide security and continuity for the recessional order in the present political landscape, to be both historical ward and warden of a Great House that is only partly or tenuously one's own.

Does this make Leatherstocking a Loyalist? Any answer is speculative, but such speculation invites us to reflect more deeply on our understanding of Leatherstocking's relationship to the broader "world" of the Tales, as well as on our own participation in cultural formulations of "Loyalism," a term as slippery as "Tory" or "Jacobite" in its original eighteenth-century context. As Edward Larkin remarks, most "patriot accounts . . . dissolve the category of loyalism by emphasizing the individual loyalist over the shared vision of loyalism . . . using the term as an *ad hominem* that empties loyalism of any ideological, political, or conceptual meaning."[4] Moreover, Larkin sees this bifurcation at the heart of Cooper's attempts to make "affective relations between family members, friends, and neighbors supersede the political debates of the Revolution" in novels such as *The Spy* (1821).[5] Speculations about Leatherstocking's Revolution thus tend to resolve according to how we conceptualize him as an "affective" or "political" character in the Tales. However, neither formulation of "Loyalism" or the "Loyalist" adequately accounts for the complex character introduced in *The Pioneers*. Nor, I would suggest, does it accurately reflect the conceptual matrix of "Loyalism" as understood and lived by the Johnson Establishment anywhere near as well as Cooper's figuration of their fictional retainer, Leatherstocking.

While Edward Oliver's account of Leatherstocking complicates some of the biographical details that appear in Cooper's later novels, it historicizes Bumppo as an "affective" flesh-and-blood figure instead of the epithetical romance hero of the pre-Revolutionary Tales. At the same time, *The Pioneers* highlights the fact that Leatherstocking's once-heroic landscape, his sphere of action, was not only the *physical* landscape of the pre-Revolutionary Tales, but also the *social* landscape of the First Empire's "Middle Ground," where "expedient and creative misunderstanding[s]" between William Johnson's white frontier elites and corresponding Iroquois Confederacy elites produced social textures of "hybrid empire" based on "a rough balance of power and mutual need."[6] In the pre-Revolutionary Tales, Leatherstocking thus operates within the "*relationality* of the frontiersman's stoic 'self-reliance' and the collective ethos of the British colonial world—the Loyalist Effinghams in *The Pioneers*, Colonel Munro in *The Last of the Mohicans*, the garrison soldiers in *The Deerslayer*—that he both serves and shuns."[7] To borrow Roland Mousnier's term for seventeenth-century French social hierarchies, the "common ethos" of Colonial Johnson elites was akin to that of a "society of orders," a system of "social stratification . . . dependent on a group of value judgments which constitute the fundamental principle of society" and have no *dependent* relationship on "activities producing material goods."[8] Johnsonian elites, both British and Iroquois, organized the fundamental social relationships of the Middle Ground around the substitutional representation, rhetorical production, and intercultural translation of the Crown's legitimacy by specific actors, families, and hierarchies that occupied metonymic corresponding roles in the Imperial bureaucracy, particularly the Johnson-controlled Superintendency of Indian Affairs. Just as the character-driven negotiations between affective loyalties and conceptual Loyalism are not the same in *The Spy* and the Leatherstocking Tales, the ideological "Loyalism" of Johnson elites, even at its most conceptual, thus had a human face—a number of familiar human faces—in a way that Westchester political Loyalism did not necessarily require. In this light, Bumppo's significance in *The Pioneers* is the extent to which his position *in locum tenens* correctly identifies the common experiential continuities between the pre-Revolutionary Johnson Establishment, the Johnson Country "Loyalist" turn in the 1770s, and Leatherstocking's individualistic, elegiac iconoclasm in the Early Republic of *The Pioneers*—all of which maintain a substitutional relationship with each other, all of which were intrinsically dependent on the performance of conceptual/interpersonal political substitutions.

With the Revolution, however, Bumppo loses the "relationality" between his heroic personal identity and the social tableau that affirmed it. Leatherstocking's own potential "Loyalist claim" in *The Pioneers* is thus far more ambiguous than that of the Effingham family because it is *purely* representational and substitutional. He internalizes the Johnson/Loyalist communal ethos, but that ethos no longer has a public correlative in the frontier "society of orders." Moreover, unlike the fictional Effinghams or historical Johnsons, his loss cannot be quantified in Pounds Sterling to organs such as the Loyalist Claims Commission. Although Loyalist petitions, official and otherwise, used autobiographical narratives to establish lists of monies and properties lost, the opposite was equally true. Enumerated losses, accompanied by personal testimonies, provided a register for describing psychosocial trauma, autobiographical witness, and a sense of felt commonwealth—a representational *empire of sufferers*. Bumppo's lack of physical capital thus excludes him from the unique *narrative* and *autobiographical* spaces afforded to men like the Effinghams in the 1790s. Conversely, his personal investment in the social capital of the Effinghams means that he must continue enacting pre-Revolutionary social fealties to them in order to preserve his own autobiographical space as "Deerslayer," "Leatherstocking," and so forth. He holds a deferred right to speak and administer *on behalf* from Major Effingham and his descendants. However, he stands *in locum tenens* for more than just the Effinghams, Cooper's emblematic and sympathetic Loyalists. By extension, Leatherstocking also proxies the central practices of transcultural imperialism and substitutional cultural brokerage that characterized New York backcountry elites under Sir William Johnson, for whom Effingham is supposed to have worked, and whose fictionalized persona seems to occupy much of Bumppo's social, historical, and ethical imagination in the Tales. Consequently, the very quality that makes Leatherstocking a trustworthy representative of Effingham interests, namely that he remains a psychological tenant of the "Effingham" order, is what makes his own loss, his own claim to historical justice, elegiac, tragic, and ultimately insoluble in the Early Republic.

"UNDER SIR WILLIAM": LEATHERSTOCKING'S SOCIAL IMAGINATION

Cooper was intimately familiar with Sir William Johnson's circle through childhood stories, family gossip, and firsthand accounts. Cooper's Loyalist in-laws, the prominent De Lanceys, had connections to Johnson through marriage and, like many frontier real estate speculators, James's father, William, had frequent business dealings with Johnson associates. And while Cooper never directly represents Sir William in the Leatherstocking novels (possibly due to his negative appraisal of James Kirke Paulding's "Leather-Stocking" Johnson in *The Dutchman's Fireside* [1831]), Johnson nevertheless functions as "a landmark in Natty's imaginative terrain . . . the frame within which his stories—and, by implication, the Leather-Stocking Tales as a whole—unfold."[9] In fact, Bumppo's persistent self-identification with Sir William is one of the few consistent elements of his characterization. Despite his many epithetical roles—"Hawkeye," "Deerslayer," "Pathfinder," "Trapper," "Leather-Stocking"—Bumppo is most consistent as a psychological character when he recalls "years agone, in the old war, when I was out under Sir William."[10] In *The Pioneers*, he unfolds a tale of how he once "travelled seventy miles alone in the howling wilderness, with a rifle bullet in my thigh, and then cut it out with a jack-knife." Similarly, in *The Prairie*, the defeat of the squatter, Ishmael Bush, inspires recollections of the time when "Sir William push'd the German, Dieskau, thro' the defiles at the foot of the Hori—" before Bumppo's travelling companion cuts him off.[11] Throughout the Tales, Bumppo's companions interrupt him when he tries to recount his time "under Sir William." On the one hand, this underscores how little currency the social capital of Sir William's world, which Leatherstocking finds so meaningful, has in "normal" Colonial Anglo-America and the Early Republic. For Leatherstocking, Johnson is always simply "Sir William," as though his companions simply ought to know who "Sir William" is—and, therefore, who Bumppo is and why he is worthy of regard. At the same time, Bumppo's "Sir William" mantra highlights his function as a product and producer of historical *locum tenens*; for Bumppo, the temporally present plot crises in the Leatherstocking Tales serve as psychological substitutions for his service in the Seven Years' War. Equally, they provide opportunities for him to enunciate selfhood through narrative self-identification as someone who had been, and who psychologically remains, "out under Sir William."

Since his appointment as the Superintendent of Indian Affairs in 1756, Johnson had used the British Empire's administrative bureaucracy to establish a *de facto* fiefdom in Mohawk Country, surrounding himself with men like the Irish fur trader and land speculator, George Croghan; the German-born Deputy Secretary of Indian Affairs, Daniel Claus; and Joseph Brant's older sister, "Miss Molly" (the politically influential stepdaughter of a Turtle Clan sachem, as well as Johnson's common-law wife). During the Seven Years' War, Johnson served as a military commander of Mohawk war parties and Colonial irregulars. After the War, he managed to translate his wartime power into social authority along the same New York frontiers where he had fought. To the patchwork of tribes, speculators, backwoodsmen, tenant settlers, and immigrants—many of whom were Irish Catholic, Germans, or Jacobites—that lived in Johnson's sphere of influence throughout the New York Province, Johnson's authority was not unlike that of a feudal lord. From London's perspective, he was a useful and necessary frontier administrator, even in spite of his Irish background, ties to Catholic traitors, "Indian" lifestyle, and scandalous sexual appetites. Thus, by 1774, when an ailing Johnson reminded Lord Gordon that "the Chiefs" feared a "Successor appointed who may be a Stranger to the regular duties of my Office . . . in which Cases they fear that Troubles may arise,"[12] he could uniquely assert the importance of *his* role in choosing a successor for the Department, both as a matter of the Crown's convenience and legitimacy in the eyes of Indian nations under the Department's nominal jurisdiction.

Johnson selected his nephew, Guy, who had emigrated from County Meath, Ireland, at the beginning of the Seven Years' War, served "His Majesty at the close of the Campaign of 1758,'" and remained alongside "his worthy kinsman" throughout the remainder of the conflict. When peace came, Guy married his cousin Polly, Sir William's daughter by his indentured housekeeper, Catherine Weisenberg. His new father-in-law gave the young couple a full square mile of land on the Mohawk and began grooming his son-in-law for succession in the Department of Indian Affairs. Guy mirrored Johnson by building a fine Georgian house called "Guy Park" where his three daughters were born and tending to Sir William's professional affairs. Unlike Sir William's biological son, Sir John Johnson, Guy shared the Superintendent's peculiar combination of diplomatic and martial instincts, as well as something of his canny, volatile temperament, a perfect *substitutional* heir. By the 1770s, the self-made baronet felt that "by long attention & Application & by so many years employed in the most difficult part of my Duty," Guy had "acquired so perfect a knowledge of the Indians and their affairs" as to be the only reasonable choice for Superintendent after his death. "I have mentioned Guy," he explained to Lord Gordon in 1774, "who I can truly say possesses such Advantages from Experience, the Offices he has held under me, to satisfy me that . . . I could not make so good a choice anywhere else."[13]

Technically, the Superintendent's power derived from "the Allowance and Emoulment enjoyed by Sir William Johnson, under the Commission granted to him for that Office in the Year 1764," but in practice, Department authority depended on a high degree of Iroquois coauthorship. As Anthony J. Hall remarks, this "transcultural orientation" of British North America had become a benchmark of frontier strategic policies at the close of the Seven Years' War, when "the Tory architects of British imperial Canada announced their intentions in a Royal Proclamation to polish and extend a Covenant Chain of treaty alliances with First Nations." By the 1770s, the proclamation had become an "essential strategic and ideological marker that divided the course of British colonization on the continent towards the forging of the new American republic on the one hand and the consolidation of a counterrevolutionary British North America on the other." The ritualized, symbolic, and interpersonal idea of the Covenant Chain underscored Guy's reminder to John Blackburn that, with Sir William's death "but too apparent" by 1774, "the Chiefs of the Indians . . . often Spoke to [Sir William] Concerning a Successor and that their wishes were for me." And when the Earl of Dartmouth finally sent notice confirming the *temporary* appointment of Sir William Johnson's nephew, Guy Johnson, *in locum tenens*, the Confederacy confirmed it *irrevocably* when they produced "the great old *Covenant* Chain of twenty one rowes [of beads]" and pronounced that "Brother, as you are long acquainted with our customs, and the ways of that great man your Father in Law . . . it would grieve, and trouble us to have any body else concerned in our affairs:—for others have no knowledge in them.—We love you and all Sir William's Family."[14]

What was unique about the "Johnson Establishment" and its use of the Covenant Chain as transcultural *locum tenens* was its model of practiced imperium. While the dominant historiographical approach to British imperialism since the Second World War has stressed a model of metropole-and-peripheries, the Johnson Establishment exemplified a kind of *transmetropolitan* imperialism, one in which the intermediate brokers between capitals and their dependencies did not *translate* the political will of one to the other so much as *constitute* both *as* empire by occupying the speaking positions of all respective parties to each other. In 1774, for example, when the Colonies feared that land disputes between "some of the inhabitants of Virginia and the Western Indians, particularly the Shawanese, [would] end in a general war," John Penn wrote to William, asking that Guy intercede with "the 6 Nats. and use his Influence to Accommodate Matters at this Critical Junction." On the basis of his *own* authority, Guy ordered an "enormous sum" to be paid "to the Plankashaw Nation of Indians" in the King's name: "10000 Flints," "250 Shirts," "400 Blankets," "35 dozens of Scalping Knives."[15] He formalized the agreement on a Ten-of-Hearts playing card. Of course, Lord North's Government did not account for flints or scalping knives on playing cards—or know that Johnson-as-Government kept such stores, but neither could it assess whether or not the sum was "enormous" or the land "inconsiderable," save by Johnson's representation.

This mode of commonplace imperial administration on the New York frontier depended on the *de facto* work of the Johnsons and their agents as *locum tenens*. Major Effingham, whose authority derives from a fictionalized Johnson, implicates his political authority as the "Fire-Eater" in Indian transcultural politics, and acts as patron for Bumppo, alludes to such practices of power in *Pioneers*. In the strictest sense, their Crown mandate placed Johnson and his subordinates in the traditional role of *custos sive guardianus regni* under English law, men "constituted by letters patents when the king is out of the kingdome" to serve as "keeper[s] of the kingdome."[16] In the case of British North America, however, the notion of the King's presence, rather than the *locum tenens'* substitutional "kingship," was the jurisdictional fiction. This was often the case in the British Empire, where the deferred ministerial authority that Edward Coke saw in the work of sheriffs, coroner's courts, and others who served *in locum tenens vicecomitis*, was often necessary in far-flung military chains-of-command, instances of British subjects receiving appointments in foreign states, and overseas political administrations.[17]

After the Proclamation of 1763, however, this North American iteration of an English institution that derived its original rationale from the temporary absence and distance of executive power acted a continuous executorship predicated on the *permanent* absence of Crown. In attrition to substitutional jurisdiction, Johnson's *locum tenens* imperialism assumed three characteristic features. First, it mandated a practice of substitutional narration, whereby the Superintendent could claim the position of giving account to the Indian Nations as the Crown, and vice versa. Second, it practiced substitutional identification, whereby the Superintendent could be more or less "British" or "Indian" as circumstances required. Third, it operated on a principle of deferred substitution, such as that which allowed Guy Johnson to assume the narrational and jurisdictional role of Sir William in negotiations with the Plankashaw nation—or that which allows Leatherstocking to retain the Effingham suit as an *individual* and *psychological* mandate in *The Pioneers*, even though the claim against Judge Temple's possession has no legal standing whatsoever in the Early Republic.

Just as the fictional Templeton substitutes for the evolving Early Republic of Cooper's time, Leatherstocking's insistence on inscribing that landscape with allegiances to the old Effingham estate asks readers to engage in a continuous negotiation with the potential meanings of Templeton, its residents, and their relationships. Indeed, in this sense, Bumppo's narrations and obfuscations of the past mirror Cooper's own work as an imaginative novelist whose speculations about character and plot remained rooted in the local historical detail. But whereas Cooper asks his audience to imagine the motivations of men from the past, his hero in the Tales asks that we imagine both past and present through the perspective of men belonging to the dispossessed establishment, men like himself. While many of Cooper's nineteenth-century readers, for example, must have understood Bumppo's status as *locum tenens* metaphorically, Leatherstocking's eighteenth-century "contemporaries" in Johnson Country would have recognized a commonplace social arrangement between half-pay officers and their demobilized subordinates, a peacetime continuation of the military relationships of the Seven Years' War through which most "leather-stockinged" rangers like Bumppo entered Colonial life in the first place. Cooper remarks that Major Effingham "was [at no time] . . . an admirer of the peaceful disciples of Fox," and evidently had little regard for his Colonial neighbors, and his biographical chronology in the Tales, which places him in the 60th Regiment of Foot ("Royal Americans"),[18] implies that he would have been posted to the 2nd or 3rd Battalion by Wolfe's death in 1759, one of the few English officers in a regiment that mirrored Johnson Country's cosmopolitan mix, drawn from all corners the British Empire and the Continent. As Alexander V. Campbell remarks, the "bonds formed . . . during wartime proved advantageous for both parties in the post-Treaty of Paris world," and because the backcountry land patents of men like Cooper's Effingham tended to be sparsely populated and socially remote, personally known veterans like Leather-Stocking tended to receive highly favorable terms from their landlords: nominal rent, ownership of improvements made to the estate, and perpetual freehold.[19] In short, Leatherstocking's personal allegiance to Effingham in *The Pioneers* substitutes for the kind of quasilegal relationship that would have both bound him to Johnson networks and distinguished him from members of other Colonial communities before the Revolution.

In fact, when Bumppo chides Chingachgook for neglecting Effingham interests in *The Pioneers*, he does not appeal to a *personal* sense of obligation, but to *social* and *legal* fealties that paralleled those of white tenants prior to the Revolution, asking "Why have you slain Mingo warriors . . . [if] not to keep these hunting grounds and lakes to your father's children? and were they not given in solemn council to the Fire-eater [Effingham]?"[20] Nor is it only Chingachgook for whom those loyalties have been cemented in communal violence (and Cooper hints, here, at the extent to which the Revolution implicates the unresolved prophetic tragedies of *The Last of the Mohicans*). Bumppo, for example, sees the taking of human scalps as a transgression against his white "nature," but views it as a "sign of honour in the eyes of a red-skin," and no more curious than some of the "remarkable idees consarning their honour" that he has seen "white men of great name and character" exhibit.[21] In *The Pioneers*, however, Templeton's inhabitants see no such distinction between Bumppo and Chingachgook, gossiping that "Mister Bump-ho has a handy turn with him, in taking off a scalp; and there's them in this here village who say that he larnt the trade by working on Christian men."[22]

While nothing in the Tales suggests that Leatherstocking took scalps, the townspeople's suspicions are altogether reasonable. During the Seven Years' War, Irregular troops working with Indian allies often utilized methods of war that scandalized English sensibilities about martial honor. In 1754, for example, the Mingo Half-King, Tanacharison, washed his hands in the brains of a French officer, Joseph Coulon de Jumonville, while a young George Washington watched; in 1759, General Wolfe escalated his campaign against Montcalm by threatening to "burn and lay waste [to Canada] for the future," and despite instructing his rangers to spare "only the churches," his concurrent decision to promote the taking of scalps from combatants and noncombatants alike resulted in numerous atrocities, including the murder and mutilation of a priest and his full congregation at St. Anne.[23] As one officer remarked, the "Royal Americans" responded to heavy casualties in frontier conflicts such as Pontiac's War, the Cherokee War, and Lord Dunmore's

War by "killing all [they] could find, and burning every house."[24] Leatherstocking, himself, bears witness to such practices during his description of "Bloody Pond" in *The Last of the Mohicans*.

Quite probably, Bloody Pond is one of the "skrimmages" that Bumppo tries to describe in *Pioneers*, recalling how he "cut up the French and Iroquois." In Bumppo's version, the French were "thinking only of the cravings of their appetites," but Leatherstocking's party "gave them . . . little breathing time, for they had borne hard upon us in the fight of the morning, and there were few in our party who had not lost friend or relative by their hands."[25] The recollection of the ensuing massacre haunts Leatherstocking, who muses to his companions in *Mohicans* that "these eyes have seen [the Pond's] waters coloured with blood, as natural water never yet flowed from the bowels of the 'arth," as well as how "there are them in the camp who say and think, man, to lie still, should not be buried while the breath is in the body," but how, "in the hurry of that evening, the doctors had but little time to say who was living and who was dead." Nevertheless, Bumppo's shame is mixed with an "air of military pride" as he reflects that "there are not many echoes among these hills that haven't rung with the crack of my rifle, nor is there a square mile atwixt Horican and the river, that 'kill-deer' hasn't dropped a living body on."[26] While the townspeople of Templeton might be wrong in suspecting that Bumppo committed atrocities against other whites, Bumppo's "air . . . of pride," even as he recounts the massacre, is equal parts individuating and communitarian. Templeton's residents are generally *correct* in identifying Bumppo's cultural affiliation with those who went "out under Sir William" and self-identify as such.

As Linda Colley remarks, eighteenth-century Britons who saw the treatment of prisoners as a mark of national honor were horrified by accounts like Leatherstocking's that portrayed Indian Nations "acting alongside the British . . . as unalloyed creatures of menace, raw, single-minded hunters, utterly beyond civility and sentiment. Emphatically the Other."[27] Equally threatening was the idea that Britons, themselves, became "emphatically Other" by pursuing policies of "total war" on the frontiers. In *The Last of the Mohicans*, Bumppo's description thus positions him outside of English civic values; he becomes an embodied substitute for the threatening difference of "white Indians" on distant geographical frontiers. However, for Templeton's residents in *The Pioneers*, as well as for Cooper's nineteenth-century reading audience, this emphatic "Otherness" reflected historical as well as spatial anxieties about sustainable "civility" in the Early Republic. Although Revolution-Era and Post-Revolutionary writers such as Crevecoeur and Sedgwick were often ambivalent—or even sympathetic—in their portrayals of Loyalists, there was a general agreement on both sides of the Atlantic that backcountry Tories who fought alongside Indian allies against their fellow Anglo-Americans—men like Guy Johnson and the Butlers—were beyond sympathy and redemption. Frontier romances like William Gilmore Simms's *The Partisan* (1835), which depicted a hero's quest to extract revenge from the Tories who murdered his wife, and Robert Montgomery Bird's *Nick of the Woods* (1837), which substituted Indians for Simms's Tories in the revenge-fantasy plot, depicted the "Leatherstocking" frontier as a location where those whose "tory principles and practices, and perhaps crimes and outrages" drove them "to seek refuge," and therefore a necessary landscape of punishment for Loyalist-Indian transculturation.[28] Conversely, William Kirby's Canadian epic, *The U.E.; A Tale of Upper Canada* (1859), introduced an aging, exiled "Leatherstocking" figure named "Ranger John." While Bird's "Indian hater," Nathan Slaughter, takes revenge against the Indian Nations, Ranger John celebrates his Revolutionary-Era attacks revenge against the Colonies under Sir John Johnson, Guy Johnson, Brant, and other prominent Loyalists who had fled "Effingham Country" in 1775. What both second-generation "Leatherstocking" copies share, however, is a common definition of Loyalism as a communal frontier identity, one that emerged from the ideological fault lines of British North America in 1763 and remained, throughout the Revolution, both "emphatically Other" from both Colonial and English metropolitan sensibilities.

Kirby's Canadian "Leatherstocking" in *The U.E.* recalls his Revolutionary War service under "good Sir Guy" Johnson, Joseph Brant, and other Iroquois-Loyalists as a series of bloody but chivalric contests in the company of "as brave a band as trod the woodland" and "oaken groves and haw-thorn shades, round Fort Niagara's walls and palisades."[29] Nothing could be further from works like Thomas Campbell's *Gertrude of Wyoming* (1809) or Crèvecœur's "Susquehannah," which described the infamous "Burning of the Valleys" as "the Same scheme which had been anteriorly Proposed & sat on foot by the commandant of Niagara [Johnson]," animated by the "most Vindictive passions" among Indian warriors "decorated with all the dreadfull ornaments of Plumes & colour of war with fierce & animated eyes," a harbinger of "war, cruel war, fatal propensity which converts one part of the human species into carnivorous animals avidly seeking to Glutt themselves with the blood of the other," and sad cries of "Mammy where are we going where is father, why don't we go Home, Poor Innocents don't you know that the King's Indians have Killed him & have burnt our House & all we had?[30] "Biased as such works were, they nonetheless reflected British practice of using Johnson County Loyalists Indians against Colonial frontier communities. "We need not be tender calling upon savages," General Gage had argued, "as the Rebels have shown us the example by bringing as many Indians down against us as they could collect," and Guy Johnson was ordered to convince the Nations to "take up the hatchet against His Majesty's rebellious subjects in North America" in 1775.[31]

At the beginning of the Revolution, there was every indication that Guy (who, like Leatherstocking, had little interest in "differences in political ideas") wanted to keep his Department, family, and "fiefdom" out of the growing conflict between the Crown and the Colonies. His own "character, station, and the large property [he had] in the country, and the duties, of [his] office" all inclined him toward the same calculated but untenable neutrality that the Six Nations initially pursued in response to what they saw as a British "family quarrel."[32] Johnson reassured the Committee of Safety in Tyron County that, as to their "political sentiments," he had "no occasion to enter on them or the merits of the cause," and wanted "to enjoy liberty of conscience and the exercise of [his] own judgment, and that all others should have the same privilege."[33] The Committee responded that it was "not ignorant of the very great importance of [his] office," and reassured him that it was "no more [their] duty than inclination to protect [him] in the discharge of the duties of [his] province."[34] However, such courtesies had threatening undertones on both sides as the Revolution began to unleash local grievances as ideological oppositions. At Caughnawaga, for example, Johnson and other local gentry tried to disperse a crowd of zealous patriots, but when one of the men, Jacob Sammons, began to personally insult him, the volatile Superintendent leapt off the platform and began to whip and strangle the young man.[35] By May 1775, Johnson began to receive "repeated accounts that a body of *New-Englanders* or others were to come to seize and carry away [his] person, and attack [his] family, under colour of malicious insinuation that [he] intend[ed] to set the *Indians* upon the people."[36] He fortified his "large well built new House" and began traveling under the "protection of armed men." He ordered the arrest of the New England missionary, Samuel Kirkland, detained "leather tanners" and troublesome "New-Englander[s]" on the King's Highway, and forcibly disbanded local political assemblies. The Committees, "greatly alarmed at Colonel Johnson's motions," kept him under constant observation and likely hoped to disarm or confine him, as they had successfully done with his cousin John.[37] Johnson, however, quickly proceeded northwest with his family and party of Loyalists, Confederacy warriors, and displaced backcountry gentry, abandoning Guy Park on what was ostensibly Department business. In July 1775, Johnson wrote to Peter Van Brugh Livingston, wishing "a speedy termination to the present troubles and informing him with that: "I shall have occasion to meet the Indians of my Department in different quarters this season."[38] By that time, Johnson had already crossed into Ontario.

Just as Cooper's notes for a scene at Niagara in the proposed Revolutionary War Tale potentially draw the fictional Leatherstocking into the orbit of Crèvecœur's "commandant," hints in *The Pioneers* suggest a similar alignment between the elder Effingham, to whom Bumppo and Chingachgook are both bound, and the initial flight of the Johnson retinue from the Tales' frontier landscape. Wayne Franklin remarks that "it is the father of the hero Oliver Edward Effingham, Col. Edward Effingham, who was an active Loyalist during the Revolution—not Major Effingham, Natty's sometime master and current guest" in *The Pioneers*, a fact that seems to give Cooper "more leeway" in imagining Leather-Stocking's Revolution than the advocates of a Loyalist reading allow.[39] This is true in a highly qualified sense, however. While Major Effingham's senility (which prevents him from participating in the War) undoubtedly reflects Cooper's desire to exempt Leather-Stocking's good-old-days from the ugliness of *The Spy*'s "family quarrel," Cooper's plot acrobatics bind his aging backwoodsman even tighter to the "historical" probability of Loyalism that the novels try to avoid. Major Effingham does, in fact, fight, however briefly, at the beginning of the Revolution. When the senile Major addresses Marmaduke Temple at the end of *The Pioneers*, he is clearly mentally arrested at the beginning of the Revolution, when prominent Loyalists such as Guy Johnson, Daniel Claus, and John Butler used "solemn councils" such as the one that invested Chingachgook's lands in the Effingham name to ensure support for the Crown among the Six Nations.[40] "The council will open immediately," Major Effingham declares. "Each one who loves a good and virtuous king will wish to see these colonies continue loyal."[41] In his mind, Effingham is in flight, suggesting that his attempt to secure Indian loyalty in Department lands would have occurred sometime in 1775, before Johnson's removal to Montreal. Of course, Cooper was not bound by historical facts in his characterization of Leatherstocking, Chingachgook, or the Effinghams. As a historical novelist, though, he bound his plots to historical contexts and often carefully interwove his fictional characters with the established biographies of their real-life contemporaries. The Major Effingham, for example, who spends most of the War invalided in Connecticut could not have held his "council" after Johnson's departure or before 1775. In short, at least that part of *The Pioneers* "exists" within a narrow "temporal" window, dominated by the actions of specific *historical* "characters" and their outcomes.

Ironically, the historical Loyalists who limn the edges of Leatherstocking's Revolution found their social prestige and legal standing reduced to political fictions about an increasingly romanticized past after the flight to Montreal. A decade after the Superintendent's arrival in Canada, General Gage testified that "Col Guy Johnson took an Active Part in favour of the British Government from the first appearance of a Revolt in North America, that he did his duty as became a Faithful Subject in his Department of Superintendancy of the Six nations, and kept those tribes in his Majesty's Interest." However, the new wartime authorities at Montreal did not "think it prudent to let [Johnson's Confederacy allies] go beyond the 45th deg. of Lat: or over the Province Line" to New York, in spite of Johnson's insistence that it was "extremely necessary to put the Indians as soon as possible into motion, as they were unaccustomed to remain long idle" and "could not be managed as other people." He quickly ran afoul of the Montreal establishment, purposely misconstrued orders, fought with general officers, and led his Indian allies on unsanctioned war parties. To make matters worse, few in Montreal wanted their Indian guests to stay. To the Six Nations and their Johnsonian political interlocutors, it seemed that there were "Bad Birds flying [about everywhere,] telling Lyes and Endeavouring to Break that Chain of Friendship which bound Britain to the Nations," for "some of the Inhabitants &c continued to sell liquor to the Indians and to strip them of their cloathing, propagating also many dangerous reports among them, and telling them that they approved of the rebels coming, as it was in the interest of the Colony." Despite Johnson's best efforts to manage the deteriorating situation, "the Indians almost all withdrew discontented, unwilling to credit any further promises of aid" and convinced that the British authorities had intentionally obstructed the Department's attempts to "procure them redress for sundry grievances they had often represented."[42] In effect, the negotiated, transcultural, and ultimately ephemeral authority of the Johnson Establishment suffered a double loss in the Revolution, compounding physical displacement from New York lands with final political displacement by the Crown—the symbolic "Return of the King" that effectively terminates *locum tenens* with the resumption of normal channels of power.

What Bumppo experiences in domestic microcosm during the backstory of *The Pioneers*, namely the tenuous alienation of a *locum tenens* without sanction, Johnson's Department experienced at the geopolitical level during the time of the fictional Effingham family's misfortunes, unsupported by either the British Crown or British North America, but forced to define his relationality to both in social terms that no longer possessed political or legal currency. Without a proper authority," Johnson concluded, "the Super-Intendant can be expected to do very little, and without some rank he cannot properly manage or preserve order among his own officers." Thus, in November 1775, Johnson "signified his intentions to go to England, [and] get these points in some measure adjusted before the Indians from their respective Nations could take the field next year." For the first time since the Seven Years' War, the Johnson Establishment sought to forgo the historically "organic" development of transmetropolitan empire in favor of a more clearly defined jurisdiction from Whitehall. However, even this political brinkmanship on Johnson's part suggests something about the power that Sir William's *locum tenens* rule had exerted across North America's frontiers, for in addition to a proper commission, Guy made the radical proposal of "fixing limits to the Department conformable to those Confederacys within it."[43] While this did little more than reiterate a pre-Revolutionary status quo, Johnson's design sought to give *de jure* force of English law to the Middle

Ground's *de facto* status as an autochthonous empire within the British Empire.[44]

THE "LEATHERSTOCKING" FIGURE AS A SYMBOL OF IMPERIAL ORDER AND LOSS

When Guy Johnson arrived in London in 1775, accompanied by Joseph Brant and other Confederacy leaders, he knew better than to present himself as a Colonial American, British officer, or backwoods squire with pretentions. He commissioned the American-born artist, Benjamin West, to paint him as "emphatically Other," as an intercultural *position* of authority and brokerage in which *he* was *unique locum tenens*. In the famous portrait, *Colonel Guy Johnson and Karonghyontye*, he is every bit *Uraghquadirha* ("The Rays of the Sun Enlightening the Earth"), an adoptive Iroquois name given by the sachems of the Six Nations after his assumption of Sir William Johnson's duties. He wears leather stockings with bright fringe, quill-worked moccasins after the Iroquois fashion, and a scarlet officer's coat, unmarked by braid or rank, that covers the buff waistcoat, the breeches, and the officer's sash that is wrongly knotted at the groin and draped between the thighs. A heavy fur robe, covered in repeating geometries and regular slashes of red and black, completes the effect, complimented by the ornamented black skin cap with a red feather, the thick powder-horn strap, intricately finger-woven in the Iroquois style, and the long rifle in his left hand. Indeed, despite his flushed white complexion and thick brown hair drawn back with a ribbon, it would have been easy to mistake him for a blood relation to his adoptive Indian brethren. Even Cooper mistook him for one of Sir William Johnson's "children by a squaw."[45]

Cooper's mistake was a common one during Johnson's own time. As Dror Wahrman remarks, Johnson's 1775 persona announced that such "frontier people" were "'individuals with 'stretched identities' [who] . . . proved unintelligible and unclassifiable within understandings of identity that colonists had inherited from their metropolitan homesteads" (and which, in turn, reflected back to England a "reasonable" image of Colonial subjects).[46] The West portrait not only presented such "stretched identities," it did so at the insistence of Johnson, Karonghyontye, and other highly invested members of the Department retinue because the whole point of commissioning the image was to illustrate that only such men were able to substitute for the Crown's authority on the frontiers and, in turn, adequately represent real frontier interests to Whitehall. In this sense, West's portrait is a unique representational artifact of practiced imperium in Johnson Country. Guy Johnson's political work in commissioning the painting also prefigures Leatherstocking's fictional purpose in remaining at Templeton in *The Pioneers*, for it articulates the case for a historical social order that was effectively defunct—imagined or performed at most—when Johnson arrived in London in 1775. Its image of "legitimate" power, displaced from its natural frontier landscape, both highlights the loss of the Iroquois-Loyalist historico-cultural establishment and the need for its restitution, the translation from the performed artifice of West's scene back into real-world power, through the painting's substitutional presence of Johnson as "white savage." In fact, what West's portrait presents is probably the most explicit eighteenth-century British analogue for Cooper's fictional white backwoodsman, an underpainting for the impressionistic mythologies of *The Last of the Mohicans*. Like Leatherstocking, Johnson surveys the landscape from a wilderness rock, his Chingachgook-like companion a mirror image beside him, wearing the same quillwork, powder horn, and stockings as his white companion; in the background, Iroquois warriors camp near a British tent; Niagara Falls, where Cooper hoped to end his sixth Tale, crashes behind them.

As James Franklin Beard remarks, Cooper's Niagara scene would have been "breathtaking," but the real power of this projected setting would have had less to do with the scene's Hudson River School sublimity than with the figural ironies involved in historicizing Bumppo in that location at that time.[47] Our best indication of what such an encounter between two Leatherstockings might have looked like occurs in *The Pathfinder*, where Bumppo encounters the self-made French ranger and Indian agent, Captain Sanglier. Cooper tells us that "Flint Heart, as he was usually termed on the borders, had got to be as terrible to the women and children of that part of the country, as those of Butler and Brant became at a later day." While Leatherstocking disapproves of Sanglier's calculating coldheartedness and rejection of his own "white gifts" in favor of Iroquois war-making, Cooper is careful to point out that Bumppo has "far too much of that liberality which is the result of practical knowledge, to believe half of what he heard to his prejudice," a suggestive comment in light of the text's analogy between Sanglier (who Natty regards foremost as a "brave warrior") and the infamous Tories of Edward Effingham's generation. The French "Leatherstocking" is both a double and an inversion of the Bumppo. As in the "celebrated interview between Wellington and Blucher," both frontier fighters "felt that in the other, he saw a formidable foe," and they stood "earnestly regarding each other for more than a minute without speaking." Cooper resolves the dramatic tension in the scene by observing that "each felt, while he ought to regard the other with the manly liberality due a warrior, that there was little in common between them, in the way of character, as well as interests." Sanglier serves for "money and preferment," while Leather-Stocking serves "because his life had been cast in the wilderness, and the land of his birth needed his arm and experience."[48]

In consequence, readers prefer Bumppo to Sanglier for ethical reasons, underscored by Bumppo's assertion to *The Pathfinder*'s "old salt," Charles Cap, that although he "wish[es] no enemies . . . [and is] ready to bury the hatchet with the Mingos as with the French," reconciliation depends on "one greater than either of us, so to turn the heart."[49] Just as Cooper makes the descriptive correlation between Sanglier and Butler, Leatherstocking emphasizes interpersonal connection and reconciliation over national allegiances, characteristically expressing his affective, individualistic ethic through the ritualistic social language of the Middle Ground, the "burying" and "taking-up" of "the hatchet" that distinguished the Superintendency's Loyalist rhetoric after 1774. *The Pathfinder*'s distinction between mercenary-adventurer and someone who fights "because his life had been cast in the wilderness" is harder to make in projected conflicts between Bumppo, the *locum tenens* of the Effingham family, and representative Loyalists who filled the same function for the Johnson Establishment on a historical scale. Indeed, Cooper's portrayal of both Major and Colonel Effingham indicates their Sanglier-like interest in wealth and preferment, but it is at Colonel Effingham's instructions that Bumppo remains at Templeton in the first place, a charge that coincides with Bumppo's sense of social honor. While Bumppo's frontier iconoclasm seems to distinguish him from the self-interest of a Sanglier, the less tangible forms of wealth and prestige that both he and Chingachgook do, in fact, find meaningful are intimately bound in the more obvious self-interest of the Effingham family. As in the historical cases of ostentatiously performed privilege at Johnson Hall or Guy Park, wealth does not provide a simple opposition to wilderness in the Tales. The manorial estate and its trappings provide a location for the translation of frontier valuations into more customary Anglo-American models of status and privilege, and vice versa. As much as Bumppo's presence continues to validate claims to quantifiable elements of the Effingham estate in *The Pioneers*, the former scope of Effingham's political authority, his rightful title to Indian and Anglo-American lands, and transcultural status provide Bumppo with the best opportunities to demonstrate his own virtues as frontiersman in ways that *Waverley* audiences would recognize as suitable to a Highland chief or medieval vassal—or, perhaps, a figure from a Benjamin West scene.

Perhaps what ultimately distances Leatherstocking and his audience from the potential implications of a "Loyalist" Niagara scene is Edward Effingham departure from Leatherstocking Country and death before *The Pioneers*. While Cooper's decision to have Edward hide his father in Connecticut suggests the influence of the Loyalist father-and-son pair, the Butlers, on the characterization of the Effinghams,[50] the Effinghams are an impressionistic rendering of types or amalgamations of anecdotal Loyalism. Edward Effingham's career, for example, also aligns him with the Sir William's supposed son "by a squaw." In a remarkably close parallel to the collapse of Guy

Johnson's career, the hot-headed Edward flees at the beginning of the Revolution, receives a colonelcy, and returns to command Loyalist "provincial corps" before leaving his child, "after several years of fruitless application and comparative poverty, in Nova Scotia, to obtain the compensation for his losses which the British commissioners had at length awarded."[51] Unlike Effingham, Guy Johnson ended the War bankrupt and died in 1788, still claiming losses in excess of £22,000. His wife, Polly, had died during the evacuation of Guy Park, and his daughters remained wards of the Clauses in Nova Scotia, one of whom seems to have returned incognito after the War to the former site of her childhood home—much like Edward Oliver—to retrieve what she could from the formerly "large well built new House of wrought stone 2 stories high," with the "Mahogany Stair Case & Complete Cellars under the whole," the "Household furniture all new," and the "Elegant Phaeton quite new," tended by "19 Negroes, most of them young and some valuable."[52] Colonel Effingham, on the other hand, *obtains* restitution in Pioneers, eventually securing a post in the West Indies. But en route to collect his family from Canada and Connecticut, he shipwrecks and dies, leaving Leather-Stocking as the sole protector of his son and father, as well as his Loyalist and Mohegan land claims in Templeton.

For Leatherstocking, the destruction of the "Johnsonian" Effingham estate (both literal and legal) in the Tales' fictionalized 1790s thus offers a dramatic foretaste of Cooper's own fears for the Early Republic during the 1830s, namely that "men of principle are [inevitably] defeated and the American promise evaporates in the decay of American civilization."[53] In fact, while critics often emphasize *The Pioneers*'s treatment of a *new* social order at Templeton, the physical landscape of 1790s New York still bore dramatic witnesses to the postcolonial destruction and repurposing of Johnson's "Middle Ground," the *old* order that still echoed in vestiges of its physical artifacts and their claims to legal, social, and historical precedence. In 1793, for example, Simon Desjardins and Pierre Pharoux, two French agents for the Compagnie de New York, remarked on the routine desolation upheaval between Albany and Cooperstown, the "charming residence[s]" of exiled Tories "bought from the State," the "establishment[s] . . . burned down by Indians during the War," and the "rustic scene[s], wild and romantic" everywhere, that seemed so "suitable for nourishing melancholy ideas of ruin, chaos, and destruction." At Caughnawaga, they passed Guy Park, which had since been "defaced out of hatred for its owner, as were the fine orchard and plantations also."[54] For most Loyalist refugees, any relationality with the Leatherstocking landscape continued as memory and narration, recorded through often-unsatisfied testimonials and petitions to the Loyalist Claims Commission.[55] In *The Pioneers*, the Effingham "claim" has a notable exception: Leatherstocking still occupies the former estate on their behalf in defiance of dialectical history. Just as Desjardins's tragic natural landscape acted as a metonym for the postcolonial ruin of the Johnson Establishment, Bumppo's continued presence in Templeton argues for the ethical and historical debt owed to the British Imperial world of the Effinghams. In one sense, Leatherstocking regenerates the frontier iconoclasm of Johnsonian "Loyalism" in the Early Republic, but as David W. Noble remarks, Leatherstocking's myth of regeneration is, itself, "a prisoner of time; it is a prisoner of the historical culture which gave it birth."[56]

NOTES

1. Wayne Franklin, "'One More Scene': The Marketing Context of Cooper's 'Sixth' Leather-Stocking Tale," in *Leather-Stocking Redux; or, Old Tales, New Essays*, ed. Jeffrey Walker (New York: AMS Press, 2011), 245–246.

2. Steven P. Harthorn, "What Happened to Cooper's Sixth Leatherstocking Tale?" (paper presented at the 15th Cooper Seminar, *James Fenimore Cooper: His Country and His Art*, State University of New York College at Oneota, July 2005), http://external.oneonta.edu/cooper/articles/suny/2005suny-harthorn.html.

3. Harthorn, "What Happened," Apart from a few scattered references in Cooper's novels, the speculative details of Bumppo's early life come primarily from Susan Fenimore Cooper's Introduction to *The Deerslayer* (New York: Houghton, Mifflin and Co., 1876), xxiv–xxix; for "biographical" continuity and context, see Sandra Gustafson, "Cooper and the Idea of the Indian," in *The Cambridge History of the American Novel*, vol. 6, edited by Leonard Cassuto (Cambridge: Cambridge University Press, 2011), 103–116.

4. Edward Larkin, "What Is a Loyalist?" *Common-Place* 8, no. 1 (2007). http://www.common-place-archives.org/vol-08/no-01/larkin/

5. Larkin, "What Is a Loyalist?"

6. Richard White, *The Middle Ground: Indians, Empires, and Republics in the Great Lakes Region, 1650–1815* (Cambridge: Cambridge University Press, 2011), xiii.

7. William V. Spanos. *American Exceptionalism in the Age of Globalization: The Specter of Vietnam* (Albany: SUNY Press, 2008), 201

8. Roland Mousnier, qtd. in William Beik, *Absolutism and Society in Seventeenth-century France: State Power and Provincial Aristocracy in Languedoc* (Cambridge: Cambridge University Press, 1985), 9. For a general outline of Mousnier's concept of the "society of orders," see "Les concepts d'*ordres*," 289–312. I should clarify that I am not suggesting that the production of the British Empire was not tied to material production. I am arguing that the Johnson Establishment and the Superintendency, in part because of Britain's relative weakness on the frontier, was primarily concerned with the representational production of political legitimacy/imperium. Indeed, what is striking in the contemporary accounts of both Sir William and Guy is the extent to which their "fiefdoms" possessed, utilized, and exchanged real property, monies, and trade goods in a primarily ritualistic and symbolic fashion.

9. Fintan O'Toole, *White Savage: William Johnson and the Invention of America* (New York: Farrar, Strauss, and Giroux, 2005), 341. For Cooper's take on Paulding's book, see Wayne Franklin, *James Fenimore Cooper: The Early Years* (New Haven: Yale University Press, 2007), 460–461. For William Cooper's connections to Johnson associates, see Alan Taylor, *William Cooper's Town* (New York: Vintage, 1996).

10. James Fenimore Cooper, *The Pioneers, or the Sources of the Susquehanna; a Descriptive Tale*, in Blake Nevins, ed., *The Leatherstocking Tales*, vol. 1 (New York: Penguin Putnam, 1985), 25.

11. James Fenimore Cooper, *The Prairie; A Tale*, in Blake Nevins, ed., *The Leatherstocking Tales*, vol. 1 (New York: Penguin Putnam, 1985), 1072.

12. Sir William Johnson, Letter to Lord Adam Gordon, 6 April 1774, GEN MSS 494, Guy Johnson Papers. Series I: Box 1, Folder 3. Beinecke Rare Book & Manuscript Library, Yale University, New Haven, CT, hereinafter referred to as "GJP." For "Miss Molly," see Gail D.

MacLeitch, *Imperial Entanglements: Iroquois Change and Persistence on the Frontiers of Empire* (Philadelphia: University of Pennsylvania Press, 2011), 113–146; for Croghan, see Nicholas B. Wainwright, *George Croghan: Wilderness Diplomat* (Chapel Hill: University of North Carolina Press, 1959); for Claus, see Louis Livingston Seaman, ed., *Daniel Claus' Narrative of His Relations with Sir William Johnson and Experiences in the Lake George Fight* (New York: General Society of Colonial Wars, 1904).

13. Sir William Johnson, Letter to Thomas Gage, 20 April 1774, GJP I:1:6; Sir William Johnson, Letter to Lord Adam Gordon, 6 April 1774, GJP I:1:3.

14. William Legge, Earl of Dartmouth, Letter to Guy Johnson, 28 June 1774, GJP I:1:10; Hall, *The American Empire and the Fourth World* (Montreal: McGill-Queen's University Press, 2005), 155–156; Guy Johnson, Letter to John Blackburn, 12 September 1774, GJP: I:1:11; "Proceedings at a Meeting with the Chiefs & Warriors of the Six Nations Held at Johnstown in September 1774," in E .B. O'Callaghan, ed., *Documents Relative to the Colonial History of the State of New York*, London Documents, XLVI (Albany: Weed, Parson, 1854) 7:500.

15. See Anthony Webster, *The Debate on the Rise of the British Empire* (Manchester: Manchester University Press, 2006), 68–93; Guy Johnson, Letter to John Penn, 22 August 1774, GJP I:1:7; John Penn, Letter to Sir William Johnson, 28 June 1774, GJP I:1:7; Guy Johnson, "List of Articles in Payment to Plankashaw Indians for Land on the Wabash," GJP III:1:37. For context, see Stuart Banner, *How the Indians Lost Their Land: Law and Power on the Frontier* (Cambridge: Harvard University Press, 2005).

16. Edward Coke, *The Second Part of the Laws of England, Containing the Exposition of Many Ancient and Other Statutes*, vol. 2 (Union: Lawbook Exchange, LTD, 2008), 26.

17. Edward Coke, *The Fourth Part of the Institutes of the Laws of England: Concerning the Jurisdiction of Courts* (London: W. Clarck and Sons, 1817), 270–271. For uses in the British Empire, see, for example, John Nathan Hutchins, *Gaine's Universal Register; or, American and British Kalendar, for the Year 1782* (New York: H. Gaine, 1782); C. H. Sampson, *A Manual of Rules and Regulations Applicable to Members of the Indian Civil Service . . . Eligible* (Calcutta: Home Office, 1891); Parliament of the Dominion of Canada, *Sessional Papers. Volume 5. Second Session of the Sixth Parliament of the Dominion of Canada* (Ottawa: A. Senecal, 1888), ix.

18. Cooper, *Pioneers*, 32.

19. Alexander V. Campbell, "Atlantic Microcosm: The Royal American Regiment, 1755–1772," in *English Atlantics Revisited: Essays Honoring Ian K. Steele*, ed. Nancy L. Rhoden (Montreal: McGill University Press, 2007), 292. For the organization and service of the 60th Foot ("Royal Americans"), see Nesbit Willoughby Wallace, *A Regimental Chronicle and List of Officers of the 60th, or the King's Royal Rifle Corps, Formerly the 62nd or the Royal American Regiment of Foot* (London: Harrison, 1879); in part, this dynamic also reflects the Provincial culture of temporary (if often repeated) military service that Andrew Farry describes in "Regulars and 'Irregulars': British and Provincial Variability among Eighteenth-Century Military Frontiers," *Historical Archaeology* 39, 2 (2005): 16–32.

20. Cooper, *Pioneers*, 166.

21. James Fenimore Cooper, *The Pathfinder, or, The Inland Sea*, in Blake Nevius, ed., *The Leatherstocking Tales*, vol. 2 (New York: Penguin, 1985), 81.

22. Cooper, *Pioneers*, 111.

23. Horace Walpole, *Memoires of the Last Ten Years of the Reign of George the Second*, vol. 1 (London: John Murray, 1822), 347; White, *Middle Ground*, 240–241.

24. James Grant, "Part of a Letter to His Honor the Lieutenant Governor, from Major Grant," *Gentleman's Magazine* (1760); for context, see John K. Mahon, "Anglo-American Methods of Indian Warfare," *The Mississippi Valley Historical Review* 45, 2 (1958): 254–275; Brian D. Carroll, "'Savages' in the Service of Empire: Native American Soldiers in Gorham's Rangers, 1744–1762," *New England Quarterly* 85, 3 (2012): 383–429; John Parmenter, "After the Mourning Wars: The Iroquois as Allies in Colonial North American Campaigns, 1676–1760," *William and Mary Quarterly* 64, 1 (2007): 39–76.

25. Cooper, *Pioneers*, 154.

26. James Fenimore Cooper, *The Last of the Mohicans: A Narrative of 1757*. In Blake Nevins, ed., *The Leatherstocking Tales*, vol. 1 (New York: Penguin Putnam, 1985), 626.
27. Linda Colley, *Captives: Britain, Empire, and the World, 1650-1800* (New York: Anchor Books, 2004), 182.
28. Robert Montgomery Bird, *Nick of the Woods: A Story of Kentucky* (London: Richard Bentley, 1837), 223.
29. William Kirby, *The U.E., A Tale of Upper Canada* (Niagara, 1859), 57–58.
30. Hector St. John Crèvecœur, "Susquehanna," in Dennis D. Moore, ed., *More Letters from the American Farmer: An Edition of the Essays in English Left Unpublished* (Athens: University of Georgia Press, 1995), 196–202.
31. Thomas Gage, Letter to Lord Dartmouth, 12 June 1775, in ; Lord Dartmouth, Letter to Guy Johnson, 24 July 1775, in K. G. Davies, *Documents of the American Revolution, 1770–1783*, Colonial Office Series (Shannon: Irish University Press, 1972–1981) 9:170.
32. Guy Johnson, "Colonel Guy Johnson to the Magistrates of Palatine, Etc., Tyron County New York [20 May 1775]," in Peter Force, ed., *American Archives: Consisting of a Collection of Authentik Records, State Papers, Debates, and Letters and Other Notices of Public Affairs* (Washington, DC: U.S. Congress, 1837–1853), 2:661. Hereinafter referred to as "*AA*."
33. Guy Johnson, "Letter from Colonel Guy Johnson to the Committee for Tyron County, New York [5 June 1775]," in *AA* 2:911.
34. Tyron County Committee of Safety, Letter to Colonel Guy Johnson, 24 June 1775, in Samuel W. Durant, *History of Oneida County, New York. With Illustrations and Biographical Sketches of Its Prominent Men and Pioneers* (Philadelphia: Everts & Fariss, 1878), 78.
35. Jacob Sammons, "Narrative of Jacob Sammons," in Cuyler Reynolds, ed., *Hudson-Mohawk Geneological and Family Memoirs* (New York: Lewis, 1911), 987–990.
36. Guy Johnson, "Letter of Colonel Guy Johnson to the Magistrates and Committee of Schenectady," in *AA* 2:661.
37. Edward Wall, Letter to the Palatine Committee of Safety, 8 June 1775, in William Leete Stone, *Border Wars of the American Revolution* (New York: Harper & Brothers, 1816), 77. For John Johnson, see Mabel Walker, "Sir John Johnson," *Mississippi Valley Historical Review* 3, 3 (1916): 318–346.
38. Guy Johnson, "Letter from Colonel Guy Johnson to the New-York Congress: opened and read by the Albany Committee, and a copy sent to General Schuyler [8 July 1777]," in *AA*, 2:1669.
39. Franklin, "One More Scene," 244.
40. For the Butlers, see Wilbur H. Siebert, "The Dispersion of the American Tories," *Mississippi Valley Historical Review* 1, 2 (1914): 185–197; Paul H. Smith, "The American Loyalists: Notes on Their Organization and Numerical Strength," *William and Mary Quarterly* 25, 2 (1968): 259–277.
41. Cooper, *Pioneers*, 445.
42. Thomas Gage, "Copy of Testimonial by Thomas Gage on Johnson's Behalf [21 June 1785]," GJP III:3:52; Frans Le Maistre, "Extracts from the Records," in Douglas Irymner, ed., *Report Concerning Canadian Archives for the Year 1904 (Being an Appendix to the Report of the Minister of Agriculture). Printed on Order of Parliament* (Ottawa: S. E. Dawson, 1905), 348; Guy Johnson, "Journal of Colonel Guy Johnson from May to November, 1775," in *DRCH* 8:660; Guy Johnson, "Journal," *DRCH* 8:351.
43. Guy Johnson, Letter to Lord George Germain, 26 January 1776, *DRCH* 8:657.
44. See, among others, Daniel P. Bard, ed., *Boundaries between Us: Natives and Newcomers along the Frontiers of the Old Northwest Territory, 1750–1850* (Kent: Ohio University Press, 2006); Robert S. Allen, *His Majesty's Indian Allies: British Indian Policy in the Defense of Canada, 1774–1815* (Toronto: University of Toronto Press, 1992); Eliga H. Gould, *The Persistence of Empire: British Political Culture in the Age of the American Revolution* (Chapel Hill: UNC Press, 2000); Eric Guest Nellis, *An Empire of Regions: A Brief History of Colonial British America* (Toronto: University of Toronto Press, 2010).
45. James Fenimore Cooper in James Franklin Beard, ed., *The Letters and Journals of James Fenimore Cooper* (Cambridge: Harvard University Press, 2004), 2:151.

46. Dror Wahrman, *The Making of the Modern Self: Identity and Culture in Eighteenth-Century England* (New Haven: Yale University Press, 2004), 216.

47. James Franklin Beard, "Cooper and the Revolutionary Mythos," *Early American Literature* 11.1 (1976): 104.

48. Cooper, *Pathfinder*, 182.

49. Cooper, *Pathfinder*, 182.

50. Francis Manwaring Caulkins, *History of New London, Connecticut: From the First Survey of the Coast in 1612 to 1860* (New London: H.H. Utley, 1895), 342–343.

51. Cooper, *Pioneers*, 446.

52. Colonel Guy Johnson, *Memorial to the Loyalist Claims Commission, 23 March 1784*, Public Record Office, London, AO 12/22/22-46, AO 12/109/176. Microfilm, Library of Congress. When his daughter, Mary Campbell, tried to pursue her father's claim in 1825, she estimated his pre-Revolutionary estate at £30,000 of which £5,370 had been compensated. See Campbell, "Memorial," GJP III:3:42.

53. Daniel Marder, "Cooper's Second Cycle," *South Central Review* 2, 2 (1985): 23.

54. Simon Desjardins and Pierre Pharoux, *Castorland Journal: An Account of the Exploration and Settlement of Northern New York State by French Emigres in the Years 1793 to 1797*, tr. John A. Gallucci (Ithaca: Cornell University Press, 2010), 245–258.

55. For context, see the voluminous archives of the American Loyalist Claims Commission, 1777–1841, in The National Archives, Kew, 151 vols., AO 12, AO 13, FO 304, T 50, FO 95/302. Of the five million pounds in losses claimed by the American Loyalists, only £659,493 were ultimately paid out as restitution; see, also, Eugene R. Fingerhut, "Uses and Abuses of the American Loyalists' Claims: A Critique of Quantitative Analysis," *William and Mary Quarterly* 25, 2 (1968): 245–258.

56. David W. Noble, "Cooper, Leatherstocking, and the Death of the American Adam," *American Quarterly* 16, 3 (1964): 421.

Chapter Four

"Revolution is a work of blood"

Nationalism, Horror, and Mercantile Empire in Frederick Marryat's The Phantom Ship

To be a captive of the times or to be captivated by them—perhaps they are not altogether dissimilar. If Frederick Marryat was a prisoner of his own historical culture in the 1830s, he was at least a happy one, much like the speaker in Wordsworth's "Prefatory Sonnet" who shudders at "the weight of too much liberty."[1] His motives for a North American tour had been muddled to begin with—writer's block, copyright disputes, political curiosity, a failed marriage, a characteristic boredom with civilian life[2]—but in December 1837, the sea-captain-turned-novelist found himself in the midst of the chaotic Lower Canada Rebellion, a brief but bitter revolt in Lower Canada that pitted Franco-Québécois radicals, known as the *Patriotes*, against a British Empire supported by the Franco-Québécois hierarchy of the Roman Catholic Church.[3] As a spectator during the decisive *Patriotes* defeat at the Battle of Saint-Eustache, which marked the end of the possibility of an independent Lower Canada, Marryat felt "about as much use as the fifth wheel of a coach."[4] It was an understandable response. Since 1806, he had lived for the British Empire's use, serving first as a midshipman aboard Lord Cochrane's frigate, the *HMS Imperieuse*, where he saw extensive action in the Napoleonic Wars until 1809. Thereafter, he served throughout the globe until retirement in 1830. Marryat captured American ships during the War of 1812; he fought river campaigns in the First Anglo-Burmese War (1824–1826); he saved a sailor's life aboard the *Imperieuse*; he saved the *HMS Aeolus*; he discovered a new species of sea snail, the *Cyclostrema cancellatum*; he invented a lifeboat; he invented a system of maritime signaling called Marryat's Code.[5] In 1820, he carried the news of Bonaparte's death aboard the

HMS Rosario and sketched the Emperor's corpse.[6] More so than most early sea novelists, including his famous American counterpart, Cooper, who popularized the genre for *Waverley* audiences with the publication of *The Pilot* in 1824, Frederick Marryat lived his out his protagonists' lives before he wrote them.[7]

To Marryat, whose worldview had been shaped by the realities of naval life and the presence of "multiethnic communities of autonomous individuals" on ships, empire-building and novel-writing bore clear similarities.[8] As Patrick Brantlinger remarks, the consistent worldview of the Marryat Cycle imagines social life as "a series of pyramids; at any given moment Marryat's characters always belong to several [potentially conflicting] hierarchies" at once.[9] As such, Marryat's sea novels portrayed the proper ship as being less a microcosm of the nation than of the broader empire that provided the naval ship with its usual sphere of operations. Coupled with this, Marryat's authorial practices admitted little distinction between the professional writing of sea-captaining—dispatches, logs, field notes, and the like—and the production of imaginative novels like *The Phantom Ship*, a supernatural sea romance first published serially in *The Metropolitan Magazine* during Marryat's North American trip. As a romancer, these habits gave him license to explore the ambiguities of his own firsthand experiences without threatening the underlying foundations of his historical outlook, situating his response to the Lower Canada Rebellion within *Phantom*'s production process. And just as the seamen of *Midshipman Easy* or *The Naval Officer* operate within multiple social hierarchies at once,[10] *Phantom* bridged multiple literary genres and cultural formations. It provided a concentrated image of its author's broader critique of the Early Republic, one in which Marryat's interventions as writer replicated the work of *Phantom*'s colonial agents: revaluation, translation, and adjudication.

For his part, Marryat was not particularly skilled at code-switching between his public personae of hard-charging naval officer and man of letters. And although Saint-Eustache foregrounded the uncomfortable fact that he was no longer the vital author of historical outcomes that he wished to be, his North American tour had been marked by public controversies surrounding his new role as romancer. While *Phantom* was a popular success, his *Diary in America*, which offered harsh critiques of the Republic, offended American fans, as did a series of newspaper scandals that depicted him as arrogant, boorish, and adulterous; worse still, reports surfaced that he had offered a toast in honor of British troops who burned an American vessel, the *Caroline*. By 1839, outraged American readers had hanged the nautical hero in effigy and organized bonfires of his novels in protest.[11] It is hard to trace Marryat's response to these events because his daughter, Florence, burned her father's private papers after his death.[12] However, Marryat's time spent in North America unquestionably influenced his creative development, serving as catalyst for a turn toward frontier stories in *Monsieur Violet*, *Settlers in Canada*, and the thematically connected tale, *Children of the New Forest*, which transposed elements of Cooper romance onto a tale of hunted children during the English Civil War.[13] Most of all, though, Marryat's North American tour left him convinced that although "Washington [had] left America as an infant nation, a pure ... and virtuous republic ... fifty years [had] afforded another proof, were it necessary, how short-sighted and fallible are men—how impossible it is to keep anything in a state of perfection here below."[14]

Although Marryat criticized James Fenimore Cooper for being a "disappointed democrat, with a determined hostility to England and the English,"[15] he admired the populist traditionalism he saw celebrated in the Leatherstocking Tales, and defended Cooper's "justly popular" use of Scott's style against the judgment of "certain cliques in [America's] principal cities and towns, who make *themselves* the medium of interpretation—their own modes of life, the representation of those of the *élite* of the country."[16] If Marryat's own commentaries on American institutions made him seem like a "disappointed democrat" of the 1830s, as well, it was perhaps because he shared Cooper's deep cultural and familial ties to the Loyalists. Frederick's father, Joseph, a prominent merchant capitalist with extensive Colonial connections, had married Charlotte von Geyer, the Hessian-American daughter of a prominent Boston Loyalist, in 1790. Consequently, Frederick's 1837 trip across the Atlantic often seemed to have the flavor an awkward homecoming, much like Cooper's fictional Effinghams, who return to a greatly altered America in the *Home* novels.[17] In fact, Cooper's political turn in *The American Democrat*, which provided the ideological template for his novel *Homeward Bound* and its sequel, *Home as Found*, also provided Marryat with a model for his own critiques of the Early Republic.[18] A decade earlier, Cooper had used the fictional persona of a British traveler in his *Notions of the Americans* to provide a "vigilant defense of his young country against European cynicism,"[19] but the *Home* novels shifted to a more critical tone, one mirrored by Marryat's complaints. For *Home*'s Effinghams, the return to North America illustrated Cooper's frustrations with the Early Republic's unfulfilled promise; for Marryat, "homecoming" meant revisiting the stage of civil war, rebellion, and failure. And while Cooper increasingly saw himself as "a foreigner in his own country" in the *Democrat*,[20] Marryat's "American" writings of 1837–1839 had the tenor of an unwelcome *insider*, an alienated native. His firsthand experience with the Lower Canada Rebellion, reflected in *Phantom*, evoked a similar response to Cooper's historical re-creation of the American Revolution in *The Spy*, namely that "of all wars, a civil war is the most cruel, the most unrelenting, and the most exterminating,"[21] but it did so with a British Imperial consciousness of vast, multivalent political spaces in the *present*. Indeed, *The Phantom Ship*—and, more broadly, Marryat's North American turn in the late 1830s—presented a counterfactual vision of what an "American" romancer might have looked like if Leatherstocking's Loyalists had won the Revolution, and how such a writer might have imagined their historical position in the British Empire.

"WHAT AMBASSADORS ARE IN THE POLITICK WORLD": COMMERCE, VARIATION, AND NARRATIVE

The Phantom Ship tells the story of a seventeenth-century Catholic sailor, Philip Vanderdecken, who pursues the famous ghost ship *The Flying Dutchman* throughout the Indian Ocean in a quest to save his doomed father's soul. While crossing the Cape of Good Hope, Philip's father, Captain William Vanderdecken, killed his ship's pilot and blasphemed a relic of the True Cross, swearing against it to gain his "point in defiance of storm and seas, of heaven, or of hell, even if [he] should beat about until the Day of Judgment."[22] As punishment, Captain Vanderdecken must "hover between this world and the world of Spirits" until Judgment Day.[23] Marryat's novel quickly takes shape as a maritime religious allegory, presenting the "legend of the Flying Dutchman as a modern version of the Biblical archetype of the fall of man as a result of succumbing to Satan's temptation."[24] Throughout the tale, the "evil-eyed" pilot, Schriften, serves as his irrational antagonist.[25] Marryat, however, also frustrates Philip's pursuit of the *Dutchman* with the introduction of a parallel plot that focuses on the adventures of Philip's Muslim wife, Amine, the daughter of the acquisitive ex-slave, Mynheer Poots, and a Near Eastern witch, as she attempts to rejoin Philip at Goa. Accompanied by the Portuguese missionary priest, Father Mathias, Amine eventually reaches her destination in spite of numerous shipwrecks, narrow escapes, and a period of captivity among New Guinean tribes, only to be charged, tried, and burned at the stake as a witch by the Inquisition. After a long fit of madness, Philip continues his quest, forgives Schriften, and reunites with his father. Philip and his father are assumed into heaven as the *Dutchman* disintegrates, and "all nature [smiles] as if it rejoiced that the charm was dissolved forever, and that 'The Phantom Ship' was no more."[26] Finis.

As with Captain Vanderdecken, real-world financial pressures likely informed Marryat's supernatural turn in *The Phantom Ship*. He may have gleaned inspiration from Edward Howard, a literary collaborator, naval officer, and subeditor at *The Metropolitan Magazine*, who described an encounter with a West Indian phantom ship in *Outward Bound, or A Merchant's Adventures*.[27] Stories about a ghostly Dutch man-o-war were widespread in British maritime circles as early as 1795, when the Irish criminal, writer, and Botany Bay settler, George Barrington, remarked that there were "very few Indiamen but what has some one on board who pretends to have seen the apparition."[28] Although most modern-day readers know the Dutchman legend from Richard Wagner's opera, *Der fliegende Holländer*, *Dutchman* stories were very much a part of the Romantic literary vernacular by the late 1830s, making ominous appearances in Walter Scott's *Rokeby*, Samuel Taylor Coleridge's "Rime of the Ancient Mariner," and Thomas Moore's "Written on Passing Dead-Man's Island."[29] Other treatments, such as Edgar Allan Poe's "MS. Found in a Bottle," jettisoned the specifics of the Indiamen's tale but retained the basic premise.[30] Marryat may have been familiar with any number of these, including variants from the maritime oral culture he shared with sailors on Barrington's Indiamen, but he derived much of *The Phantom Ship*'s basic premise from an 1821 *Blackwood's* story called "Vanderdecken's Message Home," written by John Howison, an assistant surgeon for the East India Company.[31] By the time Marryat employed the *Dutchman* motif in 1837, Howison's short story had been translated into a long-running theatrical melodrama, well-received on both sides of the Atlantic,[32] and Marryat, whose plans for an American tour included the production of his own nautical play, *The Ocean Wolf*, must have been keenly aware of the lucrative crossover appeal between novelistic and stage spectacles.[33] Although sales of Marryat's fiction averaged well over a thousand copies annually per novel, by 1836 his monetary woes had escalated to the point of threatening to "break every bone in [one publisher's] body" over unpaid royalties.[34]

At the same time, the apparitional logic of the *Dutchman* premise also provided Marryat with a recursive plot structure that was well-suited to writing practices honed in serial publication markets such as *The Metropolitan*. As early as 1832, he described the production of sea novels in terms much like Philip's frustrating hunt for the *Dutchman*. Writing, Marryat reflected, was a "ramble hand-in-hand with Fancy" in which his "whole wallet, when [he] set off, contain[ed] but one single idea" that soon became a "hermaphrodite . . . [one of those] creatures of the brain [which] are most prolific."[35] Thus he "never . . . made any arrangement of plot when [he] commenced a work of fiction, and often finish[ed] a chapter without having the slightest idea of what materials the ensuing one [was] to be constructed."[36] In a sense, Phantom's real topic was writing *through* mercantile empires. For the Faustian Captain Vanderdecken, "enormous pride and . . . [a] passion for discovery" compelled him to "usurp the Absolute's demiurgic power" by "discovering new lands, crossing frontiers, and staking out new territories as an imitation of God's creative act."[37] However, Vanderdecken's mimetic failure produces a blockage at Cape Horn that keeps his artifice, *The Dutchman*, bound to certain repetitious patterns, gestures, and revisionary attempts. For Marryat, this was also the case with his own attempts to convey experience through fiction. The completion of *The King's Own*, for example, written at sea while in pursuit of a phantom island,[38] was marked by an agony of isolation that characterized his "voluntary slavery" to a craft that failed him until "it seem[ed] to have imbibed fresh vigour from its protestation."[39] This recursive mode of production allowed Marryat to exhaust different aspects of the same idea across multiple novels. Yet, like Philip's episodic encounters with the *Dutchman*, Marryat's writing habits tended to lend sequences of his novels the air of drafts or rehearsals. *The Ocean Wolf*, with its dramatization of English Channel smuggling, retread much the same ground as Marryat's 1837 historical novel, *Snarleyyow*.[40] Philip's search for his prodigal father in *The Phantom Ship* echoed the Dickensian "foundling" premise of *Japhet, in Search of a Father*,[41] refiguring *Japhet*'s picaresque elements in terms of *Snarleyyow*'s decided focus on terror. Moreover, *Snarleyyow*'s wicked Jacobite-hunting sea captain, the "tall, meagre-looking . . . gaunt" Cornelius Vanslyperken, and his demonic, one-eyed hound, Snarleyyow—"one of the meanest, ugliest-looking curs which had ever been produced from promiscuous intercourse"[42]—reconstituted *Phantom*'s unholy pairing of Vanderdecken, and Schriften.

In *Phantom*, this correspondence between the recursive frustrations of writing and maritime life suspends any resolution to Captain Vanderdecken's curse for the novel's duration. This allows Marryat to retain *Phantom*'s allegorical archnarrative as a supernatural situation while focusing on earthbound reversals of fortune in the Indian Ocean's imperial economies. When Philip leaves Amsterdam aboard the Dutch East India Company merchantman, *Ter Schilling*, his translation from folktale landscape to the commercial world makes him subject to both the ambivalent natural world, where "fortunes are made, and fortunes are swallowed up, too, by the ocean,"[43] as well as corresponding imperial geographies where "the English and Dutch had been trading . . . for more than fifty years; and the Portuguese had lost nearly all their power, from the alliances and friendships which their rivals had formed with the potentates of the East."[44] Like Marryat's habit of writing without a clearly-mapped plot, Philip's simple quest to reach the *Dutchman* becomes contingent on the favorable resolution of many possible unforeseen concerns. Both author and protagonist must accept to enough risk to place their success in doubt, no less than the Company merchant-sailors who understand that they might spend "five years away [from home] . . . [and return] unfortunate, [having] brought home nothing, not even [their] ship."[45] As Dwight Codr remarks, this willingness to accept mercantile risk was a characteristic theological justification for eighteenth-century venture capitalism, through which "an economic practice was seen as acceptable if it placed the individual in a sufficiently powerless position relative to the outcome, which, in a world defined by Christians, was ultimately a matter of providential grace."[46] Conversely, what made practices like usury "the worst form of gain in the eyes of countless thinkers in the Protestant tradition was that it implied the making a claim on the future that could not be reconciled with the providentialist view of personal and human history."[47] In fact, the *Dutch-*

man quest is almost redundant—both for Philip and his author—because Marryat makes Philip so powerless throughout the novel's "real-world" episodes that day-to-day matters of shipping, commercial trade, and administering colonies gain parity with the supernatural romance-quest. But Philip also lives in an unquestioned Catholic cosmological order; in *Phantom*, the transactional nature of East Indian mercantile imperialism extends to spiritual negotiations on the supernatural plane.

By the late 1830s, such analogues between commerce and cosmology were used as a means to describe the practice, functions, and management of imperialism. "Money," the East India claimed in 1809, "when it enters into the Company's treasury, forms part of the general circulation of the empire, and thus contributes to the political as well as the commercial operations of the supreme government."[48] As early as 1711, Joseph Addison's description of the Royal Exchange described colonial trade agents—or *factors*—as being "in the Trading World . . . what Ambassadors are in the Politick World," for whom Britain's global trade was "a kind of additional empire," presided over by the distant, godlike figurehead of "one of our old kings . . . represented in effigy."[49] In the 1770s, Edmund Burke made the cosmological underpinnings more explicit when he condemned the Irish Parliament's support for Lord North's American policies as a lost opportunity for the Irish to act "as the Guardian Angels of the whole Empire."[50] Conversely, he attacked George III as a political Satan, whose "ministers of vengeance" carried his "bolts in their pounces," an unnatural antagonist to a British Empire described in the most organic, biological terms as one of history's "large bodies, [in which] circulation must be less vigorous at the extremities."[51] For Burke, this biological metaphor quickly elided with rhetoric of God's interaction with the soul. "As the seas roll, and months pass, between the order and the execution," Burke argued, "a power steps in, that limits the arrogance of raging passions and furious elements, and says, 'So far shalt thou go, and no farther.'"[52] However, Marryat, whose own sympathies were more with "the 'Ships, Colonies, and Commerce' interest" than with "a refined and aristocratic branch of [Tory] diplomacy,"[53] tended to view the moral implications of this with ambivalence. On the one hand, he distrusted political interference in West Indian plantation economies by British abolitionists, labor reformers, and progressive Christians. At the same time, he was a staunch protectionist, decrying "self-styled philanthropists" who advocated abolition while "voting for the importation of foreign sugar, to the direct injury of [West Indian] colonies, although that foreign sugar was the produce of the labour of new-made slaves."[54] For Marryat, it was not that the British Empire was an ideological end. It was that he viewed imperial commerce as a kind of improvisational mimesis—much like his own writing—that best made clear the contingencies and uncertainties of the human experience. God, in this sense, is *Phantom*'s ultimate colonial factor.

By extension, *Phantom* counterpointed its overt hero-quest with the idea that human life-stories are commodities in the moral economies of salvation. However unconsciously, Marryat's digressive plot alluded to eighteenth-century "it-narratives," which traced the global adventures of nonhuman creatures and things such as a guinea coin, "a Cat, Dog, a Monkey, a Hackney-Coach, a Louse, a Shilling, a Rupee, or—anything else,"[55] and "subordinate[d] the individual (and that individual's moral or immoral acts) to impersonal patterns of [socioeconomic] circulation."[56] While nineteenth-century variants such as the popular *Adventures of a Doll* often had a sentimental bent, others, such as Henri L. Dubois's *History of a French Dagger*, Henry Harcourt's *Adventures of a Sugar-Plantation*, and Cooper's *Autobiography of a Pocket-Handkerchief*[57] viewed historical and cultural systems through the surprising global circulation of objects, reflecting the subgenre's roots in the cultural dissonances of the Seven Years War.[58] *Phantom* returned readers, accustomed to the parochial horizon of most Gothic tales, to the cacophonous revaluations of cultural landscape that first *produced* the force of it-narrative in the 1750s.

In doing so, *Phantom* not only humanized the narrative logic of it-narratives, it also offered a sociological context, arguing that personal identities circulated like trade goods through maritime imperial economies. When Philip, for example, promises to release the crew and passengers of a captured Spanish vessel, he allows an African slave to remain aboard "at his own request," infuriating the slave's former master. "You prove my right by your own words," Philip informs the Spaniards. "I agreed to deliver up all passengers, but no *property*; the slave will remain on board."[59] Paradoxically, it is the slave's legal status as object that enables his manumission. The same is largely true for Mynheer Poots, who was captured as a child by Barbary pirates and exchanged through the slave economies of the Maghreb. Whereas the Spanish slave's manumission resulted from his conscious performance of self-commodification at the right moment, Poots abrogates his chattel status through conversion to Islam.[60] In both cases, slaves are able to assert their will because they understood how circumstances offer opportune moments for revaluating their object-status. As a British seaman, Marryat was acutely aware that North African captivity remained possible for European sailors as late as Lord Exmouth's expedition of 1816–1817.[61] And as Linda Colley remarks, these experiences varied based on "the captives' own characteristics and qualifications," as well as by "*when* in time they were captured, by *where* exactly they were captured, and by *who* took control of them."[62] Thus Poots, "sold as a slave to a Hakim, or physician . . . who brought him up as an assistant," grew rich "and "much celebrated," and eventually married Amine's mother, "the daughter of a [Bedouin] chief whom he had restored to health," before returning to Europe.[63] Just as Philip's success depends on his response to events outside his quest, *Phantom*'s slaves are able to reinvent themselves through understanding how shifting socioeconomic relationships recast their value.

This principle of "object"-transformation and self-revaluation extends to the highest levels of the mercantile-imperial social world in *Phantom*. The Dutch official, Mynheer Jacob Janz Von Stroom, for example, "supercargo of the Hon. Company, appointed to the good ship Ter Schilling,"[64] is one of *Phantom*'s most suggestive examples. A "supercargo," Captain Kloots explains to Philip, has a "duty . . . to look after the cargo and the traffic," and, like Addison's superintending statue at the Exchange, "play[s] the king on board [the ship] knowing that we dare not affront."[65] But the supercargo merely personifies and mediates actual corporate, imperial authority; his attempts to *manifest* that power individually simply disrupt the functional hierarchies of the ship, itself. A necessary absurdity, Mynheer Von Stroom, a "small, spare, wizen-faced man" dressed in "broad gold lace" and "white silk, worked in coloured flowers," with "gold buckles at his knees, and in his shoes, lace ruffles to his wrists, and a silver-mounted cane in his hand,"[66] boards the *Ter Schilling* "surrounded by the captain, officers and men of the ship, with their caps in their hands . . . [like] the 'Monkey who had seen the World' surrounded by his tribe."[67] But in that moment, he is the object of their need and desire, just as they are the objects of the Company's will.

In this context, the novel's counterplot—Amine's quest to find Philip—is an it-narrative gone wrong. Amine's life is as much the pure product of Poot's maritime circulation as Philip's life is a result of Captain Vanderdecken's blockage at Cape Horn. She is the embodiment of exchange. After shipwrecking in New Guinea, for example, local tribes begin "rid[ding] her of her garments," and attempt to seize "a diamond of great value" from her by "sawing [it off] at the finger." The "Tidore people," who frequent the Portuguese factory "to exchange European finery and trash for the more useful productions of the island," intervene, arguing that her value will be greater if she is returned unharmed.[68] When Amine reaches the factory, the Portuguese Commandant falls in love with her and, "had it not been for the arrival of Father Mathias, he would never have let her go . . . although she was another man's wife."[69] At each step, her relational value exchanges between different systems—economic, erotic, political, ethnic, and religious—like the "useful productions" and "European finery and trash" traded at New Guinea. Conversely, the acquisitive gestures and gazes of the Tidore cultivate her reciprocal awareness of how their persons—"their woolly hair . . . sometimes powdered white with chunam . . . [the] palmetto leaves round the waist and descending the knee . . . [the] rings through the nose and ears, and feathers of birds, particularly the bird of paradise . . . [as] their ornaments"—act as canvases for cultural commodification as well as expression. This awakens Amine's memories of her dead mother at a witch doctress's hut, and the occult "arts, which [she] had forgotten."[70] As she later informs Philip, her witchcraft has "no power over perfect spirits, but over those which are working evil, and which are bound to obey and do good, if those who master them require it."[71] Amine's tale becomes Marryat's example of a genuinely *tragic* it-narrative. Amine can only "master and require" good if she, herself, is a "perfect spirit" and not as susceptible to commodification, exchange, and narrative uncertainties as the rest of her world. Of course, this is not the case in *Phantom*. Nor, from Marryat's perspective, was such a certain conviction of purpose and rightness a viable political ethic in the world of *Phantom*'s production.

"EVERY POPULAR REVOLUTION IS A WORK OF BLOOD": WEREWOLVES, FIRES AND SAINT-EUSTACHE

In spite of its baroque plot, *The Phantom Ship* is best known for a single episode, "The White Wolf of the Hartz Mountains," a chilling *Blackwood's*-style werewolf tale narrated by a fellow sailor named Krantz. Philip's companion recounts how his father, a Transylvanian peasant, murdered his unfaithful wife and fled with his children to the Hartz Mountains. There, Krantz's father meets a woodsman's daughter, Christina, and marries her. Although Christina can soothe the rages of Krantz's abusive father, her appearance coincides with a series of nocturnal attacks by the White Wolf, a creature that kills and dismembers Krantz's siblings. Suspicious that his stepmother is somehow tied to the Wolf, Krantz follows Christina into the woods and discovers her crouching on all fours, cannibalizing his sister's corpse. Krantz wakes his father and together they kill Christina, who transforms back into her "true" state, the White Wolf. What makes Marryat's tale unique is not so much the introduction of a female werewolf—although that was a first for the genre—but the fact that Marryat's werewolf is not a human shape-shifter, cursed or otherwise. Instead, Christina is the White Wolf. Unlike others whose lives constitute endlessly shifting it-narratives in *Phantom*'s mercantile-imperial world, Christina's identity is fixed, static, and therefore antisocial. In this, she prefigures Amine's hubristic self-understanding as a "perfect spirit." Moreover, the White Wolf trope aligns with Marryat's fundamental critique of the Lower Canada Rebellion—and revolutionary ideologies more broadly—as a fixed and therefore "unnatural" complex of ideologies.

As Krantz begins his tale, Vanderdecken informs him that he has "read of [the Hartz Mountains] in some book, and of the strange things which have occurred there."[72] Marryat probably had an 1821 tale, "Hallowe'en in Germany," in mind, and it is certainly possible that Marryat was familiar with folktales of the Hartz Mountains through his Hessian-American family.[73] But although the tale's general form probably reflected the broader influence of

German Romanticism on the *Blackwood's* market,[74] Marryat had few precedents for his tale in British popular literature.[75] The closest Romantic analogue to *The Phantom Ship*'s cosmological context for lycanthropy was Walter Scott's *Letters on Demonology and Witchcraft*,[76] which briefly described the public trials conducted by the French witch-hunter and judge Pierre de Lancre in 1609.[77] As Scott notes, De Lancre's account of prosecuting supposed witches, sorcerers, and lycanthropes "assumes the form of a narrative of a direct war between Satan on the one side, and the Royal Commissioners on the other, 'because,' says Councillor de Lancre . . . 'nothing is so calculated to strike terror into the fiend and his dominions, as a commission with such plenary powers.'"[78] Scott was joking, but the inverse seemed nonetheless true to Marryat and other Tories. Like his friend, Charles Dickens, Marryat belonged to a political culture that presented "a bewildering array of possible ideological positions—Tory, Tory-Radical, Conservative, Liberal-Conservative, Liberal, Radical and Ultra-Radical."[79] On the other hand, European werewolf myths suggested that the "lupization of man and humanization of the wolf [was] at every moment possible in the dissolutio civitatis," and that "this threshold . . . is the always present and always operative presupposition of sovereignty."[80] In essence, political "lupinization" in North America horrified Marryat not because it attacked a fixed social order, but because it attacked the social open-endedness that he felt was best supported by commercial and cultural apparatuses like the British Empire.

Whereas Scott's werewolves belonged to *Demonology*'s antiquarian past, *Phantom*'s lycanthropy aligned with Marryat's peculiar use of Roman Catholicism as vernacular for political critiques of the North American present. By 1839, Marryat was convinced that "all America west of the Alleghanies [would] eventually be a Catholic country,"[81] and he tended to view this as a corrective for the Republic. "Washington and his coadjutors," Marryat remarked, "had no power to control the nature of man," and thus Americans had "deteriorate[d]," growing "more vicious" and debasing "their [own] institutions."[82] On the other hand, the sort of "equality professed by the Catholic Church" seemed more like the "equality of death" through which "all must fall before its power; whether it be to excommunicate an individual or an empire is to it indifferent; it assumes the power of the Godhead, giving and taking away."[83] Although he was a Protestant, Catholicism appealed to Marryat as a surrogate for the British Empire, a future-possible rejoinder to the Early Republic's growth in North America. Consequently, he tended to frame Westward Expansion as variations on this theme—Church and Republic, priest and monster. His 1843 Western, *Monsieur Violet*, for example, pitted a Mexican Jesuit against a puma; the puma drove the priest mad and turned his hair "to the whiteness of the snow," but Comanche warriors found the puma dead "at the bottom of [a] chasm, completely wrapped in the blanket, and with most of its bones broken."[84] Similarly, *Diary* imagined the consequences of American expansion in terms of smallpox, with Leatherstocking's boundless prairies converted into a Gothic "grave yard. . . poisoned by the stench of hundreds of corpses unburied [and] appalling beyond the powers of the imagination to conceive," where wolves "fatten[ed] on the dead carcasses."[85] Like wolves, *Diary*'s Mandan orphans prowled "without food . . . howling over the dead"; the formerly "handsome Arickarees" suffered physical transformations through disease, and, seeing the inhuman "disfiguration of their [own] features," killed themselves, "some by throwing themselves from rocks" like *Violet*'s puma, and "others by stabbing, shooting, &c."[86] Their bodies had been violently transformed by rapacious nationalism as much as disease; their physical "curse" rendered them visible signs of America's debt to Burke's Jacobins, the "tygers" and "hyenas" of Revolution's "national menagerie"[87] who waited, like *Phantom*'s Christine, "to prey upon carcasses" and "deny, even to the departed, the sad immunities of the grave."[88]

Marryat's rhetorical turn to the "White Wolf" first entered his narrative register during the Lower Canada Rebellion. There, his Toryism aligned with local Franco-Québécois contexts that framed Jean-Olivier Chenier, the mercenary adventurer, Amury Girod, and other rebels as figurative werewolves. Werewolf stories had circulated in Canada since the 1760s, when Franco-Québécois audiences read accounts of the Beast of Gévaudan, a wolflike animal reported to have been responsible for over a hundred deaths in the Margeride Mountains of France.[89] By 1767, newspapers like *La Gazette* had begun reporting a similar creature stalking the roads between Quebec and Montreal, dressed in a beggar's skin.[90] Such accounts quickly fused with corresponding Algonquin legends about the *wendigo*, a cannibalistic beastman, as well as with accounts of famous criminals. The Québécois mariticide, Marie-Josephte Corriveau, for example, whose body was left exposed in a gibbet on the Plains of Abraham, quickly became part of a traditional stock of beastlike practitioners of black arts.[91] By the 1860s, Canadian writers described Corriveau in broadly lycanthropic terms. In Philippe Aubert de Gaspé's *The Canadians of Old*, her caged corpse attacks a priest's father, who feels "two great hands as lean as a bear's paws, laying hold of his shoulders," and turns to discover *la Corriveau* "scrambling up on to him . . . trying to climb on to his back."[92] La Corriveau and others did not transform into animals in these tales, but lycanthropic figures did not *have* to. Although some Canadian priests capitalized on folktales about werewolves for pedagogical and sermonic use, Catholic demonologists tended to reject an idea of literal transformation "based on the neo-Aristotelian conception of the nonseparability of the body and soul, the body constituting the form of the soul."[93] Lycanthropic figures were animal-*like* because they stood opposed to hierarchical social order—spiritual, temporal, political, economic, and so forth—in which transformations and revaluations were supposed to occur. In

Franco-Québécois folk culture, this involved a theological attack against the Church's mechanisms of salvation, as well as a rejection of "universal" political economies that safeguarded the status of Franco-Québécois social hierarchies in the British Empire.

Although the majority of *Patriotes* were Roman Catholic, the Church sided with the British authorities for numerous reasons, chief of which was an entrenched resistance to liberalization and ideological revolution.[94] Jacques Paquin, the conservative pastor of Saint-Eustache, condemned the *Patriote* movement as heretical, spurned the political overtures of Chénier and Girod, and de facto excommunicated the rebels. Ultimately, Saint-Eustache was forcibly occupied while Paquin, like Marryat, accompanied Lord Colborne's force, following his archbishop's charge to reflect on how "almost without exception, every popular revolution is a work of blood."[95] The aftermath of Saint-Eustache illustrated the extent to which British Loyalists were willing to press this point. In some cases, *Patriote* dead were formally excommunicated postmortem and denied burial in consecrated ground. The corpse of Amury Girod, who committed suicide shortly after fleeing from Saint-Eustache, was beheaded and staked through the heart like a monster.[96] The remains of Chénier, who was killed by British troops in the Saint-Eustache graveyard, met a similar fate. Under pretense of conducting an autopsy, Government partisans mutilated his corpse and displayed it in a local tavern.[97] His skull was bludgeoned after death with rifle butts, his limbs severed, his chest cut open, and his heart removed and displayed as a trophy.[98] According to contemporary accounts, Chénier's wife recovered the remains, sewed the body together again, and buried it secretly in an undisclosed location.[99] In total, Saint-Eustache's aftermath was a Gothic public drama of lycanthrope-expulsion that did not require claims about the literality of werewolf transformations. Similarly, Christina's spiritual wolfishness in "The White Wolf" is a mainly a postmortem representation of her human acts and their symbolic nature as violations of *Phantom*'s paterfamilias. In *Phantom*, Christina's death also templates the death of Amine, through whose execution the Inquisition exposes the "hearts of wolves."[100]

Contemporaneous with Marryat's depiction of Amine's punishment, Catholic authorities in Lower Canada "carried [their] support for the English crown to extremes" after Saint-Eustache, "at one point asking . . . priests to explain to the people that the fiery destruction in the rebellion's aftermath was necessary 'for the protection of the . . . loyal subjects.'"[101] For Marryat, the Church's rhetoric of "fiery destruction" corresponded with the genesis of his Gothic Toryism. "Let it not be supposed," he wrote immediately after the Battle of Saint-Eustache, "that I am about to write a regular dispatch."[102] Such conceits were part of the framing language for *Blackwood's*-style horror, a formal counterpoint to Charles Maturin's recognition in *Melmoth the Wanderer* (1820) that "terror has no *diary*."[103] According to Marryat, the disorganized *Patriote* rebels at the village of Saint-Eustache, commanded by Jean-Olivier Chénier and the mercenary adventurer, Amury Girod, had hoped to conceal their retreat from the fortified village church by burning one of the adjoining houses. However, the fire soon spread to the church, its rectory, and the new convent built for the *Congrégation de Notre Dame*, all of which were consumed in a common "blaze of fire, and threw out volumes of smoke, which passed over the face of the bright moon, and gave to her a lurid reddish tinge, as if she too had assisted in these deeds of blood."[104] By midnight, "the Catholic priests in their splendid stoles, the altar, its candlesticks and ornaments, the solemn music, the incense, and all that" had become a vision of "bare and blackened walls, the glowing beams and rafters," and "the remains of human creatures, injured in various degrees or destroyed by fire." Some had been burned naked "to a deep brown tinge," and others were "so far consumed that the viscera were exposed; while here and there the blackened ribs and vertebra were all that the fierce flames had spared." In the adjoining mortuary, Marryat came across an equally "revolting spectacle." Unburied corpses, "heaped one upon the other," still burned—"the tressels which had once supported the coffins serving as fuel"—while "further off were bodies still unscathed by fire, but frozen hard by the severity of the weather."[105]

This might account for Philip's peculiar willingness to start fires in *The Phantom Ship*. He attempts to burn his enemies alive in their homes multiple times. First, when Philip realizes that Mynheer Poots has stolen his fragment of the True Cross, he piles "several armsful of fodder" at the door and "fans the pile into a flame" until, as at Saint-Eustache, the smoke "had ascended in columns up to the rafters of the roof while the fire raged below."[106] Later, when assaulting the Portuguese trading outpost at Tidore, he lights fires all around until the inhabitants are "stifled by the smoke, which poured volumes in upon them," and "compelled to quit the ramparts to avoid suffocation" before "the flames mounting in the air, swe[ep] over . . . [begin] to attack the factory and the houses."[107] Throughout the novel, Marryat's descriptive fascination with enemies burning alive mirrors the firsthand horror he witnessed in the Rebellion. Moreover, Phantom's account is more accurate than *Diary*'s insofar as it assigns blame to assailants rather than defenders.[108] Freed from real-world proprieties, fiction seems to have provided a space for Marryat to imagine the destructive potential of his own mercantile-imperial protagonists—both real and imagined—through the operation of flames, the purest symbolic force of transmutation. Just as the revelation of the "White Wolf" uncovered Christina's static, antisocial nature in death, Amine's execution serves as reminder of the unspeakableness of rebellion. "At the request of the priest," Amine's executioner throws "a quantity of wet straw upon Amine's pile," which causes it to release "a dense smoke" before catching fire; as at Saint-Eustache, "when the burning embers covered the ground, a few fragments of bones hanging on the chain were all that remained of the once peerless and high-minded" rebel.[109] As Marryat remarked shortly after the battle, he "could not help thinking that if Mr. Hume or Mr. Roebuck had been by [his] side, they might have repented their inflammatory and liberal opinions, as they beheld the frightful effects of them."[110] But it was also Marryat who found himself silenced by Saint-Eustache, apart from his works of imagination. The following Sunday, he was in Burlington, Vermont, "pressed into service" by "young ladies . . . dressing up [a] . . . church with festoons and garlands of evergreens for the celebration of Christmas."[111] His *Diary* records his impression thus: "Last Sunday I was meditating over the blackened walls of the church at St. Eustache, and the roasted corses lying within its precincts; now I am in another church, weaving laurel and cypress, in company with some of the prettiest creatures in creation. Like the copy book says, *variety is charming!*"[112] Perhaps he had more to say, but not to the "prettiest creatures" in New England to whom he was simply a self-consciously bright foreign object in circulation.

NOTES

1. William Wordsworth, "Nuns Fret Not," *William Wordsworth's Poetry and Prose* (New York: W. W. Norton, 2013), 401.
2. David Hannay, *Life of Marryat* (London: Walter Scott, 1889), 98–99
3. For a partial record of civilian property damages, see *Copy of the Report of the Commissioners appointed in Lower Canada, under an Ordinance . . . and the Amount of Their Claims* (London: Colonial Department, 1840); see, also, Robert Christie, *A History of the Late Province of Lower Canada, Parliamentary and Political . . . by Act of the Imperial Parliament* (Quebec: John Lovell, 1854).
4. Frederick Marryat, *A Diary in America, with Remarks on Its Institutions* (London: Longman, Orme, Brown, Green, & Longmans, 1839), first series, 1:364–365.
5. No critical biography of Marryat exists; for Marryat's life and career, see Hannay, as well as Florence Marryat, *Life and Letters of Captain Marryat* (London: Richard Bentley & Son, 1872); Tom Pocock, *Captain Marryat: Seaman, Writer, and Adventurer* (London: Chatham Publishing, 2000). For Marryat's Code, see Frederick Marryat, *A Code of Signals for the Use of Vessels Employed in the Merchant Service; Including a Cypher for Secret Correspondence* (London: J. M. Richardson, 1826); for Marryat's lifeboat, see Frederick Marryat, letter to Jonathan Barber, in *The Gentleman's Magazine* 90, no. 13 (1820), 444–445; for letters certifying Marryat's personal valor aboard the *Impérieuse*, see Mss. NMM MRY/11, National Maritime Museum, Greenwich, London.
6. Frederick Marryat, "Napoleon Bonaparte as he appeared on Sunday morning on the 6th of May, 14 hours after his death, laying upon the bed that he died in," MYR/7, National Maritime Museum, Greenwich, London.
7. James Fenimore Cooper, *The Pilot: A Tale of the Sea* (New York: Charles Wiley, 1823). As Susan Cooper noted, the idea for *The Pilot* derived from Cooper's dissatisfaction with Walter Scott's maritime descriptions in *The Pirate*, published in 1821; see Susan Fenimore Cooper, *Pages and Pictures from the Writings of James Fenimore Cooper, with Notes by Susan Fenimore Cooper* (New York: W. A. Townsend and Co, 1861), 72. As such, it represents a significant turn to the maritime life as a subject for the Romantic historical novel, as opposed to a simple setting for romance plots.
8. Ayse Celikkol, *Romances of Free Trade: British Literature, Laissez-Faire, and the Global Nineteenth Century* (Oxford: Oxford University Press, 2011), 44.

9. Patrick Brantlinger, *Rule of Darkness: British Literature and Imperialism, 1830–1914* (Cornell: Cornell University Press, 1988), 63. There are no definitive scholarly editions of Marryat's novels. While I use texts published with his approval throughout this chapter, I follow the editorial decision of Fireship Press in distinguishing between Marryat's sea novels—the Marryat Cycle—and his later historical and children's fiction.

10. Frederick Marryat, *Frank Mildmay, or The Naval* Officer (London: Richard Edward King, 1829); *Mr. Midshipman Easy* (London: Saunders and Otley, 1836). That Marryat celebrates the virtues of traditional British social hierarchy, transposed onto the social world of the sea ship, is a fairly standard—and broadly accurate—characterization of his novels. See, for example, Tim Fulford, "Romanticizing the Empire: The Naval Heroes of Southey, Coleridge, Austen, and Marryat," *MLQ: Modern Language Quarterly* 60, no. 2 (1999): 191–196; Sarah H. Ficke, "Pirates and Patriots," in Kevin Douglas Hutchings and Julia M. Wright, eds., *Transatlantic Literary Exchanges, 1790–1870* (Farnham: Ashgate, 2011): 115–133.

11. Pocock, *Captain Marryat*, 157–160.

12. For most of the surviving papers of Frederick Marryat, including a personal journal and some correspondence, see the Frederick Marryat Papers at the National Maritime Museum, Greenwich; see, also, Series I and IV of the Florence Marryat Collection, GEN MSS 994, Stirling Memorial Library, Yale University, New Haven, CT.

13. Frederick Marryat, *Narrative of the Travels and Adventures of Monsieur Violet, in California, Sonora, & Western Texas* (London: Longman, Browne, Greene, & Longmans, 1843); *The Settlers in Canada: Written for Young People* (London: Longman, Brown, Green, & Longmans, 1844); *The Children of the New Forest* (London: Routledge, 1847).

14. Marryat, *Diary*, 1:1:29.

15. Marryat, *Diary*, 2:2:109.

16. Marryat, *Diary*, 2:1:205.

17. Florence Marryat, *Life and Letters*, 6.

18. Florence Marryat, *Life and Letters*, 2:1:201; for the perspective of Cooper's *Home* novels, see John P. McWilliams, Jr., *Political Justice in a Republic: James Fenimore Cooper's America* (Berkeley: University of California Press, 1972), 185–238; see also James Fenimore Cooper, *The American Democrat, or, Hints on the Social and Civic Relations of the United Stated of America* (Cooperstown: H. & E. Phinney, 1838); *Homeward Bound, or The Chase* [1838] (New York: W.A. Townsend, 1860); *Home as Found. Sequel to "Homeward Bound"* [1838] (New York: W.A. Townsend, 1860).

19. Warren Motley, *The American Abraham: James Fenimore Cooper and the Frontier Patriarch* (Cambridge: Cambridge University Press, 1987), 127.

20. Cooper, *The American Democrat*, 6.

21. Florence Marryat, *Life and Letters*, 263.

22. Frederick Marryat, *The Phantom Ship* (Paris: Baudry's European Library, 1839), 10.

23. Marryat, *Phantom*, 9.

24. Joanna Mstowska, "The Flying Dutchman's Mimetic Desire. Crossing Geographical and Moral Boundaries in Frederick Marryat's *The Phantom Ship*," *Crossroads in Language and Literature*, edited by Jacek Fabiszak, Ewa Urbaniak-Rybicka, and Bartosz Wolski (Berlin: Springer-Verlag, 2013), 433.

25. See Bernard Rosenthal, "Melville, Marryat, and the Evil-Eyed Villain," *Nineteenth-Century Fiction* 25, no. 2 (1970): 221–224.

26. Marryat, *Phantom*, 319.

27. Edward Howard, *Outward Bound, or A Merchant's Adventures. (Ardent Troughton.)* (Paris: Baudry's European Library, 1838), 44; first published as "Ardent Troughton" in *The Metropolitan Magazine* serially throughout 1837. Howard served as a subeditor during Marryat's tenure at the *Metropolitan*, and Marryat fostered Howard's career as a writer of sea fiction; see Pocock, *Captain Marryat*, 112.

28. George Barrington, *A Voyage to New South Wales; with a Description of the Country; the Manners, Customs, Religion, &c. of the Natives, in the Vicinity of Botany Bay* (London: H. D. Symonds, 1795), 46.

29. Walter Scott, *Rokeby; A Poem* (Edinburgh: John Ballantyne and Co., 1813) 332–333; Samuel Taylor Coleridge, "The Ryme of the Ancyent Marinere, in Seven Parts," in William

Wordsworth and Samuel Taylor Coleridge, *Lyrical Ballads, with a Few Other Poems* (London: J. & A. Arch, 1798): 1–53; Thomas Moore, "Written on Passing Dead-Man's Island, in the Gulf of St. Lawrence, Late in the Evening, September, 1804," *Epistles, Odes, and Other Poems* (London: James Carpenter, 1806), 88.

30. Edgar Allen Poe, "MS. Found in a Bottle," *Southern Literary Messenger* 2 (1835): 33–37.

31. [John Howison], "Vanderdecken's Message Home; Or, the Tenacity of Natural Affection," *Blackwood's Edinburgh Magazine* 9, no. 50 (1821): 127–131.

32. Edward Fitzball, *The Flying Dutchman; or, The Phantom Ship, a Nautical Drama in Three Acts* (London: John Cumberland, 1829); for performances, see, among others, *The American Advocate*, 6 February 1830; *Baltimore Gazette and Daily Advertiser*, 10 November 1830; *Public Ledger*, 23 September 1836; a musical version of Moore's poem, written for one to three voices, was also widely popular; see *City Gazette & Commercial Daily Advertiser*, 28 November 1832.

33. Marryat's unpublished *The Orphan Wolf, or, The Channel Outlaw* was performed at the Bowery Theater, New York, in October, 1837.

34. Frederick Marryat, letter to Osmond de Beauvier Priaulx, 27 November 1836, in Florence Marryat, *Life and Letters*, 244; For works published in 1835–1836, Florence Marryat gives the following accounting as of her father's departure for America: *The Pacha of Many Tales* (1196); *Japhet, in Search of a Father* (1468); *Mr. Midshipman Easy* (1548), in *Life and Letters*, 243.

35. Frederick Marryat, *Newton Forster; or, The Merchant Service* (London: John Cochrane and Co., 1832), 7.

36. Marryat, *Newton Forster*, 7.

37. Mstowska, "Mimetic Desire," 433.

38. Marryat's description is as follows: "Where was I then? I recollect; within two days of the Lizard, returning home, after a six weeks' cruise to discover a rock in the Atlantic, which never existed except in the terrified or intoxicated noddle of some master of a merchant vessel," in *Newton Forster*, 7; this may account for Marryat's undertone of disdain for merchants, merchant vessels, and merchant captains in *The King's Own* (Paris: Baudry's European Library, 1834), 39, 238.

39. Marryat, *Newton Forster*, 7.

40. Frederick Marryat, *Snarleyyow; or the Dog Fiend* (Philadelphia: E. L. Carey and A. Hart, 1837), first serialized beginning in *The Metropolitan Magazine* 1 (1836), 15–21.

41. Frederick Marryat, *Japhet, in Search of a Father* (London: Saunders and Otley, 1836).

42. Marryat, *Snarleyyow*, 14–15.

43. Marryat, *Phantom*, 62.

44. Marryat, *Phantom*, 59.

45. Marryat, *Phantom*, 63.

46. Dwight Codr, *Raving at Usurers: Anti-finance and the Ethics of Uncertainty in England, 1690–1750* (Charlottesville: University of Virginia Press, 2016), 57.

47. Codr, *Raving*, 57.

48. Anonymous, *Reports and Papers on the Impolicy of Employing Indian Built Ships in the Trade of the East India Company, and of Admitting Them to British Registry . . . British-built Ships* (London: Blacks and Parry, 1809), 167.

49. Joseph Addison, "The Royal Exchange," *The Spectator*, 19 May 1711, no. 69, in *The Spectator*, vol. 1 of 8 (London: S. Buckley, 1712–1715), 392. All further references are to this edition.

50. Edmund Burke, letter to Charles O'Hara, 7 January 1776, in John Ross Swartz Hoffman, *Edmund Burke, New York Agent: With His Letters to the New York Assembly and Intimate Correspondence with Charles O'Hara, 1761–1776* (Philadelphia: American Philosophical Society, 1956), 613.

51. Edmund Burke, *The Speech of Edmund Burke, Esq; On Moving His Resolutions for Conciliation with the Colonies, March 22, 1775* (Dublin: J. Exshaw, 1775), 27.

52. Burke, *Speech*, 27.

53. Burke, *Speech*, 201.

54. Florence Marryat, *Life and Letters*, 205–206.

55. [Review of] "The Adventures of a Rupee," *The Critical Review: Or, Annals of Literature* 52 (1781), 477; Charles Johnstone, *Chrysal; Or the Adventures of a Guinea* (London: T. Becket, 1760).

56. Aileen Douglas, "Britannia's Rule and the It-Narrator," in Mark Blackwell, ed., *The Secret Life of Things: Animals, Objects, and It-Narratives in Eighteenth-Century England* (Cranbury: Associated University Presses, 2007), 150.

57. Mary Mister, *The Adventures of a Doll* (London: Darton and Harvey, 1816); Henri L. Dubois, *The History of a French Dagger; an Anecdote of the French Revolution. From the French* (London, 1828); Henry Harcourt, *The Adventures of a Sugar-Plantation* (London: Westley and Davis, 1836); James Fenimore Cooper, "The Autobiography of a Pocket-Handkerchief," *Graham's Magazine* 22, nos. 1–4 (1843): 1–18, 89–102, 158–167, 205–213.

58. Douglas, "Britannia's Rule," 149.

59. Marryat, *Phantom*, 173.

60. Traditional prohibitions against retaining fellow Muslims in slave status gave rise to numerous conversions among captured European sailors, but also led to restrictions against conversion in the Barbary States; see W. G. Clarence Smith, *Islam and the Abolition of Slavery* (Oxford: Oxford University Press, 2006), 69; Daniel J. Vitkus, ed., *Piracy, Slavery, and Redemption: Captivity Narratives from Early Modern England* (New York: Columbia University Press, 2001).

61. For contemporary responses, see, for example, G. A. Jackson, *Algiers: Being a Complete Picture of the Barbary States . . . Including a faithful Detail of the late Glorious Victory of Lord Exmouth* (London: R. Edwards, 1817); Charles Sumner, *White Slavery in the Barbary States. A Lecture Before the Boston Mercantile Library Association, Feb. 17, 1847* (Boston: William D. Ticknor and Company, 1847); Filippo Pananti, *A Narrative of a Residence in Algiers . . . and the Necessity and Importance of their Complete Subjugation* (London: Henry Colburn, 1818).

62. Linda Colley, *Captives: Britain, Empire, and the World, 1600–1850* (New York: Anchor, 2004), 60.

63. Marryat, *Phantom*, 42.
64. Marryat, *Phantom*, 65.
65. Marryat, *Phantom*, 62.
66. Marryat, *Phantom*, 64.
67. Marryat, *Phantom*, 64–65.
68. Marryat, *Phantom*, 225.
69. Marryat, *Phantom*, 245.
70. Marryat, *Phantom*, 226.
71. Marryat, *Phantom*, 189.
72. Marryat, *Phantom*, 281.

73. Anonymous, "Hallowe'en in Germany, or The Walpurgis Night," *The European Magazine and London Review* 80 (1821), 526–527.

74. For context, see, for example, James Pipkin, ed., *English and German Romanticism* (Heidelberg: Carl Winter, 1985); Bayard Quincy, ed., *German Literature in British Magazines, 1750–1860* (Madison: University of Wisconsin Press, 1949); Robert Morrison and Daniel S. Roberts, eds., *Romanticism and Blackwood's Magazine: 'An Unprecedented Phenomenon'* (New York: Palgrave Macmillan, 2013).

75. For precedents, see Charles Maturin, *The Albigenses, a Romance* (London: Hurst, Robinson, and Co., 1824); H. Laurence, "Norman of the Strong Arm: A Tale of the Sanctuary of Westminster. Thirteenth Century," *London in Olden Time; or, Tales Intended to Illustrate the Manners and Superstitions of Its Inhabitants from the Twelfth to the Sixteenth Century* (London: Longman, Rees, Orme, Brown, and Green, 1827): 3–79; Leitch Ritchie, "The Man-Wolf," *The Romance of History. France* (New York: J. & J. Harper, 1831): 117–147.

76. Walter Scott, *Letters on Demonology and Witchcraft, Addressed to J.G. Lockhart, Esq.* (London: John Murray, 1830); Marryat was probably familiar with Scott's *Demonology*, which served as a standard for the "striking incident[s]" and "horrible circumstances" of J. H. Jung-Stilling's *Interesting Tales* in *The Metropolitan Magazine* 20 (1837), 81.

77. See Jonathan L. Pearl, *The Crime of Crimes: Demonology and Politics in France, 1560–1620* (Waterloo: Waterloo Laurier University Press, 1999), 127–149.
78. Scott, *Demonology*, 208.
79. Michael Sanders, "Politics," in Sally Ledger and Holly Furneaux, eds., *Charles Dickens in Context* (Cambridge: Cambridge University Press, 2011), 236.
80. Giorgio Agamben, *Homo Sacer: Sovereign Power and Bare Life*, trans. Daniel Heller-Roazen (Stanford: Stanford University Press, 1998), 106.
81. Marryat, *Diary*, first series, 3:157–158.
82. Marryat, *Diary*, 1:1:29.
83. Marryat, *Diary*, 159.
84. Marryat, *Narrative of the Travels and Adventures of Monsieur Violet*, 267.
85. Marryat, *Diary*, first series, 1: 228–229.
86. Marryat, *Diary*, first series, 1: 228.
87. While "lycanthrope" literally means "wolf-man," it is important to note that as late as 1865, both the number of behaviors and the types of beastly transformations that denominated someone as a werewolf were broader and more fluid than current definitions, and often included Burke's symbolic tigers and hyenas; see Sabine Baring-Gould, *The Book of Werewolves: Being an Account of a Terrible Superstition* (London: Smith, Elder and Co., 1865); see also an account of hyena transformations in Nathaniel Pearce, *The Life and Adventures of Nathaniel Pearce . . . His Visit to Gondar* (London: Henry Colburn and Richard Bentley, 1831), 288.
88. Edmund Burke, *A Letter to the Right Honourable Edmund Burke to a Noble Lord . . . Early in the present Sessions of Parliament* (London: 1796), 4; see, also, Mark Parker, *Literary Magazines and British Romanticism* (Cambridge: Cambridge University Press, 2004); Matt Salyer, "'Nae mortal man should be entrusted wi' sic an ingine': *Blackwood's Edinburgh Magazine* and the Tory Problem of Romantic Genius," *Victorian Periodicals Review* 46, no. 1 (2013): 92–115.
89. Jay M. Smith, *Monsters of the Gévaudan: The Making of a Beast* (Harvard: Harvard University Press, 2011), 5.
90. *La Gazette de Québec*, 10 December, 1764; 16 July 1767.
91. "La Corriveau" was eventually buried, but in the 1850s, her cage and remains were excavated and briefly displayed in Canada before being sold to the Barnum Museum. For popular treatments of the Corriveau case, see Philippe Aubert de Gaspé's *The Canadians of Old [Les Anciens Canadiens]*, trans. Georgianna M. Pennee (Quebec: G. & G. E. Desbarats, 1864); William Kirby, *The Chien D'Or: The Golden Dog; a Legend of Quebec* (New York: Lovell, Adam, Wesson & Company, 1877); see, also, Louis-Philippe Bonneau, *Josephte Corriveau-Dodier, la Corriveau, 1733–1763: Une énigma non résolue* (Quebec: Société de conservation du patromoine de St-Francois de la Rivière de Sud).
92. Gaspé, *Canadians*, 42.
93. Nicole Jacques-Lefèvre, "Such an Impure, Cruel, and Savage Beast: Images of the Werewolf in Demonological Works," in Kathryn A. Edwards, ed., *Werewolves, Witches, and Wandering Spirits: Traditional Belief & Folklore in Early Modern Europe* (Kirksville: Truman State University Press, 2002), 185.
94. See Philippe Sylvain, "Libéralisme et ultramontanisme au Canada français: affrontment idéologique et doctrinal (1840–1865)," in W. L. Morton, ed., *Le Bouclier d'Achille. Regards sur le Canada à l'ère victorienne* (Toronto: McClelland and Stewart, 1968): 111–138.
95. Qtd. in Beverley Boissery, *A Deep Sense of Wrong: The Treason, Trials, and Deportation to New South Wales of Lower Canadian Rebels after the 1838 Rebellion* (Toronto: Dundurn, 1995), 21.
96. Edward Alexander Theller, *Canada in 1837–38 . . . Together with the Personal Adventures of the Author and Others Who Were Connected with the Revolution* (Philadelphia: Henry F. Anners, 1841), 64.
97. Theller, *Canada in 1837–38*, 65–66.
98. While there remains much controversy over the nature and extent of Chénier's mutilation, the general outlines of the account were widely reported in both Canada and the United States. In addition to Theller, see, for example, *The Caroline Almanac and Freeman's Chroni-*

cle (Rochester: Mackenzie's Gazette Press, 1840); Donald McLeod, *A Brief Review of the Settlement of Upper Canada by the U.E. Loyalists and Scotch Highlanders in 1783 . . . during the Commotion of 1837 and '38* (Cleveland: F. Penniman, 1841), 203.

99. Theller, *Canada in 1837–38*, 66.
100. Marryat, *Phantom*, 305.
101. Boissery, *A Deep Sense*, 21.
102. Marryat, *Diary*, 1:1:264.
103. Charles Robert Maturin, *Melmoth the Wanderer* (New York: Penguin, 2000), 213.
104. Marryat, *Diary*, 1:1:270.
105. Marryat, *Diary*, 271.
106. Marryat, *Phantom*, 17.
107. Marryat, *Phantom*, 237.
108. There were, in fact, two fires that produced the church fire—one started by overturning a stove in an adjoining house, and the other started at the high altar; see Sir Daniel Lysons, *Early Reminiscences* (London: John Murray, 1896), 86–87; "Editor's Portfolio," *The United Service Journal and Naval and Military Magazine* 26, 1 (1838): 281.
109. Marryat, *Phantom*, 308–309.
110. Marryat, *Diary*, first series, 1:272.
111. Marryat, *Diary*, 283.
112. Marryat, *Diary*, 283.

Chapter Five

"Buried in their strange decay"

Lost Letters, Lost Races, and Imperial (Mis)translations

In *Monsieur Violet*, Frederick Marryat needed a plot device, a way to place his European narrator among the Indian nations of California, Texas, and the North American plains. He chose, as his catalyst, the "Revolution of 1830, which deprived Charles the Tenth of the throne of France, [and] like all other great and sudden changes, proved the ruin of many individuals, more especially of many ancient families who were attached to the Court."[1] In the space of three years, Monsieur Violet follows his exiled Bourbonist father to "the ancient royal residence of Holyrood," Rome, Prague, "Sicily, Greece, Turkey, Egypt, and the Holy Land."[2] There is "no repose," Marryat reminds us, "for an exile attached to his country,"[3] and no repose in the present for history's losers. Having finally exhausted their Grand Tour of sites from the West's mythic, monarchical past, the Violets thus agree to share in the scheme of their Italian friend, Prince Seravalle, who plans to sail to North America and live among the Shoshone. For Violet, the cultures of North American Indians seem "very much like a romance," so this amounts to more of the same—more medieval Holyrood, more Grail-quest Orient.[4] Watching the Shoshone warriors and their "squires" joust, for example, he is easily able to "imagine that [he is] among the knights of ancient days."[5] Indeed, his knowledge of "Asiatic lore," his sense of felt continuities between the "ancient origins" of Christendom and the "Western Apaches or the Shoshones, with their antiquities and ruins of departed glory," make the transition between feudal aristocrat and tribal life seem far less dissonant to Marryat's protagonist than the position of Charles X's retinue in bourgeois, nineteenth-century Europe.[6] Right away, Marryat encamps Violet and his companions "at the foot of an obelisk in the centre of some noble ruins" near Monterrey, a "sacred spot with the Shoshones" whose "traditions told of another race, who had formerly lived there."[7] Although Violet and his priest companion are "anxious to discover any drawings or hieroglyphics" that might clarify the site's origin, practical exigencies force their departure as they contemplate "the high degree of civilization which must have existed among the lost race who had been the architects."[8]

In one sense, *Monsieur Violet* never becomes a true "lost race" romance because it already is one. There is no need for the discovery of, say, Prince Madoc's descendants or the Lost Tribes of Israel because Violet and his Bourbonist companions already ritually reenact the exilic and quest motifs of the genre in Marryat's historical present. The geographical American West, then, is pure historicized backdrop for a story that plays out after its meaningful conclusions have already been reached. This is perhaps why the novel, though rich with episodic adventure and scrupulously narrated ethnographic detail, seemed both "boring and chaotic" to audiences.[9] *Violet* excoriated Americans, particularly Texans, but the novel's commercial failure on both sides of the Atlantic in 1843 had more to do with such aesthetic imbalances. These, in turn, largely resulted from Marryat's overscrupulous use of source material, which relied heavily on correspondence with an American adventurer and "most accomplished swindler," Edward Lasalle, who "described himself as a British subject from among the N.W. of upper Canada, and as being an agent, & a kind of Chief among the Sioux."[10] Marryat seems to have used Lasalle's accounts of his Western travels verbatim, but Lasalle, in turn, had plagiarized his "experiences" from the Leatherstocking Tales, "Farnham, Lewis and Clark, and almost every other writer on [the] Western Prairies and wildernesses."[11] One source, George Wilkins Kendall, was forced to include a note in subsequent editions of his *Narrative of the Texan Santa Fe Expedition* defending himself from plagiarizing the "wondrous tale of Violet" and laying the countercharge of "larceny" at "the door of either the Captain or the Monsieur—a matter they must decide between themselves."[12] However inadvertently, Kendall locates the problem that later Victorian lost-race romances tried to quarantine by making the lost-race monarch the character who explains survivance, thereby providing the plot with a moment of discovery and the "real-world" protagonists with sufficient distance from lost-world dissonances to remain, relatively speaking, "objective." *Monsieur Violet*, however, both in terms of its production and narration, reflects the *confessional* mode of lost-race romances, which depended on the professionalism of ostensibly skilled translators and correspondents like Violet or Lasalle whose authority as firsthand speakers was often tied to their self-representation as monarchs or chiefs. The failure, then, of successfully translating firsthand descriptions of the non-West into British (and American) romance tropes, which was tied to the failure of the monarchial speaker's positional authority of the monarchical speaker, highlights the problem that was often at the heart of the lost-race romance: the representation of cultural-historical similitude.

Critics tend to dismiss "lost world" or "lost race" romances as a "brand of racist, imperialist, masculinist, and violent adventure stories [that] mapped British colonies, including settlement colonies,"[13] a narrative guise for faith in a "pre-historical mandate for empire [that was] articulated in the blood and sinews of the male body."[14] At the same time, Bradley Deane suggests that lost-race romancers were "engrossed as never before in charting vectors of convergence between the British and those they regarded as primitive, and in imagining the ways in which barbarians might make the best imperialists of all."[15] But what accounts for this apparent contradiction? What led the imperialist to emulate the barbarian's political professionalism or expertise? In part, the "imperial barbarian" motif reflected the routine cognitive dissonances involved in British encounters with the non-West as travelers, soldiers, adventurers, and administrators found that powerful, preexisting imperial states existed in locations where metropolitan sensibilities had anticipated "the savage." Like descriptions of shipboard life in the naval romances of writers like Marryat and Cooper, lost-race romances presented social hierarchies that appeared archaic and inhumane at a distance, but rational and familiar when encountered "firsthand." And in notable instances, this "shock of the civilized" accompanied a simultaneous "shock of the real" as the material cultures and traditions of "imperial barbarians" seemed to implicate Western legends and figures from romance in the actual politics of intercultural exchange, diplomatic negotiation, and conquest.

Two ostensibly disparate instances of attempts to chart these "vectors of convergence" in the "imperial barbarian" discourse—one African, one North American—illustrate the contradictory range of pressures that these encounters placed on formulations of the British Empire and its global neighbors—and non-Western rivals—as coherent "imagined communities."[16] Beginning with the 1809 expedition of the Cairo-based archaeologist and diplomat, Henry Salt, Britain's involvement in Ethiopian affairs during the period of the *Zemene Mesafint* (1769–1855), a feudal interregnum between Ethiopian centralized monarchies, and the subsequent reign of Téwodros II (1855–1868), a minor warlord who assumed the Imperial mantle, implicated Imperial foreign policy beyond what the British traveler John Leyden termed the "fearful and mysterious barrier, drawn round the narrow limits of the civilized nations" of Africa.[17] "Every object which appeared through this veil," Leyden remarked, "tended to heighten this impression—the human race, under an aspect and hue nowhere else seen on the globe; animals of strange form and magnitude; forms of society altogether uncouth and peculiar."[18] In the case of Ethiopia, however, nineteenth-century British writers were confronted with the existence of a "civilized nation" beyond the "mysterious barrier" of both a nineteenth-century imagined Africa and an imagined Medieval Europe: the Arthurian "Land of Prester John."[19] Ethiopian (re)encounters led British observers to view Téwodros II's administration in terms of a secular statecraft, historical anthropology, and progressive Protestant "higher criticism," so that by 1868, the British ethnologist, James Camden Hotten, characterized Ethiopian history through "such recitals as abound in the chronicles of the Old Testament—a weary, and almost never-ending series of small fights and petty battles, carried on senselessly and without reasonable cause or provocation, betwixt tribes and families."[20] Similarly, Henry Stern highlighted Téwodros's bildungsroman-like humble origins and social progress from "a poor boy, in a reed-built convent" to "the chief of a few freebooters, and, from the chief of a few freebooters, the conqueror of numerous and extensive provinces, and the Sovereign of a great and extensive realm."[21] Ironically, Imperial policy failures in Ethiopia, which led to the expensive Abyssinian Campaign of 1868, were largely a result of British reluctance to take the "Prester John" state-building myths of Téwodros II at face value, insisting, instead, that the Emperor of Ethiopia might, "with certain surroundings . . . make a respectable King, but who, when these were removed, would make a very bad one, and should therefore be deposed as soon as possible."[22] Had British authorities—including Hormuzd Rassam's failed diplomatic mission to parlay for the release of the British Consul, Charles Cameron, Henry Stern, and others—been more willing to play the role of a mystical-chivalric Court, Britain's Imperial involvement in Sudan, the Red Sea, and the Horn might have taken quite a different course.

As it was, the motives and character of Téwodros II struck Britons as "a mass of inconsistencies very difficult to European comprehension."[23] The more British press observers focused on Ethiopian affairs, the less tenable African caricatures, which portrayed Téwodros as "a mere remove from an orang-outang," a "negro of the lowest sort, with flat nose and huge lips," or a "music-hall Jim Crow, crouching and yelping at the feet of Lord Stanley, or somebody else, who presents him with an ultimatum at the point of a bayonet," seemed.[24] However, characterizations of Téwodros as an "exceedingly crafty" and "clever savage," whose letters were "perfect models of diplomatic composition," reframed his persona as being "not at all unlike that of many [American] Indian chiefs," and an index of how "the national character and customs of Abyssinia resemble[d] those of certain tribes of the North American Indians."[25] By the 1860s, defining the "crafty savage" through Indian analogues reflected familiar tropes from popular historical adventure fiction—the "Byronic or Ossianic" link between Walter Scott's Highlanders and James Fenimore Cooper's Mohicans[26]—as well as numerous instances of cultural rapport between Highland soldier-settlers in North America and their Indian neighbors.[27] In *Waverley*, Scott astutely identified this as a perspectival, rather than essential, alignment, noting that "so little was the condition of the Highlands known at that late period [1745], that the character and appearance of their population, sallying forth as military adventurers, conveyed to the south-country Lowlanders as much surprise as if an invasion of African Negroes or Esquimaux Indians had issued forth."[28] Nevertheless, Scott was careful to retain group distinctions as relative markers of "barbarism," noting, for example, how Jean-Jacques Audubon "very justly" preferred "associating with the Indians to the company of the Black Settlers . . . for a civilized man of the lower order—that is, the dregs, of civilization—when thrust back on the savage state becomes worse than a savage."[29] Audubon, the illegitimate son of a West Indian planter, was perhaps sensitive in these instances about the mulatto status of his half-brothers, preferring to flirt with the persona of the "lost Dauphin," to which a *Last of the Mohicans*-style "Indian" setting was better suited.[30] Scott, in turn, was interested in Audubon's knowledge of a different myth of lost, kingly pasts, namely "the idea that the Red Indians were ever a more civilized people than at this day, or that a more civilized people had preceded them in North America."[31]

The idea that North American tribes might be the inheritors of lost civilizations, which underlies the theological historiographies of Joseph Smith, had remarkable purchase in the early nineteenth century, conflating a range of cultural ideologies and traditions with archaeological speculations about the Mound Builders and other "lost races" of the Mississippi Valley.[32] In 1845, for example, the Southern historical novelist, William Gilmore Simms, definitively announced that "an American antiquity is now beyond all question," and that the United States, rising "as from the ruins of magnificent Rome," would one day "resuscitate the wondrous past" of American empires "now buried in their strange decay."[33] James Camden Hotten, in turn, grounded his characterization of Téwodros as a "crafty savage" by alluding to the claims of "certain bold speculatists" who suggested that Ethiopians and American Indians shared a common descent "from the lost tribes of the Jews."[34] Téwodros's assertion of central state authority after the *Zemene Mesafint* did, in fact, depend on Ethiopian traditions that traced the lineage of the Imperial House to the Old Testament's House of David, found mainly in the *Kebra Nagast*, a medieval text that recounts the story of King Solomon's illegitimate son with the Queen of Sheba/Ethiopia, Menelik I, including his theft of the Ark of the Covenant, subsequent conquests, and establishment of the Kingdom of Aksum.[35] British and American speculations about preColumbian America found a similar template in Romantic retellings of Welsh folklore, casting Prince Madoc, the self-exiled son of King Owain ap Gruffydd, as a transatlantic voyager, settler, and North American conqueror of the 1170s.[36] For writers such as Robert Southey, author of an 1805 epic poem on the subject,[37] Madoc's legend viewed Anglo-American imperial projects and the question of historical justice for conquered peoples through the lens of an "allure of the same" that "functioned to allay the anxieties of an era beset by the horrors of colonial mismanagement by stressing the naturalness ... of imperialism,"[38] just as Téwodros's nation-building policy reforms and self-projection on the world stage sought to align the Imperial State with a mythopoetic narrative of Old Testament anointings, dynasties, and covenants. Grand-scale "lost race" narratives such as these highlight the asymmetry of Anglo-American responses to empire-building. While attitudes about race undoubtedly influenced the relative willingness of Britons and Americans to project a kind of "whiteness" into Indian history but not the African present, the rhetoric of race was, in many instances, situational and flexible when confronted with exemplary figures of nonwhite power. The central disparity between the way Britons and Americans received the fictional "lost race" monarch, Madoc, and the historical "lost race" claimant, Téwodros, reflects the range of cultural misalignments that resulted from the use of romance narrative—in this case, racially inflected, medievalist ones—as a mutual means of intercultural brokerage between Anglo-American imperialists and nonwhite peoples. In the case of the Madoc myth, this intercultural-brokerage demonstrated a surprising openness of British Imperial policy-makers to nonwhite powers that fit within a recognizable model of the imperial civitas drawn from legend. In the case of Téwodros, the refusal to approach Abyssinian affairs *through* romance accelerated the Crisis of 1868 and undermined the British Empire's strategic latitude in the Red Sea region.

PRESTER JOHN AT MOUNT GILBOA: THE LETTERS OF TÉWODROS II AND THE ABYSSINIAN EXPEDITION

In the Old Testament, the House of David carries God's anointing. It establishes the national monarchy after a long period of decentralized rule described in the Book of Judges. However, when the Israelites first ask God to appoint a king so that they can live more like their Canaanite neighbors, the prophet, Samuel, anoints Saul. King Saul's reign, marked by madness, civil unrest, military defeat, and God's cryptic displeasure, ends at Mount Gilboa, where Saul witnesses the utter defeat of his army by the Philistines, the death of his children, and the inevitability of the claim made by Samuel's ghost that Saul will soon join him in Sheol. The I Samuel redactor describes how Saul then "took a sword, and fell upon it. And when his armourbearer saw that Saul was dead, he likewise fell upon his sword, and died with him. So Saul died, and his three sons, and his armourbearer, and all his men, that same day together."[39] For Northrop Frye, Saul is "the one great tragic hero of the Bible."[40] For Adam Welch, King Saul is a "great soul face to face with a raveled world who refuses to turn his back on what he has taken upon him, but also a great soul with a fatal defect, not quite big enough to do the thing which his time demanded from its leader, but doing all which it was left possible for him to do."[41] Such characterizations have great merit, but they imagine Saul in terms of a character from a historical novel, in which "what we [first] attend to . . . is the individual, the unique and particular case," and not "a great deal of generalized, representative value" attached to it.[42] As an Old Testament depiction of Saul's typological kingship, rather than his psychologized humanity, the implicit crisis in I Samuel is the inherently terrible or incomprehensible nature of an anointing. Just as David retains his kingly anointing in spite of the fact that he is a traitor, an adulterer, and a murderer, Saul, who is in some respects a much better man than either David or Solomon, loses his with a word from Samuel. Thus, he is positioned in such a way that he is "forced to represent incompatible themes: the need to establish a centralized state and the sense that there is something blasphemous about the emergence of a monarch."[43]

When the presiding *Abun* of the Orthodox Church, Salama III, crowned the ambitious outlaw and warlord, Kassa Haile Giorgas, as Emperor Téwodros II in 1855, the new monarch would hardly have wanted to liken his own prospects to the terrible fate of Saul.[44] Kassa's decision to assume the name "Téwodros," the prophesied Solomonic king, reflected the importance of Biblical typology in Ethiopian historiography and statecraft, but he sought to reassert connections between the Imperial House and the bloodline of King Saul's successor, David. Indeed, "just as European colonial rulers drew on the invented symbols of 'imperial monarchy' to establish hegemony over Asian and African subjects," Ethiopian monarchs of the nineteenth century sought to solidify their claims to power through "reference to the imperial past and the [mystical Orthodox] ideology that had supported it."[45] Ethiopian writers framed the *longue durée* of internecine tribal conflicts between regional warlords and competing claimants to the Imperial Throne as the *Zemene Mesafint*, after the Old Testament's "Age of Judges," and this historiographical typology corresponded with a widespread belief in the prophecies of the eschatological text *Fikkare Iyesus*,[46] which associated Biblical prophecies of one "who was to come, called by David and the Prophets, Messiah," with the imminent rule of a redeemer-monarch named Téwodros who would restore the Imperial House, expel Islam from Ethiopia, and "subdue all the world to his empire."[47]

Unlike later nineteenth-century monarchs such as the British-supported Tekle Giyorgas II, Yohannes IV, and Menelik II, Téwodros initially avoided explicit and highly tenuous claims about "Solomonic" lineage, asserting, instead, his personal claim as the radical embodiment of the *Fikkare Iyesus* typology.[48] Few of Téwodros's European contacts doubted his sincerity. As Walter Plowden, the British Consul at Massawa, remarked, Téwodros was firmly convinced that Christ had "destined [him] to restore the glories of Ethiopian Empire, and to achieve great conquests," as well as "purify and reform [the] distracted kingdom, with His aid."[49] As early as 1856, though, Téwodros's relationship with his powerful supporter, Salama III, began to show strains over the issue of Church taxation.⁵⁰ In addition, the regional noble classes, unsettled by Téwodros's reassertion of "Solomonic" imperium, increasingly favored potential usurpers, prompting Téwodros to imprison the future Menelik II, a grandson of Shewa's King Sahle Selassie, at Mäqdäla.⁵¹ British political agents such as Plowden initially supported Téwodros's move toward "feudal centralization, administrative, military and social reforms, and diplomatic relations with Queen Victoria,"⁵² however unsettled they were by the effects of Téwodros's eschatological self-confidence on regional diplomacy. As Plowden informed the Foreign Secretary, Lord Clarendon, in 1855: "Sometimes he is on the point of not caring for human assistance at all, and this is one reason why he will not seek with much avidity for assistance from or alliance with Europe."⁵³

The British diplomats at Massawa badly misread the Ethiopian situation. Although as late as 1871 some prominent Ethiopians remained convinced that "the English, the French, and the Christians" pursued regional diplomacy "subject to the orders of [the Ottoman] *Sultān* 'Abdülaziz, the son of the great *Sultān* Mahmud . . . like slaves,"⁵⁴ Téwodros "naïvely tried to revive the defunct Prester John myth," which hypothesized a powerful Christian priest-king beyond the Islamic world, as part of an effort to garner European support against the Ottoman Empire and the East African ambitions of the Egyptian *wāli*, Muhammad Sa'id Pasha.⁵⁵ Partly, Téwodros's "Prester John" rhetoric, directed against the Egyptians and Ottomans, served his state-building ambitions, which depended on the regular importation of Western technology, weapons, and craftsmen. As Richard Pankhurst remarks, Téwodros's 1856 request for "20,000 guns" and "several powder machines" was "prevented, or greatly curtailed, to Téwodros' immense displeasure, by difficulties in the Sudan. He therefore had to resort to purchasing weapons smuggled into his domains through hostile territories."⁵⁶ A British alliance against the Egyptian regime would have opened the Ethiopian markets of the Upper Nile to much-needed supplies. At the same time, Téwodros's state-building typologies depended on a medieval idea of militant "Christendom" with a far grander scope than regional disputes in the Sudan or the Horn. It had its historical terminus in Crusade, the end of Islam, the destruction of the Ottoman Empire, and the conquest of Jerusalem. Albeit for different reasons, Téwodros thus shared the concern of many Britons with what was called the "Great Eastern Question," and the idea that the progress and historical identity of his nation was irrevocably tied to the life and death of empires in the Near East. He showed particular interest, for example, in the course of the Crimean War and ordered the construction of a six-ton artillery mortar named "Sevastopol" in honor of the British victory.⁵⁷ However, his repeated attempts to attract Western interest in the East African dimensions of the emergent geopolitical landscape of the Great Game, which included extensive correspondence with Britain as well as the dispatch of numerous gifts for Queen Victoria through Plowden's successor, Duncan Cameron, were met with scorn or confusion, lost in the bureaucracies of British India, or simply ignored.[58]

One of the curious ironies in Téwodros's use of "Prester John" diplomacy—and, in fact, the cause of the Abyssinian crisis of 1867–1868—was the treatment of his "Prester John" letters to the West by the Foreign Office. Whereas the unquestionably fictitious correspondence of Prester John provoked a reconsideration of Europe's position in world affairs during the Middle Ages, British bureaucratic disregard for Téwodros's letters to his fellow "Christian" monarch, Victoria, meant that the Emperor "could only regard the refusal of the Government of Bombay to treat him as they had formerly treated the King of Shoa, now his vassal, as an additional proof of [a] ... change of feeling and conduct towards him."[59] Medieval stories about the powerful Christian monarch, Prester John, were probably inspired by a number of sources, including the third-century *Acts of Thomas*, accounts of the Nestorian Church, news of Yelü Dashi's defeat of the Seljuk Turks in 1141, and the presence of Christian dynastic states in medieval Armenia and Georgia.[60] In the 1170s, a supposed *Letter of Prester John*, addressed to the Byzantine Emperor, Manuel Comnenus, circulated in the West, describing the fabulous romance-landscape and tall-tale wonders of Prester John's kingdom.[61] While the *Letter*, as well as subsequent "letters" addressed to Frederick Barabosa and Pope Eugenius IV, amalgamated Christian legends, *Alixandre* romances, and Sinbad the Sailor tales from the Crusader States,[62] its basic outline, which included descriptions of Prester John's kingly Biblical lineage, sacerdotal person, use of the title "King of Kings," and rule over the Lost Tribes of Israel, also corresponded with Coptic-Solomonic ideologies that Crusader imperialists would have first encountered during the short-lived Kingdom of Jerusalem.[63] These contacts happened with surprising frequency during the Middle Ages. By the 1330s, a number of Western missionaries reported expeditions to Ethiopia and the Horn of Africa; conversely, Ethiopian delegations traveled to Rome and Avignon in 1309 and attended the Council of Florence in 1441.[64] By the time of the Portuguese expeditions of Pêro da Covillã and Francisco Álvarez, the Crusaders' vague association between the Horn of Africa and the "Third India" as a possible location for Prester John's kingdom had given way to confident identifications of the Indies' priest-king with the "King of Kings of Zion in Ethiopia."

Latin-Ethiopic contacts appear to have corresponded with an exchange of chivalric political myths and a hybrid conception of imperial "Christendom." Wolfram von Escherbach's Grail romance, *Parzival*, which filters Cretien de Troyes's Arthurian cycle through the cultural lens of Outremer, suggests a certain degree of "borrowing" from Ethiopian materials, including the introduction of an African kingdom, "Zazamanc," as the location of knightly quests and home of Parzival's African half-brother, Feirefiz, as well as the apparent use of Ethiopic names and place-names, and the signal representation of the Grail as a sacred stone retained in an ark, rather than as a chalice, reminiscent of the prominent ritual *tabots* of Ethiopian Orthodox churches.[65] Other Grail romances, such as Robert de Boron's *Joseph* and the prose Vulgate Cycle's *Lancelot* and *L'Estoire del Sant Graal*, show evidence of Ethiopian source material pertaining to the Coptic-Solomonic narrative as well as "the Ethiopian Middle Ages, the semi-historical period with the towering figure of King Caleb."[66] Conversely, Salah al-Din's conquest of the Crusader Kingdom of Jerusalem in 1187 may have inspired similar ripples within Ethiopian culture. Although Salah al-Din opened numerous churches in Jerusalem to Ethiopian Orthodox clergy and pilgrims, Jerusalem's fall seems to have sparked a definitional shift for many Ethiopians in the symbolic ideology of "the Holy Land" or "Christendom." During a familial contest over succession, the canonized Zagwe monarch, Gebre Mesqel Lalibela, likely fled to the Kingdom of Jerusalem for some period before 1181, an event recorded in the hagiographic *Zena Lalibela* as an angelic vision of the Holy Land.[67] Shortly after the death of Baldwin IV and the Crusader defeat at Hattin, Lalibela began an unprecedented reconstruction of his capital city, Roha, in accordance with his vision of Roha, renamed "Lalibela," as the eschatological New Jerusalem.[68] Just as European accounts placed Prester John's land within the symbolic geography of the Garden of Eden, Ethiopian tradition by Téwodros's day attributed the construction of Lalibela's New Jerusalem to angels, who assisted the saint-king "as masons and ordinary labourers," crafting the rock-hewn churches as a symbolic replicas of Christian Jerusalem's holy sites, where "traditional celebrations were held annually . . . re-enacting the baptism, the passion and crucifixion of Christ."[69] In short, both sides in medieval encounters between Ethiopia and European Crusader States reflected some element of their own cultural anxieties back through the patterns of intercultural exchange. For the Latin West, the myth of Prester John's imperium suggested that the strategic failures of the Crusades were not the only possible outcome of military and political conflicts with the Islamic world. Conversely, the collapse of Latin Outremer reinforced the Coptic-Solomonic ideology of Ethiopia's unique role in prophetic history. For the self-made monarch, Téwodros, Lalibela's contribution to the tradition of the Imperial House was part of the burden of anointing. However, it was also one of numerous precedents for enduring political self-definition through creative responses to the West.

Téwodros approached the West with the wrong kingly myth at the wrong time. While "Prester John" diplomacy was a vital component of Téwodros's restoration of the Imperial House, the West regarded it as an ethnographic curiosity, an antiquarian matter, or a component of Romantic medievalism. Walter Scott, for example, used Prester John as an example of the dangerously untenable in history. In Scott's *Tales of a Grandfather*, the French Crusader King, Louis, remains in Outremer because "the Christians, or Latins, of Syria, found it in their interest to foster his enthusiasm by holding out remote and fanciful prospects of his receiving assistance" from this "imaginary prince, Christian by profession, and a Tartar by birth."[70] In Téwodros's case, however, a real prince offered assistance for a political Crusade that the British Empire neither understood nor wanted. In fact, one of the surprising factors in Anglo-Ethiopian relations prior to 1868 was the *minor* role that racial ideology played in British perspectives on the Imperial House and its geopolitical ambitions. Even in the captivity narrative of Téwodros's hostage, Henry Blanc, which freely described the manner in which Téwodros tortured and executed his enemies, his character is presented in an evenhanded and often sympathetic manner, and discussions of "race" serve almost exclusively as metonyms for "tribe," or else distinguish the "Abyssinian [and] . . . the white man" against "tough race[s]" such as "the Takruries . . . [who] resist well the noxious influences of the climate."[71] In fact, the most resonant image of Ethiopian monarchy in nineteenth-century British culture was still Samuel Johnson's *Rasselas*, which presented Ethiopia as a veritable Eden but an allegorical one, ruled by a *Candide*-like philosopher-king of Johnson's invention.[72] More pertinently, nineteenth-century Britons during the *Zemene Mesafint* were often highly disposed to viewing violent political actors, including Britain's enemies, with a certain degree of Romantic or Byronic sympathy. John Gibson Lockhart, for example, in his "party-spirited" *History of Napoleon Buonaparte*,[73] nonetheless described Napoleon's birth as that of "the future hero of his age, [occurring] on a temporary couch covered with tapestry, representing the heroes of the Iliad."[74] Scott praised the "liberality of conduct and political views which were sometimes expressed by old Haider Ally," as well as the "resolved and dogged spirit of resolution which induced Tippoo Saib to die manfully upon the breach of his capital city with his sabre clenched in his hand."[75] Notably, however, this was not the case after Téwodros's death at Mäqdäla. However colored British sympathies with foreign opponents may have been by Byronic and/or Orientalist tropes, Britons such as Walter Scott felt that they understood non-Western actors such as Tipu Sultan of Mysore, partly due to the proliferation of an "Oriental" perspective in translated works such as Muhammad Firishtah's *History of the Rise of the Mahomedan Power in India*.[76] As late as 1868, however, writers such as Richard Chandler admitted that "an almost insuperable difficulty in dealing with Abyssinia arises from the uncertainty of its boundaries, as well ancient as modern, and the vague nature of our acquaintance with its system of government."[77]

In an 1829 review of James Justinian Morier's *Hajji Baba of Ispahan in England*, Walter Scott remarked on the extent to which intercultural narrative exchanges—unlike the cultural misalignments evident in the Ethiopian case—provoked occasions for cultural self-reflection, noting that "when a civilized people have gazed, at their leisure, upon . . . [those] whom they term barbarians, the next object of natural curiosity is, to learn what opinion the barbarian has formed of the new state of society . . . what the *lion* thinks of his visitors."[78] Morier, a Smyrna-born British diplomat and author of several romances set in Qajar Persia, hardly viewed his subjects as "barbarians." Neither, for that matter, did the tongue-in-cheek Scott. The *Waverley* author was keenly interested, however, in the possibility, foregrounded by the overwhelmingly negative Persian response to Morier's novel, of "a certain literary influence being exercised by the English press" in the non-Western world, which "would, twenty years ago [1800–1810], have sounded as absurd as to have affirmed that Prester John had studied Sir John Mandeville's Travels."[79] However, Téwodros's response to British portrayals and misperceptions of his reign illustrated how accurate this assessment was by midcentury. Téwodros, highly conversant in "theological subjects" as well as "the mystic Abyssinian history,"[80] also took a keen interest in European affairs and Western written accounts of his kingdom.[81] In fact, it is quite possible that his "Prester John" approach to European alliances was, in part, a response to the sheer volume of nineteenth-century *Western* literature that noted this historical association, as well as its functional centrality to his regional ambitions. As early as 1855, the Massawa Consulate was well aware that Téwodros's plans included the reclamation of "all the provinces lately conquered by Egypt along his northern frontier; even Khartoum, as his by right: nor does his military ardour hesitate to dream of the conquest of Egypt, and a triumphant march to the Holy Sepulchre."[82] Plowden and his successor, Cameron, simply failed to draw the connection between Téwodros's stated ambitions and their quasi-historical template. In effect, the Abyssinian Crisis occurred because the Foreign Office lacked the Romantic novelistic imagination of writers like Scott and Morier, as well as sufficient political acumen to wonder what, in Scott's metaphor, "the *lion* thinks of his visitors"—or what the anointed "Lion of Judah" might think of the "Lion of Judah."

By 1862, Téwodros became increasingly frustrated with British missionaries and concerned about the Ottoman presence along the Red Sea and the Horn. He dispatched letters to Queen Victoria, Napoleon III, Pope Pius IX, and other European monarchs asking for assistance, inverting the old epistolary romance dynamic of "Prester John," "Christendom," and Crusade.[83] The replies, when forthcoming, were cursory. Téwodros was particularly insulted by what he saw as a slight by the British, with whom he believed he had cultivated good relations through Massawa. In consequence, he seems to have blamed missionaries such as Henry Stern, whose *Wanderings among the Falashas* inadvertently snubbed the Solomonic claims of the Imperial House, and an increasing number of British political agents who fell under the administrative jurisdiction of the Raj, resulting in Téwodros's decision to take Stern, Consul Cameron, and a number of other Britons hostage until such time as Victoria's government addressed his concerns about the Ottomans. However, a "series of misunderstandings and untactful acts so infuriated Tewodros that he did not pay attention to the ultimatum of the British government," and took Rassam, the agent sent to negotiate for the hostages' release, prisoner as well.[84] There is also some basis for understanding Téwodros's decision to retain hostages as an attempt to unify regional nobles in support of his proposed Crusade at the cost of a war with Britain; Rassam, for example, advised Government to "have nothing to do with the Turks, because alliance with the unbelievers will bring on religious war."[85]

Just as the Foreign Office misconstrued Téwodros's sense of imperium, "Prester John" understood British Imperial *events* in great detail without understanding their underlying systems and causes. In the first place, the British Empire was increasingly invested in its own quasi-mystical geopolitics, the Great Game, which sought to limit Russian expansion across Eurasia. In consequence, Britain supported the regional stability of Islamic states such as the Ottoman Empire and Qajar Persia. The British Empire was also economically threatened by the uncertain outcome of the American Civil War, and viewed Téwodros's immediate enemy, Egypt, as a viable alternate source for much-needed raw cotton.[86] Second, Téwodros grossly overrated the significance of Christianity as unifying ideology among nineteenth-century European states, a medieval notion of "Christendom." For example, Parliament took seriously the accusations made by the German missionary, Wilhelm Staiger, to the effect that "the Roman missionaries at Massawah [had] . . . added to the present difficulty and critical circumstances between the English and Abyssinian Governments" by suggesting to Téwodros that "the British Government want[ed] nothing but his utter ruin, on which he put Mr. Rassam into chains."[87] Lastly, Téwodros understood Victoria's regal pomp as a mirror of his own absolute power. In reality, Victoria knew little about Téwodros. For that matter, few competent strategic thinkers in London were even remotely cognizant of Ethiopian affairs until after the hostage crisis had reached a boiling point. In part, this was a result of shifting British administrations during the 1860s. The Third Derby Ministry and subsequent First Disraeli Ministry (1866–1868), laid blame for the Abyssinian Crisis on the Liberal Foreign Secretary, John Russell, whose "term in office (1859–1865) had been marked by a series of crises which had brought Britain into dangerous or ignominious confrontation with the United States over the Trent incident, with Russia over the Polish rebellion, and with Prussia over Schleswig-Holstein."[88] Although the Derby Ministry made initial overtures to Téwodros, promising craftsmen and renewed support, domestic pressure in England for a military solution, coupled with reports of growing dissent in Téwodros's kingdom (including his excommunication by Salama

III), resulted in the dispatch of an expeditionary force from India under the command of Sir Robert Napier.[89]

Téwodros, who controlled relatively little of his own kingdom by 1868, retreated to Mäqdäla. He appears to have laid plans for converting the mountain stronghold into a new Lalibela, but it became, instead, the dramatic setting for an expression of British, rather than Ethiopian, imperium. Indeed, it was at Mäqdäla that the Anglo-American explorer, journalist, and adventurer, Henry Morton Stanley, wrote what was, in effect, a popularized "lost race" novel ending to Téwodros's reign, recording the violent death of a mystical African king, surrounded by ancient Solomonic treasures, on "a platform of rock, oval in shape, a mile and a half in length, and from half to three-quarters of a mile in width, rising 500 feet perpendicularly above a narrow plateau."[90] While Ethiopian writers after Mäqdäla quickly integrated Napier's victory and Téwodros's concurrent suicide into the typologies of Biblical-Ethiopian history, portraying the Emperor as Saul, and his hostage, Menelik II as an anointed David,[91] Stanley's description of the storming of Mäqdäla foreshadows Rudyard Kipling's narrative aesthetic of the imperial grotesque. Once Napier's forces breached Mäqdäla, Stanley records that two "excited Irishmen... Drummer McGuire and Private Bergin," heard a revolver fire and discovered Téwodros behind a haystack, "lying prostrate on the ground, dying, with the revolver still convulsively clutched in his right hand" and the back of his skull blown off.[92] Considering the revolver "but their proper loot, and without any ceremony, they took what they considered their own; but on a silver plate on the stock, during an examination of it, they perceived an inscription which read thus:

PRESENTED
BY
VICTORIA
QUEEN OF GREAT BRITAIN AND IRELAND
TO
THEODORUS
EMPEROR OF ABYSINNIA
AS A SLIGHT TOKEN OF HER GRATITUDE
FOR HIS KINDNESS TO HER SERVANT PLOWDEN
1854[93]

BROKERING THE MYTH OF PRINCE MADOC AT THE TURN OF THE NINETEENTH CENTURY

The Ethiopian kingship narratives that Téwodros inherited repeat, as their essential action, the return of Zion to the domain of history. Conversely, the Madoc legend and other stories about North American "lost races" portray the departure from history to Zion. Like the *Zena Lalibela*'s saint-king, Madoc is a princely refugee from twelfth-century civil war. However, Madoc's return to Wales does not restore spiritual economy to the broken order and violent history of the medieval chroniclers. Instead, Madoc collects his Welsh followers and vanishes, once again, into the West. As Derrick Spradlin remarks, Early American accounts, reverberating the Elizabethan vogue for this imperial legend,[94] depict Madoc's journey "as primeval in that the journey is the root of British-American identity and activity in North America, the root of Britain's successful geographical expansion into North America and establishment of British cultural hegemony therein."[95] This is a standard reading of the legend's surprising longevity in Britain and America, in no small part because it reorients the "long-standing fondness [of cultural historians] for themes of wilderness, land, nature, settlement, and civilization in early Anglo-America" in terms of a "complex but in important ways colonialist process of territorialization" in North America.[96] Readings of Southey's pantisocratic fantasy, *Madoc*, for example, in which Prince Madoc conquers the Aztecs, often present the epic in an "unattractive guise as an example of the 'aggressive and expansionist' schoolboy fantasies so characteristic of early nineteenth century apologias for Britain's imperial policy."[97] This argument equally extends to the American historico-imperial narratives of Simms, Robert Montgomery Bird, Robert Sands, and William H. Prescott, all of whom inflected their treatments of Hernán Cortés and the Aztecs through the lens of Southey's poem. As John P. McWilliams remarks, Madoc was "the kind of hero whom distant writers wished Cortes might have been."[98]

That said, an overemphasis on the colonialist-fantasy aspects of *Madoc* and its heirs neglects key historical constraints that define the nineteenth-century reception of the legend. Foremost, Prince Madoc is not an effective imperialist or colonizer. While numerous British and American eighteenth-century frontier writers described artifacts, secondhand stories, and occasional encounters with "white Indians," few seem to have had any expectation of encountering an actual "hidden" Welsh nation, akin to the Coptic-Solomonic Ethiopia of "Prester John," beyond the Appalachians. Even the Kentucky writer, John Filson, one of the most vocal proponents of the Madoc hypothesis, limited his enthusiasm to speculating on the continued existence of a tribe "at a great distance up the Missouri, resembling the other Indians, but speaking Welsh, and retaining some ceremonies of the Christian worship."[99] Similarly, in response to inquiries about the existence of Welsh tribes, the Tennessee statesman, John Sevier, informed Major Amos Stoddard in 1810 that, while Madoc's band existed, "they are no more a white people: they are now all become Indians, and look like other red people of the Country."[100] The Madoc legend's cultural logic of miscegenation echoed William Byrd's dismissal of English "squeamish[ness]" about Indian intermarriage, which Byrd suggested preserved a British racial-national identity at the expense of the British Empire's real "advantage ... on the northern continent of America."[101] In addition to limiting the growth of French and Spanish ambitions, Byrd argued that "the poor Indians would have had less reason to complain that the English took away their land, if they had received it by way of portion with their daughters."[102] Had "such affinities been contracted in the beginning," Byrd speculated, "how much bloodshed would have been prevented, and how populous would the country have been, and, consequently, how considerable?"[103] Madoc stories provided Anglo-American settlement with a medieval precedent, but that precedent, when taken seriously, also suggested a critique of Antebellum America and its Westward expansion. After all, Madoc's descendants, regardless of their "white" appearance, Welsh speech, or cargo-cult Christianity, were supposedly interspersed among "the other red people of the Country." Frontier encounters with North American tribes, in this context, also involved an encounter with the equally uncertain frontier of the Early Republic's origin and sense of exceptional purpose. Madoc legends argued that the West terminated in what was essentially a recapitulated translation of the old settlement, the British Empire, through an "Indian" lens.

As Tim Fulford remarks, Southey's version of the tale "was written in the context of Britain's North American defeat," and "offers no simplistic opposition between savage (and exploited) natives and 'civilized'" (enslaving) colonizers but instead dramatizes a three-way contest between the colonizing Welsh, who have themselves arrived in America in flight from the imperialist Saxons, the Aztecs—new imperialists who exact tribute from the local Indian tribes in the form of sacrificial victims—and the Hoamen, one of those local tribes demoralized by defeat and internally divided."[104] Madoc, triumphant, "emerges in the last chapter of the epic out of an apocalyptic lava landscape ... [as] the Aztecan remnants of the eruption crawl from the lake water and regroup like Satan and his subordinates," but it is ultimately clear that the "one city taken [by Madoc] is only a fraction of the Aztec empire."[105] The frustrated conclusion to Southey's epic illustrates the nineteenth-century trouble with Madoc-as-imperialist. Unlike Prester John's kingdom or the prophetic imperial state of Téwodros, Madoc's North American "settlement" had to be imagined within a recorded history that testified to the success of the Aztec Empire (and others), as well as a political landscape of North American Indian tribes that both anteceded British permanent settlement and absorbed Madoc's ostensible "settlement" in its entirety. Frontier accounts like those of Morgan Jones or Owen Chapelain, both of whom claimed to have been welcomed by the Tuscaroras because they knew Welsh, foreshadow the fortuitous escapes of later "lost race" narratives such as Rudyard Kipling's "The Man Who Would Be King," in which the unlikely schemes of Daniel Dravot and Peachey Carnehan succeed because the two adventurers understand the Masonic symbols used by Kafiristan's "lost" white tribe.[106]

The key difference is one of scale. Whereas Kipling's tale, like nineteenth-century alignments between Ethiopian society and Prester John's kingdom, emphasized geographic isolation and unbroken traditional continuities, Madoc stories depended on a sense of intercultural diffusion. George Catlin, for example, proposed the Madoc tale as "the remote and rational cause for such striking singularities" as he discovered in Mandan customs and material culture.[107] In 1847, the British military adventurer and *Blackwood's* writer, George Ruxton, gave credence to the "belief of the trappers, that the Moquis [and Navajo] Indians are descendants of the followers of Prince Madoc," on the basis of material culture.[108] Potential sites for mythopoetic "settlement" of Prince Madoc spanned the North American continent. Moreover, because the narrative premise of intermarriage, which, in *Waverley* fiction reconciled historical conflicts, embodied by individuals, through the production of a new paterfamilias, had a communal, intercultural scale in Welsh-Indian diffusion, claims such as Catlin's did not necessarily preclude those of Ruxton or others.

In fact, Madoc stories tended to imagine this "white tribe" within a complex, if mostly fictitious, pre-Columbian cultural landscape that tended to minimize racial or cultural distinctions between Anglo-Americans and North American Indians by emphasizing their common participation in global-imperial systems. As Alexander von Humboldt remarks, Europeans "fancied they saw in [the 'structure of American idioms'] . . . Hebrew (Semetic or Arameen); the Spanish colonists, Basque (or Iberian); the English and French planters, Welsh, Irish, and Bas-breton. The pretensions of the Basques, and the inhabitants of Wales, who regard[ed] their languages not only as mother-tongues, but as the source of all other tongues, extend[ed] far beyond America, to the Isles of the South Seas."[109] It was not uncommon for speculative historians to argue that all these pre-Columbian contacts occurred, and with great regularity. Simms, in fact, extended this paradigm to include the "coeval" settlement of Britain and Ireland, arguing for a common descent from "travelers and warriors . . . familiar with the people of different countries," and "in all probability of Carthaginian race—a people with whom the planting of distant colonies was part of the commercial policy—who are known to have sent forth immense colonies beyond the Pillars of Hercules—who made large settlements in Spain, procured tin and amber from the coasts of Great Britain, and are likely to have left their seed in Ireland."[110] Indeed, "Madoc" is less about the idea of building and justifying colonialist nations than it is about the impermanence of national identities within underlying imperial political economies. In "what may be called the first cycle of the myth," the inimical Cherokee drive Madoc's followers deeper into North America until nearly all of them are killed during a last stand at the Falls of the Ohio, after which the survivors "broke up into different groups and their chiefs led them in various directions—for in various directions there are mounds, earthworks, and mysterious artifacts that signalize their passing."[111]

But in the hodge-podge of nineteenth-century "lost race" Amerindian history, these survivors were not always portrayed as unusually "civilized" men in an unusually "savage" New World. "Madoc" presented, on a very small scale, a generally accepted dynamic of the growth, imperial expansion, and diffusion or collapse of North American Indian cultures. James Bradley Finley, for example, described the course of Iroquois history in these terms, claiming that "when the tide of civilization overflowed most of their ancient central territory, and drove them westward to mingle with the other Indian nations already occupying the country, they lost much of their preeminence."[112] In *Last of the Mohicans*, Cooper's Delaware sage, Tamenund, describes a similar situation in which "the tribes of the Lenape [have been] driven from their council fires and scattered, like broken herds of deer, among the hills of the Iroquois."[113] Humboldt situates Madoc within earlier iterations of this historical cycle, describing traditions about "a powerful nation, of gigantic stature, called *Tallegewi*, *Talligeu*, or *Allighewi* . . . more civilized than any of the other tribes found in the northern climate by the Europeans," who "inhabited towns founded on the banks of the Mississippi."[114] After "a long struggle," they were "vanquished by . . . [Cooper's] Lenni-Lenapes," who "came from the west, and were allied at that period with the Mengwis (Iroquois)."[115] By 1860, British and American writers who envisioned North American history beyond the Republic's birth, which still retained the Waverley living-memory horizon of "sixty years since," did so through an emergent mythopoetic narrative, inclusive of Prince Madoc and Cooper's Uncas, that depicted the rise and destruction of civilizations on the immense scale and with the cyclical repetitions of Gibbon's *Decline and Fall*.

It is not surprising, then, that Southey's reintroduction of the Madoc tale occurred in response to the First Empire's collapse during the 1780s. Nor should it be surprising that few writers in the Early Republic seemed remotely surprised by supposed—or anticipated—encounters with "white Indians," who were neither exclusively.[116] One of the enduring legacies of the eighteenth-century British Empire in North America was the proliferation and cultural significance of "white Indians," particularly in the South. Much of the British enthusiasm for Madoc tales during the 1790s came from the claims made by the self-styled "Director General of the Muskogee Nation," William Augustus Bowles.[117] Bowles, a Maryland-born adventurer of Irish descent, had briefly served with James Chalmers's First Battalion of Maryland Loyalists during the Revolution. When the Battalion was assigned to garrison Pensacola, Bowles resigned his commission and was adopted into the Creek Nation, taking the name *Estajoca*. After the Revolution, Lord Dunmore employed Bowles to secure West Indian commercial interests with the Gulf Coast tribes, but Bowles, who married the daughter of a Hitchiti chief, William Perryman, had grander designs. At the close of the Revolution, the Cherokee and Creek nations shared a common concern about the Early Republic's expansionist ideology. However, differing responses, many of them generational, to Anglo-American settlement, exposed "deep fissures in the Cherokee nation, mirroring those occurring simultaneously among the Iroquois confederacy."[118] The Lower Creek chief, Dragging Canoe, for example, lamented the Treaty of Watauga, which ceded Cherokee lands to Colonial speculators, and left Richard Henderson with the threat that he had purchased "bloody ground and [it] would be dark and difficult to settle."[119] In 1789, Bowles proposed reconstituting the Trans-Appalachian jurisdiction of the British Empire's Indian Department, which, under the Johnsons, had operated semi-autonomously, and extending its jurisdiction to the Cherokee Nation and Lower Creeks.

Although the West Indian press denounced Bowles as "a rogue, a plunderer, and petty chief with no following among the Indians," Bowles diplomatic mission to London, during which he received George III's assurances of support, was a surprising success.[120] Partly, this was due to the fact that such visits from "white Indians" and "Indian kings" had precedent in the ritual statecraft of the British Empire. In 1710, the famous London visit of the Four Mohawk Kings, organized by Pieter Schuyler, established the intercultural context for Sir William Johnson's ascendency during the Seven Years' War; in 1775–1776, a similar visit by Johnson's successor, Guy Johnson, reestablished the Indian Department's autonomy in North America, largely against the wishes of Guy Carleton and the British military authorities in Montreal. Partly, Bowles's success can also be attributed to his canny use of the Madoc story. Bowles and his companions sought out William Owen-Pughe, a Welsh antiquarian writer, translator of the *Mabinogion*, and avid promoter of Madoc's historicity. Bowles regaled Owen-Pughe with accounts of his dealings with the "'Padoucas' or 'White Indians,' a numerous and warlike nation well known to the Creeks," adding details such as "that their language was Welsh and that they kept as religious objects books, wrapped in skins, that described their origins."[121] During his drafting of *Madoc*, Southey used Owen-Pughe as a source for accurate historical details about Wales, fretting, for example, over "where the Court [of Owen Cyveilioc] was, whether at Mathraval? & . . . some little sketch of Cyveilocs history."[122] Owen-Pughe, in turn, depended on "General" Bowles for accurate ethnographic information that validated the historicity of Welsh romances. Bowles, in turn, wanted to establish a real "Madoc" settlement on the Gulf Coast, wrought from the jurisdictional ambiguity of his tribal status, and under the auspices of the British Empire's protection. In a sense, the maritime device that enabled the Madoc myth to seem historically viable—the home-and-away dynamics of sea travel that writers such as Cooper and Marryat utilized as a means of depicting political economies in historical flux—brought (or almost brought, in Bowles's case) the "offspring" client empire back into the fold of the "parental" British Empire. But this imperial "homecoming" suggested a more complex interrelationship between the British Empire and its analogues, namely that the former would invariably transform into the latter—and perhaps in many geographical variations—just as a patriarch recedes in the differentiated maturity of his offspring.

Bowles's general disreputability, at least from a British perspective, probably served him in this regard. *The Gentleman's Magazine*, for example, carried a letter that reiterated the usual West Indian attacks on Bowles's trustworthiness, describing him as "an Indian pack-horse man . . . [who] always so much affected the manner and dress of his colleagues, that he never could be induced even to speak English, although it was supposed at the time that he was an Irishman."[123] This projected Gaelic "white Indian" persona, however, aligned him with popular notions of how Prince Madoc's descendants might appear to "civilized" eyes. It also lent credence to the somewhat outlandish claims made by Bowles in a 1791 letter to Lord Grenville. As William C. Sturtevant remarks, Bowles's account of the "United Nation of Creeks & Cherrokees," fully allied with the Choktaw and Chiksaw tribes, was "a masterpiece, skillfully combining some grains of truth with a great deal of imagination (or optimism) that Bowles hoped would appeal to English conceptions and prejudices."[124] Bowles's letter described what was, in effect, an Amerindian mirror of the British First Empire, in which the "United Nation" fielded rank-and-file armies, constructed sea ships, produced a trade surplus, instituted taxes, tariffs, public services, and sought reconciliation with the Empire.[125] Like the medieval letters of Prester John, Bowles's "Representation" did not simply describe a surprisingly advanced "lost race" ally of European imperialism; it capitalized on and magnified rumors that a "Prester John" nation had defeated a distant enemy and sought further support. His "representation to the King of England respecting the advantage to be derived from opening the Ports in north America belonging to the Crown . . . to the Creek Nation" corresponded to "Accounts . . . received in February 1791 of the entire defeat of the Americans by United Nations of the Creeks & Cherokees & a Treaty of Peace . . . then negotiating between them Americans & the Creeks as well as the Spaniards & that Nation & their Allies."[126]

As in the case of the Ethiopian monarch, Téwodros, Bowles's letter never reached the British monarch.[127] However, Bowles's appearance in London, accompanied by "five Indian Chiefs of the nations that border the Mississippi," was sufficient to establish his popular credentials. A short biography, *The Authentic Memoirs of William Augustus Bowles*, appeared in print almost immediately. Like Stern's account of Téwodros's rise to power from humble origins, the *Authentic Memoirs* present their Bowles's bildungsroman transformation from an "artless school-boy, perfectly acquainted with any mode of life beyond what he had learnt at his father's farm," to the white leader anointed by "the unanimous voice of twenty thousand warriors, ready to hazard their lives at the command of their beloved father, son, and chief."[128] British readers were, at least in some instances, skeptical of *Memoirs*' claims, as well as their anonymous authorship. "Memoirs written by nobody," one reviewer remarked, "are worthy of nobody's attention: for what assurance can we have that there is a single word of truth in an anonymous publication, for which no one can be found to answer?"[129] Another reviewer remarked that "by what means the writer of these Memoirs has collected his information we know not; but he gives such an improbable account of Mr. Bowles' natural ingenuity respecting different arts and sciences, as cannot impress us with any great opinion of the authenticity of the narrative."[130] Ironically, British writers, beginning with Samuel Johnson, were far more willing to reserve judgment about the fantastic historical claims of Téwodros's Imperial House than give credence to the somewhat more verifiable and limited claims put forth by Bowles. However, the more that Bowles's claims about the "Padoucas" seemed to invest his "Indianness" in the Madoc tale, the more likely figures such as Owen-Pughe, Southey, and the Madoc enthusiast-explorers, John Evans and Iolo Morganwg, were to certify Bowles's own authenticity.[131] By the turn of the nineteenth century, scholarly treatises on Madoc unquestioningly identified the Irish-American adventurer as "General Bowles, a Cherokee Chief, who was in London a few years ago . . . and [had] travelled all along the southern boundary of the country inhabited by the Welch Indians."[132] Bowles, in turn, elaborated his political-esoteric role in the minds of Owen-Pughe's circle by acquiring the title of "Provincial Grand Master" of the Freemasons for the "Creek, Cherokee, Chicksaw, & Choctaw Nations, in N. America."[133]

Ultimately, most Britons familiar with Bowles's state visit do not seem to have cared one way or the other about the improbability of his Indian "kingship." *The Monthly Review* declared that "Mr. Bowles, who, at this time, appears in London in the character of an Indian chief . . . being of an unsettled, roving, and enterprising disposition, attached himself to one of the Indian nations, became enamoured of the savage life, and, which is perhaps more excusable, a savage girl, whom he married; then settled among her friends; and is now, by adoption, though not by birth, an '*Indian Warrior*.'"[134] Nevertheless, *The Critical Review* determined that "Mr. Bowles is a gentleman of great merit, and [we] are happy to think that Great Britain has so faithful and zealous a friend among the Creek Indians."[135] In contrast to the 1775 visit of Guy Johnson and his ally, Joseph Brant, who struck his British contemporaries as a "genteel Englishman," Bowles "represented the opposite phenomenon of an Englishman who had gone native,"[136] an individuated, flesh-and-blood template of the historical-imperial cycles of North

American history implied in retellings of the Madoc legend. As Timothy J. Shannon remarks, Bowles replaced "the culturally and physically distant figure of the Indian king" with that of "the adroit negotiator of imperial subjecthood," personifying the paradox of "separation and amalgamation that constituted the British imperial enterprise."[137] Unlike "Prester John" statecraft, which could not be translated into a nineteenth-century British Imperial context, Bowles's turn-of-the-century performance of the imperialist "barbarian" was, in fact, far more appealing to British spectators and relevant to a British Empire in crisis than the "civilized" persona projected by the eighteenth-century Mohawk Joseph Brant or the nineteenth-century Ethiopian Téwodros.

In fact, as one reader for *The Analytic Review* remarked, Bowles's *Authentic Memoirs* were almost exclusively a series of "preparatory elogiums" meant to establish that persona, rather than recount "the wonderful atchievements of the hero of the tale," which never finally materialized.[138] The authorship of *Memoirs* illustrates the kind of reasons that led at least some British subjects to imaginatively invest in Bowles, the Madoc-like "imperial barbarian," as a form of political, personal, and financial speculation. The anonymous author claimed to have no "political motives . . . [as] a man, the circumstances of whose situation peculiarly abstract him from parties of any kind," and little knowledge of Bowles's design beyond what was reported in the press, although this was absolutely untrue.[139] *Memoirs* was written, quite possibly at Bowles's instigation well ahead of time, by Benjamin Baynton, a Loyalist officer who had served with Bowles in British West Florida.[140] Unlike the largely self-made Bowles, Baynton came from a family that had been part of the Tory frontier elites, supported by the patronage of William Johnson's Indian Department. In 1768, Johnson had arranged for Baynton to receive title to "an immense tract of Land (Comprising one of the finest and most fertile Countries in the world)" as "indemnification for goods belonging to his Father, and amounting to near One Hundred Thousand Pounds Pennsylvania Currency."[141] However, Baynton lacked legal title to his land grant after the Revolution. When Bowles arrived in London, Baynton, then an overleveraged half-pay officer, was busy petitioning the Loyalist Claims Commission for redress of "debts, unavoidably incurred, during his Stay of two Years in America (where he was treated as an alien and an enemy) as well as . . . [the redemption of his] mortgage" on the Johnson tract.[142] The establishment of Bowles's authority over a United Nation, as well as the promise of renewed frontier war in America must have appealed to Baynton immediately, just as the "historicity" of Madoc's conquest appealed to Southey's circle in the abstract. Indeed, one of the features of Bowles's "Relation" was its emphasis on the United Nation as a haven for British Loyalists. Just as the spurious Prester John correspondence reinvigorated Crusader ideology after the collapse of the Latin imperial project of Outremer by suggesting a second frontier "Christendom," Bowles's letter, "sent to assure the king of [the United Nation's] continued loyalty, and to ask for a renewal of the old alliance," proved the "pro-British sentiment of the United Nation . . . by their admitting and protecting over one thousand Loyalist refugees, from whom the Indians expected to learn 'their skill, their arts, & their manners."[143]

But although Bowles's diplomatic mission to London was successful, ultimately providing him with the necessary political clout to establish the short-lived State of Muskogee in 1799,[144] his push to realize a sovereign British-Indian nation in North America failed because, like the mythical Padouca tribe that enchanted the Welsh antiquarians, Bowles's settlement existed within a larger framework of competitive North American empires. At the turn of the century, "Madoc" lands, particularly those identified with the Prince's "landfall" in the Gulf Coast, were subject to the rapidly shifting, overlapping, and often quickly abandoned claims of Britain, France, Spain, and the Early Republic, as well as semi-autonomous commercial networks such as the Scottish firm of Panton, Leslie & Company, which operated in the West Indies and the Gulf Coast settlements very much like the British East India Company.[145] As early as 1792, Washington's Secretary of War, Henry Knox, reiterated to the Indian agent, James Seagrove, the "utter disavowal of the court of London of having any communication whatever with Bowles."[146] While this was patently untrue, it was, in fact, the case that the Foreign Office had informed Washington "in the most explicit manner" that the "assertions said to have been made by Mr. Bowles, of his pretentions having been encouraged or countenanced by the Government of Great Britain," as well as "his having received authority to promise to the Indians protection and assistance" were groundless.[147] Nevertheless, Bowles capitalized on the fact that many Lower Creek "men of note still cherished the memory of the British," and "he had the art to avail himself" of this, just as he had exhibited an equal aptitude to "avail himself" of Britons' desire for a Madoc-like white chief during his London embassy.[148] He attacked the shipping concerns of Panton, Leslie & Company; he issued death warrants for American Indian agents and opened lands under his control to runaway slaves from Georgian plantations; he asserted that the Treaty of San Ildefonso, which transferred Indian lands from Spain to America, was illegal and, in 1800, declared war on the Spanish Empire.[149]

During this period, Bowles continued to maintain the support of at least a sizable minority of Lower Creeks, as well as displaced "favorites of the former British Governors of the Floridas, [who had] been reduced to an inferior situation by their departure," based partly on his continued promises that "the British were sending supplies to support the nation in a war with the United States."[150] However, in 1802, Britain, France, and Spain signed the Treaty of Amiens, temporarily settling affairs between their empires in North

America. The British Empire's tentative support for Bowles's schemes—what little there actually was—completely evaporated. The following year, the American Indian agent, Benjamin Hawkins, arranged with Creek factions for Bowles's capture and delivery to the Spanish authorities.[151] Indeed, the implicit argument of the Madoc legend, namely that "white Indians" were not radical outliers, was particularly true in the case of the Creeks, where figures such as Bowles's long-standing rival, the half-Scottish Alexander McGillivray, and his nephews, William McIntosh and William Weatherford, occupied positions of tribal authority and, at turns, supported the efforts of Hawkins.[152] Bowles, who had survived numerous captures and escaped in the 1790s, died of starvation in 1805, still a prisoner in the dungeons of Havana's Castilo de los Tres Reyes Magos del Morro, so named in honor of the legendary Magi who, it was believed, had founded Prester John's kingdom in the Indies. As Maya Jasanoff remarks, Bowles's "adopted people, the Creeks, would end up paying a terrible price for their relationship with the American republic, when they fractured into civil war . . . with Americans hysterically denouncing their enemies as 'British savages,' just like a generation before, [Andrew] Jackson commenced his ascent to the status of national icon on a pile of Creek bodies."[153]

"LOST RACE," LOST STORIES, POLITICAL LOSSES

Both Téwodros II and William Augustus Bowles brokered power between the British Empire and its limits of influence through diplomacy that depended on a shared vernacular of the historically poetic. In both instances, the translation failed. In Téwodros's case, this was largely a matter of misrecognition on both sides. Téwodros failed to understand that Britain was not a "Christian" power in the medieval sense; Britain, in large part because Ethiopia *was* a sophisticated nation state, expected Téwodros to operate as a "modern" political actor in the Victorian sense. Perversely, Téwodros's violent defeat at Mäqdäla resulted in the continued British "custodianship" of thousands of manuscripts, icons, and other artifacts that comprised Téwodros's "lost race" claims.[154] Conversely, Bowles's London appearance worked in part because, despite his tenuous claim to represent American Indian nations, he was able to frame his actual tribal status in terms that aligned an immediate political culture of "Indian Kings," a Romantic myth of the Matter of Britain as transatlantic *longue durée*, and the clearly defined regional interests of the British Empire in the Gulf Coast region. Ironically, it was the least exotic of these pressures—British Imperial statecraft—that lent the course of Bowles's life features that seem better suited to nineteenth-century historical romance than nineteenth-century political history: pirate expeditions, multiple prison escapes, daring raids, rivalries, betrayals, blood vendettas, and "adventures" that took him as far as the Philippines and Sierra Leone as a Spanish prisoner. The fact that the British Empire, enveloped in the Napoleonic Wars, was *not* willing to substantively support Bowles, meant that his personal fate and the tenuous existence of the State of Muskogee were as closely linked as that of Madoc and his "lost race."

On the one hand, the absence of nineteenth-century fiction surrounding the careers of Téwodros and Bowles marks a blind spot in attempts to render the figure of the "imperial barbarian" and its implications for British—and American—empire-building. Why, for example, did a writer like H. Rider Haggard, author of *King Solomon's Mines*, utterly ignore the meticulously recorded historical template of Stanley's encounter with the Coptic-Solomonic Emperor in 1868? Indeed, the literary imagination of Ethiopian chroniclers, who quickly rewrote the messianic Téwodros myth to accommodate the British "Philistine" victory at Mäqdäla over "King Saul," was far more historically responsive in this regard. Similarly, why did American romancers like William Gilmore Simms, whose elegiac, sympathetic presentation of the Southern tribes "presaged the sense of profound loss—a sense that dominated American scholarship in the twentieth century—that accompanied the tragic decline of Indian civilizations,"[155] ignore the obvious material presented by Bowles's life and the twinned fate of Muskogee? He was certainly aware of Bowles's existence, describing him in thinly veiled allusions to white men among the "Muscoghee" who "enter the nation, take wives from among the tribe, possess themselves of lands . . . acquire influence enough among the savages to become their advisors . . . their chiefs," and prepare "their speeches and letters."[156] Why, for that matter, did he not choose to write a romance about Prince Madoc? He was certainly conscious of the artistic mandate to do so, observing in 1845 that "a judicious artist might make a most romantic tale of the colony of Green Erin upon the shores of Carolina and Georgia; showing how . . . the wandering Irishmen pitched their tents for good; how they built cities; how they flourished . . . how, suddenly, the fierce red men of the southwest came down upon them in howling thousands, captured their women, slaughtered their men, and drove them to their fortresses; how they fought to the last, and perished to a man!"[157]

In part, it might be a case of the narrative principles of lost-race romance pushing writers into a corner. The more the imperialist-adventurer and lost-race monarch approximate one another in their actions and speech, the more completely the figure of the "imperial barbarian" speaks with authority on the metropolitan political stage. By the time of Simms's elegiac poem, "The Broken Arrow," which lamented the murder of Chief William McIntosh in 1825, it was the "fierce white men" of Jacksonian America who had "c[o]me down upon" the Indian nations "howling in thousands," not the other way around.[158] And to the extent that Simms imagined Madoc's descendants as having "all become Indian, and look[ing] like the other red people of the Country," it indicted Indian Removal and Westward Expansion in the historical present as a self-inflicted violence on an Early Republic with British origins and "historical" mandate on the North American continent. As a subject for romance-writing, the Coptic-Solomonic myth's close connection to the Matter of Britain would have argued for similar kind of cultural suicide on Britain's part. Think of the relationship between politico-historical uses of imperial mythmaking and the myths, themselves, as a kind of insoluble equation. The more the imperialist-adventurer and lost-race monarch dissolve into one other, the more the figure of the "imperial barbarian" lays bare the historical tenuousness of the intercultural brokerage on which its power depends. The imperialist's assumed kingship implies his ever-present potential for downfall at the hands of the world that birthed him.

NOTES

1. Frederick Marryat, *Narrative of the Travels and Adventures of Monsieur Violet, in California, Sonora, & Western Texas* (London: Longman, Browne, Greene, & Longmans, 1843), 1.
2. Marryat, *Narrative*, 1.
3. Marryat, *Narrative*, 2.
4. Marryat, *Narrative*, 151.
5. Marryat, *Narrative*, 145.
6. Marryat, *Narrative*, 21.
7. Marryat, *Narrative*, 26.
8. Marryat, *Narrative*, 27.
9. Jules Zanger, "Marryat, Monsieur Violet, and Edward La Salle," *Nineteenth-Century Fiction* 12, no. 3 (1957): 226.
10. Charles Augustus Murray, "Letter to Pierre Choteau, 25 March 1846," qtd. in Zanger, 229.
11. Thomas Falconer, letter in *The Spectator*, 18 November 1843, qtd. in Zanger, 226.
12. George Wilkins Kendall, *Narrative of the Texan Santa Fe Expedition, Containing a Description of a Tour through Texas . . . and Final Capture of the Texans, and Their March, as Prisoners, to the City of Mexico* (New York: Harper and Brothers, 1844), ii.
13. Richard Phillips, *Mapping Men and Empire: A Geography of Adventure* (New York: Routledge, 1997), 70.
14. Bradley Deane, "Imperial Barbarians: Primitive Masculinity in Lost World Fiction," *Victorian Literature and Culture* 36, no. 1 (2008), 220.
15. Deane, "Imperial Barbarians," 205.
16. See Benedict Anderson, *Imagined Communities: Reflections on the Origin and Spread of Nationalism* (London: Verso, 1991).
17. John Leyden, *Historical Account of the Discoveries and Travels in Africa, by the Late John Leyden, M.D. Enlarged, and Completed to the Present Time, with Illustrations of Its Geography, Natural History, as Well as of the Moral and Social Conditions of Its Inhabitants*, vol. 1, ed., Hugh Murray (Edinburgh: George Ramsay and Company, 1817), 29.
18. Leyden, *Historical Account*, 29.
19. For a sense of the historical range of British associations of Ethiopia with Prester John's kingdom during the *Zemene Mesafint*, see Samuel Johnson's translation of *A Voyage to Abyssinia, by Father Jerome Lobo, a Portuguese Missionary . . . Published by Sir John Hawkins or Mr Stockdale* (London: Elliot and Kay, 1789), 63, 231–249; John Wilkes, *Encyclopedia Londinensis . . . in All Ages of the World* 21 (London: G. Jones, 1826), 377; Richard Pankhurst, ed.,

Diary of a Journey to Abyssinia, 1868: With the Expedition under Sir Robert Napier, K.C.S.I.: The Diary and Observations of William Simpson of the Illustrated London News (Newburyport: Newburyport Press, 2002), 108–109. It should be noted, here, that "Ethiopia" and "Abyssinia" were used interchangeably in the nineteenth century; its borders were roughly contiguous with those of the present day.

20. John Camden Hotten, ed., *Abyssinia and Its People; or, Life in the Land of Prester John* (London: John Camden Hotten, 1868), 7–8.

21. Henry Aaron Stern, *Wanderings among the Falashas in Abyssinia; Together with a Description of the Country and Its Various Inhabitants. Illustrated by a Map and Twenty Engravings of Scenes and Persons, Taken on the Spot* (London: Wertheim, Macintosh, and Hunt, 1862), 62.

22. Hotten, *Abyssinia*, 6.

23. Hotten, *Abyssinia*, 6.

24. Hotten, *Abyssinia*, 6. See, for example, John Tenniel, "The Abyssinian Question," *Punch, or The London Charivari*, 10 August 1867.

25. Hotten, *Abyssinia*, 6–7.

26. Barrie Hayne, "*Ossian*, Scott and Cooper's Indians," *Journal of American Studies* 3, no. 1 (1969): 73.

27. See Colin G. Calloway, *White People, Indians, and Highlanders: Tribal Peoples and Colonial Encounters in Scotland and America* (Oxford: Oxford University Press, 2008). My use of the term "Indian" throughout this chapter, when not referring to members of a specific tribal nation, is in spite of my concurrence with Calloway's statement that neither "Indian" nor "Native American" are "adequate, and both are problematic in some ways" (xix). Similarly, my use of the term "Anglo-American" refers to cultural continuities between the nineteenth-century British Empire and the Antebellum United States, rather than to a specific ethnic category within the United States. While "Ethiopian" was used in the nineteenth century to mean "sub-Saharan African" as well as specifically "Abyssinian," I have chosen to use "Ethiopian" in its current sense, unless responding in context.

28. Walter Scott, *Waverley; or, 'Tis Sixty Years Since*, ed. Claire Lamont (Oxford: Oxford University Press, 1986), 212.

29. Walter Scott, *The Journal of Sir Walter Scott: 1825–1832, from the Original Manuscript at Abbotsford* (Edinburgh: David Douglas, 1891), 345.

30. See Francis H. Herrick, "Audubon and the Dauphin," *The Auk* 54, no. 4 (1937): 476–499.

31. Scott, *Journal*, 345.

32. For a survey of relevant nineteenth century approaches to the Mound Builders, see Charles E. Orser, Jr., *Race and Practice in Archaeological Interpretation* (Philadelphia: University of Pennsylvania Press, 2004), especially 39–74.

33. William Gilmore Simms, "The American Sagas of the Northmen," *Views and Reviews in American Literature, History and Fiction* (New York: Wiley and Putnam, 1845), 3.

34. Hotten, *Abyssinia*, 6.

35. The most reliable English translation of the *Kebra Nagast* (*Book of Kings*) is E. A. Wallis Budge, *The Queen of Sheba and Her Son Menyelek: The Kebra Nagast* (New York: Routledge, 2010). For premedieval origins of the Kebra Nagast and its traditions, see J. T. Pawlikowski, "The Judaic Spirit of the Ethiopian Orthodox Church: A Case Study in Religious Acculturation," *Journal of Religion in Africa* 4, fasc. 3 (1971): 178–199; David W. Phillipson, "The Aksumite Roots of Medieval Ethiopia," *Azania: Archaeological Research in Africa* 39, no. 1 (2004): 77–89.

36. See Gwyn A. Williams, *Madoc: The Making of a Myth* (Oxford: Oxford University Press, 1997).

37. Robert Southey, *Madoc* (London: Longman, Hurst, Rees, Orme, and Brown, 1805).

38. Rebecca Cole Heinowitz, "The Allure of the Same: Robert Southey's Welsh Indians and the Rhetoric of Good Colonialism," *Romantic Circles Praxis Series: Sullen Fires across the Atlantic: Essays in Transatlantic Romanticism*, 02 March 2014, http://www.rc.umd.edu/praxis/sullenfires/heinowitz/heinowitz.html.

39. I Samuel 31:4-6.

40. Northrop Frye, *The Bible and Literature* (London: Routledge & Keegan Paul, 1982), 181.

41. Adam Welch, "Saul," *Kings and Prophets of Israel*, ed. Norman W. Proteous (London: Lutterworth, 1952), 78.

42. W. J. Harvey, *Character and the Novel* (Ithaca: Cornell University Press, 1965), 67.

43. Francesca Aran Murphy, *I Samuel* (Grand Rapids: Brazos Press, 2010), 107–108.

44. For Abuna Salama III and his role in Orthodox controversies that likely influenced his political alliance with Giorgas, see Donald Crummey, "Doctrine and Authority: Abuna Sālāma, 1841–1854," *PICES* 4, no. 1 (1974): 567–578.

45. Izabela Orlowska, "Mining the Wisdom of Solomon: The Coronation of Yohannas IV," *Proceedings of the XV International Conference of Ethiopian Studies* (Wiesbaden: Otto Harrassowitz GmbH & Co. KG, 2006), 315.

46. Russel A. Berman, *Enlightenment or Empire: Colonial Discourse in German Culture* (Lincoln: University of Nebraska Press, 1998), 76.

47. Samuel Gobat, *Journal of Three Years' Residence in Abyssinia, in Furtherance of the Objects of the Church Missionary Society* (London: Hatchard & Son, 1834), 172–173.

48. Edmond J. Keller, *Revolutionary Ethiopia: From Empire to People's Republic* (Bloomington: Indiana University Press, 1988), 24. Téwodros nevertheless came to style himself as "King of Kings of Zion in Ethiopia" and used the conquering Lion of Judah seal; see, for example, the seal affixed to the *Däräsge Maryam*, confiscated in the Expedition of 1868 and in the collections of the British Museum, photographic record housed in the Institute of Ethiopian Studies, Addis Ababa, and the University of Toronto's Mazgaba Seelat database at http://www.utoronto.ca/deeds/.

49. Walter Plowden, letter to Clarendon, 5 March 1856, in *Parliamentary Papers, Correspondence Respecting Abyssinia, 1846–1848* (London: Harrison and Sons, 1868), 165.

50. Donald Crummey, *Land and Society in the Christian Kingdom of Ethiopia: From the Thirteenth to the Twentieth Century* (Urbana-Champaign, University of Illinois Press, 2000), 204–205.

51. For Menelik II, see Harold Marcus, *The Life and Times of Menelik II* (Oxford: Clarendon, 1975).

52. Tasema Ta'a, "The Macca Oromo States and the Creation of Modern Ethiopian Empire," in *The Political Economy of an African Society in Transformation: The Case of Macca Oromo (Ethiopia)*, ed. Catherine Griefenow-Mewis (Wiesbaden: Otto Harrassowitz GmbH & Co. KG, 2006), 70–71.

53. Plowden, *Parliamentary Papers*, 165.

54. Abū Bakr Ibrāhīm, letter to Minīlik, March 1871, *Acta Æthiopica, Volume III: Internal Rivalries and Foreign Threats, 1869–1879*, ed. Sven Rubenson (Addis Ababa: Addis Ababa University Press, 2000), 82.

55. Hagai Erlikh, *The Cross and the River: Ethiopia, Egypt, and the Nile* (London: Lynne Rienner, 2002), 65.

56. Richard Pankhurst, "Imperial Orders in a Command or Pre-Market Economy," *Proceedings of the XVth International Conference of Ethiopian Studies: Hamburg 2003*, ed. Siegbert Uhlig (Wiesbaden: Otto Harrassowitz GmbH & Co. KG, 2006), 322.

57. Richard Pankhurst, "A 'Missing' Letter from Emperor Tewodros II to Queen Victoria's Special Envoy Hormuzd Rassam," *Afrikas Horn*, ed. Walter Raunig and Steffen Wenig (Wiesbaden: Otto Harrassowitz GmbH & Co. KG, 2005), 109.

58. Mengiste Desta, *Ethiopia's Role in African History* (Addis Ababa: Shama Books, 2007), 25.

59. Charles Beke, letter to Lord Stanley, 29 June 1867, in *Accounts and Papers of the House of Commons: Slave Trade. State Papers:—Abyssinia. Session: 5 February–21 August 1867*, vol. 35 (London: Harrison and Sons, 1867), 178.

60. See Maurizio Paolillo, "White Tatars: The Problem of the Origin of the Ongut Conversion to *Jingjiao* and the Uighur Connection," *From the Oxus River to the Chinese Shores: Studies on East Syriac Christianity in China and Central Asia*, ed. Li Tang and Dietmar W. Winkler (Berlin: Lit Verlag, 2013), 238–239; L. N. Gumilev, *Searches for an Imaginary Kingdom: The Legend of the Kingdom of Prester John*, trans. R. E. F. Smith (Cambridge:

Cambridge University Press, 1987); Charles E. Nowell, "The Historical Prester John," *Speculum* 28, no. 3 (1953): 435–445.

61. See Vsevolod Slessarev, trans., *Prester John: The Letter and the Legend* (Minneapolis: University of Minnesota Press, 1959).

62. See Malcolm Letts, "Prester John: A Fourteenth-Century Manuscript at Cambridge," *Transactions of the Royal Historical Society*, Series 4, 29 (1947): 19–26.

63. The *Letter*'s designation of Prester John as "[*rex regnum et*] *dominus dominantium* (Prester John, [King of kings and] lord of lords), analogous to that of the author of the canonical *Apocalypse* (*Presbyteros Ioannis*), recalls the priestly nature of the imperial ruler . . . unequivocally endowing him with the characteristics of *Cosmocrator*, resulting from the merging of the two ecumenical figures of power, Alexander and Jesus Christ"; see Christopher J. Tribe, trans., *Pedro Paez's* History of Ethiopia, *1622*, vol. II (London: Hakluyt Society, 2011), 385.

64. J. R. S. Phillips, *The Medieval Expansion of Europe* (Oxford: Oxford University Press, 1998), 143–145.

65. Helen Adolf, "New Light on Oriental Sources for Wolfrram's *Parzival* and Other Grail Romances," *PMLA* 62, no. 2 (1947): 306–324.

66. Adolf, "New Light," 322.

67. See Dejazmach Berhane-Meskel Deseta, *Zena-Lalibela* (Addis Ababa: Berthanena Selam Matemia Bet tatame, 1951); for the traditional account of Lalibela's construction, see Richard Pankhurst, ed., *Gadla Lalibela* in *The Ethiopian Royal Chronicles* (Addis Ababa: Oxford University Press, 1967).

68. See Niall Finneran, "Built by Angels? Towards a Buildings Archaeology Context for the Rock-Hewn Medieval Churches of Ethiopia," *World Archaeology* 41, no. 3 (2009): 415–429; Marilyn E. Heldman, "Architectural Symbolism, Sacred Geography and the Ethiopian Church," *Journal of Religion in Africa* 22, no. 3 (1992): 221–241.

69. Ivan Hrbek, "Ethiopia, the Red Sea and the Horn," *The Cambridge History of Africa, Volume 3: c. 1000–1650*, ed. Roland Oliver (Cambridge: Cambridge University Press, 1977), 115–116.

70. Walter Scott, *Tales of a Grandfather. Vol. VI. France*, in *The Miscellaneous Works of Sir Walter Scott, Bart.*, Vol. XXVII (Edinburgh: Robert Cadell, 1836), 326.

71. Henry Blanc, *A Narrative of Captivity in Abyssinia; With Some Account of the Emperor Theodore, His Country and People* (London: Smith, Elder and Co., 1868), 116.

72. Samuel Johnson, [*Rasselas*] *The Prince of Abyssinia. A Tale* (London: J. Dodsley, 1759); for the Ethiopian origins of Johnson's tale, see Wendy Laura Belcher, *Abyssinia's Samuel Johnson: Ethiopian Thought in the Making of an English Author* (Oxford: Oxford University Press, 2012). *Rasselas* appears in novels by British and American writers including Brontë, Alcott, Eliot, Hawthorne, Gaskell, and others.

73. Richard Henry Horne, *The History of Napoleon*, vol. II (London: Robert Tyas, 1841), 392.

74. John Gibson Lockhart, *The History of Napoleon Buonaparte, with Engravings on Steel and Wood*, vol. I (London: John Murray, 1829), 2.

75. Walter Scott, letter to Robert Southey, 17 June 1814, in *The Letters of Sir Walter Scott*, ed. H. J. C. Grierson (London: Constable and Company, Limited, 1932–1937), 3:451.

76. John Briggs, trans., *The Rise of the Mahomedan Power in India . . . With Copious Notes* (London: Longman, Rees, Orme, Brown, and Green, 1829).

77. Richard Chandler, *Abyssinia: Mythical and Historical* (London: C. J. Skeet, 1868), 7.

78. Walter Scott, "Hajji Baba in England," *The Miscellaneous Prose Works of Sir Walter Scott, Bart.*, vol. 18: Periodical Criticism, vol. 2: Romance (Edinburgh: Robert Cadell, 1835), 354.

79. Scott, "Hajji Baba," 364.

80. Blanc, *Captivity*, 2.

81. Stern, *Wanderings*, 122.

82. Plowden, qtd. in Sven Rubenson, *King of Kings: Tewodros of Ethiopia* (Addis Ababa: Haile Sellassie University Press, 1966), 61.

83. Franz Amadeus Dombrowski, *Ethiopia's Access to the Sea* (Leiden: E.J. Brill, 1985), 49.

84. Dombrowski, *Ethiopia's Access*, 50.

85. Rassam, qtd. in *Accounts and Papers*, 131.

86. Frederic A. Sharf, David Northrop, and Richard Pankhurst, *Abyssinia, 1867–1868: Artists on Campaign: Watercolors and Drawings from the British Expedition under Sir Robert Napier* (Tsehai: Hollywood, 2003), 24.

87. Wilhelm Staiger, letter to British Foreign Office, 2 January 1867, *Accounts and Papers*, 130.

88. Nini Rodgers, "The Abyssinian Expedition of 1867–1868: Disraeli's Imperialism or James Murray's War?" *The Historical Journal* 27, no. 1 (1984): 129.

89. Simpson, *Diary* (ed. Pankhurst), 13–14.

90. Henry Morton Stanley, *Coomassie and Magdala: The Story of Two British Campaigns in Africa* (London: Sampson, Low, Marston, Low, & Searle, 1874), 444.

91. Gebre-Igziabiher Elyas, *Power, Piety, and Politics: The Chronicle of Abeto Iyaso and Empress Zewditu (1909–1930)* (Cologne: Rüdiger Köppe Verlag, 1994), 304; Bairu Tafla, ed., *A Chronicle of Emperor Yohannes IV* (Wiesbaden: Steiner, 1977), 59.

92. Stanley, *Coomassie*, 449.

93. Stanley, *Coomassie*, 449.

94. See John Dee, *Brytanici Imperii Limites*, British Library Additional MS 59681; Charlotte Artese, "King Arthur in America: Making Space in History for The Faerie Queen and John Dee's Brytanici Imperii Limites," *Journal of Medieval and Early Modern Studies* 33, no. 1 (2003): 125–141.

95. Derrick Spradlin, "'GOD ne'er brings to pass such Things for nought': Empire and Prince Madoc of Wales in Eighteenth-Century America," *Early American Literature* 44, no. 1 (2009): 40

96. Michael Warner, qtd. in Spradlin, "*GOD*," 40.

97. Linda Pratt, "Revising the National Epic: Coleridge, Southey, and Madoc," *Romanticism* 2, no. 2 (1996): 149.

98. John P. McWilliams, Jr., *The American Epic: Transforming a Genre, 1770–1860* (Cambridge: Cambridge University Press, 1989), 168.

99. John Filson, *The Discovery, Settlement, and Present State of Kentucky . . . and Several Other Places* (London: John Stockdale, 1793), 56.

100. John Sevier, letter to Amos Stoddard, 9 October 1810, in Zella Armstrong, ed., *The History of Hamilton County and Chattanooga, Tennessee*, vol. 2 (Johnson City: Overmountain Press, 1993), 280.

101. William Byrd, *The Westover Manuscripts: Containing* The History of the Dividing Line betwixt Virginia and North Carolina; A Journey to the Land of Eden, A.D. 1733; and A Progress to the Mines. *Written from 1728 to 1736, and Nor First Published* (Petersburg: Edmund and Julian C. Ruffian, 1841), 3.

102. Byrd, *Westover Manuscripts*, 3.

103. Byrd, *Westover Manuscripts*, 3.

104. Tim Fulford, "Prophets of Resistance: Native American Shamans and Anglophone Writers," *Transatlantic Literary Exchange, 1790–1870: Gender, Race, and Nation*, ed. Kevin Hutchings and Julia M. Wright (Burlington: Ashgate, 2011), 91.

105. Christopher J. P. Smith, *A Quest for Home: Reading Robert Southey* (Liverpool: Liverpool University Press, 1997), 325–326.

106. For Jones's account, first published in *The Gentleman's Magazine* (1740), see Peter Deroo, *History of America before Columbus, according to Documents and Approved Authors*, vol. 2 (Philadelphia: J.B. Lippincott, 1900), 330–331; for Chapelain, see Alexander von Humboldt, *Personal Narrative of Travels to the Equinoctial Regions of the New Continent, during the Years 1799–1804 . . . Translated into English by Helen Maria Williams* (London: Longman, Rees, Orme, Brown, and Green, 1826), 324.

107. George Catlin, *North American Indians* (New York: Penguin, 2004), 183.

108. George F. Ruxton, *Adventures in Mexico and the Rocky Mountains* (London: John Murray, 1847), 195.

109. Humboldt, *Personal Narrative*, 326.
110. Simms, "American Sagas," 97.
111. Bernard DeVoto, *The Course of Empire* (New York: Houghton Mifflin, 1998), 70.
112. James Bradley Finley, *Life among the Indians; or, Personal Reminiscences and Historical Incidents Illustrative of Indian Life and Character* (Cincinnati: Methodist Book Concern, 1860), 106.
113. James Fenimore Cooper, *The Last of the Mohicans; A Narrative of 1757*, in *The Leatherstocking Tales*, vol. 1 (Penguin: New York, 1985), 828.
114. Humboldt, *Personal Narrative*, 327.
115. Humboldt, *Personal Narrative*, 327.
116. See, for example, W. Raymond Wood, *Prologue to Lewis and Clark: The Mackay and Evans Expedition* (Norman: University of Oklahoma Press, 2003), 42.
117. For the standard biography of Bowles and context for his career, see James Leitch Wright, Jr., *William Augustus Bowles: Director General of the Creek Nation* (Athens: University of Georgia Press, 2010).
118. Gary B. Nash, *The Unknown American Revolution: The Unruly Birth of Democracy and the Struggle to Create America* (New York: Viking, 2005), 258.
119. Lucas Moore, ed., *Twelfth Biennial Report of the Bureau of Agriculture, Labor, and Statistics. Of the State of Kentucky* (Louisville: George G. Fetter, 1897), 78.
120. Wright, *William Augustus Bowles*, 39.
121. William C. Sturtevant, "The Cherokee Frontiers, the French Revolution, and William Augustus Bowles," *The Cherokee Indian Nation: A Troubled History*, ed. Duane H. King (Knoxville: University of Tennessee Press, 1979), 79.
122. Robert Southey, letter to William Owen-Pughe, 9 August 1797, National Library of Wales, MS 13222C, 469; see also, for context, Shawna Lichtenwalner, *Claiming Cambria: Invoking the Welsh in the Romantic Era* (Cranbury: Rosemont, 2008).
123. *The Gentleman's Magazine* 61 (1791): 800.
124. Sturtevant, "Cherokee Frontiers," 80.
125. "The Representation of William Augustus Bowles . . . to His Brittanic Majesty," 3 January 1791, Public Records Office, F.O. L/9, S/J.9756, fols. 5–17, London.
126. Manuscript notes to Benjamin Baynton, *The Authentic Memoirs of William Augustus Bowles, Esquire, Ambassador from the United Nations of Creeks and Cherokees, to the Court of London* (London: R. Faulder, 1791), in the collection of the British Museum, transcribed in E. Alfred Jones, "The Real Author of the 'Authentic Memoirs of William Augustus Bowles,'" *Maryland Historical Magazine* 18, no. 4 (1923): 308.
127. Count Paulo Andreani, letter to Gian Mario Andreani, 26 May 1790, trans. Cesare Marino, Fondo Sormani-Andreani, Archivo di State, Milan, Italy, in Cesare Marino and Karim M. Tiro, eds., *Along the Hudson and Mohawk: The 1790 Journey of Count Paulo Andreani* (Philadelphia: University of Pennsylvania Press, 2006), 97.
128. Baynton, *Authentic Memoirs*, 3, 67.
129. "Monthly Catalogue," *The Monthly Review, or, Literary Journal* 4 (1791): 356.
130. "Monthly Catalogue," *The Critical Review; or Annals of Literature, Extended and Improved. By a Society of Gentlemen. A New Arrangement* 1 (1791): 238.
131. See Prys Morgan, "From a Death to a View: The Hunt for the Welsh Past in the Romantic Period," Eric Hobsbawm and Terence Ranger, eds., *The Invention of Tradition* (Cambridge: Cambridge University Press, 2012): 43–101.
132. George Burder, *The Welch Indians or A Collection of Papers Respecting a People Whose Ancestors Emigrated from Wales to America, in the Year 1170, with Prince Madoc . . . West Side of the Mississippi* (London: T. Chapman, 1787 [?]), reprinted in its entirety in *The Magazine of History with Notes and Queries* 78 (1922): 41.
133. "A Gentleman," *Jachin and Boaz; or, An Authentic Key to the Door of Free-Masonry, Both Ancient and Modern . . . and Days of Meeting* (London: E. Newbery, 1800), 56.
134. "Catalogue," *Monthly Review*, 356.
135. "Catalogue," *Critical Review*, 238.

136. Timothy J. Shannon, "'This Wretched Scene of British Curiosity and Savage Debauchery': Performing Indian Kingship in Eighteenth-Century Britain," *Native Acts: Indian Performance, 1603–1832* (Lincoln: University of Nebraska Press, 2011), 241.

137. Shannon, "'Wretched Scene,'" 241.

138. "Politics. Article XVI," *The Analytical Review, or History of Literature . . . and the Literary Intelligence of Europe, &c.* 9 (1791): 312.

139. Baynton, *Memoirs*, iii.

140. King, ed., *Cherokee Indian Nation*, 79.

141. "Petition of Captain Benjamin Baynton, of His Majesties Late Regiment of Pennsylvania Loyalists," Loyalist Claims, Public Record Office, Audit Office, Class 13, Volume 70B, folio 158, London.

142. "Petition of Captain Benjamin Baynton," folio 58.

143. Sturtevant, "Cherokee Frontiers," 82.

144. See Lyle N. McAlister, "William Augustus Bowles and the State of Muskogee," *Florida Historical Quarterly* (1962): 317–328.

145. See William S. Coker and Thomas D. Watson, *Indian Traders of the Southeast Spanish Borderlands: Panton, Leslie & Company and John Forbes & Company, 1783–1847* (Gainesville: University Presses of Florida, 1986); Lawrence Kinnaird, "The Significance of William Augustus Bowles' Seizure of Panton's Apalachee Store in 1792," *The Florida Historical Society Quarterly* (1931): 156–192.

146. Henry Knox, letter to James Seagrove, 11 April 1792, in Walter Lowrie and Matthew St. Claire Clarke, eds., *American State Papers: Documents, Legislative and Executive, of the Congress of the United States*, vol 4: Indian Affairs (Washington, DC: Gales and Seaton, 1832), 251.

147. George Hammond, letter to Thomas Jefferson, *State Papers*, 251.

148. Alexander McGillivray, letter to Henry Knox, 18 May 1792, *State Papers*, 315.

149. David W. Miller, *The Taking of American Indian Lands in the Southeast: A History of Territorial Cessions and Forced Relocations, 1607–1840* (Jefferson: McFarland & Company, 2011), 95.

150. McGillivray, *State Papers*, 315.

151. See, for Hawkins's relations with McGillivray and others, *Letters of Benjamin Hawkins, 1796–1806*, ed. Stephen Beauregard Hawkins (Savannah: Geographical Historical Society, 1915).

152. See Amos J. Wright, Jr., *The McGillivray and McIntosh Traders: On the Old Southwest Frontier, 1716–1815* (Montgomery: NewSouth Books, 2007); Linda Langley, "The Tribal Identity of Alexander McGillivray: A Review of the Historical and Ethnographic Data," *Louisiana History: The Journal of the Louisiana Historical Association* 46, no. 2 (2005): 231–239.

153. Maya Jasanoff, *Liberty's Exiles: American Loyalists in the Revolutionary World* (New York: Vintage, 2012), 322.

154. See Rita Parkhurst, "The Library of Emperor Tewodros II at Mäqdäla (Magdala)," *Bulletin of the School of Oriental and African Studies, University of London* 36, no. 1 (1973): 15–42; AFROMET, Memorandum from the Association for the Return of Maqdala Ethiopian Treasures, House of Commons, Culture, Media, and Sport Committee, Seventh Report on Cultural Property: Return and Illicit Trade, vol. 3 (London, 2000), 354–358.

155. John Caldwell Guilds, "William Gilmore Simms and the Portrayal of the American Indian: A Literary View," in John Caldwell Guilds and Charles Hudson, eds., *An Early and Strong Sympathy: The Indian Writings of William Gilmore Simms* (Columbia: University of South Carolina Press, 2003), xxxii.

156. William Gilmore Simms, "Thle-cath-cha," in Guilds, *Strong Sympathy*, 62.

157. Simms, "American Sagas," 100.

158. William Gilmore Simms, "The Broken Arrow," *The Book of My Lady: A Melange. By a Bachelor Knight* (Philadelphia: Key & Biddle, 1833), 122–126. For Simms proximity to the Georgia Treaty and McIntosh's death, see his handwritten notes to a copy of "The Broken Arrow" in Scrapbook G, Charles Gilmore Simms Collection, South Caroliniana Library, Charleston, South Carolina.

Chapter Six

"Just as Government's a mere matter of form"

Blackwood's Edinburgh Magazine, *Imperial Romanticism, and the Art of "Personation"*

For exhibit, consider the curious afterlives of the Scottish-born William Brydon, an "Assistant Surgeon in the Shah's Service" during the First Anglo-Afghan War (1839–1842). By the early 1840s, the East India Company was at war beyond the Khyber Pass, but the military effort, led by the aging General Elphinstone, had completely failed to legitimize their client monarch in Kabul, Shuja Shah Durani, or implement successful counterinsurgency policies against his rival, Dost Mohammed. And after finally abandoning the Shah, British authorities had failed to adequately ensure the safe withdrawal of over sixteen thousand soldiers and camp followers, nearly all of whom were massacred during the infamous Retreat from Kabul in 1842.[1] When Brydon reached the British garrison at Jalalabad during the brutally cold January of 1842 "(on a horse scarcely able to move another yard) wounded and bruised from head to foot with stones," he, alone, had "arrived to tell the fearful tale" of the column's demise.[2] Simultaneously, he *was* the fearful tale. Brydon arrived "wounded in the knee, badly in the left hand, cut across by a sabre, and seriously in the head by an Affghan knife, which, but for a *Blackwood's Magazine* [stuffed] in his forage-cap, must certainly have killed him."[3] He had been quite literally saved by the sheer number of "fearful tales" very much like his own that filled *Blackwood's*' thick pages.

Brydon fit the mold of those imperialists whom George Orwell later described as "Kipling's official admirers . . . the 'service' middle classes, the people who read *Blackwood's*."[4] But by Kipling's time, *Blackwood's* readers, particularly those with strong connections abroad, had become Brydon's official admirers, as well. When British troops again crossed the Northwest Frontier in what became the Second Anglo-Afghan War, among them were men like Major J. J. Bailey, a paymaster for the 4th Battalion, Rifle Brigade, who had been present at Jalalabad forty years prior, and whose presence testified to the cyclical patterns of imperial time. Also present were others like William Simpson, an embedded artist for the *Illustrated London Times*, for whom the Second Anglo-Afghan War offered an experience of "living history," an opportunity to access the romanticized *Blackwood's* past firsthand as well as participate in a fully analogous present.

Indeed, the renewed interest in Brydon's tale had much to do with the parallels offered between fiction and fact, past and present at the close of the 1870s. It is possible, for example, that the Brydon "revival" of the late 1870s influenced the backstory for Arthur Conan Doyle's famous narrator, Dr. John Watson, a former military surgeon who survived the stunning British defeat at Maiwand in 1880.[5] Doyle knew the publisher, William Blackwood, whose younger brother died at Maiwand, through family connections, but his keen interest in accounts of a wounded surgeon present at the battle would have been thoroughly in step with numerous *Blackwood's* readers who saw Brydon, the Retreat from Kabul, and the First Anglo-Afghan War, more generally, as a template for present affairs. In 1879, for example, Lady Elizabeth Butler had exhibited her famous painting of Brydon's arrival, *The Remnants of the Army*, at the Royal Academy. That same year, Simpson displayed a watercolor of Brydon's arrival that he had "painted from sketches [done] on the spot and descriptions furnished to the artist by Major Bailey, an eyewitness of Dr. Brydon's arrival." Although identical in many respects to Butler's preceding work, it had the additional warrant of having been based on narrative descriptions given by the aging Bailey, who warranted that "after a lapse of thirty seven years [he] consider[ed] it a very fine representation of both man and pony."[6]

It is not difficult to see how someone of Major Bailey's years and particular set of experiences might imagine continuities between events at different points in their lives. Nor is it difficult to imagine the recursive circulation between *Blackwood's* stories about the Northwest Frontier and the collective experience of numerous Imperial Britons of the 1870s–1880s who found themselves enacting and repeating often-told narratives of the past as much as their Afghan counterparts. The "*Blackwood's*" Brydon, like other valorized imperial(ist) figures, served as a sort of prism for collective memories that informed a range of possible narratives and experiential analogues. But to extend the metaphor, a prism is an object used by an observer for the purpose of seeing the multifarious strains of a spectrum. On the other side of the metaphor, it is an obvious enough thing to claim that public figures and figures from stories express a collective set of historical experiences, voices, and valuations. But if the central professional act of the British Imperial agent was interlocution, then the essential question comes into focus through a different kind of refraction: what did it mean to *be* the prism? To put it another way, how was selfhood understood, not through recourse to another's value as a vessel for collective traditions, but to one's own self-understanding as the protagonist, object, and narrator of a tale all at once? Moreover, what avenues would engines of popular culture like *Blackwood's* have offered to someone like William Brydon for understanding both the uniqueness and collective commonalities of his own "fearful tale?"

However much this sort of imaginative circulation might have made sense to far-flung *Blackwood's* readers in the British Empire, it had little to do with what Matthew Arnold meant when he articulated his call for the "free play of the mind" in literary criticism in 1865, drawing a stark contrast between Continental "organ[s] like the *Revue des Deux Mondes*" and a vibrant culture of British periodical reviews that had emerged by the early nineteenth century.[7] These British "organs of criticism," he reflected, "are organs of men and parties having practical ends to serve, and with them those practical ends are the first thing and the play of the mind second."[8] Arnold enumerated these journals and their corresponding factions: the *Times* was as "an organ of the common, satisfied, well-to-do Englishman"; the *British Quarterly Review* belonged to the "political Dissenters"; the *Edinburgh Review* remained the "organ of the old Whigs," and the *Quarterly Review* was "an organ of the Tories, and for as much play of mind as may suit its being that."[9] *Blackwood's Edinburgh Magazine*, however, the Tory periodical notorious for "its record of critical irresponsibility, political bias, and personal slander"—and so increasingly tied to the imperialist classes abroad—was noticeably absent from the list.[10] Undoubtedly, the omission of *Blackwood's* from Arnold's tidy list of partisan journals had much to do with what Peter T. Murphy identifies as the "hermeneutically challenging situation" of *Blackwood's* writing.[11] The problem for Arnold, reviewing at midcentury, was largely the same as the problem faced by *Blackwood's* metropolitan readers—and targets—throughout its early years. The *Blackwood's* style, always more than reductively partisan, was notoriously difficult to define. The Tory journal's pages combined a serious "free play of the [critical] mind" with a highly polemical, wildly imaginative, and often violent "free play" of fiction, pseudonymous authorship, and metatextual sleight-of-hand.

By avoiding *Blackwood's*, though, Arnold's critique ignored the pivotal role that the journal played in the early nineteenth century's virulent debates about the relationship between political culture, literature, and individual expression—debates that ended up drawing keen distinctions between reading sensibilities in metropolitan Britain and the Empire. As Richard Cronin remarks, Waterloo's cultural aftermath gave rise to three distinct literary phenomena: the "extraordinary celebrity of Lord Byron," the "development of a new and distinctively modern variety of literary magazine" best exemplified by journals like *Blackwood's*, and the enormous popularity of Sir Walter Scott's historical novels, which, "according to William St. Clair's extraordinary calculation, outsold the work of all other novelists put together."[12] *Blackwood's* writers routinely chose the private lives and public personae of literary celebrities as their subject matter, alternately describing, praising, and attacking figures like Byron and Wordsworth and inveighing against "Cockney School" writers like John Keats and Leigh Hunt in a series of scathing satires. Invariably, the *Blackwood's* reviews complicated their readers' sense of what it meant to be a writer of "genius" in the Romantic period. Higgins notes that in the case of Wordsworth, for example, *Blackwood's* "interest in 'personality' both underpinned and ironized its account of [the poet] as . . . transcendent genius. For although this account was based, in part, on representations of him as a private man, the very existence of those representations in the pages of the magazine complicated its claim that he stood above the literary marketplace," occupying a position of privileged repose.[13]

While critics since Arnold have recognized *Blackwood's* importance as a site where a new periodical form interrogated a new ideal of Romantic authorship, little attention has been paid to the importance of Cronin's third literary phenomenon, the *Waverly* effect, in *Blackwood's* approach to the problem of Romantic genius. *Blackwood's* promoted literary figures like Sir Walter Scott and Edmund Burke as model writers whose emphasis on the dialogic, corporate, and inherited nature of cultural tradition placed them in stark contrast to the individualistic lyric personae of Romantic writers like Lord Byron. While this preference aligns neatly with the Tory cultural sensibility of *Blackwood's*, steeped in the backward glances of Scottish Romanticism, it also reveals much about how principal contributors like John Gibson Lockhart and James Hogg wrestled with the emergent forms of periodical writing that allowed individual authors to both build and maintain the collective imaginative project of *Blackwood's* and its literary "ingine o' five hundred elephant power."[14]

The collaborative, dialogic nature of periodical writing and publishing in Romantic Britain provided the *Blackwood's* circle with a powerful metaphor for describing the polyphonic "voice" and "genius" of inherited traditions beyond the dominant metropolitan purview. At the same time, the regular *practice* of writing and editing *Blackwood's*—as well as its startling array of shifting, pseudonymous authorial personae—provided writers like John Wilson, John Gibson Lockhart, and James Hogg with a laboratory for working out what it meant to operate as individual talents bound by the common strictures of tradition. In short, throughout its early years, *Blackwood's* treated the production of periodical form and the reception of cultural forms interchangeably. The journal's reviewers valorized conservative literary figures such as Edmund Burke and Sir Walter Scott, but they also looked to writers like Burke and Scott as models of what it might mean to reconcile Romantic individualism with their own brand of populist, nonmetropolitan traditionalism. They wanted one "ingine 'o" Romantic genius—*Blackwood's*—but they also wanted to be invisible among its "five hundred elephants."

On the one hand, the *Blackwood's* "elephant-power" editorial formula alluded to accounts of the Indian juggernaut, an immense cart meant to carry statues of Hindu deities during the *Ratha Yatra* precessions at Jagganath Temple, which supposedly crushed worshipers beneath its "ingine" as it passed. At the same time, it aligned the scope of *Blackwood's* with *jagannātha*—or, the "world-lord"—one of the attributes of Krishna. Like the loanword, juggernaut, itself, this framework of allusion reflected the Imperial networks that influenced *Blackwood's* editorial material, as well as the lives and livelihoods of numerous readers. As Walter Scott remarked, Scotland was Britain's "corn-chest," and its "live articles of exportation" were "black cattle and our children, and though England furnishes a demand for our quadrupeds, we are forced to send our bipeds as far as Bengal."[15] Like Captain Marryat, Scott's political-historical worldview inclined him to view this kind of political-economic commodification as a form of signification, one that not only illustrated Britain's interrelationship with the broader Imperial world, but provided a mode of speech and self-representation for Imperial subjects whose lives bore the striking passages, reversals, and uses of it-narratives and could speak from within their matrix. However, in *Blackwood's*, the editorial act radically conflated the imperial rhetorical situation with its speakers (who are all corporate, pseudonymous, easily interchangeable) and the objects of their speech. Like the British Empire, *Blackwood's* coauthored the "lives" of its personae as just as much as they produced and serviced its "ingine." Indeed, the circulation of this image, itself, within British Imperial networks and reading audiences abroad speaks to the astuteness of the *Blackwood's* circle in this regard. In 1847, for example, an article in the United Service Magazine remarked that developments in technologies and Imperial politics were such that no one could "tell but soon, instead of talking of horse-strength in steam, we shall be boasting of engines of four or five hundred-elephant power!"[16]

Of course, the immediate context for *Blackwood's*' emergence in Regency cultural arguments had much to do with the simultaneous rise of London-based, politically progressive literary cultures such as Hunt's circle. Whereas the "Cockney School" represented the metropole, progress, and radical individualism, the *Blackwood's* circle performed province, tradition, and communitarian ideals of Scottish Romanticism. But as Daniel Sanjiv Roberts remarks, the journal's "ambitions to shape public opinion in the political arena and to voice a distinctively Edinburgh-based regional critique of British letters were underpinned by its consciousness of the spectacular growth of empire" during its formation, particularly in South Asia.[17] In fact, the journal's central "self"-characterization as an "ingine o' five hundred elephant power" reflects how easily the Romantic provincial traditionalism of Scott's circle provided a rhetorical situation for emergent Imperial speech, identities, and historical consciousness.

THE *BLACKWOOD'S* HERMENEUTIC OF COMMUNAL PERSONALITY

Blackwood's resists easy categorization. It switched between the political, the personal, and the aesthetic in its invective rhetoric, blurring the lines between imaginative literature and the form of the critical essay. As Robert Morrison remarks, *Blackwood's* was the "finest contemporary critic of Shelley and his circle and the most wide-ranging and penetrating publication of the age."[18] Yet, as many of *Blackwood's*'s contemporaries lamented, the magazine's reviews left "all the privacies of life . . . ransacked" and "all the sanctuaries of nature explored and violated."[19] During the magazine's riotous early years, regular contributors like John Wilson and Walter Scott's son-in-law, John Gibson Lockhart, turned their "wicked ingenuity" against the radical politics and literary aesthetics of writers like Leigh Hunt, William Hazlitt, and John Keats, utilizing a dizzying range of satirical and often shared personae to do so.[20] In fact, there is much to recommend Alan Lang Strout's assessment that there remains "no better example of political malignity in the periodical criticism of the early nineteenth century" than the reviews in *Blackwood's* and its imitators.[21]

Yet the inner circle of *Blackwood's* tended to view their metropolitan Tory counterparts in London—satirists and critics like William Gifford of the *Quarterly*—with some suspicion, sensing their respectable distaste for *Blackwood's* "locality of allusion" and "audacious puffery."[22] To contributor William Maginn, for example, Gifford seemed a rather "fanatical Ministerialist."[23] And just as *Blackwood's* writers bristled next to their London counterparts, radicals whose work was often the subject of *Blackwood's* censure found cause to acknowledge the merit of their critics. Byron, for example, congratulated Walter Scott on his daughter's union with Lockhart, "her lord" about whom the poet claims to have heard "much good."[24] Unlike the respectable nineteenth-century conservatism of literate English elites—whether the "fanatical Ministerialism" of Regency writers like William Gifford and Robert Southey or, by Arnold's day, the *Quarterly* reviewers—the early contributors to *Blackwood's* had more in common with their cultural opponents than with they did with many of their own political allies. *Blackwood's* Tory stance—both overtly reactionary and oriented toward the "free play of the mind"—was, in effect, a highly Romantic project, one that asked readers and members of the magazine's community of writers to struggle with the relationship between individual artistic expression and a common, largely Gothic, historical past. Indeed, the Blackwood's ethos enacted both of the great caveats to Whig national-historical ideologies, performing and diffusing both the voice of the traditional "Tory" past and situating that voice in peripheral British landscapes—the Scottish Highlands, Edinburgh, Ireland, the Indies—that were decidedly nonnational and nonmetropolitan.

By Arnold's day, this was both a recognizably Romantic and reactionary stance in periodical culture. Thus, his omission of *Blackwood's* from its pantheon of early nineteenth-century periodicals is particularly strange given his criticism of Byron, Wordsworth, Keats, and other Romantic writers who "had their source in a great movement of feeling."[25] Writing in 1864, Arnold echoes *Blackwood's* Regency-era concerns about the literary influence of the French Revolution, "that object of so much blind love and so much blind hatred," which "found undoubtedly its motive-power in the intelligence of men and not in their common sense."[26] Curiously, his assessment of Romantic poetics also relied, in part, on the kind of literary figuration of Edmund Burke that British readers could have expected to find in *Blackwood's* during the 1820s, where reviewers placed the Anglo-Irish orator at the center of a great *agon* of British responses to the French Revolution. For *Blackwood's* in the 1820s as well as Arnold in the 1860s, Burke straddled the divide between an eighteenth- and early nineteenth-century "intellectual sphere" and "political sphere" that "created, in opposition to itself . . . an *epoch of concentration.*"[27] Burke was thus a contradictory figure, but also a wholly characteristic one for his era, as well as a kind of curative for dissonant strains in the Romantic imagination that competed in early nineteenth-century periodical cultures. "The great force of that epoch of concentration was England," Arnold wrote, "and the great voice of that epoch of concentration was Burke."[28]

Like the echo of Burke in Arnold's criticism, *Blackwood's* early writing straddled the apparent contradictions between a Tory political rhetoric in support of traditional social forms and a Romantic literary interest in the lyric speaker, both as the focus of the poet's work and as a projection of the writer's personality and individual "genius." As David Higgins remarks, Romantic writers and their critics celebrated the figure of the "creative artist" as "never before, largely through the valorization of genius as the highest form of human subjectivity."[29] To a great degree, Romantic arguments about the nature and quality of "original genius," neglected or otherwise, reacted to the "perceived degradation of literary production in contemporary Britain," in particular, the "increasing popularity and cultural power of the periodical press."[30] The infamous "Cockney School" attacks, for example, "constituted an enormously powerful act of cultural definition."[31] The *Blackwood's* reviews challenged a "claim for cultural power by the liberal Hunt circle,"[32] but in doing so, they nearly always focused on dismantling Romantic claims about the radical *individuality* of artistic "genius." Behind *Blackwood's* "open character assassination" against Romantic writers of "genius,"[33] Kim Wheatley sees the "unsettling tendency of fictions to take on a life of their own."[34] What began as periodical satire, Wheatley argues, quickly became something "more primitive and Romantic" than the "ostensible attitude" of "amusingly blatant class snobbery"[35] adopted by writers like Lockhart and Wilson in their reviews.[36] By the 1820s, *Blackwood's* critical rhetoric had also become a creative literature, one driven, like the Cockney School reviews, by the "doubling and splitting of personalities."[37]

However, *Blackwood's* infamous critical attacks, like Arnold's critical reluctance to characterize its "practical ends," illustrated the problem of trying to interpret the collective "genius" and character of the magazine. If antagonists like John Scott tried to exchange the "hermeneutically challenging" situation of pseudonymous authorship for a "(potentially) clearer one," one that challenged the "insulter to replace word with body, insult with action," then *Blackwood's* Tory Romanticism tried to do quite the opposite.[38] As Robert Morrison notes, *Blackwood's* domesticated "into one context both conservative politics and radical poetics," and perhaps nowhere is the expression of this strange conjunction more evident than in the magazine's notions of authorship and "original genius."[39] In its early years, *Blackwood's* substituted the collective "genius" of the periodical format for a Romantic ideal of inspired individual authorship, and the journal's collective metafiction of identity—the common inheritance of "Maga"—reflected a serious attempt to reconcile Burkean rhetoric about the organic "genius" of tradition with an ascendant Romantic model of originality and individual talent, an admixture jarring to metropolitan readers but completely in line with the experiential realities of empire-building, "adventurism," and intercultural brokerage in the Empire.

Periodical publications imposed a range of literal and imaginative forms on the individual expressions contained in their pages. In the case of *Blackwood's*, the magazine's regular contributors in the early years foregrounded the constraints and possibilities of periodical writing until the publication itself became a sort of metonym for the poetic idea of an organic unity. The verse, critical pieces, local notices, histories, and political essays that appeared in an anthologized, edited format also enacted an idea of a common culture, a corporate project that lent authority and coherence to individual pieces. This idea of the magazine-as-such also became the central character and speaker of contributors' fictions and the overarching fiction of editorial practice, a shape-shifting, voracious, self-reflexive personification known as "Maga." At times, "Maga" appears as a beautiful "matron . . . flung wildly across her bed, and moaning under the weight of the monster," a Whig that squats devilishly on her "breast."[40] The magazine itself and the whole process of writing and editing is no less a gothic fiction than the weird stories it showcased. "Maga," the magazine, elided with the "sweet body" whose "bare-white breasts" received the killer's knife in Wilson's "Extracts from Gosschen's Diary" (1818).[41] At other times, "Maga" herself was the "monster," a "hell-cat from the kingdom of Pluto," next to which "the Fates, the Furies, the Harpies, and the Gorgons, in the world's distressed fancy, made but one Venus."[42] Both muse and demon, *Blackwood's* was ultimately an "omnipresence," whose "visits are hailed by the heart-acclamation of young and old alike," by the "fire-light reflected from brass mirrors bright as gold" as well as "by the peat-low frae the ingle o' the 'auld clay biggin.'"[43] It was also, the magazine's quasi-fictional contributors reflected, a self-perpetuating "Ingine o' five hundred elephant power," and "nae mortal man," remarks the "Ettrick Shepherd" of the collaborative "Noctes Ambrosianae" colloquies, "should be entrusted wi' sic an ingine."[44] It was autochthonous as the British Imperial networks of circulation that quickly came to serve as Maga's significant readership and source of narrative material.

Beginning in 1818, the "Noctes" series enunciated the fictional argument of "Maga" as "Ingine" and form. Written primarily by *Blackwood's*'s early luminaries—John Gibson Lockhart, John Wilson, James Hogg, and William Maginn—the "Noctes" crystallized the self-referential playfulness and anonymous quasi-fictions of the magazine into a single recurrent conceit: *none* of the actual contributors to *Blackwood's* would be entrusted with "sic an Ingine." Instead, the "Noctes" stage the wide-ranging conversations of fictional personae such as "Christopher North," "Timothy Tickler," and the "Ettrick Shepherd" as they drink at Ambrose's tavern and prepare *Blackwood's*. As much as this metafiction was an exercise in the "art of personation"[45] and an "experiment in fluid romantic criticism,"[46] it was also an argument for the subordination of individual talents—even "Brobdingnagian" ones[47]—to tradition, community, and received forms. *Blackwood's*, claimed "Christopher North," was "Moon-Maga," and the fictional writers throughout its pages "her Star-satellites."[48] And "just as government's a mere matter of form," Wilson's persona explained, "so too with Maga. On she goes, and on she would go, if editors and contributors were all asleep, nay, all dead and buried."[49] Because individual speakers in *Blackwood's* orbit "Moon-Maga," they, too, share its qualities. Thus, the fictional "Christopher North" responds to *Blackwood's* real critics by "taking notice of the one supposed feature of our character which our enemies represent as excessively unbecoming, but of which our friends deny the existence—we mean, our PERSONALITY."[50] As Murphy remarks, "[the persona's] friends know that he does exist (that he can be "personal," and be criticized for it); his friends know that he doesn't exist, and that criticism of him flies off into some no-man's land of discourse, the verbal equivalent of a dead letter office."[51] Collectively, though, they existed as *Blackwood's* "personality," and their elusiveness was the by-product of their immersion in a common form and rhetorical speaking position: "We have a personal existence and our name is North."[52]

One of the remarkable characteristics of *Blackwood's* writing was the extent to which this periodical model of corporate "personality," wherein an editor or narrator spoke for a parish, tradition, or family, was replicated in highly individual works of fiction. The *Blackwood's* circle was a remarkably prolific one, pursuing Wilson's metaphor of the "Ingine" through numerous novels and collections of short stories, typically united by a common metafiction or editorial "personality" who observes manners and records antiquarian tales. In *Peter's Letters to His Kinsfolk* (1819), for example, Lockhart assumes the epistolary fiction of an outsider describing Edinburgh in a series of letters meant for his provincial relatives. Among the characters "Peter" encounters is a "Mr. L--- who, as well as Mr. W---n is supposed to be one of the principal supporters of this Magazine [*Blackwoood's*]."[53] But "Peter" and "Mr. L---" are more than individual fictional personae of the actual John Gibson Lockhart. They are locations of communal speech and translation: "Peter" stands in the place of his family, and "Mr. L---" stands in for "Maga" and Edinburgh. Lockhart, moreover, constructs "Mr. L---" as a kind of phantom, a creature of gossip, misapprehension, and common opinion. "Most persons whom I have heard speak of him," "Peter" remarks, "seemed to have been impressed with the notion that the bias of his character inclined towards an unrelenting subversion of the pretensions of others. But I soon perceived that here was another instance of the incompetency of the crowd to form any rational opinion about persons of whom they see only partial glimpses, and hear only distorted impressions."[54]

In *Peter's Letters*, individuals are understood only through a social hermeneutic, one made more complicated by the fact that Lockhart, the writer, invents the "crowd" as much as they, in turn, invent him. On one level, the combined fictions of the "crowd," Peter's country kin, and the closed, parochial world of misunderstood Edinburgh literati, allow the real Lockhart to hide behind the Romantic tropes of local identity and national character. To *Blackwood's* contributors, though, these imaginative allegiances constitute what Charles Snodgrass describes as a "subversive Scottishness."[55] The homespun, regional identity evoked by Lockhart is a mask for something far more complex, corporate, and ultimately elusive. The unfortunate John Scott understood as much, warning readers of the *London Magazine* that "Peter is the Editors [of Blackwood's], puffing their own magazine . . . and professing contrition while hatching fresh offences," with "Peter Morris, the hypocrite in front, and Christopher North, the ruffian behind."[56] This "Scottishness" is hardly an identity at all; it is a hermeneutic of deconstruction, and one to which John Scott ultimately falls victim, wrongly looking for a single meaning and a single speaker, conflating "Peter Morris" with "Christopher North," and John Gibson Lockhart with John Wilson.

Obviously, it would have been simpler for the actual Lockhart to defend his own personal character in some less baroque fashion. Moving under the same power as *Blackwood's* "Ingine," though, Lockhart's expressive projection of his own real identity in *Peter's Letters* cannot help but suggest a slew of social contexts, layered one atop the other, that dominate his own self-portrayal. *Blackwood's* contributor John Galt felt the same impetus, the dialogic power of tradition and community, when he began writing *The Ayrshire Legatees* (1821), a similar work told through the common frame of one family's correspondence. It quickly became "necessary," Galt told William Blackwood, "in order to prepare the reader for the tone of the observations that I mean to ascribe to several characters to frame somewhat more of a story than I first intended. This however will not diminish the interest of the work, but it has forced me to make as it were an earlier beginning."[57] The work, the familial "Ingine," has taken mastery over the individual writer, no less than "Maga" has in the "Noctes." Significantly, the living Galt asks the living Blackwood to "tell my friend [the fictional] Mr North not to touch one of the Scotticisms."[58] Do not, in other words, *simplify*; do not grant any single voice too much authority over the others. In the metaphorical geography of *Blackwood's*, to do so would be to make the work and its speakers less "Scottish."

ROMANTIC GENIUS AND THE PROBLEM OF THE "TRADITIONARY" SELF

James Hogg's *Private Memoirs and Confessions of a Justified Sinner* (1824), with its return of "Mr. L---," is one of the most striking and sustained examples of *Blackwood's*'s "Ingine" at work. In the "Ettrick Shepherd's" gothic horror tale, the diabolical possession of the "justified sinner" is only one level of ventriloquism, just as the sinner's confession is simply one record contained within the hermeneutical knot of local legend, parish records, and editorial interlocutors. The "printed pamphlet" confession, found with a corpse at a "vacant space" in "that part of the grave that had never been opened before," alone establishes nothing.[59] This "vacant space," like the "personalities" and general form of *Blackwood's*, becomes a method for interpreting and coauthoring meaning, rather than a terminus for it. Suddenly, the novel seems to shift to the "Noctes" world of *Blackwood's* personae. "Mr L---t," the narrator recalls, "picked up a leathern case, which seemed to be wrapped round and round by some ribbon, or cord, that had rotten from it, for the swaddling marks still remained. . . . On opening it out, we found to our great astonishment, that it contained *a printed pamphlet*."[60] "Mr L---w . . . requested Mr L---t to give it to me," the narrator continues, "as he had so many things of literature and law to attend to."[61] It does not particularly matter, Hogg seems to suggest, who occupies the role of "editor." What matters is the writer-editor's subordination to the work as a whole and his work in subordinating the sinner's individual voice to the "authentic" detail of curious "traditionary facts" compiled for the reader.[62] This is a *Blackwood's* ethos: individual identities are less intelligible than communal identities, and their utterances are usually corporate, interchangeable, or else utterly obscure.

On one level, nothing could be farther from what Jerome McGann describes as "one of the basic illusions of Romantic Ideology," namely that "only a poet and his works can transcend a corrupting appropriation by 'the world' of politics and money."[63] Instead, the *Blackwood's* circle advocated a kind of "traditionary" romanticism, a Burkean rhetoric of the self that relocated the chivalric speaking authority of declining elites squarely in the hands of "service middle-class" writers and their readers. Just as the "appearance of proper authority and good government" retained its old forms in Tory thought, "even as they passed from the exclusive grasp of the nobility," the eccentric, absurdly elitist, and highly individuated "appearances" of the *Blackwood's* "personalities" masked the genuine interest of these writers in a Romantic poetics of "the world" they shared with their readers.[64] In Hogg's *Confessions*, for example, "Mr. L---t," ostensibly the first choice to write the novel, must attend to "so many things" beforehand, and thus the task falls to Hogg. Among the *Blackwood's* set, it is a mark of seriousness to have, as Lockhart does, "so many things" of both "literature and law to attend to."[65] Of course, this is a far cry from what Lockhart characterized as the "very nature and genius" of a writer—and "personality"—like Lord Byron, whose poetic imagination remained "forever occupied intensely with the Self, as the great centre and source of its strength."[66] To this Romantic ideal of "self-concentration," Lockhart continues, "there is, of course, no such disturbing and fatal enemy as those sympathies and affections that draw the mind out actively towards others."[67]

Elsewhere, however, Lockhart "denotes . . . a disengaged ideal" of writing "by the phrase 'literature *as his occupation*,'" hence equating professionalism, which one might associate with a down-to-earth and businesslike attitude, with the dreamy aestheticism of the Romantic poets."[68] "That one word *genius*," he remarked, "has done more harm than anything in the vocabulary."[69] Unlike the cultivated persona of the Romantic poet as one "possessed of more than usual organic sensibility"[70] or as one who "participates in the eternal, the infinite, and the one,"[71] Lockhart portrayed Lord Byron, for example, as a poet of the "MOPING SCHOOL" who "permitted some wounds of vanity (inflicted by base hands) to drive him out of the society for which he was born, and from the duties which his rank entailed on him," bestowing on "eternal journeyings, pistol-practicing, and gin-twist, the time which the time which might have been, with at least as much advantage to his genius, bestowed upon the proper occupations of an English landlord and legislator."⁷² This was more than a personal criticism of Lord Byron's private affairs and public notoriety. The key phrase in Lockhart's critique of Byron is "with at least as much advantage to his genius." Arguing against the Byronic model, Lockhart evoked a litany of writers from Homer and Aeschylus to his father-in-law, Sir Walter Scott, who took a "hearty part in the active business of life" as soldiers, planters, advocates, politicians, clerics, and ploughmen.⁷³ The real question for Lockhart was whether or not "these men of genius have done what they have done in spite of their situations, and would have done much better things had they been merely men of genius."⁷⁴ Like the imagined community of "Maga," the poet's occupation, as conceived of in the pages of *Blackwood's*, binds the individual talent to a received tradition of literature, the "real great Geniuses of the world," as well as to an equally inherited compact of "proper occupations," the "ordinary society and business of the world" that "blend" the poet's imaginative labor into the "common streams of life."⁷⁵

Lockhart also associated the ideal of individual Romantic "genius" with a series of adverse effects on the serious writer's work. First, there was the "genuine cruelty" of cutting the poet off from the "ordinary occupations of life as unworthy of genius," a "delusion" that leads the poet to "undervalue entirely the reception" his work may have with the general public.⁷⁶ Second, Lockhart suggested, this ideal leads to a "high contempt" for "the *vox populi*" and a "sovereign disgust for almost everything that happens, in our own particular time, to be excessively popular."⁷⁷ Popular novels, he observed, become the singular objects of "scorn."⁷⁸ It is hard to read Lockhart's special defense of the popular novel without recalling his own ambitions as a writer of popular fiction or his unwavering admiration for his famous father-in-law, Sir Walter Scott. And while Lockhart's sense of Romantic elitism seems out of step with the overt political ideologies and poetics of Hunt's circle and other popular *Blackwood's* targets, it is a keen insight into urbane posturing or "Cockney School" writers who viewed Walter Scott's popularity with disdain or suspicion. John Scott, for example, remarked that while Sir Walter Scott's "mind" presented "no obstacles, in the shape of pre-conceptions or pre-dispositions, to the free and fair development of his story and characters," his "compositions [were] not marked by particular veins of thought of language," unlike the "studiously moody" Lord Byron or "involuntarily mystical" Wordsworth."⁷⁹ Similarly, William Hazlitt remarked that Scott represented "just half of what the human intellect is capable of being," an ultimately dangerous "prophesier of things past" to whom the present and future are one "dull, hateful blank."⁸⁰ To both critics, Scott was as an example of a skilled writer who lacks *individual* genius. Critics like Hazlitt suggested that his imagination did not extend either politically or artistically—and the two were often interchangeable in "liberal" periodical reviews of

Scott's work—beyond a remarkable skill at mimesis. His writings "all pass as more or less lucky seizures of the actual lineaments of nature," John Scott opined, but the "writer of the Scotch novels betrays nothing of himself."[81]

If a radical political aesthetic of Romantic transcendence led prominent early nineteenth-century reviewers to brand Scott as an example of "degraded" genius, and one that "did not project itself beyond this into the world unknown," then Scott's historical imagination, which "receive[d] and treasure[d] up every thing brought to it by tradition or custom," made him an equally exemplary writer for the *Blackwood's* circle.[82] The very characteristics that made Scott suspicious to liberal writers of Hunt's circle—his transparency as a literary "personality," his use of personae and anonymity, and, most of all, his tendency in the *Waverley* novels to subordinate individual imagination to a received framework of Hogg's "curious traditionary facts"—embodied Lockhart's ideal of a writer who was concerned with "proper occupations" as much as literary ones, and one willing to take his own "hearty part in the active business of life."[83] Like the "schoolboys" who bound the endless discourse of their *Blackwood's* personae to the fetters of a common literary and social fiction called the "Maga"—or, for that matter, the "Ettrick Shepherd's" characters in the *Confessions*—Scott's novel cycles displayed an author "lost in the idea of the characters which he represents."[84] But if Scott, the writer, was somehow emptied out by his own fictions—a name used to mark a particular mode of cultural recording and transmission—he nonetheless remained a Romantic figure to *Blackwood's*. As Hazlitt keenly observed, Scott's ethos of "tradition and custom" was a weight of "romantic association," if not necessarily the kind of individuated Romantic inspiration enunciated by writers like Hunt, Shelley, or Keats.[85] To the *Blackwood's* writers, the "author of *Waverly*," like "Maga," embodied an idea of "the world" of politics, commerce, and history. But to writers like Lockhart and Wilson, that "world," whether called "Maga" or "Scott," served the one truly sublime, transcendent, and corporate self, one that imagines and invents, displacing as "genius" whatever individual writer happened to be "entrusted wi' sic an ingine" at any given moment.

BURKE, SCOTT, AND "TRADITIONARY" GENIUS: GESTURING TOWARD THE IMPERIAL RHETORICAL SITUATION

This same world of "traditionary" sensibilities was also the measure of a given writer's unique "genius" in *Blackwood's*. If "Scott" marked a poetic mode of subordinating Romantic "fancy" to the "traditionary" imagination—individual declarations of selfhood to the roles played in pursuit of one's "proper occupations," the "blank" future to the common past, and the private impulses of inspiration to the inherited associations of the "vox populi"—

then the inextricably literary and political "personality" of Edmund Burke served as *Blackwood's*'s template for redefining "genius" within tradition as a particular aptitude for negotiating and giving voice to Hazlitt's web of "romantic association[s]."[86] As such, the *Blackwood's* figure of Burke was a striking counterpoint to the conflation made by Hunt and others between the "reclining poet topos," a lyrical stance assumed by a poem's speaker, and the position assumed by the poet himself with respect to the political and social affairs of the "world." In an 1825 review of James Prior's *Memoir of the Life and Character of the Right Honourable Edmund Burke* (1824), *Blackwood's*'s chief political essayist of the decade, the impoverished and largely self-educated David Robinson who wrote under the pseudonym "Y. Y. Y.," characterized Burke as a uniquely transformational figure in British political culture. "Perhaps the empire stands more deeply indebted to Burke," he remarked, "looking at what it has been preserved from, at what it has been preserved to, and what it has been obtained, than to any other individual—perhaps no other individual ever equaled him in great and extraordinary achievements, accomplished by mere force of intellect."[87]

Robinson made it clear that, rather than an aptitude for "martial victories," a "splendid series of ministerial labours," or "scarcely any of the things which generally give shape and perpetuity to the highest kind of fame," Burke's peculiar genius was an essentially poetic one.[88] His speeches and political writings were "compositions . . . inimitable in literary beauty, and this, if they had possessed no other recommendation, ought to have obtained for them constant perusal and powerful influence."[89] Burke's less admiring critics, of course, would have agreed with this characterization of him as a literary stylist. Mary Wollstonecraft, for example, famously attacked the "desultory writer" and his predilection for following his own poetic "fancy" in the place of any "grand [ideological] principles."[90] Similarly, Hazlitt's description of Burke's literary style echoed Lockhart's insight about a distrust of popular prose writers. Burke, Hazlitt remarked, was one of the "most poetical of prose writers," but he was not a poet, for he "always aims at overpowering rather than pleasing; and consequently sacrifices beauty and grandeur to force and vividness."[91] There are shades of Hazlitt's critique of Scott in this. Both Burke and Scott, equally the objects of *Blackwood's* praise and liberal distrust, trumped "beauty" and other "pleasing" projections of the imagination with the "overpowering" rhetoric of vividness, descriptive minutiae, violence, and the familiar that drew the reader's sense of the present into an inextricable relationship with the problem of the history. Thus, for the poet Richard Cumberland, Burke's skill was not merely "retrospection" but the ability to convert the civic poetics of the classical world into a living British vernacular.[92] For Sir Samuel Egerton Brydges, whose recollections occasioned Lockhart's critique of Romantic "genius," Burke was, like Addison, "Cowley the poet," and Walter Scott's "Glorious John" Dryden, a master of what Auden would later call the broad "middle style" of English speech.[93]

In *Blackwood's*, though, Burke was not simply an inheritor of a tradition, literary or otherwise. "The grave," Robinson remarked, "has made him a wonderful prophet."[94] There was little about the *Blackwood's* prophet-poet that aligned the magazine's notions of "literary beauty" with, for example, the urbane pastoral poses of Hunt's circle. If anything, the "undead" poet Burke was closer to the Byronic archetype of individual genius, with its undertones of brooding secrecy, forbidden knowledge, and imminent violence. Like Byron, the *Blackwood's* Burke was "mad, bad, and dangerous to know," for "though his ashes slumber in the tomb, his voice is still heard to confound" his enemies, and "his spirit still walks the earth to scatter their dogmas and schemes to the winds, and to hold them up to the derision of mankind."[95] This Gothic figuration—a creature that belonged to *Blackwood's* horror fiction as much as to its reviews—inherited a very particular mode of Burkean rhetoric. Robinson wanted the enraged Burke of the 1790s, full of hyperbolic, proto-Byronic fury in works like *Letters on a Regicide Peace*, wherein the epistolary speaker asks to "die with my pen in my hand and . . . mark out the dreadful consequences of receiving an arrangement of Empire dictated by the despotism of Regicide."[96] *Blackwood's* wanted the Senecan apocalypse of *Letter to a Noble Lord*, where Burke's "Prophetic dead," drawn from their doomed repose by the sorceries of "revolutionists," utter wild predictions of "disastrous fate."[97]

By the time of the *Letter to a Noble Lord*, the imagined political world of *Regicide Peace* has only grown more surreal; it is, in effect, a kind of posthistorical nightmare, no less than Byron's "Darkness" (1816) or Mary Shelley's gloomy historical novel, *The Last Man* (1826), which contemporary readers recognized as a "sort of detailed and prose copy of Byron's terrible painting of darkness."[98] Despite its own interest promoting literature of the supernatural, the "dark," and the apocalyptic, *Blackwood's* took a particular dislike to the "huge unmixed nonsense under which the poor ill-used Last Man has been buried," singling Shelley's work out as an "abortion," and dismissing Byron's poem as a "mere daub."[99] In part, this is surely due to the distinctly radical tenor of "Last Man" works at a time when, from *Blackwood's* Tory vantage point, history had already taken its apocalyptic turn at the end of the eighteenth century. *Blackwood's* had already chosen its own "Last Man," Edmund Burke, and, in good gothic fashion, it was sufficient to leave him among the noisy "Prophetic dead." It is surprising to see Byron's work simply dismissed in *Blackwood's* as a "mere daub," but the inescapable solipsism of the poem, touched on by Walter Scott's review in the *Quarterly*, emphasized the qualities of Byron's genius that were most antithetical to the ideal of authorship promoted by *Blackwood's*. Insofar as Byron's "Darkness" transformed the world into a metonym for his own "irritable feelings," it also privileged a kind of radical autonomy for its speaker that sought to unseat the already "Prophetic" voice of tradition and continuity in *Blackwood's*.[100]

In *Noble Lord*, the political economy of Europe has already self-annihilated. The famous argument of the *Reflections*, that the "age of chivalry is gone," succeeded by "sophisters, economists, and calculators," is already a decided and irrevocable anterior event in the text.[101] Thus in *Lord*, the "national menagerie" replaces parliaments, and reformers have become wild "hyenas to prey upon the carcasses" and "unplumb the dead."[102] And with the winding-down of history in Burke's late writings, there is also a decided shift in the stance of the speaker who moves from an awareness of his own impending death in *Regicide Peace* to a sense that death is immediately upon him in *Lord*, or, stranger still, has already effectively occurred beforehand. "Are they apprehensive," asks the Burke of *Lord*, "that if even an atom of me remains, the sect has something to fear? Must I be annihilated, lest, like old John Zisca's, my skin might be made into a drum to animate Europe to eternal battle?"[103] This is a ghost's question or the question of a "last man," directed toward an inhuman posterity. Like the lyric speaker of Byron's "Darkness"—or, for that matter, the narrating protagonist of Hogg's *Memoirs*—the Burke of the *Letter to a Noble Lord* utters his judgments in the fevered pitch of a "dream, that was not a dream."[104] But a work like Hogg's is fundamentally antiquarian; its confessional gothic centerpiece is always held at arm's length as a suspect narrative that the editor and his friends may or may not be able to correlate with the existent mass of "traditionary" knowledge. And for the doomed Byronic speaker who alone sees the world run "seasonless, herbless, treeless, manless, lifeless," until it has become a "lump of death," the power of visionary speech only heightens the certitude of his own impotence and the crushing transcendence of the annihilating "Universe."[105]

In the *Letter to a Noble Lord*, Burke modeled a different relationship between the confessional human consciousness and an antagonistic historical world. Unlike the Byronic speaker, his "Prophetic dead" have the power to reformulate the hideous landscape of the "wonderful" present.[106] For both speakers, the common past of a human order in dramatic, rapid decline has become the exclusive psychological terrain of the solitary rhetorical consciousness. But the terror of Byron's dream of oblivion is a decidedly lyric terror, a deep violence done to the "reclining poet topos," and, by extension, to lyric poetry's particular enactment of the idea of the poet's individual "genius." By the poem's end, "Darkness" has "no need of aid" from natural elements; it also has no need of any elements of the poet's work. "She was," the Byronic speaker concludes, the "Universe," and one in which the dreamer's individuated "genius" is wholly annihilated. But much of what—for *Blackwood's* at least—characterizes the "striking peculiarities of [Burke's] late works, the chain of predictions, respecting some of the most momentous, novel, and complicated of human events," can be attributed to the decidedly *novelistic* quality of Burke's confessional speakers in his late works.[107] As Alison Milbank remarks, an "understanding of national developments as organic, *a la* Edmund Burke, precludes organized change," and thus a "conservative Gothic eschews an extensive symbolization of Britain as the prison that one finds in more radical writers."[108] Instead, Milbank continues, Gothicism in the pages of *Blackwood's* displayed a "new preoccupation with individual psychology."[109]

This psychological turn in Tory literary imagination allowed a political reviewer like Robinson—who was also engaged in a fictional conceit of personalities when he writes as "Y. Y. Y."—to imagine Burke as a very different kind of individual "genius" from Lockhart's Byron. By accepting the historically "prophetic" quality of Burke's highly gothic and apocalyptic rhetoric in the "late work," *Blackwood's* conceded that the reader's eschatological present is one in which "passion, convulsion, and chaos" go hand in hand with a false hope in "glorious days of gorgeous names and wonderful systems."[110] Yet because of this, Burke's confessional mode in his late works is radically unlike the dead Robert Wringham's narrative in Hogg's *Confessions*. Burke's prophetic speech does not need to be correlated to the common political affairs of the world because in the post-Revolutionary age, they are only so many "gorgeous names" and "systems." Nor is there any appeal to the "traditionary" because its final location is not to be found in the post-revolutionary world at all, but rather in the private psychology and expressive rhetoric of the ghostly literary speaker, Burke.

On the one hand, the *Blackwood's* Burke is a Gothic figure *possessed* by the "traditionary," much like Hogg's protagonist or, for that matter, "Christopher North" and his compatriots who were all presented as individual personalities driven by the voracious collective "ingine" of "Maga." At the same time, Burke's "genius," like Scott's, was seen as being like "Maga," herself. By the late Burke, the eighteenth-century logic of social sensibilities has twisted into a gothic image of the cultural "ingine" of revolution and the much distrusted "wonderful" constitution of the era, including "all its members and its organs from the very beginnings," extending "even to the constitution of the mind of man."[111] But this strange, easy, and often frightening translation between the psychological self and the communal life of others—a theme that dominated Scott's heroes in the Waverly novels, the pseudonymous dialogues of Wilson's "Noctes," Hogg's tales of hauntings and possession, as well as Robinson's Tory populism and Lockhart's critiques of Hunt and Byron—allowed the individual writer to speak in the persona of the same "world" of politics, commerce, and "traditionary" society that, for the *Blackwood's* circle, was the measure of a writer's true merit. Not surprisingly, the parlance of the *Blackwood's* circle is replete with the rhetoric of corporate identity. As Wilson's persona stated, "we have a personal existence and our name is North."[112] Scott tuned his humor to a similar key in an 1827 letter to Lockhart in which he asked whether the Royal Society of Literature had fallen in love with merely a single one of his "bad parts" or the "whole politic state of evil,"[113] distinguishing between his coherent public persona and the messier "politic state" beneath. The former was a poor copy, a "body Balaam" in *Blackwood's* terminology, while the latter, the incoherent corporate self beneath, was the real "Scott."[114]

Lockhart, for his part, "attached high values to imaginative writing, attributing at various times great power of moral suasion and philosophical insight to the productions of writers from Cicero to Scott; on the other [hand] he felt that writers should somehow be unaware of their powers."[115] Individual "genius," in other words, is proven by its transparency, just as in *Blackwood's* Burke's merit as a literary prophet was proven by the proximity of his imagined narratives to the actual course of political events as they had unfolded by the 1820s. Indeed, like Robinson's Burke, Lockhart's Scott was a writer of tremendous "power" because his novels could "make plain matter of fact infinitely brighter than all the inventions in the world could ever render a fictitious event."[116] The *Blackwood's* writers were aware of the tremendous paradox inherent in the idea of Scott, the fantasist of "plain matter of fact," as well as Burke, "who abandoned the study of the law to become an author by profession," and ended his life, nonetheless, amid the "struggle" of an "active and exalted political existence."[117] Even Burke's "political existence" takes on the poetic character of the *Blackwood's* ideal of a Romantic genius that is both radically individuated and nearly invisible as a "traditionary" cultural expression.

Robinson's analysis of Burke presents the Anglo-Irish orator as a curiously elusive "personality" who both "overthrew the Toryism of the day, and harmonized Whiggism with the reason, right feeling, and interests of the nation," and whose "creed," nonetheless, was "in several points a higher Toryism than that which now exists."[118] Burke's ideological slipperiness, which endlessly frustrated his late eighteenth- and early nineteenth-century critics, made sense in the context of *Blackwood's*'s similarly poetic and contradictory Toryism, where "creeds are but words, the meaning of which men change at pleasure; they are the tools of men, but not the guides."[119] To the *Blackwood's* circle of the early nineteenth century, Burke's idiosyncratic character lent him a kind of "subversive Scottishness" all his own. As Ian Duncan remarks, Scottish Romanticism—of which *Blackwood's* was undoubtedly a chief "ingine"—"condenses the problematic of evolutionary discontinuity and cultural disintegration" into the "aesthetic salvage of tradition."[120] In Duncan's assessment, the "Romantic ideology of national culture" salved the tendency of early nineteenth-century writers to imagine Scottish history—and British modernity—as a "series of disjunctions and dismemberments (the Reformation, the Acts of Union)."[121] It promised the "eternal recurrence of a spiritual unity that wipes out the divisions between past and present (as well as contemporary social divisions) even in its reiteration of the figures of historical loss."[122]

On closer inspection, though, it is clear that for writers like Lockhart, Wilson, and Robinson, the idea of an inherited national culture was never simply an ideal of union, stability, or coherence. To the *Blackwood's* circle, the "traditionary" was fundamentally multivocal. As a mode of historiography, it exerted, like Hogg's several speakers and editors in the *Memoirs*, highly *tentative* claims about the past and its relationship to the present. Insofar as the "traditionary" imagination of *Blackwood's* tended toward the "reiteration of the figures of historical loss," those figures never argued exclusively for a "spiritual unity." Robinson's "prophetic" Burke, for example, presented in *Blackwood's* as the quintessential political figure of "historical loss," radically *emphasized* the "divisions between past and present." The "spiritual unity" suggested by Burke as kind of medium of the "traditionary" mode veers toward the apocalyptic, the necromantic, and the supernatural. Unlike Byron's apocalyptic speaker in "Darkness," there is nothing elegiac about Robinson's evocation of Burke; the Burke of *Blackwood's* did not so much lament the loss of the past as use it to commit violence against the ideological metropolitanism of the present. The "prophetic" function of this figure was fundamentally synched, then, to the purpose of the *Blackwood's* personae. As a political specter, these "traditionary" figures sought to shatter rational Whig ideas about the progress of history into thousands of pieces that could only be understood through recourse to the past. As poetic identities, they attempted to dismember the Romantic lyric speaker, who served, as often as not, as a metonym for an idea of the poet as a kind of uniquely privileged "personality" and individual genius.

But although the heterogeneity of the *Blackwood's* "traditionary" stood largely at odds with the more universalizing ideologies of Whig History, as well as with the ethos of progressive literary circles like Hunt's, it articulated a nascent model of "Greater Britain" that was perhaps far more in line with how the "service classes" of the British Empire experienced their own relationship to the metropole. A few months before the Retreat from Kabul, for example, *Blackwood's* drew a sharp distinction between trajectories in national politics and imperial practice. In an essay titled "The World of London," *Blackwood's* remarked that "the grand distinction between the world of London and the world of the provinces is one of extreme indifference, wherewith in the former objects of particular indifference are regarded."[123] At first glance, "The World of London" seems to echo standard *Blackwood's* antimetropolitan rhetoric from the 1810s–1820s. By the 1840s, however, the "world of the provinces" increasingly had a double meaning for *Blackwood's* contributors and their reading audiences, eliding the "traditionary" landscapes of Scotland or Ireland that dominated the sensibilities of Maga's early years with more distant Imperial ones, such as India and Afghanistan. In consequence, treatments of London in *Blackwood's* began to seem more like Addison's "Great Exchange"—emphasizing Whitehall and the City of London—and less like the Whiggish national metropole satirized in the "Cockney School" attacks.

As the author of "The World of London" remarked, in "the *city* alone has the public opinion of London any weight of authority—and the opinion of the city of London has materially influenced, and continues to influence, the public opinion of the empire."[124] In effect, London as administrative center brokered "Britishness" between Britain and the Empire, representing each to the other. Moreover, the *Blackwood's* "London" of 1841 represented a complete world-system in microcosm, one that aligned it both with Maga's early editorial principles and Burke's formula of "mediatorial" empire. On the one hand, *Blackwood's* suggested that the Imperial center "took its tone and character from a thousand clashing and conflicting interests; extreme ends of the town represent[ing] extreme opinions, ever changing their extremes," much like the journal—or the Empire—itself.[125] At the same time, it was an impersonal "ingine," a "mighty motive power" that remained "permanent, revolving steadily in a moderate but decided course."[126] Although *Blackwood's* had marked its emergence in Romantic literary culture with a rejection of metropolitan London, by the early Victorian period, it began to mirror the cultural drift of Imperial audiences by imaginatively remaking London and "Britishness" after its own image. And while we do not know what issue of *Blackwood's* from 1841 Major Brydon brought to Jalalabad, bloodstained and stuffed into his hat, on 13 January 1842, it was undoubtedly one that reflected both Britain and British culture as a mirror of the Empire's "public opinion." It was also one that increasingly "took its tone and character from a thousand clashing and conflicting" stories such as his, just as much as he took his sense of Britain from *Blackwood's*.

NOTES

1. For contemporary accounts, see, among numerous others, John William Kaye, *History of the War in Afghanistan* (London: Richard Bentley, 1851); Vincent Eyre, *The Military Operations at Cabul, Which Ended in the Destruction of the British Army, January 1842. With a Journal of Imprisonment in Afghanistan* (London: John Murray, 1843); Charles Nash, ed., *History of the War in Affghanistan, from the Commencement to Its Close; from the Journals and Letters of an Officer High in Rank* (London: Brooks, 1843).

2. Julius Brockman Backhouse, "Journal Kept at the Headquarters of the Artillery Brigade of the Army of the Indus," a manuscript diary in the possession of William Trousdale, who quotes it in "Dr. Brydon's Report of the Kabul Disaster and the Documentation of History," *Military Affairs* 47, 1 (1983): 27.

3. Anonymous, "Miscellany: An Adventurous Life" [obituary], *The Medical Times and Register: A Weekly Journal of Medical and Surgical Science* 3 (Philadelphia: J. B. Lippincott, 1873), 574.

4. George Orwell, "Rudyard Kipling," in George Packer, ed., *All Art Is Propaganda: Critical Essays* (New York: Houghton Mifflin Harcourt, 2009), 182.

5. See Thaddeus Holt, "you have been in Afghanistan, I perceive," *Military History Quarterly* 6, 2 (1988): 32–38; see also Ian Gordon Brown, "Conan Doyle, Blackwood's and Two Afghan Disasters," https://www.nls.uk/about-us/publications/discover/2009/conan-doyle.

6. J. J. Bailey, letter to William Simpson, 29 December 1878, Special Collections, Uncategorized, Anne S. K. Brown Military Collection, Brown University, RI.

7. Matthew Arnold, "The Function of Criticism in the Present Time," *Essays in Criticism* (London: Macmillan, 1865): 19.

8. Arnold, "Function of Criticism," 19.

9. Arnold, "Function of Criticism," 19–20.

10. John Hayden, *The Romantic Reviewers: 1802–1824* (London: Routledge, 1969), 258. Of course, the legacy of *Blackwood's Magazine*'s early years did not escape Arnold's notice altogether. In *The English Poets* (1880), even the dispassionate Arnold finds himself "tempted to speak even as Blackwood or the Quarterly were in the old days wont to speak" about John Keats. His own ad hominem criticism of the Romantics, wherein "Keats's love-letter is the love-letter of a surgeon's apprentice," goes farther in some ways than John Gibson Lockhart's satirical attacks on Keats, Hunt, and the "Cockney School" of poetry in the early issues of *Blackwood's*.

11. Peter T. Murphy, "Impersonation and Authorship in Romantic Britain," *ELH* 59, 3 (1992): 625.

12. Richard Cronin, *Paper Pellets: British Literary Culture after Waterloo* (Oxford: Oxford University Press, 2010), 11.

13. David Higgins, "*Blackwood's Edinburgh Magazine* and the Construction of Wordsworth's Genius," in Kim Wheatley, ed., *Romantic Periodicals and Print Culture* (London: Frank Cass, 2003), 124.

14. "Noctes Ambrosianae. No. XL," *Blackwood's Edinburgh Magazine* 24 (December 1828): 696.

15. Walter Scott, letter to Lady Abercorn, 31 December 1809, in David Douglas, ed., *Familiar Letters of Walter Scott*, vol. 1 (Boston: Houghton Mifflin, 1894), 157.

16. "Strictures on Whewell's Inductive Sciences," *Colburn's United Service Magazine and Naval and Military Journal* (London: H. Hurst, 1847), 380

17. Daniel Sanjiv Roberts, "Mediating Indian Letters in an Age of Empire: *Blackwood's* and Orientalism, in Robert Morrison, ed., *Romanticism and Blackwood's Magazine: "An Unprecedented Phenomenon"* (New York: Palgrave MacMillan, 2013), 255.

18. Robert Morrison, "'To Abuse Wickedness but Acknowledge Wit': 'Blackwood's' and the Shelley Circle," *Victorian Periodicals Review* 34, 2 (2001): 161.

19. James Grahame and Macvey Napier, *Hypocrisy Unveiled and Calumny Detected: in a Review of Blackwood's Magazine* (Edinburgh: Francis Pillans, 1818), 1, 8.

20. Alan Lang Strout, "Hunt, Hazlitt, and *Maga*: I. Leigh Hunt and *Maga*: The Lighter Side of 'Cockney'-Killing," *ELH* 4, 2 (1937): 152.

21. Strout, "Hunt," 151.

22. William Maginn, Letter to William Blackwood, July 30, 1822. In Margaret Oliphant, ed., *William Blackwood and His Sons: Their Magazine and Friends*, vol. 1 (Edinburgh: Blackwood, 1897), 397.

23. Oliphant, *William Blackwood*, 397.

24. [Lord] Byron, letter to Walter Scott, January 27, 1822. In George Gordon, Lord Byron, *Letters and Journals*, vol. 6 of Rowland Edmund Prothero, ed., *The Works of Lord Byron* (London: John Murray, 1901), 5.

25. Arnold, "The Function of Criticism," 9.

26. Arnold, "The Function of Criticism," 9.

27. Arnold, "The Function of Criticism," 13–14.

28. Arnold, "The Function of Criticism," 14.

29. Higgins, *Romantic Genius and the Literary Magazine: Biography, Celebrity, Politics* (New York: Routledge, 2005), 12.

30. Higgins, *Romantic Genius*, 12.

31. Jeffrey N. Cox, *Poetry and Politics in the Cockney School: Keats, Shelley, Hunt and Their Circle* (Cambridge: Cambridge University Press, 2004), 19.
32. Cox, *Poetry and Politics*, 20.
33. David Reiman, *The Romantics Reviewed: Contemporary Reviews of British Romantic Writers* (New York: Garland, 1972), 47.
34. Kim Wheatley, "The Blackwood's Attacks on Leigh Hunt," *Nineteenth-Century Literature* 47, 1 (1992): 2.
35. Wheatley, "Blackwood's Attacks," 5–6.
36. Wheatley, "Blackwood's Attacks," 6.
37. Wheatley, "Blackwood's Attacks," 5–6.
38. Murphy, "Impersonation," 625.
39. Morrison, "To Abuse Wickedness," 147.
40. [John Wilson], "Reformers and Anti-Reformers—A Word to the Wise from Old Christopher," *Blackwood's Edinburgh Magazine* 29 (May 1831): 723.
41. [John Wilson], "Extracts from Gosschen's Diary," *Blackwood's Edinburgh Magazine* 3 (August 1818): 597.
42. John Gibson Lockhart, "The Lord Advocate on Reform," *Blackwood's Edinburgh Magazine* 29 (June 1831): 981.
43. "Noctes Ambrosianae. No. XL," 696.
44. "Noctes Ambrosianae. No. XL," 696.
45. J. H. Alexander, "Hogg in the Noctes Ambrosianae," *Studies in Hogg and His World* 4 (1993), 45.
46. J. H. Alexander, "Literary Criticism in the Later 'Noctes Ambrosianae,'" *Yearbook of English Studies* 16 (1986), 17.
47. Alan Lang Strout, "Purple Patches in the *Noctes Ambrosianae*," *ELH* 2, 4 (1935): 327.
48. "Noctes Ambrosianae. No. XLVII," *Blackwood's Edinburgh Magazine* 26 (December 1829): 861.
49. "Noctes Ambrosianae. No. XXXII," *Blackwood's Edinburgh Magazine* 21 (April 1827): 489.
50. [John Wilson], "An Hour's Tete-a-Tete with the Public," *Blackwood's Edinburgh Magazine* 8 (October 1820): 99.
51. Murphy, "Impersonation," 639.
52. [John Wilson], "Tete-a-Tete," 99.
53. [John Gibson Lockhart], *Peter's Letters to His Kinfolk* (Edinburgh: William Blackwood, 1819): 135.
54. [Lockhart], *Peter's Letters*, 135.
55. Charles Snodgrass, "Blackwood's Subversive Scottishness," in David Finkelstein, ed., *Print Culture and the Blackwood Tradition, 1805–1930* (Toronto: University of Toronto Press, 2006), 90–119.
56. John Scott, "Blackwood's Magazine," *London Magazine* 9 (November 1820): 511–514.
57. John Galt, Letter to William Blackwood, May 1, 1820, Publishing Papers, E, MS 4005, fol. 82. In P. D. Garside, ed., *British Fiction, 1800–1829: A Database of Production, Circulation & Reception*. http://www.british-fiction.cf.au.uk.
58. Galt, Letter to Blackwood.
59. James Hogg, *The Private Memoirs and Confessions of a Justified Sinner: Written by Himself: With a detail of curious traditionary facts and other evidences by the editor*. Ed. John Carey (Oxford: Oxford University Press, 1999), 250.
60. Hogg, *Private Memoirs*, 252.
61. Hogg, *Private Memoirs*, 252.
62. Hogg, *Private Memoirs*, 255.
63. Jerome McGann, *The Romantic Ideology: A Critical Investigation* (Chicago: University of Chicago Press, 1983), 13.
64. Tim Fulford, *Romanticism and Masculinity: Gender, Politics and Poetics in the Writings of Burke, Coleridge, Wordsworth, De Quincey and Hazlitt* (New York: St. Martin's, 1999), 9.
65. Hogg, *Memoirs*, 252.

66. John Gibson Lockhart, "More's Life of Lord Byron," *Quarterly Review* 44 (January 1831): 189–190.
67. Lockhart, "More's," 190–191.
68. Barton Swaim, "'What Is Scott?': John Gibson Lockhart's Professional Amateurism," *Victorian Periodicals Review* 39, 3 (2006): 280.
69. John Gibson Lockhart, "Sir Egerton Brydges' Recollections," *Blackwood's Edinburgh Magazine* 17 (May 1825): 506.
70. William Wordsworth, "Preface to Lyrical Ballads," *Lyrical Ballads, with Other Poems. In Two Volumes* (London: T. N. Longman, 1800), xiv.
71. Percy Bysshe Shelley, "A Defense of Poetry," in *Essays, Letters from Abroad, Translations and Fragments, by Percy Bysshe Shelley*, ed. Mary Shelley (London: Edward Moxon, 1840), 7.
72. Lockhart, "Sir Egerton Brydges," 507.
73. Lockhart, "Sir Egerton Brydges," 507.
74. Lockhart, "Sir Egerton Brydges," 507.
75. Lockhart, "Sir Egerton Brydges," 506.
76. Lockhart, "Sir Egerton Brydges," 506.
77. Lockhart, "Sir Egerton Brydges," 510.
78. Lockhart, "Sir Egerton Brydges," 510.
79. John Scott, "The Author of the Scotch Novels," *London Magazine* 1 (January 1820): 12.
80. William Hazlitt, "Sir Walter Scott," in *The Spirit of the Age; or, Contemporary Portraits* (Paris: A. and W. Galignani, 1825), 27–28.
81. Scott, "Scotch Novels," 13.
82. Hazlitt, "Sir Walter Scott," 28.
83. Lockhart, "Sir Egerton Brydges," 507.
84. Scott, "Scotch Novels," 13.
85. Hazlitt, "Sir Walter Scott," 28.
86. Hazlitt, "Sir Walter Scott," 28.
87. [David Robinson], "Life of Burke," *Blackwood's Edinburgh Magazine* 17 (January 1825): 1.
88. Robinson, "Life of Burke," 1.
89. Robinson, "Life of Burke," 1.
90. Mary Wollstonecraft, *A Vindication of the Rights of Men, in a Letter to the Right Honourable Edmund Burke; Occasioned by His Reflections on the Revolution in France* (London: J. Johnson, 1790), iv.
91. William Hazlitt, "Character of Mr. Burke," in *Political Essays, with Sketches of Public Characters* (London: William Hone, 1819), 269.
92. Richard Cumberland, *Retrospection: A Poem in Familiar Verse* (London: W. Bulmer, 1811), 31–36.
93. Samuel Egerton Brydges, *Censura Literaria: Containing Titles, Abstracts, and Opinions of Old English Books: With Original Disquisitions, Articles of Biography* (London: Longman, Hurst, Rees, and Orme, 1808), 94–95.
94. [Robinson], "Life of Burke," 2.
95. [Robinson], "Life of Burke," 2.
96. Edmund Burke, *Letters on a Regicide Peace; Letter Four, to the Earl Fitzwilliam, in vol. 6 of The Works of the Right Honourable Edmund Burke* (London: F. C. and J. Rivington, 1812), 23–24.
97. Burke, *A Letter from the Right Honourable Edmund Burke to a Noble Lord, on the Attacks Made upon Him and his Pension, in the House of Lords, by the Duke of Bedford and the Earl of Lauderdale, Early in the Present Sessions of Parliament* (London: J. Owen, 1796), 5.
98. Anonymous, "The Last Man," *The Knickerbocker: Or, New-York Monthly Magazine* 2 (1833), 315.
99. Anonymous, "Hood's Whims and Oddities," *Blackwood's Edinburgh Magazine* 21 (January 1827): 54.

100. Sir Walter Scott, "Review of Childe Harold's Pilgrimage and The Prisoner of Chillon," The Quarterly Review 16 (October 1816), 172–208.
101. Burke, *Reflections*, 113.
102. Burke, *Noble Lord*, 4–5.
103. Burke, *Noble Lord*, 3.
104. George Gordon, Lord Byron, "Darkness," *The Prisoner of Chillon, and Other Poems* (London: John Murray, 1816), 27.
105. Byron, "Darkness," 30–31.
106. Burke, *Noble Lord*, 5.
107. [Robinson], "Life of Burke," 1.
108. Milbank, "The Victorian Gothic," 150.
109. Milbank, "The Victorian Gothic," 150.
110. [Robinson], "Life of Burke," 8.
111. Burke, *Noble Lord*, 4.
112. Wilson, "Tete-a-Tete," 99.
113. Walter Scott, Letter to John Gibson Lockhart, April 5, 1826, in Andrew Lang, *The Life and Letters of John Gibson Lockhart* (London: C. Nimmo, 1897), 2:14.
114. Scott, Letter to Lockhart, 2:14.
115. Swaim, "'What Is Scott?'" 280.
116. John Gibson Lockhart, Letter to Christie, December 22, 1816, in Lang, *Life and Letters,* 1:116.
117. [Robinson], "Life of Burke," 7.
118. [Robinson], "Life of Burke," 14.
119. [Robinson], "Life of Burke," 12.
120. Ian Duncan, *Scott's Shadow: The Novel in Romantic Edinburgh* (Princeton: Princeton University Press, 2007), 186–187.
121. Duncan, *Scott's Shadow*, 186.
122. Duncan, *Scott's Shadow*, 186.
123. "The World of London. Part V," *Blackwood's Edinburgh Magazine* 50 (September 1841): 528.
124. "The World of London," 528.
125. "The World of London," 528.
126. "The World of London," 528.

Chapter Seven

Coda

"And to show us your books": Kipling's Peachey Taliaferro Carnehan as "Romance-Monger" and Reader

In his 1840 lecture, "The Hero as Poet," Thomas Carlyle concluded that the "Indian Empire will go, at any rate, someday; but this Shakespeare does not go, he lasts forever with us."[1] As Jyostna Singh remarks, Carlyle thus "acknowledges the temporary, even arbitrary, political power of the rulers, but nevertheless promotes their cultural authority by universalizing the bard's popularity."[2] For nineteenth-century readers, this imagined "universalization" of Anglophone "high culture" was perhaps metonymic for mythologies of the nation state as "true" commonwealth, a buttress against the experiential arbitrariness of political enfranchisement at home and imperial dissonances abroad. Elizabeth Samet, for example, remarks that the nineteenth-century "citizen-soldier" found such literary paragons helpful insofar as he "found himself compelled to negotiate a dual identity as he acquired a political consciousness."[3] This may have been the case in some circumstances, such as the mythologizing of "the Union" during the American Civil War, and for some populations—British or American military officers, for example, for whom the "literary" served as a white-gloved class marker—but the "administrators, soldiers, and engineers whose praises [Kipling] sings" seem to have had relatively little interest in the "universal" value of writers like the Bard.[4] It is true that commentators on Indian affairs used plays like *Macbeth*, "so steeped in blood," as analogies for depicting the "sadomasochistic psychological and social logic" of "suffering imperialists" to metropolitans, but there was little sense of high culture's role in "war's 'rhetorical stakes' . . . [or] important linguistic or thematic correspondences" waiting to be mined.[5] To a great degree, this is because the "imperial" political consciousness was not in the process of being "acquired" in the mid-nineteenth century, at least not by those involved in the regular production and administration of imperium, which lacked the citizen-soldier's nationalistic *agon* that Samet describes.

Kipling's "The Man Who Would Be King," which serves as a "small compendium of his most characteristic concerns" about culture,[6] and an imaginative "recapitulate[ion] the [entire] British conquest" in microcosm,"[7] is nothing if not a sketch of a kind of alternate political consciousness, one that is effectively posthistorical in the nineteenth-century sense of the "citizen-soldier," for instead of attempting to negotiate tensions between political arbitrariness and literary-cultural "universality," it understands both as precedent for radical self-definition between these two givens. In this sense, Kipling's tale forms an extended commentary on what *Blackwood's* called the art of "personation," that "took its tone and character from a thousand clashing and conflicting" examples at hand for Daniel Dravot and Peachey Taliaferro Carnehan, whether historical, fictional, or quasi-fictional. What distinguishes the wildly irresponsible schemes of Kipling's antiheroes is their peculiar historiographical focus, beginning with their rise as self-made conquerors like their hero, Robert Clive, and concluding with the would-be kings' own violent defeat in an analogue to the Indian Mutiny of 1857. It is important to recognize that the self-imposed cultural exile of Carnehan and Dravot is ultimately a *voluntary* recursion into the "primordial" history of the British Raj. But how are the "worst muckers" of the 1880s, Dravot and Carnehan, able to imagine themselves as part of a pre-1857 historical milieu in the first place? Not by reading the nineteenth-century Canon of what "does not go." But despite E. M. Forster's doubts as to whether Kipling's "strong silent men," all "putty, brass and paint," are really capable of "feel[ing] anything at all,"[8] and George Orwell's middle-class conviction that Kipling's real-life models were univocally "tawdry and shallow,"[9] Kipling's would-be kings are sophisticated storytellers and highly imaginative readers, as well as killers and tramps. Their temporary military conquest and subsequent political failure in Kafiristan align the story that Peachey eventually returns to tell with popular accounts of soldiers, spies, and adventurers who were active during the rise of what Kipling retrospectively called "the Great Game" of the 1830s–1850s.[10] Moreover, Kipling's sense of the interconnection between the stories that Peachey and Daniel have read, their plans of action, and Carnehan's role as narrator recapitulates the Romantic literary practice of true-life "romance-mongering," one in which active producers of the British Empire articulated both the personal licensure and historical liabilities of conquest.

"THINK US A LITTLE MORE MAD": READING PEACHEY'S "PERSONATION"

How do Carnehan and Dravot come to entertain the idea of conquering Kafiristan? During the Second Anglo-Afghan War (1878–1881), they "there with Robert's Army" at least as far as the mountain passes at Jagdalak, a landscape haunted by the desperate stand of the British retreat column in 1842.[11] Daniel and Peachey may have learned of Kafiristan during their Afghan War service, but it is just as likely that they read about their destination. They consciously model their imperialist scheme on accounts of the life of James Brooke, the EIC soldier, sailor, and failed businessman who became an independent monarch in Malay Archipelago by 1842. By 1850, extracts from Brooke's letters and journals circulated widely throughout the British Empire, and subsequently provided the inspiration for Charles Kingsley's 1855 pirate novel, *Westward Ho!*,[12] but accounts of similar adventures in India and Afghanistan circulated with equal profligacy by midcentury. The American-born Quaker, Josiah Harlan, had worked throughout the 1820s as an EIC surgeon and mercenary soldier in the Punjab before Maharaja Ranjit Singh installed him as the governor of two border provinces in 1829. By the start of the First Afghan War, Harlan had subverted the Afghan dynasty of Mohammad Reffee Beg Hazara, assuming the hereditary title, "Prince of Ghor."[13] Harlan's adventure was widely known in EIC circles, partly from firsthand encounters with the Prince, but mostly through the publication of his *Memoir of India and Afghanistan* (1842), which caused an international sensation. In 1853, the *Journal of the Asiatic Society of Bengal* published even more remarkable extracts from the journals of Alexander Gardner, an American or Irishman of improbable background who styled himself "Gordana Khan."[14] A likely source for Kipling's physical descriptions of the would-be kings, the immense, thick-bearded Gardner seemed to exist wholly in a borderland between romance and reality. By the time he received a commission as Ranjit Singh's Commandant of Artillery in 1831, he had already spent thirteen years as a mercenary, prisoner, outlaw, spy, and vagabond, travelling through Astrakan, Afghanistan, Badakhshan, Shignan, Yarkan, and the Kokcha, accumulating fourteen wounds, subsisting on salt and raw hyena, and keeping his often-incomprehensible journal tied around his neck in a copy of the Koran.[15] To readers "who [had] in them the divine spark of enterprise," Gardner's editor remarked, his journals were not "without a suggestion and a lesson."[16] To Daniel and Peachey, Gardner's account of traveling through Kafiristan in "successful disguise" and encountering obliging holy men and "ample stores of everything" would have provided a template for their own ambitions; Gardner's description of the death of Europeans "under the supposition that they were evil spirits" ought to have provided a warning.[17]

Because the erstwhile kings introduce themselves as "boiler-fitters, engine-drivers, petty contractors, and all that,"[18] Kipling's audiences often tend to overlook the fact that Peachey and Daniel are voracious readers. Indeed, this is most likely an extension of the fact that most of *their* present-day readers tend to view Peachey and Daniel's destination, Kafiristan, through the lens of literary and/or political allegory. As Edward Marx notes, "many current 'postcolonialist' readings [of the tale] tend to continue or replicate New Critical separation between text and context," ignoring the fact it is "Kipling's evident intention [as well as Dravot and Carnehan's] to leave a careful paper trail [to Kafiristan] traceable by any schoolchild with access to the Encyclopaedia Britannica."[19] For their part, the two rough-and-tumble imperialists are aware of how strange their own literacy, which encompasses a wide range of historical, religious, political, and professional literatures, must seem. But their apparent discontinuity suggests more about how Kipling's readers, then and now, perceive class, than it does about whether the tale's portrayal of imaginative pragmatists is a viable one.

When they arrive unannounced at the Narrator's office, for example, to solemnize their "Contrack" and raid his library, they inform him that they "would be more pleased" if he could "think [them] a little more mad."[20] As Dravot explains. "We have come to you to know about this country, to read a book about it, and to be shown maps. We want you to tell us that we are fools and to show us your books."[21] Some of the Narrator's books—studies produced by the United Services Institution, George Henry Raverty's *Notes of Afghanistan and Baluchistan* and Walter Henry Bellew's *Our Punjab Frontier*—are indicative of the type of sources which "had become crucial for planning military campaigns in lesser-known places like Kafiristan" by the 1880s.[22] Others such as John Wood's 1841 narrative, *Sources of Oxus*, contextualize the technical information contained in these kinds of works within the earlier political—and literary—culture of the Conolly era. Ultimately, Dravot and Carnehan want certain kinds of books: accounts by other adventurers, soldiers, intelligence agents, provocateurs. Like the British Imperial audiences cultivated by *Blackwood's* and the soldier-romance-mongers, they want to read books by men like themselves. Kipling's tale as a whole thus acts as a coda to geopolitical shifts in midcentury romancing, projecting the narrative logic of late Company-Era historical fiction, memoirs, anecdotal campaign histories, and hybrid travelogues against the incongruous social background of the Raj.

By the 1830s, a surprising number of Britain's bright young men devoted themselves to speculative political adventurism in Central Asia, casting themselves as spies, military advisors, intercultural brokers, and kingmakers in a dangerous game of imperial influence that played out across the bramble of failed states between Russia, the British East India Company (EIC), and Qajar Persia.[23] Men like the Sandhurst-educated Charles Stoddart, an Anglo-

Irish soldier "distinguished alike for his talent, character and enterprise,"[24] and the Irish intelligence agent, traveler, and writer Arthur Conolly (who often traveled incognito under the name "Khan Ali") were popular figures in British circles both at home and abroad, yoking the Orientalized appeal of Lord Byron's romances to the "new" imperialism's progressive ethos of "play[ing] the part that the first Christian nation of the world ought to fill."[25] At the same time, Company agents like Stoddart and Conolly operated entirely within older mercantilist imperial systems that were based on patronage, diplomatic pragmatism, and—whenever possible—an unapologetic "the nakedness of the sword."[26] Stoddart, for example, was a career soldier from a family of career soldiers, and moved from staff positions at the United Services Institution to influential diplomatic posts abroad under the patronage of Sir Henry Ellis, Sir John McNeill, and others. Conolly's family of professional empire-builders included two brothers abroad as well as the calculating Sir William Macnaghten, Secretary of the EIC's Secret and Political Department, whose aggressive pursuit of regime change in Kabul aggravated the severity of Britain's debacle during the First Anglo-Afghan War (1839–1842).[27]

As a traveler and sometimes-anthropologist, Conolly was fascinated by the idea of play—the "great game[s]" of "unsophisticated children of nature" who ran about "in glee like so many imps, screaming and flinging dust on each other," the sociable division of "the price of a dead horse" over a game of chess near Khiva[28]—and he famously extended this sense of gamesmanship to the idea of a "finer order of things for every party involved" in Central Asian affairs, a "grand game" which would satisfy Russia, get the Czar to "shake hands with Persia," secure India, and keep the "man-stealers and savages" from the border tribes and khanates "in wholesome check."[29] None of Conolly's plans prospered. By 1843, when Joseph Wolff, the Messianic Jewish Anglo-Catholic missionary adventurer, traveled to Bukhara in search of Stoddart and Conolly (both of whom had disappeared during diplomatic intrigues the year before), the EIC had bungled the First Anglo-Afghan War, and stories of overwhelming defeat, such the bloody Retreat from Kabul, filled the London press. British readers were perhaps most struck, however, by the violent death of so many prominent architect-players in the nascent Game including William Macnaghten, Alexander "Bokhara" Burnes, two of Conolly's brothers (a third would die by beheading in 1855), as well as Lt. Col. Stoddart and Arthur Conolly, himself, both of whom were convicted on espionage charges by the Emir of Bukhara, Nasrullah Khan, after which they were suspended in cages, mutilated, and publically beheaded.[30] As the Bengali intelligence operative, Hurree Chunder Mookerjee, explains in *Kim*: "When everyone is dead the Great Game is finished. Not before."[31]

In this sense, Kipling's project of describing narrative continuities between the past and present—which is the common argument of nineteenth-century historical romancing—parallels an implicit argument made by the conqueror-readers, Carnehan and Dravot, about literary reception and cultural tradition. For Kipling's "kings," the impetus for their attempt to live in the past in the present is an extension of the *Blackwood's*-style idea of the "insider" audience to the domain of historiography, a conversion of the British Empire's cultural geography during the 1840s or 1850s into what Kipling presents as a vibrant received tradition. This imposes a burden of belonging on the Narrator's readers, whose relationship to the tale's imperialist social group also distinguishes them as being either "inside" or "outside" of history, as well. The account of Kafiristan's conquest and loss, doubly embedded in the immediate past by Carnehan and the frame-story's Narrator, thus becomes more or less coherent based on a reader's proximity to the literary-political culture of Conolly-era adventurism and geopolitical speculation. Moreover, Kipling's willingness to portray rank-and-file readers like Peachey and Daniel suggests a flexibility to his social imagination that is often given short shrift. Although he was often more than willing to critique elites of the Raj, Kipling admired the paternalistic social traditions and perceived historical continuities of Anglo-Indian officer and civil servant classes.[32] Even so, "Would Be King" suggests that these social hierarchies provided meaningful and surprisingly flexible imaginative hierarchies of geographical and personal mobility for lower-class figures like Carnehan and Dravot.

Some instances of this historiographical, social, and literary cross-contamination in the text are comparatively minor hints at particular works that may have inspired Dravot and Carnehan's plan. The pronunciation of "Sar-a-*whack*," for example, while clearly intended to function as a pun, also suggests that the two adventurers may have first encountered the story of James Brooke through Henry Keppel's 1847 work, *The Expedition of H.M.S. Dido for the Suppression of Piracy*, which uses a similar phonetic spelling.[33] Other instances potentially complicate our understanding of the "kings," themselves. To an "outsider" audience, Dravot's fixation on his Central Asian subjects' whiteness is a crass and obvious enactment of late Victorian racial ideologies. However, "insiders" of the 1840s would have likely recognized a context for Daniel's racial fixation in Moghul ethnographic claims about the Lost Tribes of Israel, which entered Anglophone literature in 1829 through the publication of Bernhard Dorn's translation of Nimat Allah al-Harawi's *History of the Afghans*, and corresponded with numerous Company-Era surveys that recorded folk accounts of the "White Huns" and "Beni Afghana."[34] More significant are those elements of the plot which become clearer in proximity to Imperial audiences of the Company period. The central ruse upon which the story turns—Dravot's self-identification as a Kafiristani demigod, the son of Alexander the Great and Queen Semiramis—actually has remarkably little foundation in the text. The Narrator's readers must contextualize both Daniel's charade and its positive reception by the tribes through an external body of knowledge in order for either to make much sense, and the closer that body of knowledge is to the period of the First Afghan War, the more reasonable both Daniel and his Afghan subjects appear.

As Jonathan Lee remarks, the EIC's Central Asian policies reflected an "obsession with classical history, and Alexander the Great in particular," largely due to "successive generations of British political and military officers . . . [who had been] educated in system which was steeped in the Greek and Latin works which Alexander's conquests spawned . . . [and] it was to these sources that officials turned for information about the human and military geography of the regions beyond the Khyber."[35] In addition to the frontier classicism of Conolly and his contemporaries (whose journals are "shot through with references to Herodotus, Plutarch, Quintus Curtius Rufius, etc."),[36] British travelers often encountered stories about Alexander, as well as what appeared to be archeological traces of his brief campaigns, in a region where numerous ruling families including those in Hunza, Nager, Badakhshan, Gilgit claimed the same divine descent from Alexander as Daniel Dravot.[37] British military studies also made occasional reference to Semiramis, the legendary Assyrian sensualist, in connection with Central Asia, but Kipling's pairing of Semiramis with Alexander provides an allusive metacommentary on Dravot's religious hucksterism and doomed monarchic ambitions, tying both through Dravot's "mother" to Alexander Hislop's description of Semiramis in his popular 1853 treatise, *The Two Babylons*, in which she appears as the Old Testament wife of Nimrod, a coconspirator in the construction of the Tower of Babel, and the self-interested inventor of paganism.[38] While Hislop's Semiramis is an utterly unique reinvention of the legendary figure, it shares the common elision of political imperialism and religious mysticism present in midcentury romances as diverse as Disraeli's *Tancred*, John Henry Newman's *Callista*, and Charles Kingsley's *Hypatia*. By Kipling's day, the mystical connection between syncretistic religious visions of time and the cyclic geopolitical model of the Great Game was largely a given for many British, Russian, and Central Asian spies and politicians. When Agvan Lobsan Dorjieff, for example, an influential Tibetan statesman, spy, and tutor to the Dali Lama, revived old legends at the turn of the twentieth century that associated Moscow with the mystical kingdom of Shambala and declared that the Romanovs were incarnations of the White Tara, he opened the Himalayas to Russian influence and upset the fragile balance of power in the region.[39] But during the early decades of the Game, political adventurers often framed their mystical espionage on Central Asian frontiers with Christian myths of origins and ends. Gardiner affirmed the Alai Valley as "no other than the site of the Garden of Eden and the birthplace of the human race,"[40] and in 1842, his American counterpart, Harlan, described the "present exciting and critical state" of the Great Game as a foreshock of the "present prophetic condition" of end-times history.[41]

Despite the fact that Britons often viewed the Empire in terms of liberal Christian ideologies, it is hard to avoid the impression that the God most commonly reflected back by the midcentury literary cultures of the Great Game was the Old Testament God of historical reversals, cataclysms, dispensational punishments, and obscure intentions.[42] Fittingly, Kipling's tale about 1880s readers who want to essentially time travel back to the 1840s unfolds against a "background constructed of kingly acts, both temporal and spiritual, legalistic and symbolic, Hebraic and Christian, of the Bible."[43] But the background is not Kipling's; that it to say, it is not an objective common landscape within the fiction. The escalating religious rhetoric of the piece belongs almost exclusively to Carnehan's narration of the conquest and loss of Kafiristan. For Dravot, the tribal mysticism that his kingship depends on is nothing more than a "master-stroke 'o policy" that makes "running the country as easy as a four-wheeled bogie on a down grade."[44] The irony is that Dravot does very little actual running of his "hugeous great state," apart from leading "the priest of each village up to the idol, and say[ing] he must sit there and judge the people, and if anything goes wrong he is to be shot."[45] Carnehan is Kafiristan's Disraeli, the architect of Daniel's power; it is Carnehan, the "first-class Commander-in-Chief," who has "drilled the men and showed the people how to stack their oats better," and "brought in those tinware rifles from Ghorband."[46] It is also Carnehan who takes the mysticism of political authority in the Game seriously, warning his partner that "the Bible says that Kings ain't to waste their strength on women, 'specially when they've got a raw new Kingdom to work over."[47] But if Carnehan is a Disraeli, he is one whose biography operates in reverse. He moves from practicing the art of imperial politics to practicing the art of imperialist narrative upon his return to the Narrator's world.

Daniel, who dies with his "body caught on a rock with the gold crown close beside,"[48] recapitulates familiar stories of failed Central Asian interventionists of the 1840s, men like Conolly, Stoddart, and Macnaghten who quite literally lost their heads. Indeed, Dravot's fall from power compresses the entire ethos of EIC policy in the early nineteenth century into a cautionary romance biography that revolves around a single quest. Peachey, on the other hand, completes the symbolic recursion to Conolly's world through the fact of his survival. The outraged tribes "crucified him, sir," Carnehan explains to the Narrator, "as Peachey's hands will show. They used wooden pegs for his hands and feet; and he didn't die. He hung there and screamed and they took him down the next day, and said it was a miracle that he wasn't dead."[49] It is always "him, sir," the third person, when Peachey talks about his torture, survival, and return. By the end of Kipling's story, he has become, like Brydon, Sale, Campbell, and others, both the "fearful tale" and its teller. "They was cruel enough to feed him in the temple," Peachey continues, "because they said he was more of a God than old Daniel was a man."[50] While the mutilated and possibly insane Carnehan is potentially an unreliable narrator, his passage from retrospective "outsider" to 1840s imperialist "insider" and soldier-romance-monger is unquestionable.[51] *Something* happened and Carnehan, both actor and author, is the sole legitimate witness. The Christ metaphor clarifies nothing. Instead, its air of factuality simply frustrates attempts to neatly allegorize the story's final perspective on the British Empire, further complicating *Idylls*'s uncertainty as to what "the tone of empire" is or ought to be. Nevertheless, it involves both Carnehan's adventure and his narration in the central associative functions of romance, aligning realistic political speculations with the regenerative spiritual transformations of a knightly quest. This complicates rather than clarifies the historical-literary paradox of soldier-romance-mongering and the symbolic identity of the British Empire. Thus the last words convert Reginald Heber's famous Anglo-Indian hymn into question: "The Son of God goes forth to war, / A kingly crown to gain; / His blood-red banner streams afar! / Who follows in his train?"[52]

Peachey's last words are pregnant with meaning, but their value is different based on whether one reads them from the Narrator's perspective, which remains hermetically sealed within the textual present, or through the imagined historical continuities that Peachey feels with his EIC-era predecessors. Like Arthur Conolly, the Oxford-educated Hebert was a beneficiary of the EIC patronage system. After the death of Thomas Middleton in 1822, Heber received an appointment to the bishopric of Calcutta through his former schoolmate, Charles Watkins Williams-Wynn, who had been appointed to the Board of Control earlier that year.[53] Young, poetical, and traditionalist, the charismatic Heber embodied a religious adventurism that appealed to many of the fresh EIC officers and bureaucrats produced by the Military Seminary, including a sixteen-year-old Arthur Conolly, who accompanied Heber to India aboard the Indiaman, *Grenville*, and "showed themselves glad to read with him."[54] As John William Kaye remarks, "In those days, the first voyage to India of a young writer or a young cadet often exercised an important influence over his whole after-career," and this was certainly true in the case of Conolly, whose practical scheme to unite the khanates of Khiva, Bokhara, and Kokand into a single buffer entity against Russian influence corresponded with his *Tancred*-like vision of Central Asia as the future site of Christian civilization.[55] There is an echo of this mentality during Daniel's charade as a mad priest, when he declares that "from Roum have I come . . . from Roum, blown by the breath of a hundred devils across the sea,"[56] superimposing the beginning of his personal quest north of the Khyber onto the Christian eschatological politics of the Game. Carnehan's last words similarly provide both a beginning and a conclusion but reverse this dynamic. His literal quest ends in failure, madness and death, but he has also successfully aligned himself with the cyclical nature of the Game; he has symbolically returned to the "true-romance" landscape of the 1840s, making the Narrator's reflection that "to-day, I greatly fear that my King is dead, and if I want a crown I must go hunt it for myself,"[57] entirely viable.

Which "Son of God" has gone forth to war, Peachey or Daniel? In a sense, the answer is that both have. Daniel performs his divinity as an imperialist political calculation; Peachey comes by the appearance of his through violent accidents that are utterly outside of his control. The pair thus refracts the symbiotic dualism of power and powerlessness that so heavily marked accounts of the Game during the period of the First Afghan War. Much of the foreshadowing in "Would Be King" revolves around this equivalency of life and death, conquest and loss. When Daniel and Peachey masquerade as clerics to gain safe passage north, a horse trader in the marketplace warns that because they are "mad," they "will either be raised to honour or have [their] head[s] cut off" by "HH the Amir of Bokhara."[58] The fulfillment of the latter possibility, of course, aligns Daniel's eventual fate with that of Conolly. However, it also conflates the narrative of Joseph Wolff, the "eminent and eccentric missionary," writer, and adventurer who discovered Conolly's eventual fate in 1843, with Carnehan's firsthand relation of Daniel's demise.[59] The son of a German rabbi, Wolff converted to Christianity, was baptized Catholic in 1812, and converted to High Church Anglicanism in 1818. For the next two decades, Wolff traveled extensively in East Africa, America, and Central Asia, proselytizing Jews, searching for the Lost Tribes of Israel, and, according to *The Spectator*, acting the apologist for "tithes, tories, taxes, bishops, bigots, [and] boroughmongers."[60] In 1843, Wolff announced his plans for an expedition to ascertain the fate of Conolly and Stoddart, funded largely by private donations from religious philanthropists and military officers. Like Carnehan and Dravot, who penetrate Afghanistan dressed as dervishes, concealing their twenty Martini rifles "and ammunition to correspond, under the whirligigs and the mud dolls,"[61] Wolff's plan for safe passage across Central Asia largely revolved around his own wild religious theatricality. Dressed in clerical robes and laden with trinkets and trade goods, Wolff, who assumed the title of "Grand Dervish of England, and Ireland, and the whole of Europe, and America" for the duration of his trip, survived because—like Peachey's captors—the Emir of Bokhara, Nasrullah Khan, was unsure as to whether his strange guest was insane, duplicitous, or able to make the dead rise.[62]

For Wolff, who disavowed figurative, "phantomming" interpretations of scripture, the rotations of the Great Game in the 1830s and 1840s certified his own "grammatical, historical" predictions that 1847 would mark the Biblical eschaton.[63] For Carnehan, the rotations have a different verifiability. It is the figurative historicity of the First Afghan War which validates both the historical logic of his own adventures and the spiritual apocalypse of the Raj. Just as Wolff's adventure narrative testified to Conolly's ultimate fate as well as Wolff's own role as firsthand witness, writer, and mystical hero, Carnehan's recovery of Dravot's fate is both a narrative and self-declarative act; Peachey can only validate what transpired in Kafiristan because, as a storyteller, he shares Dravot's exceptional status as a player in the Game. This partly accounts for the lack of closure in "Would Be King." For the Narrator, the final disappearance of Carnehan's body and Dravot's crown illustrate the pressure of narrative covetousness produced by the interplay of event, testimony, and literary reception in the British Imperial culture of the Conolly era. Carnehan's narrative presents Dravot's Central Asian meddling and downfall as an analogue to midcentury adventurers like Arthur Conolly, most of whom recorded their lives in popular accounts that circulated throughout—and in part defined—the British Empire of the *Tancred* era. But "Would Be King" is ultimately less about the acts narrated by Peachey than it is about the centrality of narration, itself, in delineating the imagined commonwealth of reader, writer, and adventurer that saw itself reflected through the mystical historiography of the Great Game, that saw itself *as* the British Empire, and that saw that Empire as a type of Tennyson's Camelot—"at once the most brilliant of dreams, and the most sober of realities."

"BLANK AS MORDRED'S SHIELD": KIPLING'S KINGS' ALLUSIONS

In 1845, *The Asiatic Journal* defended Macnaghten's interventionism in Central Asia by observing that "an empire which embraced the interests of a hundred millions of people, and yielded a revenue of twenty millions sterling a year," could hardly be understood by a nation for which it "excited so little interest."[64] While Britons often dismissed their Empire as something "entirely outside their experience and knowledge,"[65] members of groups actively involved in the production of the British imperium tended to regard the metropole with an equal modicum of indifference or disdain. "All the time," the Narrator remarks, "the [editorial office] telephone-bell is ringing madly, and Kings are being killed on the Continent, and Empires are saying, 'You're another,' and Mister Gladstone is calling down brimstone upon the British Dominions," but none of it matters; the "wheel of the world" just "swings through the same phases again and again."[66] Of course the mythologized "wheel of the world" also exposes the vibrant counterpoint of British Imperial affairs along the Central Asian borderlands as a kind of true romance. Carnehan's physical—if not psychological—return to the stagnant, complacently posthistorical Raj argues that the experiences behind Dravot's "tales of things that he seen and done, of out-of-the-way corners of the Empire into which he had penetrated, and of adventures in which he had risked his life for a few days' food" are in fact the substantial acts of history, rather than the principles of metropolitan political economics mimicked by Lord Lytton's establishment.[67] In effect, the anachronistic political adventurisms of the 1830s–1850s are not simply proven viable by Carnehan's witness; they are mythologized as future historical inevitabilities in the rotational course of the Game. However, because both the Narrator and his readers have not decided to "seek a crown of [their] own," they remain exiled from the intrinsic meanings of Carnehan's narrated world by a metropolitan distance that subordinates the British Empire's narrative potential to the banal repetitions of English news stories, flung from the hands of the "copy-boys . . . whining '*kaa-pi chay-ha-yeh*' [copy wanted] like tired bees," while "most of the paper is blank as Mordred's shield."[68]

The Narrator's choice of simile frames his conception of "Empires . . . [and] the British Dominions" through the romance historiography of Tennyson's "Gareth and Lynette," in which the shield of Arthur's destroyer is "blank as death."[69] Of the several tales that comprise *Idylls of the King*, "Gareth and Lynette" is ostensibly the happiest, a fanciful story in which a secret knight masquerading as a kitchen boy rescues a maiden and defeats several allegorical Knights before finally overcoming the dread Knight of Death. As James R. Kincaid remarks, the idyll "celebrates a victory over time, implying very literally that they lived happily ever after," but Tennyson's myth of Camelot ultimately distrusts the stagnation of endings and "insists in their place on the inevitability of the cycles of destruction," ultimately articulating "an unaccustomed and ironic view of what the 'ever after' looks like."[70] A decade after Lord Lytton's extravagant spectacle of Indian vassalage, the Coronation Durbar of 1877, Carnehan, Dravot, and the Narrator extend *Idylls*'s ironic distrust of political happy endings to the ostensibly settled question of India's subordination to the British administrative elite at Simla, marked throughout the 1870s by a series of legal and administrative reforms accompanied by ostentatious gestures including the proposal of an Indian peerage, the employment of South Asian medievalism in political ceremonies, and Victoria's "succession" to the last Moghul, Bahadur Shah II, who had been tried, deposed, and exiled following the Indian Mutiny of 1857.[71] Nevertheless, the underlying malaise of the Raj, of Camelot, and the shallowness of any supposed national-historical end-state, are embedded in the very premise of Kipling's tale. "This country isn't half worked out," Peachey complains, "because them that governs it won't let you touch it. They spend all their blessed time in governing it, and you can't lift a spade, nor chip a rock, nor look for oil, nor anything like that without the Government saying, 'Leave it alone, and let us govern.'"[72]

What was at stake in the 1870s–1880s for the triad of the Narrator, Dravot, and Carnehan—as well as for "them that governs"—was an ending. This is true in a literary as well as a historical sense. One of the curious features of the Raj was the fact that a number of its prominent architects were also writers. Robert Bulwer-Lytton, for example, the Viceroy who presided over the Coronation Durbar, the Second Anglo-Afghan War, and the Great Famine of 1876–1878, wrote popular verse dramas under the name "Owen Meredith." Even if he was not, as Lord Derby observed, "a little mad,"[73] his erratic personal behavior and violent mismanagement of Indian affairs suggested a radical dissociation of sensibility between the almost "theological" certitudes of his Englishness and the unfolding socioeconomic catastrophes which marked his tenure.[74] For Benjamin Disraeli, on the other hand, the Raj concluded an imaginative project begun in his political romances of the 1840s. As Miles Taylor remarks, the Victorian "image of Disraeli as an Eastern potentate, corrupting the English monarchy by turning the Queen into an Empress" obscures the fact that Victoria considered herself Empress "at least since the East India Company lost control of India in 1858, and possibly further back than that."[75] It also obscures the extent to which Disraeli the novelist came to imagine Britain as a cosmopolitan world order with an Eastern core during his prolific literary period of the 1830s and 1840s. Following the publication of his early political manifesto, *Vindication of the English Constitution* (1835), Disraeli articulated the nostalgic, populist conservatism of "Young England" in a trilogy of novels, *Coningsby* (1844), *Sybil* (1845), and *Tancred* (1847), the last of which superimposed the concerns of the contemporary social novel onto the quest form of historical romances. In *Tancred*, the young hero, Lord Montacute, retraces the footsteps of his crusader ancestors to the Levant, abandoning all things British, "whether it be religion, or government, or manners; sacred or political or social,"[76] to recover, instead, "the great Asian mystery."[77] In this sense, Montacute is an aristocratic forebear of Dravot and Carnehan, but the definitional crisis of his "new crusade"—and, by extension, theirs—is distinctively pre-Raj (or at least insofar as Kipling depicts the Raj in "King").

While *Tancred*, with its undiscriminating setting, "represents an imaginary exportation of the romance and novel to the Middle East," it also marks an apogee in the development of the historical romance of the early nineteenth century, displacing re-creations of a national past in favor of a wholly exported and reconstituted Britishness that belongs to the novel's speculative imperial future.[78] As early as John Gibson Lockhart's 1821 romance, *Valerius*, British romancers and their audiences struggled with the generically destructive potential of empires for Walter Scott's national-historical model of the novel. Scott himself set his medieval romance, *Count Robert of Paris* (heavily edited by his son-in-law, Lockhart, and his publisher, Robert Cadell), in a decaying Byzantine Empire.[79] But he did so with mixed results. As Ian Duncan remarks, Scott "bedevils the historical novel—his signature genre—with an alien history and alien races and species" in *Count Robert*,[80] a criticism of empires that often occurs *within* the Classicist romances of Scott's contemporaries and a range of successors including the anti-Catholic polemicist Charles Kingsley and the Secretary of State for the Colonies Edward Bulwer-Lytton.[81] A widespread and corresponding criticism *about* historical imperial fiction reflected the fact that *Waverley* readers did not like the impression given by works such as *Count Robert*, which suggested that history was the provenance of strange empires in which they, themselves, were strangers rather than masters. In 1863, John Blackwood wrote to the Anglo-Indian romancer, Philip Meadows Taylor, in an attempt to dissuade him from focusing on exclusively Indian historical subjects, arguing that Taylor's projected cycle about the cyclical collapse of the Moghul Empire would exhibit "for English readers a fatal want of human interest in the characters."[82] Bulwer-Lytton's introductory remarks for his *Last Days of Pompeii* provide a more ideological rationale for excluding the overwhelming Roman Empire as much as possible from a novel set in the Roman Empire. His "insight into the higher principles of art" required that the story remain "rigidly confined" to Pompeii lest "her awful fate" seem "like a petty and isolated wreck in the vast seas of imperial sway"; his insight into his market equally required that *Last Days*'s audience should feel a "natural sympathy and bond of alliance" with characters whose "struggles for liberty and justice" reflected Britain's "present institutions."[83]

The commercial failure of Lockhart's *Valerius* a decade earlier suggested that Bulwer-Lytton was right. Lockhart's novel had portrayed a colonized Britain stitched into the "ill-cemented and motley fabric" of a dying empire, an "insulated colony" distinguished by "the sullen submission of barbarians on the one hand, or the paltry vanity of provincial officials on the other."[84] But to Disraeli—and to numerous British Imperial readers—this *was* the crux of concerns about Britain's "present institutions." In 1833, Disraeli's Messianic historical romance, *The Wondrous Tale of Alroy*, argued that "universal empire must not be founded on sectarian prejudices and exclusive rights,"[85] and in 1842, he criticized Government's confounding laissez-faire attitude toward EIC interventionism by observing that "the wars in central Asia were not the wars of the East India Company, but of England."[86] In 1847, *Tancred* extended Disraeli's increasing conviction that England, "no longer a mere European power" but rather the "metropolis of a great maritime empire," was "really more an Asiatic power than a European" one, by suggesting that "Young England" must abandon England altogether to regenerate the British cultural order in the flux of history.[87]

In the Levant, Lord Montacute meets the Lebanese emir, Fakredeen, who explains that Montacute's generation "must . . . quit a petty and exhausted position [England] for a vast and prolific empire. Let the Queen of England collect a great fleet . . . and transfer the seat of her empire from London to Delhi. There she will find an immense empire ready made, a first rate army, and a large revenue."[88] The emir's fantasy reinforces Montacute's rejection of old England ("Your Queen is young," Fakredeen explains, "she has an avenir. Aberdeen and Sir Peel will never give her this advice; their habits are formed. They are too old, too rusés "[89]), as well as the centrality of the Game as the sacred political mystery of the British Imperial history ("I will arrange with Mehmet Ali," he plots. "He shall have Bagdad and Mesopotamia, and pour the Bedoueen cavalry into Persia. I will take care of Syria and Asia Minor. The only way to manage the Afghans is by Persia and by the Arabs"[90]). In *Tancred*'s Romantic Tory vision of history, the emir's ambition reinvigorates England, the dying nation, into nothing less than "the greatest empire that ever existed . . . for the only difficult part, the conquest of India, which baffled Alexander, is all done!"[91]

Tancred thus produces a temporary impasse for the treatment of empire in the nineteenth-century historical romance. By associating Tory sensibilities with a projected Oriental future rather than a British past, Disraeli effectively writes his "Young England" out of existence. Moreover, having superimposed Britain, itself, onto the political landscape of the Game through Fakredeen, the action of the novel comes to an abrupt halt. The hero's proposal of marriage is left unanswered; his family arrives in the Levant to retrieve him; we are not sure what will follow next. In 1847, Disraeli the political novelist is unsure of what follows. It remains for Disraeli to resume *Tancred*'s theme of British Imperial regeneration thirty years later through the prime minister's office, lending the eerie resonance of authorial wish-fulfillment on a real-life stage to John Tenniel's famous 1876 caricature in *Punch*, which depicts Disraeli, Orientalized as a bazaar merchant, offering Victoria "new crowns for old ones."[92] In his meticulous construction of Victoria's Raj, Disraeli had, in fact, cast himself in the role of Fakredeen, circulating the imperialist fictions of the 1840s and the novelistic imperialism of the 1870s through a politicohistorical hall of mirrors.

As a consummate imitator, Daniel Dravot's difficulty in ruling Kafiristan is that he cannot see through the "Tancred" moment of the 1840s as Disraeli does; his reign collapses largely because he begins to conceptualize his power in terms of anachronistic British respectability ("I'd hand over the crown," he muses, "this crown I'm wearing now—to Queen Victoria on my knees, and she'd say 'Rise up, Sir Daniel Dravot'") instead of the real constitution of his own "hugeous great State,"[93] its customs, traditions, and the experiential warrant of his own extensive "dealings . . . in foreign parts."[94] While he understands the process of conquest in terms of the circular Game, he fails to understand the point made by works such as *Valerius*, *Tancred*, and Tennyson's "Locksley Hall," all of which renounce a static ideology of British national purpose for a nominal Britishness that reflects an evolving mythology of the Empire.[95] *Idylls*'s mythology of Arthur's historical elusions is instructive in this context. Like Fakredeen's movable Court—or, for that matter, the sense among Disraeli's contemporaries that *Tancred* was "at once the most brilliant of dreams, and the most sober of realities"[96]—Tennyson's Camelot is an imperium "built / To music, therefore never built at all, And therefore built forever."[97]

However, Tennyson's Camelot, like the Raj, is a product of "confusion, and illusion, and relation, / Elusion, and occasion, and evasion"[98] It also shares in the evasive work of allusion, which is perhaps characteristic of all myths that posit historical continuities between empires. In the case of "Would Be King," two aspects of the Narrator's use of Tennyson are worth noting. First, he interprets *Idylls* in accordance with his own perspective as a British Imperial reader, for whom the Arthurian national epic operates primarily as a meditation on "the relationship between the loss of faith and the loss of empire."[99] Tennyson's Camelot is defined by its retention of a common moral patrimony, but that legacy rarely manifests at the center of Arthur's realm; it has the most vibrancy in the peripheral landscapes of quests and conquest, where the Once and Future King expands his dominion. Thus Arthur is undone at home by what Robert Penn Warren identifies as paradoxes of imperium that Dravot and Carnehan encounter in Kafiristan, the contradictions between "different kinds of power, internal and external, power over others and power over oneself,"[100] all of which are ultimately resolved by universal death, the blankness of Mordred, the geohistorical rotations of the Game. What begins as a rhetorical question in *Idylls*'s address to Crown—"is this the tone of empire?"[101]—thus becomes what is literally at stake in a poem that often seems, like the Narrator's account of Dravot and Carnehan's irresponsible but irrepressibly sympathetic conquest, to be "ideologically at war with itself" and even "incoherent, juxtaposing as it does elements of newly expansionist imperial 'trusteeship,' Christian humanist anti-imperial critique, Darwinian doubt, and apocalyptic dread."[102]

Second, the Narrator's use of *Idylls* as a descriptive setting for Carnehan's reappearance suggests how certain audiences came to see the cycles of destruction that characterize the Arthurian world as regenerative political, literary, and personal spheres of action. Professional imperialists were often less interested in reading metropolitan debates about an intellectually abstracted British Empire than in reading about themselves. Throughout the Anglo-Afghan War, for example, *Blackwood's* ensured a wide circulation throughout the "libraries and messes of the British empire" by publishing "articles about this campaign and the so-called Great Game," and the "regular inclusion of articles on India and other parts of the empire, as well as on the Army."[103] During the 1820s to the 1850s, *Blackwood's* also heavily promoted popular novels, memoirs, and journals written by military veterans such as George Robert Gleig, Thomas Hamilton, George Wood, and "other gentlemen who," as William Maginn remarked in 1859, had "turned the sword not into a ploughshare, but into as hard-working an instrument—a pen."[104] While *Blackwood's* audiences praised these "soldier-romance-mongers" as the "rollicking describers of fights, campaigns, sieges, carousings, riotings, [and] love-makings,"[105] London writers tended to depict their models—subalterns, cocksure imperialists, and cavalryman carousers who flashed "the extreme edges of [their] fine teeth" at proper debutantes—as being among "the proudest, the poorest, the worst educated, the most polished, and the most privileged, of all orders of people above the rank of mere bodily labour."[106] However, the public exposition of British failure in India and Central Asia throughout the 1840s and 1850s highlighted the professional imperialist's role as both quasi-fictional romance hero and firsthand witness to history. As the *Daily Intelligencer*'s foreign correspondent remarked in 1842, it was impossible to comprehend the "peculiar hardships" of the British Empire from metropolitan writing. "To form an idea of them," he informed his readers, "you must hear, as I have done, verbal narratives from subalterns who survived seven years' campaigning in every mode. It is from reading the private letters from Affghanistan that you learn the sufferings of the British expeditions to and from Cabul."[107]

Starting in 1842, numerous political and military treatises tried to explain the EIC's nation-building debacle by arguing that these "peculiar hardships" largely exempted the conduct of field officers and political agents such as Conolly and Stoddart from British judgment and reassigned blame to the strategic policy-makers.[108] These politicohistorical assessments paralleled the ethos of the "romance-mongers," who, "at the risk of being thought . . . writer[s] of romance," echoed Washington Irving's dictum in *Bracebridge Hall* to the effect that "a prosperous life, passed at home, has little incident for narrative," and that "it is only poor devils, that are tossed about the world, that are true heroes of the story."[109] Many of the confessional accounts produced by survivor-writers after the Retreat from Kabul, such as the captivity narrative of Lady Florentia Sale or John Campbell's *Lost among the Afghans*, pushed the bounds of believability at times, but nevertheless strikingly emphasized the fact that British Imperial narrator-subjects often led lives on which English social habits and mores had little bearing.[110] For other reading audiences, those who "moved in the same sphere[s]" as the active agents of British imperium, this concentrated simultaneity of focus on both firsthand witness and romance often led to an astonishingly circular correspondence between reading, writing, and participation in common cultures of work.[111] Dr. Brydon's dramatic survival and appearance at Jalalabad, as well as the prominent mention of *Blackwood's*'s role in saving his life, constitute an example par excellence.

Like many of Brydon's contemporaries during the Central Asian campaigns of the 1830s to 1840s, Carnehan and Dravot are reader-protagonists who wildly project their sympathies with the heroes of stories through their own actions into the real world. "We shall go to [Afghanistan]," Daniel explains, "and say to any King we find—'D' you want to vanquish your foes?' and we will show him how to drill men; for that we know better than anything else."[112] In the 1880s, nothing about this statement seems unreasonable coming from two veterans of the Second Anglo-Afghan War. Neither does their plan to "subvert that King and seize his Throne and establish a Dynasty."[113] The endgame is simply anachronistic, projecting a pre-Raj literacy of British policy in Central Asia and political operators like Conolly and Stoddart into the Victorian present. On the one hand, Dravot and Carnehan's scheme conceptualizes political action—like *Tancred*—as a modern-day knight's quest, wherein "trial through adventure is the real meaning of the . . . [protagonists'] ideal existence."[114] On the other hand, Dravot's assessment that "in any place where they fight, a man who knows how to drill men can always be King" had any number of historical correlatives by midcentury, including Josiah Harlan, Alexander Gardner, and Sir James Brooke, Rajah of Sarawak, from whom the would-be kings derive the idea of uncharted lands where "two strong men can Sar-a-*whack*."[115] But the very historicity of Dravot and Carnehan's scheme connects them to the British Imperial reading culture of the "soldier-romance-mongers" of the 1830s–1850s, as well as commensurate shift in historical novels toward entwined treatments of heroism and imperialism. By midcentury, this increasing literary interest in matters concerning the British Empire rather than the Matter of Britain reflected a definitional problem of social status on the frontiers. As William Buyers observed in 1848, "the conduct of European adventurers in India whose functions were not defined, and whose powers were of no settled character, is supposed to be still the model of that of the present rulers of that country."[116] Unlike the knight, for whom a "rich and pungent portrait" of courtly life "remains aloof" from the rest of feudal society, Dravot and Carnehan's self-portrayal allows them to identify with this social-professional group of "very imperfect instruments of administration"[117] in a *historical* setting that is "fixed and isolating" in the past, and yet remain "distinct from other strata of [Anglo-Indian] society" in the 1880s.[118]

Paradoxically, the certainty of this historical fatalism secures the promise of new adventures, advancement, and kingship for Conolly's Victorian heirs, Dravot and Carnehan. As Hannah Arendt remarks, the great allure of the Game is that it "has no ultimate purpose," and this is what "makes it so dangerously similar to life itself."[119] Freed from "all ordinary social ties, family, regular occupation, a definite goal, ambitions, and a guarded place in the community to which he belongs by birth," the gamesman thus undergoes the divestitures of a social death, but exchanges his identity as a member of the paterfamilias for a mimesis of complete existential freedom.[120] "Such as [the Raj] is," Kipling's erstwhile kings decide, "we will let it alone, and go away to some other place where a man isn't crowded and can come into his own. We are not little men, and there is nothing that we are afraid of except

Drink . . . *Therefore*, we are going away to be Kings."[121] Kipling has no doubt about the general plausibility of their scheme. "Men even lower than Peachey Carnehan," he observes, "made themselves kings (and kept their kingdoms too) in India not 150 years ago."[122] For all their worldly experience, though, Dravot and Carnehan concoct this scheme as readers; their ambitious departure to the Central Asian heartlands of the Great Game is a projection of popular accounts written about the circumstances of the First Afghan War. Like the EIC's spies, political agents, and military adventurers during the 1830s–1840s, they are initially successful but ultimately undone by the imaginative architecture of their conquest. Two years after their departure for Afghanistan, Carnehan reappears, alone and ghostlike, in a pressroom busy with "a night-issue and a strained waiting for something to be telegraphed from the other side of the world, exactly as had happened before."[123] Something *does* happen as before: the British adventurers lose. To the Narrator's horror, the self-made white rajah, Carnehan, has become the figure of a white *dalit*: "a rag-wrapped whining cripple . . . crying that he was come back" with his "head sunk between his shoulders" and his crucified hands, "twisted like a bird's claw[s]," clutching a horsehair sack that wraps the "dried, withered head of Daniel Dravot" who had once been king in Kafiristan.[124] Barbarous as this reads, "The Quarterly might have opined, it might not have "astonish[ed] educated Englishmen" from "the days of Burke and Fox and Pit"—Kipling's allusive "150 years ago." No one in the eighteenth century would have mistaken Dravot for one of Horace Walpole's stained-glass saints "who had their bodies cut off, and [of whom] nothing remain[ed] but the heads." But Burke, contemplating the would-be-king's forebears among the empire-brokers of his age, might have left Carnehan an epitaph for Dravot: "I have robbed upon Hounslow Heath, but hundreds have robbed there before me.

NOTES

1. Thomas Carlyle, "Lecture III: The Hero as Poet. Dante; Shakespeare," [12 May 1840] in *The Works of Thomas Carlyle* (Cambridge: Cambridge University Press, 2010), 113.

2. Jyotsna Singh, "The Postcolonial/Postmodern Shakespeare," in Heather Kerr, Robin Eaden, and Madge Miltton, *Shakespeare: World Views* (Cranbury: Associated University Presses, 1996), 29.

3. Elizabeth Samet, *Willing Obedience: Citizens, Soldiers, and the Progress of Consent in America, 1776–1898* (Stanford: Stanford University Press, 2004), 3. Samet's focus is on negotiated obligations and consent in a specifically American nineteenth-century context, primarily with respect to military conflicts and in the "literary" political self-understandings of high-ranking officers (e.g., Sherman, Grant). In the broader sense, though, the nineteenth-century figure of the "citizen-soldier"—implicitly linked to the "Great Man" model of history—speaks to the kind of nation-based and "Whig-historical" self-understandings that Kipling places Carnehan and Dravot apart from as readers and agents.

4. George Orwell, "Rudyard Kipling," *All Art Is Propaganda: Critical Essays*, ed. George Packer (New York: Houghton Mifflin Harcourt, 2009), 181.

5. John Kucich, "Sadomasochism and the Magical Group: Kipling's Middle-Class Imperialism," *Victorian Studies* 36, no. 1 (2004): 33; see, also, Kucich, *Imperial Masochism: British Fiction, Fantasy, and Social Class* (Princeton: Princeton University Press, 2006); Samet, *Willing Obedience*, 107; Charles James Fox, qtd. in "Affairs of India," *Corbett's Political Register* (London: Richard Bagshaw, 1806), 699; for *Macbeth* and the Company Era milieu, see also, for example, James Talboys Wheeler, *College History of India: Asiatic and European* (London: Macmillan and Co., 1888), 222.

6. Zohreh T. Sullivan, *Narratives of Empire: The Fictions of Rudyard Kipling* (Cambridge: Cambridge University Press, 1993). 101.

7. Louis D. Cornell, *Kipling in India* (New York: MacMillan, 1966), 163.

8. E. M. Forster, "The Poems of Kipling," *The Creator as Critic and Other Writings*, ed. Jeffrey M. Heath (Toronto: Dundurn, 2008), 29.

9. Orwell, "Kipling," 181.

10. The "classical" period of the Great Game, which entered the Anglophone popular consciousness through the publication of Kipling's >*Kim* lasted from roughly the Eastern Crisis of 1878 to the Bolshevik Revolution in 1917. See Peter Hopkirk, *The Great Game: On Secret Service in High Asia* (Oxford: Oxford University Press, 1990).

11. Rudyard Kipling, "The Man Who Would Be King," *The Man Who Would Be King* (New York: Penguin, 2011), 104.

12. Charles Kingsley, *Westward Ho! Or, The Voyages and Adventures of Sir Amyas Leigh, Knight . . . in the Reign of Her Most Gloriously Majesty Queen Elizabeth* (Cambridge: Macmillan, 1855).

13. For Harlan's Central Asian career, see Josiah Harlan, *A Memoir of India and Avghanistaun, with Observations on the Present Exciting and Critical State and Future Prospects of Those Countries . . . and the Speedy Dissolution of the Ottoman Empire* (Philadelphia: J. Dobson, 1842). Harlan wrote nearly a thousand pages of autobiographical reminiscences, divided into three sections: *Central Asia—Personal Narrative of General Josiah Harlan, Oriental Sketches*, and *Manners and Customs of the Paropamisus and Bulkh or Bactra*. See Ben Macintyre, *The Man Who Would Be King: The First American in Afghanistan* (New York: Faber, Strauss, and Giraux, 2005), 293.

14. Alexander Gardner, *Soldier and Traveller: Memoirs of Alexander Gardner, Colonel of Artillery in the Service of Maharaja Ranjit Singh*, ed. Hugh Pearse (Edinburgh: William Blackwood and Sons, 1898), 6. It is worth noting that Gardner's memoir, although published for a late Victorian audience, was produced during the same period (1830s–1850s) as similar works by writer-adventurers like Harlan and Brooke. As with many works in this vein, there are two texts: the evolving memoir produced incrementally by the late Romantic and early Victorian reader, and the edited text published after the fact, usually by traditionally Tory publishing concerns.

15. Gardner, *Soldier and Traveller*, xxxi–xxxii.

16. Gardner, *Soldier and Traveller*, 291.

17. Gardner, *Soldier and Traveller*, 83–85, 159.

18. Kipling, "King," 104.

19. Edward Marx, "How We Lost Kafiristan," *Representations* 67 (1999), 48. Marx's essay is undoubtedly the most thorough treatment in recent secondary literature of Kipling's sources.

20. Marx, "Kafiristan," 105.

21. Marx, "Kafiristan," 105.

22. James Hevia, *The Imperial Security State: British Colonial Knowledge and Empire-Building in Asia* (Cambridge: Cambridge University Press, 2012), 2.

23. For the EIC and the development of the Great Game from the 1780s through the 1850s, see vols. 1–8 of Martin Ewans, ed., *The Great Game: Britain and Russia in Central Asia* (New York: Routledge, 2004); for Qajar Persia's role as a third party in the Game, see Edward Ingram, "An Aspiring Buffer State: Anglo-Persian Relations in the Third Coalition, 1804–1807," *The Historical Journal* 16, no. 3 (1973): 509–533; Abbas Amanat, "'Russian Intrusion into the Guarded Domain': Reflections of a Qajar Statesman on European Expansion," *Journal of the American Oriental Society* 1 (1993): 35–56.

24. "Lieut.-Colonel C. Stoddart," *The Gentleman's Magazine: and Historical Review* (March 1843), 320.

25. Arthur Conolly, letter to Henry Rawlinson, 22 August 1839, in John William Kaye, *History of the War in Afghanistan. From Unpublished Letters . . . of British Connexion with That Country*, vol. 1 (London: Richard Bentley, 1851), 540.

26. Lord Salisbury, letter to Benjamin Disraeli, 7 June 1876, Hughenden Papers, Box 92/2, folio 1–45.

27. For a contemporary Anglo-Indian assessment of Macnaghten, see "Sir William Hay Macnaghten," *The Asiatic Journal and Monthly Miscellany* 4, no. 3 (1845): 479–501; 605–623. As part of a general administrative reshuffling of the EIC bureaucracy beginning in 1786, a new Secret and Political Department took as its purview "all subjects of a political nature . . .all correspondence with the Agents or Residents at foreign courts . . . and every military operation or movement of troops which is either order or undertaken; also all secret plans and views of foreign European nations or powers"; see Bankey Bihari Misra, *The Central Administration of the East India Company, 1773–1834* (Bombay: Oxford University Press, 1959), 75.

28. Arthur Conolly, *Journey to the North of India, Overland from England, through Persia, Russia, and Affghaunistaun* (London: Richard Bentley, 1838), 86, 141.

29. Conolly, letter to Rawlinson, 22 August 1839. The EIC's concerns about Central Asian instability and Russian regional influence were by no means unfounded. See John Taylor's geopolitical sense of "facilitating conjunction[s]" across Eurasia in *Letters on India, Political, Commercial, and Military; Relative to Subjects Important to The British Interests in the East* (London: S. Hamilton, 1800), 55. Taylor gets this phrase from a description of the Russian Empire given in "National Affairs," *The English Review, Or, An Abstract of English and Foreign Literature* 11 (1788), 238; Taylor's description, which sheds the *Review*'s interest in European powers altogether, illustrates a shift in the British Imperial geopolitical focus. See, also, Secret Committee of the Board of Directors, East India Company, letter to Lord Minto, Governor-General-in-Council, 24 September 1807, in A. Aspinall and E. Smith, *English Historical Documents, 1782–1832* (London: Eyre and Spottiswoode, 1969), 909; John W. Strong, "Russia's Plans for an Invasion of India in 1801," *Canadian Slavonic Papers* 7 (1965): 114–126.

30. "Stoddart," *Gentleman's Magazine*, 320–321.

31. Rudyard Kipling, *Kim* (New York: Penguin, 1984), 222.

32. See, for example, Eric Stokes, *The English Utilitarians and India* (London: Clarendon, 1959); Kipling had a high regard for administrators of the "Punjab School," most notably John and Henry Lawrence; for Kipling and the Lawrences, see Lewis Wurgaft, *The Imperial Imagination: Magic and Myth in Kipling's India* (Middletown: Wesleyan University Press, 1983).

33. Henry Keppel, *The Expedition of H.M.S. Dido for the Suppression of Piracy: with Extracts from the Journal of James Brooke, Esq. of Sarāwak* (London: Chapman and Hall, 1847).

34. Moghul historians tended to identify the Pashtun tribes with the Lost Tribes of Israel. Through works such as the *Maghzan-e-Afghani* and *Mirat-ul-Alam'* these claims entered Anglophone Orientalist literature, beginning with Bernhard Dorn's translation of Nimat Allah al-Harawi's *History of the Afghans: Translated from the Persian of Neamet Ullah* (London: Oriental Translations Fund, 1829). Numerous nineteenth-century accounts (Bellew, for example) make mentions of these claims ss well as their currency among the Afghan tribes; the most prominent treatment of the subject is George Moore, *The Lost Tribes and the Saxons of the East and of the West, with New Views of Buddhism, and Translations of Rock-Records of India* (London: Longman, Green, Longman, and Roberts, 1865).

35. Jonathan L. Lee, *The 'Ancient Supremecy': Bukhara, Afghanistan, and the Battle for Balkh* (Leiden: Brill, 1996), 74.

36. Lee, *'Ancient Supremecy,'* 74.

37. G. W. Leitner, "Notes on the Genealogy of the Divine Rajas of Nagyr," *Dardistan in 1866, 1886 and 1893 . . . and an Epitome of Part III of the Author's "The Languages and Races of Dardistan"* (New Delhi: AES Reprint, 1996), 111; see, also, Warwick Ball, "Some Talk of Alexander: Myth and Politics in the North-West Frontier of British India," in Richard Stone-

man, Kyle Erickson, and Ian Richard Netton, eds., *The Alexander Romance in Persia and the East* (Zuurstukken: Barkhuis, 2012): 127–161.

38. Alexander Hislop, *The Two Babylons; or, The Papal Worship Proved to Be the Worship of Nimrod and His Wife. With Sixty-One Woodcut Illustrations from Nineveh, Babylon, Egypt, Pompeii, &c.* (Edinburgh: James Wood, 1858), first published in a shorter pamphlet form in 1853.

39. Samplildondov Chuluun and Uradyn F. Bulag, eds., *The Thirteenth Dali Lama on the Run (1904–1906): Archival Documents from Mongolia* (Leiden: Brill), 3; see, also, Andrei Znamenski, *Red Shambala: Magic, Prophecy, and Geopolitics* (Wheaton: Quest Books, 2011).

40. Gardner, *Soldier*, 146.

41. Harlan, *Memoir*, i.

42. During Conolly's era, metropolitan Britons—if not necessarily professional imperialists, themselves—tended to self-identify with what William Arthur referred to as "enlightened, sound-hearted, liberal Christianity" in *The Extent and Moral Statistics of the British Empire* (London: Benjamin L. Green, 1848), 53; see, also, William Thorp, *The Destinies of the British Empire, and the Duties of British Christians at the Present Crisis* (London, 1831).

43. Paul Fussell, "Irony, Freemasonry, and Humane Ethics in Kipling's 'The Man Who Would Be King,'" *ELH* 25, no. 3 (1958): 221.

44. Kipling, "King," 115.

45. Kipling, "King," 113.

46. Kipling, "King," 119.

47. Kipling, "King," 120.

48. Kipling, "King," 125.

49. Kipling, "King," 125.

50. Kipling, "King," 125.

51. For Peachey's supposed madness, narrative reliability, and speech patterns, see Thomas A. Shippey and Michael Short, "Framing and Distancing in Kipling's 'The Man Who Would Be King,'" *The Journal of Narrative Technique* 2, no. 2 (1972): 79–82.

52. Peachey takes these lines from an 1812 hymn written by Reginald Heber. For Kipling's use, see Larry J. Kreitzer, "'The Son of God Goes Forth to War': Biblical Imagery in Rudyard Kipling's 'The Man Who Would Be King,'" in *Borders, Boundaries and the Bible*, ed. Martin O'Kane (New York: Sheffield Academic Press, 2002): 99–126.

53. Reginald Heber, qtd. in John William Kaye, *Lives of Indian Officers* (London: W. H. Allen & Co., 1895), 96; for Heber's Indian career and travels, see Reginald Heber and Amelia Heber, *The Life of Reginald Heber, D. D. Lord Bishop of Calcutta. By His Widow. With Selections from His Correspondence, Unpublished Poems, and Private Papers . . . and a History of the Cossacks* (London: John Murray, 1830).

54. Kaye, 96.

55. Peter Roudik, *The History of the Central Asian Republics* (Westport: Greenwood, 2007), 67.

56. Kipling, "King," 107.

57. Kipling, "King," 98.

58. Kipling, "King," 107.

59. "Dr. Wolff at Mount Sanai," *The Jewish Intelligence and Monthly Record of the London Society for Promoting Christianity amongst the Jews* (London: James Nisbet, 1885), 158.

60. "The Travels and Adventures of the Reverend Joseph," *The Spectator*, 4 August 1860.

61. Kipling, "Kings," 108.

62. Joseph Wolff, *Travels and Adventures of the Reverend Joseph Wolff, D.D., L.L.D. Vicar of Ile Brewers, Near Taunton, and Late Missionary to the Jews and Muhammadans in Persia, Bokhara, Cashmeer, Etc.* (London: Saunders, Otley, and Co., 1861), 330, 395–399; see, also, Joseph Wolff, *Journal of the Rev. Joseph Wolff. . . Containing an Account of His Missionary Labours from the Years 1827 to 1831: and from the Years 1835 to 1838* (London: James Burns, 1839); for Wolff's initial account of the Conolly/Stoddart expedition, see James Wolff, *Narrative of a Mission to Bokhara, in the Years 1843–1845, to Ascertain the Fate of Colonel Stoddart and Captain Conolly* (London: J. W. Parker, 1845).

63. "Travels," *Spectator*, 4 August 1860.

64. "Macnaghten," *Asiatic Journal*, 479.
65. Bernard Porter, *The Absent-Minded Imperialists: What the British Really Thought about Empire* (Oxford: Oxford University Press, 2005), 37.
66. Kipling, "King," 102, 109.
67. Kipling, "King," 98. For Anglo-Indian economics, see Paul R. Brumpton, *Security and Progress: Lord Salisbury at the India Office* (Westport: Greenwood, 2002).
68. Kipling, "King," 102.
69. Alfred Lord Tennyson, "Gareth and Lynette" [1872], in *Idylls of the King* (New York: Penguin, 2004), 47.
70. James R. Kincaid, "Tennyson's 'Gareth and Lynette,'" *Texas Studies in Literature and Language* 13, no. 4 (1972): 663.
71. See Bernard Cohn, "Representing Authority in Victorian India," in Eric Hobsbawm and Terence Ranger, eds., *The Invention of Tradition* (Cambridge: Cambridge University Press, 1983): 165–209; see also, Waltraud Ernst and Biswamoy Pati, *India's Princely States: Peoples, Princes, and Colonialism* (New York: Routledge, 2007); Caroline Keen, *Princely India and the British: Political Development and the Operation of Empire* (New York: Palgrave Macmillan, 2012).
72. Kipling, "King," 104.
73. Lord Derby, qtd. in David Steele, *Lord Salisbury: A Political Biography* (New York: Routledge, 2001), 126.
74. Mike Davis, *Late Victorian Holocausts: El Nino Famines and the Making of the Third World* (London: Verso, 2001), 31.
75. Miles Taylor, "Queen Victoria and India, 1837–1861," *Victorian Studies* 46, no. 2 (2004): 264.
76. Benjamin Disraeli, *Tancred; or, The New Crusade*, vol. 1 (Bern: Tauchnitz Jun, 1847), 54.
77. Disraeli, *Tancred*, vol. 2, 140.
78. Cara Murray, *Victorian Narrative Technologies in the Middle East* (New York: Routledge, 2008), 62.
79. See J. H. Alexander's commentary on his restored text of *Count Robert of Paris* (Edinburgh: Edinburgh University Press, 2006), in vol. 23a of *The Edinburgh Edition of the Waverley Novels*. For Scott's assessment of *Count Robert*'s commercial failure, see W. E. K. Anderson, *The Journal of Sir Walter Scott* (Oxford: Oxford University Press, 1972), 741.
80. Ian Duncan, "The Trouble with Man: Scott, Romance, and World History in the Age of Lamarck," in *Romantic Frictions*, ed. Theresa Kelley. *Romantic Circles: Praxis Series* (2011), 14 January 2014, http://romantic.arhu.umd.edu/praxis/frictions/HTML/praxis.2011.duncan.html
81. See, for example, Edward Bulwer-Lytton, *The Last Days of Pompeii* (Paris: Baudry's European Library, 1834; Charles Kingsley, *Hypatia, or New Foes with an Old Face* (London: John W. Parker and Son, 1853).
82. John Blackwood, letter to Philip Meadows Taylor, 2 May 1863, Blackwood's Papers 5643.D4.
83. Edward Bulwer-Lytton, *The Last Days of Pompeii* (Paris: Baudry's European Library, 1834), ii.
84. John Gibson Lockhart, *Valerius: A Roman Story* (Edinburgh: William Blackwood, 1821), 14, 4.
85. Benjamin Disraeli, *The Wondrous Tale of Alroy. The Rise of Iskander* (London: Saunders and Otley, 1833), 182.
86. Benjamin Disraeli, Speech of 22 April 1842, in *Hansard's Parliamentary Debates* 62 (London: G. Woodfall and Son, 1842), 1029.
87. Benjamin Disraeli, qtd. in Ali Parchami, *Hegemonic Peace and Empire: The Pax Romana, Britannica, and Americana* (New York: Routledge, 2009), 70.
88. Disraeli, *Tancred*, 296.
89. Disraeli, *Tancred*, 297.
90. Disraeli, *Tancred*, 296.
91. Disraeli, *Tancred*, 296.

92. John Tenniel, "New Crowns for Old Ones," *Punch* (15 April 1876): 146; see, also, Robert O'Kell, *Disraeli: The Romance of Politics* (Toronto: University of Toronto Press, 2013).

93. Kipling, "King," 119.

94. Kipling, "King," 118.

95. For the problem of empire, nation, and history in "Locksley Hall," see David G. Riede, "Tennyson's Poetics of Melancholy and the Imperial Imagination," *Studies in English Literature* 40, no. 4 (2000): 659–678; Henry Kozicki, "Philosophy of History in Tennyson's Poetry to the 1842 Poems," *ELH* 42, no. 1 (1975): 88–106.

96. Kipling, "King," 118.

97. Kipling, "King," 43.

98. Tennyson, *Idylls*, 43.

99. Christopher Hodgkins, *Reforming Empire: Protestant Colonialism and Conscience in British Literature* (Columbia: University of Missouri Press), 205; see also Inga Bryden, *Reinventing King Arthur: The Arthurian Legends in Victorian Culture* (Burlington: Ashgate, 2002).

100. Robert Penn Warren and Cleanth Brooks, *The Scope of Fiction* (New York: Appleton-Century-Crofts, 1960), 31.

101. Tenyson, *Idylls*, 301.

102. Hodgkins, *Reforming Empire*, 203.

103. David Finkelstein, "Imperial Self-Representation: Constructions of Empire in *Blackwood's Magazine*, 1880–1900," in *Imperial Co-Histories: National Identities and the British and Colonial Press*, ed. Julie F. Codell (London: Associated University Presses, 2003), 99.

104. William Maginn, forward to W. H. Maxwell, *Erin-Go-Bragh; or, Irish Life Pictures* (London: Richard Bentley, 1859), viii. Maginn gives precedence to George Robert Gleig's *The Subaltern* (William Blackwood: Edinburgh, 1825). Gleig was the author of several popular soldier romances based on the success of *The Subaltern*, including *The Light Dragoon* (London: G. Routledge, 1853), *The Hussar* (London: Henry Colburn), and *The Chelsea Pensioners* (London: Henry Colburn, 1829), among others. George Wood was the author of *The Subaltern Officer: A Narrative* (London: Septimus Prowett, 1825). Regular *Blackwood's* contributor Thomas Hamilton, who served in both the Peninsular War and the War of 1812, wrote the widely read *The Youth and Manhood of Cyril Thornton* (Edinburgh: William Blackwood, 1827).

105. Maginn, *Erin-Go-Bragh*, viii.

106. "The Miners," *New Monthly Magazine* 72 (1844), 34–35.

107. "From Our European Correspondent," *Daily National Intelligencer*, 18 October 1842.

108. Louis Dupree, "The Retreat of the British Army from Kabul to Jalalabad in 1842: History and Folklore," *Journal of the Folklore Institute* 4, no. 1 (1967): 50.

109. Wood, *Subaltern*, title page.

110. Florentia Sale, *A Journal of the Disasters in Affghanistan, 1841–2* (London, John Murray, 1843); John Campbell, *Lost among the Affghans: Being the Adventures of John Campbell, (Otherwise Feringhee Bacha), amongst the Tribes of Central Asia. Related by Himself to Hubert Oswald Fry* (London: Smith, Elder, and Co., 1865).

111. Wood, *Subaltern*, 3.

112. Kipling, "King," 105.

113. Kipling, "King," 105.

114. Erich Auerbach, "The Knight Sets Forth," *Mimesis: The Representation of Reality in Western Literature* (Princeton: Princeton University Press, 2013), 135.

115. Kipling, "King," 105. For Field Marshall Frederick Sleigh Roberts, see his *Forty-One Years in India* (London: Richard Bentley and Son, 1896).

116. William Buyers, *Recollections of Northern India; with Observations on the Origin, Customs, Moral Sentiments of the Hindoos, and Remarks on the Country, and Principal Places on the Ganges, &c.* (London: John Snow, 1848), 234.

117. Buyers, *Recollections*, 234.

118. Auerbach, *Mimesis*, 132.

119. Hannah Arendt, *The Origins of Totalitarianism* (New York: Harcourt, 1979), 217.

120. Arendt, *Origins*, 217.

121. Kipling, "King," 104.
122. Rudyard Kipling, letter to Edward White, qtd. in Gail Ching-Liang Low, *White Skins/Black Masks: Representation and Colonialism* (London: Routledge, 2005), 239.
123. Kipling, "King," 109.
124. Kipling, "King," 125.

Works Cited

Abū Bakr Ibrāhīm. "Letter to Minīlik, March 1871." *Acta Æthiopica, Volume III: Internal Rivalries and Foreign Threats, 1869–1879*. Edited by Sven Rubenson. Addis Ababa: Addis Ababa University Press, 2000.
Addison, Joseph. "The Royal Exchange." In *The Spectator*. London: S. Buckley, 1712–1715.
Adolf, Helen. "New Light on Oriental Sources for Wolfrram's *Parzival* and Other Grail Romances." *PMLA* 62, no. 2 (1947): 306–324.
Agamben, Giorgio. *Homo Sacer: Sovereign Power and Bare Life*. Translated by Daniel Heller-Roazen. Stanford: Stanford University Press, 1998.
Alexander, J. H. "Hogg in the Noctes Ambrosianae." *Studies in Hogg and His World* 4 (1993): 37–47.
Alexander, J. H. "Literary Criticism in the Later 'Noctes Ambrosianae.'" *Yearbook of English Studies* 16 (1986): 17–31.
Anderson, Benedict. *Imagined Communities: Reflections on the Origin and Spread of Nationalism*. London: Verso, 1991.
Anderson, Fred. *Crucible of War: The Seven Years War and the Fate of Empire in British North America, 1754–1766*. New York: Vintage, 2000.
Anonymous. "The Adventures of a Rupee." *The Critical Review: Or, Annals of Literature* 52 (1781): 477.
Anonymous. *An Answer to the High-Church Standers; or, A New Passive Obedience*. N.p, 1711.
Anonymous. *The Case of the Honourable James Annesley, Esq; Being a Sequel to the Memoirs of an Unfortunate Young Nobleman*. London: W. Bickerton, 1745.
Anonymous. *Case of the Honourable James Annesley, Esq. Humbly Offered to All Lovers of Truth and Justice*. N.p., 1758.
Anonymous. "Cause between J. Annesley, Esq; and the E. of Anglesey." *The London Magazine, and Monthly Chronologer* 13 (1744).
Anonymous, "Description of Dublin." In *The New Foundling Hospital for Wit. Being a Collection of Fugitive Pieces, in Prose and Verse, Not in Any Other Collection. With Several Pieces Never Before Published*. Vol 6. London: J. Debrett, 1786.
Anonymous. "Dr. Wolff at Mount Sanai." *The Jewish Intelligence and Monthly Record of the London Society for Promoting Christianity amongst the Jews*. London: James Nisbet, 1885.
Anonymous. *Elegy on the Unfortunate tho' Much Lamented Death of James Cotter, Esq., Who Was Executed at Cork on the 7th May, 1720, for Ravishing Elizabeth Squibb, a Quaker. A Broadside*. N.p., 1720.
Anonymous. "From Our European Correspondent." *Daily National Intelligencer* (18 October 1842).

Anonymous. "A Further Account of the Contest between Lord An – sey and Mr Annesley, the Supposed Son of the Late Lord Altham." *The Gentleman's Magazine and Historical Chronicle* 26 (1756).

Anonymous. "Hallowe'en in Germany, or The Walpurgis Night." *The European Magazine and London Review* 80 (1821): 526–527.

Anonymous. "Hood's Whims and Oddities." *Blackwood's Edinburgh Magazine* 21 (January 1827).

Anonymous. *Jachin and Boaz; or, An Authentic Key to the Door of Free-Masonry, Both Ancient and Modern . . . and Days of Meeting.* London: E. Newbery, 1800.

Anonymous. "Judicial Puzzles—the Annesley Case." *Blackwood's Edinburgh Magazine* 88 (1860).

Anonymous. "The Last Man." *The Knickerbocker: Or, New-York Monthly Magazine* 2 (1833).

Anonymous. *A Letter to a Nobleman in the Country on the Great Affair of Mr. Annesley: Containing a Full and Distinct Account of That Extraordinary Transaction, and All Its Circumstances. Together with Some Particulars, Not Hitherto Published. By an Impartial Hand.* London: J. Roberts, 1744.

Anonymous. "Lieut.-Colonel C. Stoddart." *The Gentleman's Magazine: and Historical Review* (March 1843).

Anonymous. "The Life of Miss Nano Nagle: Foundress of the Presentation Order." *The Bengal Catholic Herald* 7 (1844): 95–157.

Anonymous. "The Miners," *New Monthly Magazine* 72 (1844).

Anonymous. "Miscellany: An Adventurous Life" [obituary], *The Medical Times and Register: A Weekly Journal of Medical and Surgical Science* 3 (Philadelphia: J. B. Lippincott, 1873), 574.

Anonymous. "Noctes Ambrosianae. No. XXXII." *Blackwood's Edinburgh Magazine* 21 (April 1827).

Anonymous. "Noctes Ambrosianae. No. XLVII." *Blackwood's Edinburgh Magazine* 26 (December 1829).

Anonymous. *The Parallel: Or, A Collection of Extraordinary Cases, Relating to Concealed Births, and Disputed Successions.* London: J. Roberts, 1744.

Anonymous. "Politics. Article XVI." *The Analytical Review, or History of Literature . . . and the Literary Intelligence of Europe, &c.* 9 (1791).

Anonymous. "Proceedings at a Meeting with the Chiefs & Warriors of the Six Nations Held at Johnstown in September 1774." In *Documents Relative to the Colonial History of the State of New York*, edited by E. B. O'Callaghan. Albany: Weed, Parson, 1854.

Anonymous. *Reports and Papers on the Impolicy of Employing Indian Built Ships in the Trade of the East India Company, and of Admitting Them to British Registry . . . British-built Ships.* London: Blacks and Parry, 1809.

Anonymous. *Sentiments of a Corn-Factor on the Present Situation of the Corn Trade.* London: J. Richardson, 1758.

Anonymous. "Strictures on Whewell's Inductive Sciences." *Colburn's United Service Magazine and Naval and Military Journal.* London: H. Hurst, 1847.

Anonymous. *The Town Spy, or, the Devil's Factor's Discover'd. In Several Witty and Ingenious Dialogues . . . The Whole Laying Open, Their Cunning Intrigues, and Subtile and Wicked Designs.* London: Robert Gifford.

Anonymous. "The Travels and Adventures of the Reverend Joseph." *The Spectator* (August 1860).

Anonymous. *The Trial at Bar between Campbell Craig, Lessee of James Annesley, Esq; and the Right Honourable Richard Earl of Anglesea, Defendant, before the Honourable the Barons of the Exchequer, at the King's Court, Dublin, in Trinity Term, in the 16th and 17th Years of the Reign of Our Sovereign Lord George the Second, King of Great-Brotain, &c. and in the Year of Our Lord 1743.* London: R. Walker, 1744.

Anonymous. *The Trial at Large, between James Annesley, Esq; and the Right Honourable the Earl of Anglesea, before the Barons of the Court of Exchequer in Ireland . . . the Whole Taken in Court and Revived by an Eminent Counsellor in the Cause.* Newcastle Upon Tyne: John Gooding, 1744.

Anonymous. *Vertue Rewarded; or, The Irish Princess* [1693]. Edited by Ian Campbell Ross and Ann Markey. Dublin: Four Courts Press, 2010.
Anonymous. "The World of London. Part V," *Blackwood's Edinburgh Magazine* 50 (September 1841).
Arendt, Hannah. *The Origins of Totalitarianism*. New York: Harcourt, 1979.
Armstrong, Catherine. *Landscape and Identity in North America's Southern Colonies from 1600 to 1745*. New York: Routledge, 2016.
Arnold, Matthew. *Essays in Criticism*. London: Macmillan, 1865.
Auerbach, Erich. *Mimesis: The Representation of Reality in Western Literature*. Princeton: Princeton University Press, 2013.
Bailey, J. J. "Letter to William Simpson, 29 December 1878." Special Collections, Uncategorized, Anne S. K. Brown Military Collection, Brown University, RI.
Bakhtin, Mikhail. "Discourse in the Novel." In *The Dialogic Imagination: Four Essays*, edited by Michael Holquist, translated by Caryl Emerson and Michael Holquist. Austin: Texas University Press, 1981.
Barbatus, Q. Horatius. "Journal of the Proceedings and Debates in the Political Club." *The Gentleman's and London Magazine: and Monthly Chronologer*. Dublin: John Exshaw, 1757.
Baron de Montesquieu, Charles-Luis de Secondat. *The Spirit of Laws: A Compendium of the First English Edition*, ed. David Wallace Carrithers (Berkeley: University of California Press, 1977), 176.
Barrington, George. *A Voyage to New South Wales; with a Description of the Country; the Manners, Customs, Religion, &c. of the Natives, in the Vicinity of Botany Bay*. London: H. D. Symonds, 1795.
Baugh, D. *The Global Seven Years' War, 1754–1763*. New York: Routledge, 2014.
Bayly, C. A. "The British and Indigenous Peoples, 1760–1860: Power, Perception, and Identity." In *Empire and Others: British Encounters with Indigenous Peoples, 1600–1850*, edited by Martin Daunton and Rick Halpern. Philadelphia: University of Pennsylvania Press, 1999.
Baynton, Benjamin. "Petition of Captain Benjamin Baynton, of His Majesties Late Regiment of Pennsylvania Loyalists." Loyalist Claims, Public Record Office, Audit Office, Class 13, Volume 70B, folio 158, London.
Beard, James Franklin. "Cooper and the Revolutionary Mythos." *Early American Literature* 11.1 (1976): 84–104.
Beard, James Franklin ed. *The Letters and Journals of James Fenimore Cooper* (Cambridge: Harvard University Press, 2004), 2:151.
Beik, William. *Absolutism and Society in Seventeenth-century France: State Power and Provincial Aristocracy in Languedoc*. Cambridge: Cambridge University Press, 1985.
Beke, Charles. "Letter to Lord Stanley, 29 June 1867." In *Accounts and Papers of the House of Commons: Slave Trade. State Papers:—Abyssinia. Session: 5 February–21 August 1867*. London: Harrison and Sons, 1867.
Berman, Russel A. *Enlightenment or Empire: Colonial Discourse in German Culture*. Lincoln: University of Nebraska Press, 1998.
Bird, Robert Montgomery. *Nick of the Woods: A Story of Kentucky*. London: Richard Bentley, 1837.
Black, Jeremy. *A Short History of Britain*. (London: Bloomsbury Academic, 2015), 49.
Blackstone, William. *Commentaries on the Laws of England: By the Late Sir W. Blackstone. To Which Is Added an Analysis by Baron Field, Esq*. Philadelphia: John Grigg, 1827.
Blackwood, John. Letter to Philip Meadows Taylor, 2 May 1863, Blackwood's Papers 5643.D4.
Blanc, Henry. *A Narrative of Captivity in Abyssinia; With Some Account of the Emperor Theodore, His Country and People*. London: Smith, Elder and Co., 1868.
Boissery, Beverley. *A Deep Sense of Wrong: The Treason, Trials, and Deportation to New South Wales of Lower Canadian Rebels after the 1838 Rebellion*. Toronto: Dundurn, 1995.

Bolingbroke, Henry St. John. "Concerning Authority in Matters of Religion." In *The Philosophical Works of the Late Right Honorable Henry St. John, Viscount Lord Bolingbroke*. London, 1754.
Booth, Wayne C. *The Rhetoric of Irony*. Chicago: University of Chicago Press, 1974.
Bosman, William. *A New and Accurate Description of the Coast of Guinea, Divided into the Gold, the Slave, and the Ivory Coasts*. London: J. Knapton, 1705.
Boswell, James. *London Journal*. Edited by Janet B. Kopito. Mineola: Dover, 2018.
Bowles, William Augustus. "The Representation of William Augustus Bowles . . . to His Britannic Majesty." 3 January 1791, Public Records Office, F.O. L/9, S/J.9756, fols. 5–17, London.
Boyd, Elizabeth. *Altamira's Ghost; or, Justice Triumphant. A New Ballad. Occasion'd by a Certain Nobleman's Cruel Usage of His Nephew. Done Extempore*. London: Charles Corbett, 1744.
Brantlinger, Patrick. *Rule of Darkness: British Literature and Imperialism, 1830–1914*. Cornell: Cornell University Press, 1988.
Brewer, John. *The Sinews of Power: War, Money and the English State, 1688–1783*. London: Unwin Hyman, 1989.
Briggs, John, translator. *The Rise of the Mahomedan Power in India . . . With Copious Notes*. London: Longman, Rees, Orme, Brown, and Green, 1829.
"Britanicus." *Seasonable Reflections, on the Dying-Words, and Deportment, of that Great, but Unhappy Man, Arthur, Late Lord Balmerino, Who Was Beheaded . . . Published by the Authority of the Sheriffs*. London: John Noon, 1746.
Brown, Charles Brockden. "The Difference between History and Romance." In *Charles Brockden Brown's Weiland, Ormond, Arthur Mervyn, and Edgar Huntly with Related Texts*, edited by Philip Barnard and Stephen Shapiro. Indianapolis: Hackett, 2009.
Brown, Charles Brockden. *Edgar Huntly; or, Memoirs of a Sleep-Walker, with Related Texts*. Edited by Philip Barnard and Stephen Shapiro. Indianapolis: Hackett, 2006.
Brown, Charles Brockden. "Extract from 'Sky-Walk.'" *The Weekly Magazine* 1, no. 8 (1798): 228–231.
Brown, Charles Brockden. "Memoirs of Stephen Calvert." *The Monthly Magazine, and American Review* 1, no. 3 (1799): 192–193.
Brown, Charles Brockden. "Walstein's School of History." In *Charles Brockden Brown's Weiland, Ormond, Arthur Mervyn, and Edgar Huntly with Related Texts*, edited by Philip Barnard and Stephen Shapiro. Indianapolis: Hackett, 2009.
Brown, Josiah. *Reports of Cases, upon and Writs of Error, in the High Court of Parliament from the Year 1701, to the Year 1779. With Tables, Notes and References*. London: P. Uriel, 1779.
Brydges, Samuel Egerton. *Censura Literaria: Containing Titles, Abstracts, and Opinions of Old English Books: With Original Disquisitions, Articles of Biography*. London: Longman, Hurst, Rees, and Orme, 1808.
Bulwer-Lytton, Edward. *The Last Days of Pompeii*. Paris: Baudry's European Library, 1834.
Burder, George. *The Welch Indians or A Collection of Papers Respecting a People Whose Ancestors Emigrated from Wales to America, in the Year 1170, with Prince Madoc . . . West Side of the Mississippi*. London: T. Chapman, 1787.
Burke, Edmund. *The Correspondence of Edmund Burke*. Edited by Thomas W. Copeland, et al. Cambridge: Cambridge University Press, 1958–1978.
Burke, Edmund. "A Dialogue." In *A Note-Book of Edmund Burke*, edited by H.V.F. Somerset. Cambridge: Cambridge University Press, 1957.
Burke, Edmund. "A Dialogue," in H. V. F. Somerset, ed., *A Note-Book of Edmund Burke* (Cambridge: Cambridge University Press, 1957), 76.
Burke, Edmund. *The Early Life Correspondence and Writings of Rt. Hon. Edmund Burke: With a Transcript of the Minute Book of the Debating "Club" Founded by Him in Trinity College Dublin*. Edited by Arthur P. J. Samuels. Dublin: University Press, 1923.
Burke, Edmund. *A Letter from Edmund Burke, Esq; One of the Representatives in Parliament for the City of Bristol, to John Farr and John Harris, Esqrs. Sheriffs of That City, On the Affairs of America*. London: J. Dodsley, 1777.

Burke, Edmund. *A Letter from the Right Honourable Edmund Burke to a Noble Lord, on the Attacks Made upon Him and His Pension, in the House of Lords, by the Duke of Bedford and the Earl of Lauderdale, Early in the Present Sessions of Parliament*. London: J. Owen, 1796.

Burke, Edmund. *Letters on a Regicide Peace; Letter Four, to the Earl Fitzwilliam*. In *The Works of the Right Honourable Edmund Burke*. London: F.C. and J. Rivington, 1812.

Burke, Edmund. "A Letter to Charles O'Hara, 7 January 1776." In *Edmund Burke, New York Agent: With His Letters to the New York Assembly and Intimate Correspondence with Charles O'Hara, 1761–1776*, edited by John Ross Swartz Hoffman. Philadelphia: American Philosophical Society, 1956.

Burke, Edmund. "Letter to Richard Shackleton, 28 September 1752." In *The Works and Correspondence of the Right Honourable Edmund Burke*. London: Francis and John Rivington, 1852.

Burke, Edmund. "A Letter to William Smith." In *Edmund Burke: Selected Writings and Speeches*, edited by Peter Stanlis. Chicago: Regnery Gateway, 1963.

Burke, Edmund. "History of Europe." *The Annual Register, for the Year 1763*. London: J. Dodsley, 1763.

Burke, Edmund. "The History of the Present War." *The Annual Register, for the Year 1758*. London: J. Dodsley, 1758.

Burke, Edmund. "Impeachment of Warren Hastings." In *The Writings and Speeches of Edmund Burke*. New York: Cosimo, 2008.

Burke, Edmund. *A Philosophical Enquiry into the Origin of Our Ideas of the Sublime and Beautiful*. In *The Writings and Speeches of Edmund Burke*. Volume 1. Edited by T. O. McLoughlin and James T. Boulton. Oxford: Oxford University Press, 1997.

Burke, Edmund. *The Speech of Edmund Burke, Esq; On Moving His Resolutions for Conciliation with the Colonies, March 22, 1775*. Dublin: J. Exshaw, 1775.

Burke, Edmund. "Speech on Fox's East India Bill." In *On Empire, Liberty, and Reform*, edited by David Bromwich. New Haven: Yale University Press, 2000.

Burke, Edmund. *Thoughts on the Causes of the Present Discontents*. London: J. Dodsley, 1770.

Burke, Edmund. *A Vindication of Natural Society: or, A View of the Miseries and Evils Arising to Mankind from Every Species of Artificial Society*. London: M. Cooper, 1756.

Buyers, William. *Recollections of Northern India; with Observations on the Origin, Customs, Moral Sentiments of the Hindoos, and Remarks on the Country, and Principal Places on the Ganges, &c*. London: John Snow, 1848.

Byrd, William. *The Westover Manuscripts: Containing* The History of the Dividing Line betwixt Virginia and North Carolina; A Journey to the Land of Eden, A.D. 1733; *and* A Progress to the Mines. *Written from 1728 to 1736, and Nor First Published*. Petersburg: Edmund and Julian C. Ruffian, 1841.

[Lord] Byron, George Gordon. "Darkness." In *The Prisoner of Chillon, and Other Poems*. London: John Murray, 1816.

[Lord] Byron, George Gordon. "Letter to Walter Scott, January 27, 1822." In *The Works of Lord Byron*, edited by Rowland Edmund Prothero. London: John Murray, 1901.

Calloway, Colin G. *White People, Indians, and Highlanders: Tribal Peoples and Colonial Encounters in Scotland and America*. Oxford: Oxford University Press, 2008.

Camden, William. *Camden's Brittania Abridg'd . . . with above Sixty Maps Exactly Engraven*. London: Joseph Wild, 1701.

Campbell, Alexander V. "Atlantic Microcosm: The Royal American Regiment, 1755–1772." In *English Atlantics Revisited: Essays Honoring Ian K. Steele*, edited by Nancy L. Rhoden. Montreal: McGill University Press, 2007.

Campbell, John. *Lost among the Affghans: Being the Adventures of John Campbell, (Otherwise Feringhee Bacha), amongst the Tribes of Central Asia. Related by Himself to Hubert Oswald Fry*. London: Smith, Elder, and Co., 1865.

Campbell, Mary, "Memorial." GEN MSS 494, Guy Johnson Papers. Series III: Box 3, Folder 42. Beinecke Rare Book & Manuscript Library, Yale University, New Haven, CT.

Canavan, Francis. *The Political Economy of Edmund Burke: The Role of Property in His Thought*. New York: Fordham University Press, 1995.

Carleton, William. *Traits and Stories of the Irish Peasantry*. Dublin: William Curry, Jun. and Company, 1830.

Carlyle, Thomas. "Lecture III: The Hero as Poet. Dante; Shakespeare" [12 May 1840]. In *The Works of Thomas Carlyle*. Cambridge: Cambridge University Press, 2010.

Catlin, George. *North American Indians*. New York: Penguin, 2004.

Caulkins, Francis Manwaring. *History of New London, Connecticut: From the First Survey of the Coast in 1612 to 1860*. New London: H. H. Utley, 1895.

Cawelti, John C. "Cooper and the Frontier Myth and Anti-Myth." In *James Fenimore Cooper: New Historical and Literary Contexts*, edited by W. M. Verhoeven. Amsterdam: Editions Rodopi B. V., 1993.

Celikkol, Ayse. *Romances of Free Trade: British Literature, Laissez-Faire, and the Global Nineteenth Century*. Oxford: Oxford University Press, 2011.

Chandler, Richard. *Abyssinia: Mythical and Historical*. London: C.J. Skeet, 1868.

Cheadle, Eliza. *Manners of Modern Society*. London: Cassell Petter & Galpin, 1875.

Chuluun, Samplildondov, and Uradyn F. Bulag, editors. *The Thirteenth Dali Lama on the Run (1904–1906): Archival Documents from Mongolia*. Leiden: Brill, 2013.

Clark, J. C. D. "British America: What If There Had Been No American Revolution?" In *Virtual History: Alternatives and Counterfactuals*, edited by Niall Ferguson. New York: Basic Books, 1999.

Claus, William. "Letter to Frederick Halimand, 1779." National Archives of Canada, MG24, Series B, BI 14:63, D.

Clive, Robert. "Speech to the House of Commons, 30 March 1772." In Philip Henry Stanhope, *The Rise of Our Indian Empire. By Lord Mahon. Being the History of British India from Its Origin till the Peace of 1783. Extracted from Lord Mahon's History of England*. London: John Murray, 1858.

Cobbett, William. *Rural Rides . . . with Economical and Political Observations Relative to Matters Applicable to, and Illustrated by, the State of Those Counties Respectively*. London: William Cobbett, 1830.

Codr, Dwight. *Raving at Usurers: Anti-finance and the Ethics of Uncertainty in England, 1690–1750*. Charlottesville: University of Virginia Press, 2016.

Coke, Edward. *The Fourth Part of the Institutes of the Laws of England: Concerning the Jurisdiction of Courts*. London: W. Clarck and Sons, 1817.

Coke, Edward. *The Second Part of the Laws of England, Containing the Exposition of Many Ancient and Other Statutes*. Union: Lawbook Exchange, LTD, 2008.

Coleridge, Samuel Taylor. "The Ryme of the Ancyent Marinere, in Seven Parts." In *Lyrical Ballads, with a Few Other Poems*. London: J. & A. Arch, 1798.

Colley, Linda. *Captives: Britain, Empire, and the World, 1600–1850*. New York: Anchor, 2004.

Colley, Linda. "The Imperial Embrace." *The Yale Review* 81, no. 4 (1993): 92–98.

Colley, Linda. *The Ordeal of Elizabeth Marsh: A Woman in World History*. New York: Anchor, 2007.

Conolly, Arthur. *Journey to the North of India, Overland from England, through Persia, Russia, and Affghaunistaun*. London: Richard Bentley, 1838.

Conolly, Arthur. "Letter to Henry Rawlinson, 22 August 1839." In John William Kaye, *History of the War in Afghanistan. From Unpublished Letters . . . of British Connexion with That Country*. London: Richard Bentley, 1851.

Cook[e], Ebenezer. *The Sot-Weed Factor; or, A Voyage to Maryland. A Satyr. In Which Is Describ'd The Laws, Government, Courts and Constitutions of the Country, and also the Buildings, Feats, Frolicks, Entertainments and Drunken Humours of the Inhabitants of That Part of America*. London: D. Bragg, 1708.

Cooper, James Fenimore. *The American Democrat, or, Hints on the Social and Civic Relations of the United States of America*. Cooperstown: H. & E. Phinney, 1838.

Cooper, James Fenimore. "The Autobiography of a Pocket-Handkerchief." *Graham's Magazine* 22, nos. 1–4 (1843): 1–18, 89–102, 158–167, 205–213.

Cooper, James Fenimore. *The Last of the Mohicans: A Narrative of 1757*. In *The Leatherstocking Tales*, edited by Blake Nevins. New York: Penguin Putnam, 1985.

Cooper, James Fenimore, *The Letters and Journals of James Fenimore Cooper*, edited by James Franklin Beard. Cambridge: Harvard University Press, 2004.
Cooper, James Fenimore. *The Pathfinder, or, The Inland Sea*. In *The Leatherstocking Tales*, edited by Blake Nevins. New York: Penguin, 1985.
Cooper, James Fenimore. *The Pilot: A Tale of the Sea*. New York: Charles Wiley, 1823.
Cooper, James Fenimore. *The Pioneers, or the Sources of the Susquehanna; a Descriptive Tale*. In *The Leatherstocking Tales*, edited by Blake Nevins. New York: Penguin Putnam, 1985.
Cooper, James Fenimore. *The Prairie; A Tale*. In *The Leatherstocking Tales*, edited by Blake Nevins. New York: Penguin Putnam, 1985.
Coote, Charles. *Statistical Survey of the County of Armagh, with Observations on the Means of Improvement; Drawn Up in the Years 1802, and 1803, for the Consideration, and Under the Direction of the Dublin Society*. Dublin: Graisberry and Campbell, 1804.
Corp, Edward T. *A Court in Exile: The Stuarts in France, 1689–1718* (Cambridge: Cambridge University Press, 2004), 116–120.
Cornell, Louis D. *Kipling in India*. New York: MacMillan, 1966.
Courtnay, John. *A Poetical and Philosophical Essay on the French Revolution. In a Letter Addressed to the Right Hon. Edmund Burke*. London: J. Ridgway, 1793.
Cox, Jeffrey N. *Poetry and Politics in the Cockney School: Keats, Shelley, Hunt and Their Circle*. Cambridge: Cambridge University Press, 2004.
Craig, Cairns. *Out of History: Narrative Paradigms in Scottish and English Culture*. Edinburgh: Polyglon, 1996.
Crèvecoeur, J. Hector St. John. *Letters from an American Farmer and Sketches of Eighteenth-Century Life*. Edited by Albert E. Stone. New York: Penguin, 1981.
Crèvecœur, J. Hector St. John. "Susquehanna." In *More Letters from the American Farmer: An Edition of the Essays in English Left Unpublished*, edited by Dennis D. Moore. Athens: University of Georgia Press, 1995.
Cronin, Richard. *Paper Pellets: British Literary Culture after Waterloo*. Oxford: Oxford University Press, 2010.
Crowe, Ian. *Patriotism and Public Spirit: Edmund Burke and the Role of the Critic in Mid-Eighteenth-Century Britain*. Stanford: Stanford University Press, 2012.
Crummey, Donald. "Doctrine and Authority: Abuna Sālāma, 1841–1854." *PICES* 4, no. 1 (1974): 567–578.
Crummey, Donald. *Land and Society in the Christian Kingdom of Ethiopia: From the Thirteenth to the Twentieth Century*. Urbana-Champaign: University of Illinois Press, 2000.
Cumberland, Richard. *Retrospection: A Poem in Familiar Verse*. London: W. Bulmer, 1811.
Dalrymple, William. "The East India Company: The Original Corporate Raiders." *The Guardian* (4 March 2015).
Davies, K. G. *Documents of the American Revolution, 1770–1783*. Shannon: Irish University Press, 1972–1981.
Davis, Mike. *Late Victorian Holocausts: El Nino Famines and the Making of the Third World*. London: Verso, 2001.
Day, Sherman. *Historical Collections of the State of Pennsylvania; Containing a Copious Selection of the Most Interesting Facts, Traditions, Biographical Sketches, Anecdotes, etc. Relating to Its History and Antiquities, Both General and Local, with Topographical Descriptions of Every County an All the Larger Towns in the State*. Philadelphia: George W. Gorton, 1843.
Deane, Bradley. "Imperial Barbarians: Primitive Masculinity in Lost World Fiction." *Victorian Literature and Culture* 36, no. 1 (2008): 205–225.
De Bruyn, Frans. *The Literary Genres of Edmund Burke: The Political Uses of Literary Form*. Oxford: Clarendon, 1996.
Defoe, Daniel. *The Compleat English Gentleman*. In *Selected Writings of Daniel Defoe*, edited by James T. Bouldon. Cambridge: Cambridge University Press, 1975.
De Jean, Joan. *Tender Geographies: Women and the Origins of the Novel in France*. New York: Columbia University Press, 1991.
Dekker, George. *The American Historical Romance*. Cambridge: Cambridge University Press, 1987.

Dekker, George. *James Fenimore Cooper: The American Scott.* New York: Barnes and Noble, 1967.
Deroo, Peter. *History of America before Columbus, according to Documents and Approved Authors.* Philadelphia: J. B. Lippincott, 1900.
Desjardins, Simon, and Pierre Pharoux, *Castorland Journal: An Account of the Exploration and Settlement of Northern New York State by French Emigres in the Years 1793 to 1797.* Translated by John A. Gallucci. Ithaca: Cornell University Press, 2010.
Desta, Mengiste. *Ethiopia's Role in African History.* Addis Ababa: Shama Books, 2007.
DeVoto, Bernard. *The Course of Empire.* New York: Houghton Mifflin, 1998.
Dickson, David. *Old World Colony: Cork and South Munster, 1630–1830.* Cork: Cork University Press, 2005.
Dillon, Thomas Arthur. *Memoirs of Count Lally, from His Embarking for the East Indies, as Commander in Chief of the French Forces in That Country . . . to Illustrate His Civil and Military Character.* London: Charles Kiernan, 1766.
Disraeli, Benjamin. "Speech of 22 April 1842." In *Hansard's Parliamentary Debates* 62. London: G. Woodfall and Son, 1842.
Disraeli, Benjamin. *Tancred; or, The New Crusade.* Bern: Tauchnitz Jun, 1847.
Disraeli, Benjamin. *The Wondrous Tale of Alroy. The Rise of Iskander.* London: Saunders and Otley, 1833.
Dombrowski, Franz Amadeus. *Ethiopia's Access to the Sea.* Leiden: E. J. Brill, 1985.
Douglas, Aileen. "Britannia's Rule and the It-Narrator." In *The Secret Life of Things: Animals, Objects, and It-Narratives in Eighteenth-Century England*, edited by Mark Blackwell. Cranbury: Associated University Presses, 2007.
Dowling, P. J. *The Hedge Schools of Ireland.* Cork: Mercier, 1968.
Doyle, Laura. *Freedom's Empire: Race and the Rise of the Novel in Atlantic Modernity, 1640–1940.* Durham: Duke University Press, 2008.
Dubois, Henri L. *The History of a French Dagger; an Anecdote of the French Revolution. From the French.* London, 1828.
Duncan, Ian. *Modern Romance and Transformations of the Novel: The Gothic, Scott, Dickens.* Cambridge: Cambridge University Press, 1992.
Duncan, Ian. *Scott's Shadow: The Novel in Romantic Edinburgh.* Princeton: Princeton University Press, 2007.
Duncan, Ian. "The Trouble with Man: Scott, Romance, and World History in the Age of Lamarck." In *Romantic Frictions*, edited by Theresa Kelley. *Romantic Circles: Praxis Series* (2011). http://romantic.arhu.umd.edu/praxis/frictions/HTML/praxis.2011.duncan.html.
Dupree, Louis. "The Retreat of the British Army from Kabul to Jalalabad in 1842: History and Folklore." *Journal of the Folklore Institute* 4, no. 1 (1967): 50–74.
Dutton, Hely. *Statistical Survey of the County of Clare, with Observations on the Means of Improvement; Drawn up for Consideration, and by Direction of the Dublin Society.* Dublin: Graisberry and Campbell, 1808.
Eagleton, Terry. *Heathcliff and the Great Hunger: Studies in Irish Culture.* London: Verso, 1995.
Eastburn, Robert. *A Faithful Narrative, of the Many Dangers and Sufferings, as Well as Wonderful Deliverances of Robert Eastburn . . . With a Recommendatory Preface, by the Rev. Gilbert Tennent.* London: William Dunlap, 1758.
Ekirch, A. Roger. *Birthright: The True Story That Inspired Kidnapped.* W. W. Norton & Company: New York, 2010.
Elyas, Gebre-Igziabiher. *Power, Piety, and Politics: The Chronicle of Abeto Iyaso and Empress Zewditu (1909–1930).* Cologne: Rüdiger Köppe Verlag, 1994.
Emin, Joseph. *The Life and Adventures of Joseph Ēmïn, an Armenian. Written in English by Himself.* London: N.p., 1792.
Empson, William. "Tom Jones." *The Kenyon Review* 20, no. 2 (1958): 217–249.
Erlikh, Hagai. *The Cross and the River: Ethiopia, Egypt, and the Nile.* London: Lynne Rienner, 2002.

Evans, Richard J. *Altered Pasts: Counterfactual in History*. Waltham: Brandeis University Press, 2013.
Ferguson, Niall ed., *Virtual History: Alternatives and Counterfactuals* (New York: Basic Books, 1999), 89.
Fielding, Henry. *The History of Tom Jones*. Edited by R. P. C. Mutter. New York: Penguin, 1966.
Filson, John. *The Discovery, Settlement, and Present State of Kentucky . . . and Several Other Places*. London: John Stockdale, 1793.
Finkelstein, David. "Imperial Self-Representation: Constructions of Empire in *Blackwood's Magazine*, 1880–1900." In *Imperial Co-Histories: National Identities and the British and Colonial Press*, edited by Julie F. Codell. London: Associated University Presses, 2003.
Finley, James Bradley. *Life among the Indians; or, Personal Reminiscences and Historical Incidents Illustrative of Indian Life and Character*. Cincinnati: Methodist Book Concern, 1860.
Fitzball, Edward. *The Flying Dutchman; or, The Phantom Ship, a Nautical Drama in Three Acts*. London: John Cumberland, 1829.
Fortune, Robert. "Travels in China." *The Quarterly Review*. London: John Murray, 1857.
Forster, E. M. "The Poems of Kipling." In *The Creator as Critic and Other Writings*, edited by Jeffrey M. Heath. Toronto: Dundurn, 2008.
Foster, William Henry. *Gender, Mastery and Slavery: From European to Atlantic World Frontiers*. New York: Palgrave, 2010.
Franklin, Benjamin. "Information to Those Who Would Remove to America." In *Autobiography and Other Writings*, edited by Ormond Seavey. Oxford: Oxford University Press, 1993.
Franklin, Wayne. "'One More Scene': The Marketing Context of Cooper's 'Sixth' Leather-Stocking Tale." In *Leather-Stocking Redux; or, Old Tales, New Essays*, edited by Jeffrey Walker. New York: AMS Press, 2011.
Fraser, Simon. *A Candid and Impartial Account of the Behavior of Simon Lord Lovat . . . By a Gentleman Who Attended His Lordship in His Last Moments*. London: J. Newbery, 1747.
Frye, Northrop. *The Bible and Literature*. London: Routledge and Keegan Paul, 1982.
Fulford, Tim. "Prophets of Resistance: Native American Shamans and Anglophone Writers." In *Transatlantic Literary Exchange, 1790–1870: Gender, Race, and Nation*, edited by Kevin Hutchings and Julia M. Wright. Burlington: Ashgate, 2011.
Fulford, Tim. *Romanticism and Masculinity: Gender, Politics and Poetics in the Writings of Burke, Coleridge, Wordsworth, De Quincey and Hazlitt*. New York: St. Martin's, 1999.
Fussell, Paul. "Irony, Freemasonry, and Humane Ethics in Kipling's 'The Man Who Would Be King.'" *ELH* 25, no. 3 (1958): 216–233.
Gage, Thomas. "Copy of Testimonial by Thomas Gage on Johnson's Behalf [21 June 1785]." GEN MSS 494, Guy Johnson Papers. Series III: Box 3, Folder 52. Beinecke Rare Book & Manuscript Library, Yale University, New Haven, CT.
Galt, John. "Letter to William Blackwood, May 1, 1820." In *British Fiction, 1800–1829: A Database of Production, Circulation & Reception*, edited by P. D. Garside. http://www.british-fiction.cf.au.uk
Gardner, Alexander. *Soldier and Traveller: Memoirs of Alexander Gardner, Colonel of Artillery in the Service of Maharaja Ranjit Singh*. Edited by Hugh Pearse. Edinburgh: William Blackwood and Sons, 1898.
Garson, Marjorie. *Moral Taste: Aesthetics, Subjectivity, and Social Power in the Nineteenth-Century Novel*. Toronto: University of Toronto Press, 2007.
Gay, John. The Beggar's Opera *and* Polly. Oxford: Oxford University Press, 2013.
Gibbon, Edward. *The History of the Decline and Fall of the Roman Empire*. New York: Harper and Brothers, 1845.
Gillray, James. *Crumbs of Comfort* (1782). BM 6027; British Museum, London.
Gobat, Samuel. *Journal of Three Years' Residence in Abyssinia, in Furtherance of the Objects of the Church Missionary Society*. London: Hatchard & Son, 1834.
Godwin, William. *An Enquiry Concerning Political Justice and Its Influence on General Virtue and Happiness*. London: G. G. J. and J. Robinson, 1793.

Godwin, William. "Of History and Romance." *Enquirer* [1797]. http://www.english.upenn.edu/~mgamer/Etexts/godwin.history.html. 17 August 2014.

Grahame, James, and Macvey Napier. *Hypocrisy Unveiled and Calumny Detected: In a Review of Blackwood's Magazine*. Edinburgh: Francis Pillans, 1818.

Grant, James. "Part of a Letter to His Honor the Lieutenant Governor, from Major Grant." *Gentleman's Magazine* (1760).

Grosart, Alexander Balloch, editor. "On the Departure of King James yc 2d 1688." *English Jacobite Ballads, Songs & Satires, etc. From the MSS. at Towneley Hall, Lancashire*. Manchester: Charles E. Simms, 1877.

Grubb, Farley. *German Immigration and Servitude in America, 1702–1920*. London: Routledge, 2011.

Guilds, John Caldwell. "William Gilmore Simms and the Portrayal of the American Indian: A Literary View." In *An Early and Strong Sympathy: The Indian Writings of William Gilmore Simms*, edited by John Caldwell Guilds and Charles Hudson. Columbia: University of South Carolina Press, 2003.

Gumilev, L. N. *Searches for an Imaginary Kingdom: The Legend of the Kingdom of Prester John*. Translated by R. E. F. Smith. Cambridge: Cambridge University Press, 1987.

Gunn, J. A. W. *Beyond Liberty and Property: The Process of Self-Recognition in Eighteenth-Century Political Thought* (Montreal: McGill-Queen's University Press, 1983), 120–194.

Guthrie, William. *An Address to the Public, On the Dismission of a General Officer*. London: W. Nicoll, 1764.

Hall, Anthony J. *The American Empire and the Fourth World* (Montreal: McGill-Queen's University Press, 2005).

Hammond, George. "Letter to Thomas Jefferson." In *American State Papers: Documents, Legislative and Executive, of the Congress of the United States*, edited by Walter Lowrie and Matthew St. Claire Clarke. Washington, DC: Gales and Seaton, 1832.

Hannay, David. *Life of Marryat*. London: Walter Scott, 1889.

Harcourt, Henry. *The Adventures of a Sugar-Plantation*. London: Westley and Davis, 1836.

Harthorn, Stephen P. "What Happened to Cooper's Sixth Leatherstocking Tale?" Paper presented at the 15th Cooper Seminar, *James Fenimore Cooper: His Country and His Art*, State University of New York College at Oneota, July 2005. http://external.oneonta.edu/cooper/articles/suny/2005suny-harthorn.html

Harvey, Biakia. "Letter to Thomas Biakia, Esq., 30 December 1775." William Manson Papers, Orkney Island Archives, Kirkwall, Orkney.

Harvey, W. J. *Character and the Novel*. Ithaca: Cornell University Press, 1965.

Hawkins, Laetitia Matilda. *Anecdotes, Biographical Sketches and Memoirs; Collected by Laetitia Matilda Hawkins*. London: F. C. and J. Rivington, 1822.

Hayden, John, editor. *The Romantic Reviewers: 1802–1824*. London: Routledge, 1969.

Hayne, Barrie. "*Ossian*, Scott and Cooper's Indians." *Journal of American Studies* 3, no. 1 (1969): 73–87.

Haywood, Eliza. *Memoirs of an Unfortunate Young Nobleman, Return'd from a Thirteen Years Slavery in America Where He Had Been Sent by the Wicked Contrivances of His Cruel Uncle. A Story Founded on Truth, and Address'd Equally to the Head and Heart*. London: J. Freeman, 1743.

Hazlitt, William. "Character of Mr. Burke." In *Edmund Burke: Appraisals and Applications*. Edited by Daniel E. Ritchie. New Brunswick: Transaction, 1990.

Hazlitt, William. "Character of Mr. Burke," in *Political Essays, with Sketches of Public Characters* (London: William Hone, 1819), 269.

Heinowitz, Rebecca Cole. "The Allure of the Same: Robert Southey's Welsh Indians and the Rhetoric of Good Colonialism." *Romantic Circles Praxis Series: Sullen Fires across the Atlantic: Essays in Transatlantic Romanticism*, 02 March 2014. http://www.rc.umd.edu/praxis/sullenfires/heinowitz/heinowitz.html

Herbert, James Dowling. *Irish Varieties from the Last Fifty Years: Written from Recollections*. London: William Joy, 1836.

Herrick, Cheesman. *White Servitude in Pennsylvania: Indentured and Redemption Labor in Colony and Commonwealth*. New York: Negro University Press, 1969.

Herrick, Francis H. "Audubon and the Dauphin." *The Auk* 54, no. 4 (1937): 476–499.
Hevia, James. *The Imperial Security State: British Colonial Knowledge and Empire-Building in Asia*. Cambridge: Cambridge University Press, 2012.
Higgins, David. *"Blackwood's Edinburgh Magazine* and the Construction of Wordsworth's Genius." In *Romantic Periodicals and Print Culture*, edited by Kim Wheatley. London: Frank Cass, 2003.
Higgins, David. *Romantic Genius and the Literary Magazine: Biography, Celebrity, Politics*. New York: Routledge, 2005.
Hinderaker, Eric. *Elusive Empires: Constructing Colonialism in the Ohio Valley, 1673–1800*. Cambridge: Cambridge University Press, 1997.
Hinds, Elizabeth Jane Wall. *Private Property: Charles Brockden Brown's Gendered Economics of Virtue*. London: Associated University Presses, 1997.
Hislop, Alexander. *The Two Babylons; or, The Papal Worship Proved to Be the Worship of Nimrod and His Wife. With Sixty-One Woodcut Illustrations from Nineveh, Babylon, Egypt, Pompeii, &c*. Edinburgh: James Wood, 1858.
Hodgkins, Christopher. *Reforming Empire: Protestant Colonialism and Conscience in British Literature*. Columbia: University of Missouri Press.
Hogg, James. *The Private Memoirs and Confessions of a Justified Sinner: Written by Himself: With a Detail of Curious Traditionary Facts and Other Evidences by the Editor*. Edited by John Carey. Oxford: Oxford University Press, 1999.
Holt, Thaddeus. "you have been in Afghanistan, I perceive." *Military History Quarterly* 6, 2 (1988): 32–38.
Holwell, John Zephaniah. *A Genuine Narrative of the Deplorable Deaths of the English Gentlemen, and Others, Who Were Suffocated in the Black-Hole . . . in a Letter to a Friend*. London: A. Millar, 1758.
Horne, Richard Henry. *The History of Napoleon*. London: Robert Tyas, 1841.
Hotten, John Camden. *Abyssinia and Its People; or, Life in the Land of Prester John*. London: John Camden Hotten, 1868.
Howard, Edward. *Outward Bound, or A Merchant's Adventures*. Paris: Baudry's European Library, 1838.
Howell, T. B., editor. *A Complete Collection of State Trials and Proceedings for High Treason and Other Crimes and Misdemeanors from the Earliest Period to the Year 1783*, vol. 18. London: Longman, Hurst, Rees, Orme, and Brown, 1813.
Howison, John. "Vanderdecken's Message Home; Or, the Tenacity of Natural Affection." *Blackwood's Edinburgh Magazine* 9, no. 50 (1821): 127–131.
Hrbek, Ivan. "Ethiopia, the Red Sea and the Horn." In *The Cambridge History of Africa, Volume 3: c. 1000–1650*, edited by Roland Oliver. Cambridge: Cambridge University Press, 1977.
Israel, Jonathan. *The Anglo-Dutch Moment: Essays on the Glorious Revolution and Its World Impact*. Cambridge: Cambridge University Press, 2003.
Jacques-Lefèvre, Nicole. "Such an Impure, Cruel, and Savage Beast: Images of the Werewolf in Demonological Works." In *Werewolves, Witches, and Wandering Spirits: Traditional Belief & Folklore in Early Modern Europe*, edited by Kathryn A. Edwards. Kirksville: Truman State University Press, 2002.
Jasanoff, Maya. *Liberty's Exiles: American Loyalists in the Revolutionary World*. New York: Vintage, 2012.
Johnson, Guy. "Colonel Guy Johnson to the Magistrates of Palatine, Etc., Tyron County New York [20 May 1775]." In *American Archives: Consisting of a Collection of Authentik Records, State Papers, Debates, and Letters and Other Notices of Public Affairs*, edited by Peter Force. Washington, DC: U.S. Congress, 1837–1853.
Johnson, Guy. "Journal." In *Documents Relative to the Colonial History of the State of New York*, edited by E. B. O'Callaghan. Albany: Weed, Parson, 1854.
Johnson, Guy. "Journal of Colonel Guy Johnson from May to November, 1775." In *Documents Relative to the Colonial History of the State of New York*, edited by E. B. O'Callaghan. Albany: Weed, Parson, 1854.

Johnson, Guy. "Letter from Colonel Guy Johnson to the Committee for Tyron County, New York [5 June 1775]." In *American Archives: Consisting of a Collection of Authentik Records, State Papers, Debates, and Letters and Other Notices of Public Affairs*, edited by Peter Force. Washington, DC: U.S. Congress, 1837–1853.

Johnson, Guy. "Letter from Colonel Guy Johnson to the New-York Congress: Opened and Read by the Albany Committee, and a Copy Sent to General Schuyler [8 July 1777]." In *American Archives: Consisting of a Collection of Authentik Records, State Papers, Debates, and Letters and Other Notices of Public Affairs*, edited by Peter Force. Washington, DC: U.S. Congress, 1837–1853.

Johnson, Guy. "Letter of Colonel Guy Johnson to the Magistrates and Committee of Schenectady." In *American Archives: Consisting of a Collection of Authentik Records, State Papers, Debates, and Letters and Other Notices of Public Affairs*, edited by Peter Force. Washington, DC: U.S. Congress, 1837–1853.

Johnson, Guy. "Letter to John Blackburn, 12 September 1774." GEN MSS 494, Guy Johnson Papers. Series I: Box 1, Folder 11. Beinecke Rare Book & Manuscript Library, Yale University, New Haven, CT.

Johnson, Guy. "Letter to John Penn, 22 August 1774." GEN MSS 494, Guy Johnson Papers. Series I: Box 1, Folder 7. Beinecke Rare Book & Manuscript Library, Yale University, New Haven, CT.

Johnson, Guy. "Letter to Lord George Germain, 26 January 1776." In *Documents Relative to the Colonial History of the State of New York*, edited by E. B. O'Callaghan. Albany: Weed, Parson, 1854.

Johnson, Guy. "List of Articles in Payment to Plankashaw Indians for Land on the Wabash." GEN MSS 494, Guy Johnson Papers. Series III: Box 1, Folder 37. Beinecke Rare Book & Manuscript Library, Yale University, New Haven, CT.

Johnson, Guy. *Memorial to the Loyalist Claims Commission, 23 March 1784*, Public Record Office, London, AO 12/22/22-46, AO 12/109/176. Microfilm, Library of Congress.

Johnson, Samuel. *A Dictionary of the English Language: In Which the Words Are Deduced from Their Originals, and Illustrated in Their Different Significations by Examples from the Best Writers. To Which Are Prefixed a History of the Language, and an English Grammar.* London: W. Strahan, 1773.

Johnson, Samuel. [*Rasselas*] *The Prince of Abyssinia. A Tale.* London: J. Dodsley, 1759.

Johnson, William. "Letter to Lord Adam Gordon, 6 April 1774." GEN MSS 494, Guy Johnson Papers. Series I: Box 1, Folder 3. Beinecke Rare Book & Manuscript Library, Yale University, New Haven, CT.

Johnson, William. "Letter to Thomas Gage, 20 April 1774." GEN MSS 494, Guy Johnson Papers. Series I: Box 1, Folder 6. Beinecke Rare Book & Manuscript Library, Yale University, New Haven, CT.

Johnstone, Charles. *Chrysal; Or the Adventures of a Guinea.* London: T. Becket, 1760.

Jones, E. Alfred. "The Real Author of the 'Authentic Memoirs of William Augustus Bowles.'" *Maryland Historical Magazine* 18, no. 4 (1923): 300–308.

Kafer, Peter. "Charles Brockden Brown and Revolutionary Philadelphia: An Imagination in Context." *The Pennsylvania Magazine of History and Biography* 116, no. 4 (1992): 467–498.

Kafer, Peter. *Charles Brockden Brown's Revolution and the Birth of the American Gothic.* Philadelphia: University of Pennsylvania Press, 2004.

Kamrath, Mark L. "American Exceptionalism and Radicalism in the 'Annals of Europe and America.'" In *Revising Charles Brockden Brown: Culture, Politics, and Sexuality in the Early Republic*, edited by Phiip Barnard, Mark L. Kamrath, and Stephen Shapiro. Knoxville: University of Tennessee Press.

Kaye, John William. *Lives of Indian Officers.* London: W. H. Allen & Co., 1895.

Keller, Edmond J. *Revolutionary Ethiopia: From Empire to People's Republic.* Bloomington: Indiana University Press, 1988.

Kendall, George Wilkins. *Narrative of the Texan Santa Fe Expedition, Containing a Description of a Tour through Texas . . . and Final Capture of the Texans, and Their March, as Prisoners, to the City of Mexico.* New York: Harper and Brothers, 1844.

Kennedy, Michael V. "The Consequences of Cruelty: The Escalation of Servant and Slave Abuse, 1750–1780." *Essays in Economic and Business History* 22 (2012): 127–141.
Keppel, Henry. *The Expedition of H.M.S. Dido for the Suppression of Piracy: With Extracts from the Journal of James Brooke, Esq. of Sarāwak*. London: Chapman and Hall, 1847.
Kermode, Frank. *The Sense of an Ending: Studies in the Theory of Fiction with a New Epilogue*. Oxford: Oxford University Press, 2000.
Kimber, Edward. *The Life and Adventures of Joe Thompson. A Narrative Founded on Fact*. London: John Hinton, 1775.
Kingsley, Charles. *Westward Ho! Or, The Voyages and Adventures of Sir Amyas Leigh, Knight . . . in the Reign of Her Most Gloriously Majesty Queen Elizabeth*. Cambridge: Macmillan, 1855.
Kincaid, James R. "Tennyson's 'Gareth and Lynette,'" *Texas Studies in Literature and Language* 13, no. 4 (1972): 663–671.
Kipling, Rudyard. *Kim*. New York: Penguin, 1984.
Kipling, Rudyard. "Letter to Edward White." In Gail Ching-Liang Low, *White Skins/Black Masks: Representation and Colonialism*. London: Routledge, 2005.
Kipling, Rudyard. "The Man Who Would Be King." In *The Man Who Would Be King*. New York: Penguin, 2011.
Kirby, William. *The U.E., A Tale of Upper Canada*. Niagara, 1859.
Knox, Henry. "Letter to James Seagrove, 11 April 1792." In *American State Papers: Documents, Legislative and Executive, of the Congress of the United States*, edited by Walter Lowrie and Matthew St. Claire Clarke. Washington, DC: Gales and Seaton, 1832.
Krause, Sydney J. "Edgar Huntly and the American Nightmare." *Studies in the Novel* 13, no. 3 (1981): 294–302.
Krause, Sydney J. "Penn's Elm and Edgar Huntly: Dark 'Instruction to the Heart.'" *American Literature* 66, no. 3 (1994): 463–484.
Kreitzer, Larry J. "'The Son of God Goes Forth to War': Biblical Imagery in Rudyard Kipling's 'The Man Who Would Be King.'" In *Borders, Boundaries and the Bible*, edited by Martin O'Kane. New York: Sheffield Academic Press, 2002.
Kucich, John. "Sadomasochism and the Magical Group: Kipling's Middle-Class Imperialism." *Victorian Studies* 36, no. 1 (2004): 33–68.
Kuehn, Julia, editor. *Travel Writing, Form, and Empire: The Poetics and Politics of Mobility*. New York: Routledge, 2009.
Lambert, Elizabeth. *Edmund Burke of Beaconsfield*. Cranbury: Associated University Presses, 2003.
Lambert, Elizabeth. "The Law, the Nun, and Edmund Burke," in Ian Crowe, ed., *An Imaginative Whig: Reassessing the Life and Thought of Edmund Burke* (Columbia: University of Missouri Press, 2002), 158–174.
Lang, Andrew. *The Life and Letters of John Gibson Lockhart*. London: C. Nimmo, 1897.
Larkin, Edward. "What Is a Loyalist?" *Common-Place* 8, no. 1 (2007). http://www.common-place-archives.org/vol-08/no-01/larkin/
Leadbeater, Mary. *The Leadbeater Papers; A Selection from the Mss. and Correspondence of Mary Leadbeater. Vol. 2. Unpublished Letters of Edmund Burke: and the Correspondence of Mrs. Richard Trench and Rev. George Crabbe*. London: Bell and Daldy, 1862.
Mary Leadbeater, ed., *Memoirs and Letters of Richard and Elizabeth Shackleton . . . Including a Concise Biographical Sketch, and Some Letters, of her Grandfather, Abraham Shackleton* (London: Harvey and Darton, 1822), 4.
Lee, Jonathan L. *The 'Ancient Supremecy': Bukhara, Afghanistan, and the Battle for Balkh*. Leiden: Brill, 1996.
Legge, William. "Letter to Guy Johnson, 28 June 1774." GEN MSS 494, Guy Johnson Papers. Series I: Box 1, Folder 10. Beinecke Rare Book & Manuscript Library, Yale University, New Haven, CT.
Leitner, G. W. "Notes on the Genealogy of the Divine Rajas of Nagyr." In *Dardistan in 1866, 1886 and 1893 . . . and an Epitome of Part III of the Author's "The Languages and Races of Dardistan."* New Delhi: AES Reprint, 1996.

Le Maistre, Frans. "Extracts from the Records." In *Report Concerning Canadian Archives for the Year 1904 (Being an Appendix to the Report of the Minister of Agriculture). Printed on Order of Parliament*, edited by Douglas Irymner. Ottawa: S. E. Dawson, 1905.

Letts, Malcolm. "Prester John: A Fourteenth-Century Manuscript at Cambridge." *Transactions of the Royal Historical Society*, Series 4, 29 (1947): 19–26.

Leyden, John. *Historical Account of the Discoveries and Travels in Africa, by the Late John Leyden, M.D. Enlarged, and Completed to the Present Time, with Illustrations of Its Geography, Natural History, as Well as of the Moral and Social Conditions of Its Inhabitants*. Edited by Hugh Murray. Edinburgh: George Ramsay and Company, 1817.

Lockhart, John Gibson. *The History of Napoleon Buonaparte, with Engravings on Steel and Wood*. London: John Murray, 1829.

Lockhart, John Gibson. "The Lord Advocate on Reform." *Blackwood's Edinburgh Magazine* 29 (June 1831).

Lockhart, John Gibson. "More's Life of Lord Byron." *Quarterly Review* 44 (January 1831).

Lockhart, John Gibson. *Peter's Letters to His Kinfolk*. Edinburgh: William Blackwood, 1819.

Lockhart, John Gibson. "Sir Egerton Brydges' Recollections." *Blackwood's Edinburgh Magazine* 17 (May 1825).

Lockhart, John Gibson. *Valerius: A Roman Story*. Edinburgh: William Blackwood, 1821.

Lukacs, Georg. *The Historical Novel*. Lincoln: University of Nebraska Press, 1962.

Lysons, Daniel. *Early Reminiscences*. London: John Murray, 1896.

MacIntyre, Alasdair. *After Virtue*. London: Gerald Duckworth & Co., 1981.

Macintyre, Ben. *The Man Who Would Be King: The First American in Afghanistan*. New York: Faber, Strauss, and Giraux, 2005.

Madden, Kyla. *Forkhill Protestants and Forkhill Catholics, 1787–1858*. Montreal: McGill-Queen's University Press, 2005.

Magray, Mary Pekham. *The Transforming Power of Nuns: Women, Power, and Cultural Change, 1750–1900* (Oxford: Oxford University Press, 1998), 14–32.

Mair, John. *Book-Keeping Modernized: Or, Merchant-Accounts by Double Entry, according to the Italian Form. . . To Which Is Added, A Large Appendix*. Edinburgh: John Bell and William Creech, 1786.

Marder, Daniel. "Cooper's Second Cycle." *South Central Review* 2, 2 (1985): 23–37.

Marino, Cesare, and Karim M. Tiro, editors. *Along the Hudson and Mohawk: The 1790 Journey of Count Paulo Andreani*. Philadelphia: University of Pennsylvania Press, 2006.

Marryat, Frederick. *The Children of the New Forest* (London: Routledge, 1847).

Marryat, Frederick. *A Diary in America, with Remarks on Its Institutions*. London: Longman, Orme, Brown, Green, and Longmans, 1839.

Marryat, Frederick. *Frank Mildmay, or The Naval Officer*. London: Richard Edward King, 1829.

Marryat, Frederick. *Japhet, in Search of a Father*. London: Saunders and Otley, 1836.

Marryat, Frederick. *The King's Own*. Paris: Baudry's European Library, 1834.

Marryat, Frederick. *Mr. Midshipman Easy*. London: Saunders and Otley, 1836.

Marryat, Frederick. *Narrative of the Travels and Adventures of Monsieur Violet, in California, Sonora, & Western Texas*. London: Longman, Browne, Greene, and Longmans, 1843.

Marryat, Frederick. *Newton Forster; or, The Merchant Service*. London: John Cochrane and Co., 1832.

Marryat, Frederick. *The Phantom Ship*. Paris: Baudry's European Library, 1839.

Marryat, Frederick. *The Settlers in Canada: Written for Young People* (London: Longman, Brown, Green, & Longmans, 1844).

Marryat, Frederick. *Snarleyyow; or the Dog Fiend*. Philadelphia: E. L. Carey and A. Hart.

Marx, Edward. "How We Lost Kafiristan." *Representations* 67 (1999): 44–66.

Mason, William. "An Heroic Epistle to Sir William Chambers, Knight." *Specimens of the British Poets; With Biographical and Critical Notices, and an Essay of English Poetry*. Edited by Thomas Campbell. London: John Murray, 1819.

Maturin, Charles Robert. *Melmoth the Wanderer*. New York: Penguin, 2000.

Maxwell, Richard. *The Historical Novel in Europe, 1650–1950*. Cambridge: Cambridge University Press, 2009.

Maxwell, W. H. *Erin-Go-Bragh; or, Irish Life Pictures*. London: Richard Bentley, 1859.
McAlister, Lyle N. "William Augustus Bowles and the State of Muskogee." *Florida Historical Quarterly* (1962): 317–328.
McGann, Jerome. *The Romantic Ideology: A Critical Investigation*. Chicago: University of Chicago Press, 1983.
McGillivray, Alexander. "Letter to Henry Knox, 18 May 1792." In *American State Papers: Documents, Legislative and Executive, of the Congress of the United States*, edited by Walter Lowrie and Matthew St. Claire Clarke. Washington, DC: Gales and Seaton, 1832.
McManus, Antonia. *The Irish Hedge School and Its Books, 1695–1831*. Portland: International Specialized Book Service, 2004.
McMaster, John Bach. *A History of the United States, from the Revolution to the Civil War*. New York: Appleton and Company, 1900.
McWilliams, John P., Jr.*The American Epic: Transforming a Genre, 1770–1860*. Cambridge: Cambridge University Press, 1989.
Miller, David W. *The Taking of American Indian Lands in the Southeast: A History of Territorial Cessions and Forced Relocations, 1607–1840*. Jefferson: McFarland & Company, 2011.
Misra, Bankey Bihari. *The Central Administration of the East India Company, 1773–1834*. Bombay: Oxford University Press, 1959.
Mister, Mary. *The Adventures of a Doll*. London: Darton and Harvey, 1816.
Moore, Lucas, editor. *Twelfth Biennial Report of the Bureau of Agriculture, Labor, and Statistics. Of the State of Kentucky*. Louisville: George G. Fetter, 1897.
Moore, Thomas. "Written on Passing Dead-Man's Island, in the Gulf of St. Lawrence, Late in the Evening, September, 1804." In *Epistles, Odes, and Other Poems*. London: James Carpenter, 1806.
Moraley, William. *The Infortunate: The Life and Adventures of William Moraley, an Indentured Servant*. Edited by Susan E. Klepp and Billy G. Smith. University Park: Pennsylvania State University Press, 2005.
Morgan, Prys. "From a Death to a View: The Hunt for the Welsh Past in the Romantic Period." In *The Invention of Tradition*, edited by Eric Hobsbawm and Terence Ranger. Cambridge: Cambridge University Press, 2012.
Morrison, Robert. "'To Abuse Wickedness but Acknowledge Wit': 'Blackwood's' and the Shelley Circle." *Victorian Periodicals Review* 34, 2 (2001): 147–164.
Motley, Warren. *The American Abraham: James Fenimore Cooper and the Frontier Patriarch*. Cambridge: Cambridge University Press, 1987.
Mstowska, Joanna. "The Flying Dutchman's Mimetic Desire. Crossing Geographical and Moral Boundaries in Frederick Marryat's *The Phantom Ship*." In *Crossroads in Language and Literature*, edited by Jacek Fabiszak, Ewa Urbaniak-Rybicka, and Bartosz Wolski. Berlin: Springer-Verlag, 2013.
Mulvey-Roberts, Marie. *Dangerous Bodies: Historicizing the Gothic Corporeal*. Oxford: Oxford University Press, 2016.
Murphy, Francesca Aran. *I Samuel*. Grand Rapids: Brazos Press, 2010.
Murphy, Peter T. "Impersonation and Authorship in Romantic Britain." *ELH* 59, 3 (1992): 625–649.
Murray, Cara. *Victorian Narrative Technologies in the Middle East*. New York: Routledge, 2008.
Musgrave, Richard. *Memoirs of the Different Rebellions in Ireland, from the Arrival of the English . . . With the History of the Conspiracy Which Preceded it*. Dublin: Robert Marchbank, 1802.
Nash, Gary B. *The Unknown American Revolution: The Unruly Birth of Democracy and the Struggle to Create America*. New York: Viking, 2005.
Nixon, Cheryl L. *The Orphan in Eighteenth-Century Law and Literature: Estate, Blood, and Body*. London: Routledge, 2016.
Noble, David W. "Cooper, Leatherstocking, and the Death of the American Adam." *American Quarterly* 16, 3 (1964): 419–431.
"Noctes Ambrosianae. No. XL," *Blackwood's Edinburgh Magazine* 24 (December 1828): 696.
Nowell, Charles E. "The Historical Prester John." *Speculum* 28, no. 3 (1953): 435–445.

Ó Bauchalla, Breandán. "Irish Jacobite Poetry." *The Irish Review* 12 (1992): 40–49.
Ó Buachalla, Breandán. "The Making of a Cork Jacobite." In *Cork: History and Society: Interdisciplinary Studies on the History of an Irish County*, edited by P. O'Flannagan and C. G. Buttimer. Dublin: Geography Publications, 1993.
Ó Ciardha, Éamonn. "A Voice from the Jacobite Underground: Liam Inglis (1709–78," in Gerard Moran ed., *Radical Irish Priests,1690–1970* [Dublin: Four Courts Press, 1998]: 16–38.
Ó Ciardha, Éamonn. *Ireland and the Jacobite Cause: A Fatal Attachment* (Dublin: Four Courts Press, 2004), 285–286, 338–345.
Ó Colmáin, Domnhall. *Párliament na mBan*, ed. Brian Ó Cuiv (Dublin: Dublin Institute for Advanced Studies, 1952).
O'Connell, Basil. "Richard Burke and James Cotter, Jr." *The Burke Newsletter* 6, no. 1 (1964): 360–362.
O'Kell, Robert. *Disraeli: The Romance of Politics*. Toronto: University of Toronto Press, 2013.
Oliphant, Margaret, editor. *William Blackwood and His Sons: Their Magazine and Friends*. Edinburgh: Blackwood, 1897.
Orlowska, Izabela. "Mining the Wisdom of Solomon: The Coronation of Yohannas IV." *Proceedings of the XV International Conference of Ethiopian Studies*. Wiesbaden: Otto Harrassowitz GmbH & Co. KG, 2006.
Orwell, George. "Rudyard Kipling." In *All Art Is Propaganda: Critical Essays*, edited by George Packer. New York: Houghton Mifflin Harcourt, 2009.
O'Toole, Fintan. *White Savage: William Johnson and the Invention of America*. New York: Farrar, Strauss, and Giroux, 2005.
Pagano, Frank N. "Burke's Views of the Evils of Political Theory; Or, *A Vindication of Natural Society*." *Polity* 17, no. 3 (1985): 446–462.
Pagden, Anthony. "Afterward: From Empire to Federation." In *Imperialisms: Historical and Literary Investigations, 1500–1900*, edited by Balachandra Rajan and Elizabeth Sauer. New York: Palgrave MacMillan, 2004.
Pankhurst, Richard. "Imperial Orders in a Command or Pre-Market Economy." *Proceedings of the XVth International Conference of Ethiopian Studies: Hamburg 2003*, edited by Siegbert Uhlig. Wiesbaden: Otto Harrassowitz GmbH & Co. KG, 2006.
Pankhurst, Richard. "A 'Missing' Letter from Emperor Tewodros II to Queen Victoria's Special Envoy Hormuzd Rassam." In *Afrikas Horn*, edited by Walter Raunig and Steffen Wenig. Wiesbaden: Otto Harrassowitz GmbH & Co. KG, 2005.
Paolillo, Maurizio. "White Tatars: The Problem of the Origin of the Ongut Conversion to *Jingjiao* and the Uighur Connection." In *From the Oxus River to the Chinese Shores: Studies on East Syriac Christianity in China and Central Asia*, edited by Li Tang and Dietmar W. Winkler. Berlin: Lit Verlag, 2013.
Parchami, Ali. *Hegemonic Peace and Empire: The Pax Romana, Britannica, and Americana*. New York: Routledge, 2009.
Parkhurst, Rita. "The Library of Emperor Tewodros II at Mäqdäla (Magdala)." *Bulletin of the School of Oriental and African Studies, University of London* 36, no. 1 (1973): 15–42.
Pearl, Jonathan L. *The Crime of Crimes: Demonology and Politics in France, 1560–1620*. Waterloo: Waterloo Laurier University Press, 1999.
Peers, Douglas M. "Conquest Narratives: Romanticism, Orientalism and Intertextuality in the Indian Writings of Sir Walter Scott and Robert Orme." In *Romantic Representations of British India*, edited by Michael J. Franklin. New York: Routledge, 2005.
Penn, John. "Letter to Sir William Johnson, 28 June 1774." GEN MSS 494, Guy Johnson Papers. Series I: Box 1, Folder 7. Beinecke Rare Book & Manuscript Library, Yale University, New Haven, CT.
Pethers, Matthew. "The Indentured Atlantic: Bound Servitude and the Literature of American Colonization [Part Three]." *U.S. Studies Online*. British Association for American Studies, http://www.baas.ac.uk/usso/the-indentured-atlantic-bound-servitude-and-the-literature-of-american-colonization-part-three/
Phillips, J. R. S. *The Medieval Expansion of Europe*. Oxford: Oxford University Press, 1998.

Phillips, Richard. *Mapping Men and Empire: A Geography of Adventure*. New York: Routledge, 1997.
Plank, Geoffrey. *Rebellion and Savagery: The Jacobite Rising of 1745 and the British Empire*. Philadelphia: University of Pennsylvania Press, 2005.
Plowden, Walter. "Letter to Clarendon, 5 March 1856." In *Parliamentary Papers, Correspondence Respecting Abyssinia, 1846–1848*. London: Harrison and Sons, 1868.
Poe, Edgar Allen. "MS. Found in a Bottle." *Southern Literary Messenger* 2 (1835).
Porter, Bernard. *The Absent-Minded Imperialists: What the British Really Thought about Empire*. Oxford: Oxford University Press, 2005.
Pratt, Linda. "Revising the National Epic: Coleridge, Southey, and Madoc." *Romanticism* 2, no. 2 (1996): 149–163.
Prior, James. *Memoir of the Life and Character of the Rt. Hon. Edmund Burke; with Specimens of His Poetry and Letters, and an Estimate of His Genius and Talents, Compared with Those of His Contemporaries*. London: Baldwin, Cradock, and Joy, 1826.
Reiman, David. *The Romantics Reviewed: Contemporary Reviews of British Romantic Writers*. New York: Garland, 1972.
Reynolds, Joshua. *Horace Walpole*. Oil on canvas, c. 1756–1757, 50 1/8 in. x 40 1/8 in., National Portrait Gallery, UK.
Ricoeur, Paul. *Time and Narrative*. Translated by David Pellauer. Chicago: Chicago University Press, 1984.
Riddle, William. *Cherished Memories of Old Lancaster-Town and Shire*. Lancaster: Intelligencer Printing House, 1910.
Ringe, Donald. *Charles Brockden Brown*. New York: Twayne, 1966.
Roberts, Daniel Sanjiv. "Mediating Indian Letters in an Age of Empire: *Blackwood's* and Orientalism." In *Romanticism and Blackwood's Magazine: "An Unprecedented Phenomenon,"* edited by Robert Morrison. New York: Palgrave MacMillan, 2013.
Roberts, Sian Silyn. *Gothic Subjects: The Transformation of Individualism in American Fiction, 1790–1861*. Philadelphia: University of Pennsylvania Press, 2014.
[Robinson, David]. "Life of Burke." *Blackwood's Edinburgh Magazine* 17 (January 1825).
Rodgers, Nini. "The Abyssinian Expedition of 1867–1868: Disraeli's Imperialism or James Murray's War?" *The Historical Journal* 27, no. 1 (1984): 129–149.
Rosenthal, Bernard. "Melville, Marryat, and the Evil-Eyed Villain." *Nineteenth-Century Fiction* 25, no. 2 (1970): 221–224.
Roudik, Peter. *The History of the Central Asian Republics*. Westport: Greenwood, 2007.
Rubenson, Sven. *King of Kings: Tewodros of Ethiopia*. Addis Ababa: Haile Sellassie University Press, 1966.
Ruxton, George F. *Adventures in Mexico and the Rocky Mountains*. London: John Murray, 1847.
Ryan, Dermot. *Technologies of Empire: Writing, Imagination, and the Making of Imperial Networks, 1750–1820*. Newark: University of Delaware Press, 2013.
Sale, Florentia. *A Journal of the Disasters in Affghanistan, 1841–2*. London, John Murray, 1843.
Samet, Elizabeth. *Willing Obedience: Citizens, Soldiers, and the Progress of Consent in America, 1776–1898*. Stanford: Stanford University Press, 2004.
Sammons, Jacob. "Narrative of Jacob Sammons." In *Hudson-Mohawk Genealogical and Family Memoirs*, edited by Cuyler Reynolds. New York: Lewis, 1911.
Samuels, Arthur P. J., ed. *The Early Life Correspondence and Writings of Rt. Hon. Edmund Burke: With a Transcript of the Minute Book of the Debating "Club" Founded by Him in Trinity College Dublin* (Dublin: University Press, 1923), 8.
Sanders, Michael. "Politics." In *Charles Dickens in Context*, edited by Sally Ledger and Holly Furneaux. Cambridge: Cambridge University Press, 2011.
Scally, Robert James. *The End of Hidden Ireland: Rebellion, Famine, & Emigration*. Oxford: Oxford University Press, 1995.
Scott, John. "The Author of the Scotch Novels." *London Magazine* 1 (January 1820).
Scott, John. "Blackwood's Magazine." *London Magazine* 9 (November 1820).

Scott, Walter. "An Essay on Romance." In *The Miscellaneous Prose Works of Sir Walter Scott, Bart.* Vol. 6. Boston: Wells and Lilly, 1829.

Scott, Walter. "Hajji Baba in England." In *The Miscellaneous Prose Works of Sir Walter Scott, Bart.* Edinburgh: Robert Cadell, 1835.

Scott, Walter. *The Journal of Sir Walter Scott: 1825–1832, from the Original Manuscript at Abbotsford.* Edinburgh: David Douglas, 1891.

Scott, Walter. *Letters on Demonology and Witchcraft, Addressed to J.G. Lockhart, Esq..* London: John Murray, 1830.

Scott, Walter. "Letter to Lady Abercorn, 31 December 1809." In *Familiar Letters of Walter Scott*, edited by David Douglas. Boston: Houghton Mifflin, 1894.

Scott, Walter. "Letter to Robert Southey, 17 June 1814." In *The Letters of Sir Walter Scott*, edited by H. J. C. Grierson. London: Constable and Company, Limited, 1932–1937.

Scott, Walter. "Review of *Childe Harold's Pilgrimage and The Prisoner of Chillon*," *The Quarterly Review* 16 (October 1816), 172–208.

Scott, Walter. *Rokeby; A Poem.* Edinburgh: John Ballantyne and Co., 1813.

Scott, Walter. *Tales of a Grandfather. Vol. VI. France.* In *The Miscellaneous Works of Sir Walter Scott, Bart.* Edinburgh: Robert Cadell, 1836.

Scott, Walter. *Waverley; or, 'Tis Sixty Years Since.* Edited by Claire Lamont. Oxford: Oxford University Press, 1986.

Seeley, John Robert. *The Expansion of England: Two Courses of Lectures* (Cambridge: Cambridge University Press, 2010).

Sevier, John. "Letter to Amos Stoddard, 9 October 1810." In *The History of Hamilton County and Chattanooga, Tennessee*, edited by Zella Armstrong. Johnson City: Overmountain Press, 1993.

Shackleton, Richard and Elizabeth. *Memoirs and Letters of Richard and Elizabeth Shackleton . . . Including a Concise Biographical Sketch, and Some Letters, of Her Grandfather, Abraham Shackleton.* Edited by Mary Leadbeater. London: Harvey and Darton, 1822.

Shannon, Timothy J. "'This Wretched Scene of British Curiosity and Savage Debauchery': Performing Indian Kingship in Eighteenth-Century Britain." In *Native Acts: Indian Performance, 1603–1832.* Lincoln: University of Nebraska Press, 2011.

Shapiro, Stephen. "'Man to Man I Needed Not to Dread His Encounter': Edgar Huntly's End of Erotic Pessimism." In *Revising Charles Brockden Brown: Culture, Politics, and Sexuality in the Early Republic*, edited by Philip Barnard, Mark L. Kamrath, and Stephen Shapiro. Knoxville: University of Tennessee Press.

Sharf, Frederick A., David Northrop, and Richard Pankhurst. *Abyssinia, 1867–1868: Artists on Campaign: Watercolors and Drawings from the British Expedition under Sir Robert Napier.* Tsehai: Hollywood, 2003.

Shelley, Percy Bysshe. "A Defense of Poetry." In *Essays, Letters from Abroad, Translations and Fragments, by Percy Bysshe Shelley*, edited by Mary Shelley. London: Edward Moxon, 1840.

Sherman, Sandra. *Finance and Fictionality in the Early Eighteenth Century: Accounting for Defoe.* Cambridge: Cambridge University Press, 1996.

Simmons, R. C., and P. D. G. Thomas, eds. *Proceedings and Debates of the British Parliaments Regarding North America, 1754–1783.* Milkwood, 1982–1986.

Simms, William Gilmore. "The Broken Arrow." In *The Book of My Lady: A Melange. By a Bachelor Knight.* Philadelphia: Key & Biddle, 1833.

Simms, William Gilmore. "Thle-cath-cha." In *An Early and Strong Sympathy: The Indian Writings of William Gilmore Simms*, edited by John Caldwell Guilds and Charles Hudson. Columbia: University of South Carolina Press, 2003.

Simms, William Gilmore. *Views and Reviews in American Literature, History and Fiction.* New York: Wiley and Putnam, 1845.

Simpson, D. H., and E. A. Morris. *Twickenham Ferries in Story and Song.* Borough of Twickenham Local Historical Society Paper 43 (1980).

Singh, Jyotsna. "The Postcolonial/Postmodern Shakespeare." In *Shakespeare: World Views*, edited by Heather Kerr, Robin Eaden, and Madge Miltton. Cranbury: Associated University Presses, 1996.

Slotkin, Richard. *Regeneration through Violence: The Mythology of the American Frontier, 1600–1860*. Norman: University of Oklahoma Press, 1973.
Smith, Jay M. *Monsters of the Gévaudan: The Making of a Beast*. Harvard: Harvard University Press, 2011.
Smith, Christopher J. P. *A Quest for Home: Reading Robert Southey*. Liverpool: Liverpool University Press, 1997.
Smollett, Tobias. *The Adventures of Peregrine Pickle. In Which Are Included, Memoirs of a Lady of Quality*. London: D. Wilson, 1751.
Snodgrass, Charles. "Blackwood's Subversive Scottishness." In *Print Culture and the Blackwood Tradition, 1805–1930*, edited by David Finkelstein Toronto: University of Toronto Press, 2006.
Snodin, Michael, and Cynthia E. Roman, *Horace Walpole's Strawberry Hilll* (New Haven: Yale University Press, 2009).
Southey, Robert. "Letter to William Owen-Pughe, 9 August 1797." National Library of Wales, MS 13222C, 469.
Southey, Robert. *Madoc*. London: Longman, Hurst, Rees, Orme, and Brown, 1805.
Spanos, William V. *American Exceptionalism in the Age of Globalization: The Specter of Vietnam*. Albany: SUNY Press, 2008.
Spradlin, Derrick. "'*GOD* ne'er Brings to Pass Such Things for Nought': Empire and Prince Madoc of Wales in Eighteenth-Century America." *Early American Literature* 44, no. 1 (2009): 39–70.
[Speratus]. "Letter 1." *The Weekly Magazine* 1, no. 7 (1798).
Sprigs, Elizabeth. "Letter to Mr. John Spriggs in White Cross Street near Cripple Gate, London, 22 September 1756." In *Colonial Captivities, Marches, and Journeys*, edited by Isabel Calder. New York: Macmillan, 1935.
Stampone, Christopher. "A 'Spirit of Mistaken Benevolence': Civilizing the Savage in Charles Brockden Brown's *Edgar Huntly*." *Early American Literature* 50, no. 2 (2015): 415–448.
Stanley, Henry Morton. *Coomassie and Magdala: The Story of Two British Campaigns in Africa*. London: Sampson, Low, Marston, Low, and Searle, 1874.
Steele, David. *Lord Salisbury: A Political Biography*. New York: Routledge, 2001.
Stern, Henry Aaron. *Wanderings among the Falashas in Abyssinia; Together with a Description of the Country and Its Various Inhabitants. Illustrated by a Map and Twenty Engravings of Scenes and Persons, Taken on the Spot*. London: Wertheim, Macintosh, and Hunt, 1862.
Stone, William Leete. *Border Wars of the American Revolution* (New York: Harper & Brothers, 1816).
Strout, Alan Lang. "Hunt, Hazlitt, and *Maga*: I. Leigh Hunt and *Maga*: The Lighter Side of 'Cockney'-Killing." *ELH* 4, 2 (1937): 151–154.
Strout, Alan Lang. "Purple Patches in the *Noctes Ambrosianae*." *ELH* 2, 4 (1935): 327–331.
Sturtevant, William C. "The Cherokee Frontiers, the French Revolution, and William Augustus Bowles." In *The Cherokee Indian Nation: A Troubled History*, edited by Duane H. King. Knoxville: University of Tennessee Press, 1979.
Sullivan, Zohreh T. *Narratives of Empire: The Fictions of Rudyard Kipling*. Cambridge: Cambridge University Press, 1993.
Swaim, Barton. "'What Is Scott?': John Gibson Lockhart's Professional Amateurism." *Victorian Periodicals Review* 39, 3 (2006): 280–297.
Sylvain, Philippe. "Libéralisme et ultramontanisme au Canada français: affrontment idéologique et doctrinal (1840–1865)." In *Le Bouclier d'Achille. Regards sur le Canada à l'ère victorienne*, edited by W. L. Morton. Toronto: McClelland and Stewart, 1968: 111–138.
Ta'a, Tasema. "The Macca Oromo States and the Creation of Modern Ethiopian Empire." In *The Political Economy of an African Society in Transformation: The Case of Macca Oromo (Ethiopia)*, edited by Catherine Griefenow-Mewis. Wiesbaden: Otto Harrassowitz GmbH & Co. KG, 2006.
Tafla, Bairu, editor. *A Chronicle of Emperor Yohannes IV*. Wiesbaden: Steiner, 1977.
Taylor, Miles. "Queen Victoria and India, 1837–1861." *Victorian Studies* 46, no. 2 (2004): 264–272.

Tenniel, John. "New Crowns for Old Ones." *Punch* (15 April 1876).
Tennyson, Alfred. *Idylls of the King*. New York: Penguin, 2004.
The Annual Register, Or a View of the History, Politics, and Literature, for the Year1760 (London: J. Dodsley, 1760), 120.
Theller, Edward Alexander. *Canada in 1837–38 . . . Together with the Personal Adventures of the Author and Others Who Were Connected with the Revolution*. Philadelphia: Henry F. Anners, 1841.
Thompson, E. P. *The Making of the English Working Class*. New York: Vintage, 1966.
Thorne, James. *Handbook to the Environs of London, Alphabetically Arranged, Containing an Account of Every Town and Village, and of All Places of Interest, within a Circle of Twenty Miles Round London*. London: John Murray, 1876.
Tomlins, Thomas Edlyne. *The Law-Dictionary: Explaining the Rise, Progress, and Present State, of English Law, in Theory and Practice, Defining and Interpreting the Terms or Words of Art; and Comprising Copious Information, Historical, Political, and Commercial, on the Subject of Our Law, Trade, and Government*. London: Andrew Strahan, 1797.
Tribe, Christopher J., translator. *Pedro Paez's* History of Ethiopia, *1622*. London: Hakluyt Society, 2011.
Trousdale, William. "Dr. Brydon's Report of the Kabul Disaster and the Documentation of History." *Military Affairs* 47, 1 (1983): 27.
Tyler, Royall. *The Contrast*. In *The Contrast: Manners Morals, and Authority in the Early American Republic*, edited by Cynthia A. Kierner. New York: New York University Press, 2007.
Tyron County Committee of Safety, "Letter to Colonel Guy Johnson, 24 June 1775." *History of Oneida County, New York. With Illustrations and Biographical Sketches of Its Prominent Men and Pioneers*. Edited by Samuel W. Durant. Philadelphia: Everts & Fariss, 1878.
Voloshin, Beverly. "*Edgar Huntly* and the Coherence of the Self." *Early American Literature* 23, no. 3 (1988): 262–280.
Von Humboldt, Alexander. *Personal Narrative of Travels to the Equinoctial Regions of the New Continent, during the Years 1799–1804 . . . Translated into English by Helen Maria Williams*. London: Longman, Rees, Orme, Brown, and Green, 1826.
Wahrman, Dror. *The Making of the Modern Self: Identity and Culture in Eighteenth-Century England*. New Haven: Yale University Press, 2004.
Wall, Edward. Letter to the Palatine Committee of Safety, 8 June 1775, in Stone, *Border Wars*, 77.
Walpole, Horace. *Memoires of the Last Ten Years of the Reign of George the Second*. London: John Murray, 1822.
Walpole, Horace. *The Yale Editions of Horace Walpole's Correspondence*, edited by W. S. Lewis et al. New Haven: Yale, 1937–1983.
Walsh, Alexander. *Strong Representations: Narrative and Circumstantial Evidence in England*. Baltimore: Johns Hopkins University Press, 1992.
Warren, Robert Penn, and Cleanth Brooks, editors. *The Scope of Fiction*. New York: Appleton-Century-Crofts, 1960.
Watson, John Fanning. *Annals of Philadelphia in the Olden Time; Being a Collection of Memoirs, Anecdotes, and Incidents of the City and Its Inhabitants, and of the Earliest Settlements of the Inland Part of Pennsylvania from the Days of the Founders*. Philadelphia: A. Hart, 1850.
Webster, Anthony. *The Debate on the Rise of the British Empire*. Manchester: Manchester University Press, 2006.
Welch, Adam. "Saul." In *Kings and Prophets of Israel*, edited by Norman W. Proteous. London: Lutterworth, 1952.
Weston, John C., Jr. "Edmund Burke's View of History." *The Review of Politics* 23, no. 2 (1961): 203–229.
Wheatley, Kim. "The Blackwood's Attacks on Leigh Hunt." *Nineteenth-Century Literature* 47, 1 (1992): 1–31.
White, Richard. *The Middle Ground: Indians, Empires, and Republics in the Great Lakes Region, 1650–1815*. Cambridge: Cambridge University Press, 2011.

Williams, Gwyn A. *Madoc: The Making of a Myth*. Oxford: Oxford University Press, 1997.
Wilson, George. *Reports of Cases Argued and Adjudged in the King's Courts at Westminster*. London: H. Baldwin and Son, 1799.
[Wilson, John]. "An Hour's Tete-a-Tete with the Public." *Blackwood's Edinburgh Magazine* 8 (October 1820).
[Wilson, John]. "Extracts from Gosschen's Diary." *Blackwood's Edinburgh Magazine* 3 (August 1818).
[Wilson, John]. "Reformers and Anti-Reformers—A Word to the Wise from Old Christopher." *Blackwood's Edinburgh Magazine* 29 (May 1831).
Wilson, Kathleen. *A New Imperial History: Culture, Identity and Modernity in Britain and the Empire, 1660–1840*. Cambridge: Cambridge University Press, 2004.
Wokeck, Marianne S. "German and Irish Immigration to Colonial Philadelphia." *Proceedings of the American Philosophical Society* 133, no. 2: Symposium on the Demographic History of the Philadelphia Region, 1600–1860 (1989): 128–143.
Wolff, Joseph. *Travels and Adventures of the Reverend Joseph Wolff, D.D., L.L.D. Vicar of Ile Brewers, Near Taunton, and Late Missionary to the Jews and Muhammadans in Persia, Bokhara, Cashmeer, Etc*. London: Saunders, Otley, and Co., 1861.
Wollstonecraft, Mary. *A Vindication of the Rights of Men, in a Letter to the Right Honourable Edmund Burke; Occasioned by His Reflections on the Revolution in France*. London: J. Johnson, 1790.
Wood, Neal. "The Aesthetic Dimension of Burke's Political Thought." *Journal of British Studies* 4 (1964).
Wordsworth, William. "Nuns Fret Not." In *William Wordsworth's Poetry and Prose*. New York: W. W. Norton, 2013.
Wordsworth, William. "Preface to Lyrical Ballads." In *Lyrical Ballads, with Other Poems. In Two Volumes*. London: T. N. Longman, 1800.
Zanger, Jules. "Marryat, Monsieur Violet, and Edward La Salle." *Nineteenth-Century Fiction* 12, no. 3 (1957): 226–231.
Zimmerman, Doron. *The Jacobite Movement in Scotland and in Exile* (London: Palgrave Macmillan, 2003), 159.

Index

Abyssinia. *See* Ethiopia
Addison, Joseph, 60, 103, 105, 163, 168
Afghanistan, 168, 177; Anglo-Afghan Wars, 149, 177, 180, 183; Kipling's fiction and, 183, 191
Aksum, Kingdom of, 121
Anglesea, Arthur (1st Earl of), 59; estate of, 50, 57
Annesley, James, 50; accounts of, 50–54, 56, 57; Arthur Annesley and, 59–62; Charles Brockden Brown's fictions and, 62, 65; as literary "orphan," 68; Richard Annesley and, 56
Armagh Outrages, 65
Arthurian legends, 125, 190
Aubin, Penelope, 27
Audubon, Jean-Jacques, 120
Auerbach, Erich, 13

Barrington, George, 100
Baynton, Benjamin, 138
Beast of Gévaudan, 108
Biblical literature, 122; Ethiopian kingship and, 123, 124; Kipling's sources, 181, 184; *The Phantom Ship* and, 100
bildungsroman, 28, 31, 57, 119, 136
Blackburn, John, 80
Blackstone, William, 62
Blackwater (Ireland), 20, 25–27, 28–29, 30, 34–35

Blackwood's Edinburgh Magazine: collaborative "personation" in, 151–152; influence of British India on, 153; Gorge Ruxton and the Madoc legend, 132; the Lockhart Circle, 154–159; *Phantom Ship* sources, 100, 106; the Retreat from Kabul, 150; treatment of Edmund Burke, 162–164; Walter Scott's influence, 161–162
Bolingbroke, Henry St. John, 12; Burke's *Vindication* and, 31–32
Bowles, William Augustus, 135–140
Bumppo, Natty. *See* Leatherstocking
Brant, Joseph, 84; literary depictions of, 85; trip to London, 89, 137
British Empire, 2–13, 21, 29–34, 66, 126, 129, 131, 134–135; as "hybrid empire," 77, 81, 88; imperialist readership, 150–153, 168–169; and Marryat's fiction, 98, 99; organic and cosmological metaphors for, 103, 119; The Great Game, 182, 184, 188–190
Brockden Brown, Charles: Irish affairs and, 50, 55, 65; social influences on, 48; views on historical romance, 53
Brydon, William, 149–150, 182
Bulwer-Lytton, Edward, 187
Bulwer-Lytton, Robert, 186
Burke, Edmund : early life of, 22–32; *Blackwood's* representation of, 152, 155, 162–168; idea of empire, 103;

Seven Years' War, 32–34
Byron, George Gordon, Lord, 151, 154, 160, 164, 166

Camden, William, 11
Canada: American Revolution and, 83, 86, 87; Lower Canada Rebellion in, 97–98, 109
Chenier, Jean-Olivier, 108
Coke, Lord Edward, 81
Cotter, James, 24–25; Edmund Burke and, 25, 30
Cooper, James Fenimore : knowledge of the Johnsons, 78; Marryat's view of, 99; "Sixth" Leatherstocking Tale and, 75–77
Covenant Chain, 81
Crèvecœur, Hector St. John, 45, 84–85

Defoe, Daniel, 27, 50
Disraeli, Benjamin: Abyssinian Crisis and, 129; Peachey Carnehan as, 182; *Tancred* and the Raj, 187–189
Durbar of 1877, 186, 187
Dutch East India Company: *Phantom Ship*'s depiction of, 102, 105

East India Company, 5, 66, 100, 103, 139, 149, 178, 187–188
Edgar Huntly, 43–68
Ethiopia, 119, 125–126, 140

factor, 3–8, 12, 103; Marryat's depictions of, 102–103

Galt, John, 159
Gardner, Alexander, 177
genre, 7–8, 12, 29, 46, 53, 97, 106, 118
Gibbon, Edward, 11
Godwin, William, 8
Gordon, Lord Adam, 79–80
Gothic, 45, 104, 107, 109, 156, 159, 164–165

Hawkins, Benjamin, 139
Hawkins, Laetitia, 1
Haywood, Eliza, 51
Hazlitt, William, 162–163
Heber, Reginald, 182–183

hedge schools, 27–29
historical romance. *See* romance
Hogg, James, 152, 157, 159

Idylls of the King, 182, 186, 189–190
India, 12, 124, 126, 129, 169, 177, 179, 183, 188, 190, 191
Iroquois, 9, 77, 80, 89, 134
it-narratives, 104, 105–106, 106, 153

Jackson, Andrew, 139
Jacobinism, 107
Jacobitism, 3, 19–20, 23, 25, 29, 30, 34
Johnson, Guy, 80, 82, 85–87, 89
Johnson, Samuel, 60
Johnson, Sir William, 5, 9, 77, 78–79

Keats, John, 151, 154, 155, 162
Kebra Nagast, 121
Kimber, Edward, 5
Kingsley, Charles, 187
Kipling, Rudyard, 7, 176–179

Leadbeater, Mary, 20
Leatherstocking, 52, 75–84, 90–91
Leatherstocking Tales, 78, 118; *The Last of the Mohicans*, 83–84, 89; *The Pathfinder*, 90–91; *The Pioneers*, 75–78, 81–84, 86, 88–92
Lockhart, John Gibson, 126, 152, 154
locum tenens, 75–78, 76, 81, 82, 87–89
Loyalism, 76–77, 84, 86, 91
lycanthropy, 107–109

Mackercher, Douglas, 50
Macnaghten, Sir William, 179, 182
Madoc, 121, 130–134
Maginn, William, 154, 157, 190
"The Man Who Would Be King," 176–192
Muskogee, State of, 134, 139, 140

Nagle family, 25, 27; influence on Burke, 28, 30
Napoleon, 6, 126
nation state, 6–8, 98–99, 124, 140, 167, 175; empire and, 11–12, 98

objectification, 104–105
orphan, literary figure of, 52–53, 56, 68

Orientalism, 178, 189
Owen-Pughe, William, 135, 136

Paulding, James Kirk, 78
periodical culture, 151–152, 154, 155, 158
Persia, 127, 129, 178–179, 188
The Phantom Ship, 97–110

revolution, 109, 166; American Revolution, 76–92, 99, 134; French Revolution, 155
romance, 3–7, 12; Charles Brockden Brown and, 46, 53, 67; Disraeli's fiction, 188–189; Jacobitism and, 27–28, 33, 34; Kipling's fiction, 177, 182, 185–186; "lost race" fiction, 118–119, 141; Marryat's fiction, 98, 117–118; "romance-mongering," 176, 190–191; *Waverley* and, 20, 26, 29
Romanticism, 7–8, 12, 19, 100, 106, 121, 126–127, 152–153, 155–157, 160–163, 167, 176, 188
Russia, 4, 129, 178–179

Scott, Walter, 20–21, 52, 54, 106, 120, 126–127, 151, 152–153, 160–162, 166–167, 187
Shackleton, Richard, 31

Shakespeare, William, 26, 175
Shelley, Mary, 164
Shelley, Percy Bysshe, 154, 162
Simms, William Gilmore, 84, 121, 130, 133, 141
Stoddart, Charles, 178, 182, 184, 191

Tennyson, Alfred, 186, 189–190
Téwodros II, 119–130
Toryism, 9, 22, 76, 80, 84, 106, 151, 152, 154, 156, 160, 166, 188–189
transculturation, 78, 80–81, 84, 87
transportation, 48–49

Victoria, 123–125, 128, 130, 186, 189
Victorian: attitudes toward Abyssinia, 140; and imperial "Britishness," 169, 180; "imperial commons," 7; "lost race romances," 118

Walpole, Horace, 1, 9–11, 12–13, 21, 22, 32
Washington, George, 83, 98, 107
Waverley, 6–7, 19–31, 76, 91, 120, 132, 134, 162
Wordsworth, William, 151, 155, 161

About the Author

Matthew Carey Salyer is an associate professor of English at the United States Military Academy, West Point, where he is also affiliated with the Center for the Study of Civil-Military Operations. His next book project examines urban landscapes in eighteenth-century crime literature. He lives in The Bronx.

www.ingramcontent.com/pod-product-compliance
Lightning Source LLC
Chambersburg PA
CBHW050903300426
44111CB00010B/1357